"*Good Health for African Americans,* an expansive, yet concisely written work . . . is a winner of a book."
— *Quarterly Black Review of Books*

"Dixon supplies a fascinating historical explanation as to why disease and mortality rates differ between blacks and other Americans. . . . These are potentially political issues, and Dixon handles them with grace and sensitivity while mapping lifestyle changes needed for improved health."
— *Publishers Weekly*

"An intriguing mix of historical perspective and informative, valuable information."
— *Detroit Free Press*

"The most comprehensive self-help book of its kind."
— *Cleveland Plain Dealer*

"Good, solid health information."
— *The Sunday Denver Post*

"An important new book."
— *Orange County Register*

GOOD
HEALTH
FOR
AFRICAN
AMERICANS

**Introducing the 24-Week Sankofa Program for
Nutritional and Lifestyle Transformation**

**Barbara M. Dixon, R.D., L.D.N.,
with Josleen Wilson**

Foreword by Elijah Saunders, M.D.

Crown Trade Paperbacks/New York

In memory of my parents,
Bertha McIntyre and Lawrence McIntyre, Jr.

Published by Crown Publishers, Inc., 201 East 50th Street, New York, New York 10022.
Member of the Crown Publishing Group.

Random House, Inc. New York, Toronto, London, Sydney, Auckland

CROWN TRADE PAPERBACKS and colophon are trademarks of
Crown Publishers, Inc.

Originally published in hardcover by Crown Publishers, Inc., in 1994.

Manufactured in the United States of America

Library of Congress Cataloging-in-Publication Data
Dixon, Barbara M.
Good health for African Americans/Barbara M. Dixon with Josleen Wilson.
Includes index.
1. African Americans—Health and hygiene.   2. African Americans—Nutrition.   3.
African Americans—Diseases.   I. Wilson, Josleen.   II. Title.
RA776.5.D59   1994
613'.089'96073—dc20   93-24430

ISBN 0-517-88302-3

10 9 8 7 6 5 4 3 2 1

First Paperback Edition

CONTENTS

ACKNOWLEDGMENTS

Many people have inspired my professional career and encouraged me to share my experiences with a wider audience. I am most grateful for the unwavering support of my husband, Henry C. Dixon, M.D., who spent many hours looking over my shoulder and offering abundant medical advice, as well as good cheer.

I wish to thank my sister, Patricia McIntyre, for keeping things in order around me and always being willing to lend a listening ear. I thank Freddie Johnson, R.D., professor, Southern University (Baton Rouge, LA) for her friendship and professional guidance.

I particularly wish to thank my agent, Barbara Lowenstein, whose foresight and steadfast initiative brought this book into the publishing mainstream and afforded me the opportunity to work with Crown Publishers; and my editor, Joyce Engelson, whose instant, strong support and direction made this work not only possible, but a consistent pleasure.

Josleen Wilson and I would like to acknowledge the contributions of four outstanding researchers who helped gather and analyze the vast amount of information that underlies this work. Without Roslyn Tolson, Southern University Library, Baton Rouge, the lengthy historical research would not have been possible. Jeffrey Felshman (Chicago), Lee Seifman, and Shelagh Masline (New York) provided both research and editorial support for the complex chapters on AIDS, addictions, and various diseases.

I am also grateful to everybody at Crown Publishers in every department who have been so helpful throughout the editorial and production process. I've especially enjoyed working with Steve Magnuson, Andy Martin, Joan De Mayo, Robin Strashun, Catherine Collins, Phyllis Fleiss, Mannie Barron, Jason Graham, and Debra Kampel.

And, finally, I am indebted to Leon F. Kraft, M.D., Baton Rouge, and Irene Jackson, M.D., Washington, D.C., for their thorough medical review of the manuscript. Their suggestions were invaluable and their generosity profound.

FOREWORD

Elijah Saunders, M.D., F.A.C.C.

In August, 1985, the U.S. Department of Health and Human Services released an eight-volume report based on the federal government's study of the health status of American minority groups entitled "The Report of the Secretary's Task Force on Black and Minority Health." These series of reports documented what had been presumed for a long time: The gap in health status between white and black Americans was very significant. This led the secretary to conclude that more than 60,000 excess deaths occurred per year for blacks compared to the general population and there was no evidence that this gap was narrowing. (By 1993 the figure was 75,000.)

Although hypertension and cardiovascular diseases in general were primary contributors to this life-expectancy differential, other conditions described in this book by nutritionist Barbara Dixon were also significant contributors to this black–white death gap. Although there has been a decline in cardiovascular and noncardiovascular deaths in this country since the early 1970s, this decline still is less significant for African Americans.

Because of these statistics, especially as they concern cardiovascular diseases, my colleagues and I (D. Hall and N. B. Shulman) published in 1985 a textbook entitled *Hypertension in Blacks: Epidemiology, Pathophysiology and Treatment*. A number of prominent authors contributed to this text and, indeed, it pointed out, at least in the area of hypertension, some of the major problems, clinical presentation, and the lack of research in this very important area. This stimulated much interest in the subject and future research such that since 1985 there have been a number of initiatives from the National Heart, Lung and Blood Institute and other branches of the National Institutes of Health concerning the lag in the health status of black Americans.

As a cardiologist, I followed the *Hypertension in Blacks* textbook with a more recent publication, *Cardiovascular Diseases in Blacks* (1991). Again, this document continued to address many of the issues in the cardiovascular area affecting African Americans, almost all disproportionate to the incidence and prevalence among the general population.

With the publication of these two textbooks, primarily for professionals, much interest has been stirred by the general public, as well as health professionals in other areas, in addition to cardiovascular medicine. This is particularly emphasized in this very excellent book, *Good Health for African Americans*. The need for a book of this type, covering all of the major conditions disproportionately affecting black Americans, in language that can be appreciated and understood by the lay public, is overwhelming. I consider it a privilege to read and introduce this very fine work. I believe it is filling a void in the education of the general public, and more particularly, the education of black Americans regarding the major health problems contributing to their shorter life expectancy. Barbara Dixon's superbly formatted approach to the problem begins with the significant history of our African heritage, events that occurred during the African-American slave experience and continued to the post-Reconstruction era, and finally to present time. This book makes for excellent reading both for the lay public and for health professionals.

Finally, Ms. Dixon's candid and objective approach to some very sensitive issues, such as obesity among black females and the tradition of soul-food consumption, is extremely important. I would like to commend her for delving into areas not previously approached by professionals of her status. I would like to commend her, too, for meeting a necessary challenge and, in my opinion, one that can be best fulfilled by a professional of her caliber, who also happens to be an African American.

Elijah Saunders, M.D., F.A.C.C.
Associate Professor, Department of Medicine
Head, Division of Hypertension, University of Maryland,
   School of Medicine
Co-Editor: *Hypertension in Blacks: Epidemiology, Pathophysiology*
   and Treatment
Chief Editor: *Cardiovascular Diseases in Blacks*

INTRODUCTION

If you are black and live in the United States, you are more likely to die sooner, and of a major disease, than members of any other group. By an alarming margin, African Americans lead in the mortality rate from the nation's six biggest killers: heart disease, cancer, stroke, liver disease, infant mortality, accidental death, and homicide.

There's more: Diabetes and respiratory diseases also take an excessively higher death toll among blacks. Now AIDS is widening that health gap still further. African Americans comprise only 12 percent of the population, yet we now account for 30 percent of AIDS cases.

I know that these horrible statistics got your attention. And let me say right now that I believe we can change these numbers. But first, let's take a good look at our situation. What's our bottom line?

African Americans as a whole can expect to die fully six years sooner than the national average of age at death: 75.5. The life expectancy for black men is even worse: They will die eleven years sooner—this at a time when it is said that most people are living longer and the fastest-growing population in the United States is senior citizens! These few critical points on our life-span curve translate into some 75,000 more deaths among blacks each year. Statisticians call these deaths "excess," each one a death that happened too young and too soon.

The worst thing about these statistics is that there's nothing new about them. It's an old, old story. Historically, American blacks have always had a higher mortality rate than whites. But our rate of improvement over the years has at least run parallel to that of the white community. Until, bang, in 1984, we began to fall behind. The gap between blacks and the rest of the population opened, and is still continuing to do so.

Various explanations are suggested: Too many of us use drug and alcohol; we don't eat right; we fail to seek medical care soon enough; we don't follow medical instructions.

Many people blame poverty. And there's no doubt that poverty plays a major role in our poor health. But some scientists say that poverty is only part of a much more complex web of problems. Why did one study of hundreds of affluent doctors themselves reveal that hypertension was three times more common in those who were black and heart attacks ten times more common? Remember, this was among well-to-do blacks!

Other new studies raised more surprising questions. Why do black women gain more weight than white women of the same age? Why are healthy black women—regardless of age, education, or prenatal care—twice as likely to have a baby of low birth weight, the major cause of infant mortality?

The truth is that black health problems are different from those of other groups. As you'll see later in this book, specific environmental factors and the genetic predisposition to certain diseases are different for African Americans. Therefore, any approach to prevention and treatment, if it is to succeed, must also be different.

I decided to put this new information about the possible causes of our poor health profile together with what I had learned in my private practice. I am a nutritionist and my husband, Henry Dixon, is a doctor of internal medicine. Every day, we see the terrible toll diseases such as diabetes, hypertension, and heart disease take on our black patients' lives. We constantly seek new and innovative ways to turn the tide in their favor, but we have always felt that there is something more at work here than ordinary illness.

I had my own personal stake in exploring the health problems of African Americans, for, surely, my family, perhaps like yours, has been part of the gloomy story. My sister, one great-aunt, one great-uncle, and I are the only family members who have not died young.

My parents were born in the South, but since my father was a career army man, we lived all over the world, experiencing many different cultures and cuisines but treasuring traditional home cooking. My mother clung to her southern traditions, loving pork chops, chitlins, ham, mashed potatoes and grits, biscuits and fried chicken, and, well, anything fried, with lots of gravy and plenty of salt. Barbecues and cookouts were treats. These were the enemies from within. Welcoming them, relishing them, we did not know they might be killing us.

When my mother was a child, her father, then in his early thirties, died of pneumonia, a condition young people like that usually fight off, then a common respiratory ailment among blacks. Her mother was overweight and died young, at age thirty-nine, from a stroke.

My mother was overweight, too, and we didn't know her blood pressure was too high. By contrast, my father seemed to be a picture of health and fitness. When new health information began to appear in the popular press, he tried to help us change our diets to emphasize fruits, vegetables, and fish. Unfortunately, he was also a great believer in T-bone steaks.

Suddenly, at forty-five, my father died of a heart attack. Over the next two years, my mother suffered a series of strokes; and by age forty-seven, she was paralyzed on her left side, eventually dying of complications following surgery for colon cancer. My sister, also hypertensive, lost her first child during pregnancy.

After all that, I didn't need a kick to wake me up. It was obvious to me that these medical problems and early deaths were not just unlucky accidents. I began to wonder, Are we programmed to die young, or do we program ourselves? The year I completed my internship in dietetics, I was nearly forty pounds overweight. I took a hard look at myself and at my family's lifeline.

While I seemed healthy, apparently without my parents' health problems, I couldn't shake the feeling that I was sitting on a genetic time bomb. Since then, I have done everything I can to protect myself against early death by reducing my risk factors, especially the excess weight that encumbered me. In the process, I discovered that the enemies striking down my family members in their prime are the same deadly factors threatening every African American.

For rich, poor, or middle class—health problems have a greater impact on blacks than on other Americans. To overcome them, we must understand the ways in which our health problems are different—genetically and environmentally. The two aspects are connected, for environment and patterns of living can trigger the expression of genetic potential for disease in any human being.

The statistics are grim, but I believe they are not written in stone. We *can* change our health story.

Self-help has worked in the general population: In the last fifteen years, heart disease fell 33 percent; stroke was cut in half. This was primarily due to massive public-education campaigns pouring forth from government offices, hospitals, and community programs. People were urged to stop smoking and take control of their health.

The trouble was that this public-health campaign did not speak well enough to the black community. Like other Americans, we need information that takes into account our special health problems, unique needs, and particular assets. Yes, we do have assets that we can draw upon to help ourselves.

"But isn't it all the same?" someone asked me when this book was begun. "Health is health." No, it's not the same.

We African Americans have our own traditions, life experiences, and health risks.

As I hope you'll see from reading later in this book, the way we eat, live, and medicate ourselves—or don't—is rooted in our history. We can trace our modern lifestyle back to the post–Civil War Reconstruction era, back to slave days, and all the way back to Africa. These cultural footprints—the web of genetics, environment, and history—may also contribute in a major way to *solving* our modern health crisis.

Research is beginning to show *why* we suffer more than other groups from poor diet: Born in the past, but also, alas, deeply felt in the present moment, is the constant rage and stress of living in a racist society. That stress, superimposed on an American high-fat, high-salt diet and our genetic framework (evolved to handle our past environment), has proven more virulent than any disease. Indeed, it *is* a disease.

The goal of this book is to make up for all the good health information we didn't get. My own desire was to create an effective nutritional and lifestyle self-help program specifically for African Americans. I call it the Sankofa Program. To put this program together meant looking at the past in order to draw from it all the benefits of our heritage, as well as the challenges. It also meant looking at the present, to take into account all of our problems living in the United States today.

This book tries, therefore, to consider *all* the major health elements that cut across our lives:

- Old traditions that influence the foods we choose and the way we prepare them. These can be traced back to Africa, through changes that occurred in early slave days in the American South, and into modern urban life.
- Modern eating habits. Studies show that what black Americans eat may be killing them.
- Destructive lifestyle practices—smoking, alcohol, drugs— that have come to define the self-image of too many African Americans.
- Black stress: a steady, subdued rage that researchers now believe is a root cause of ill health. It can make hypertension and other diseases worse, or stimulate dormant illness.
- Genetic factors—specific markers that make blacks, like other groups, vulnerable or resistant to certain diseases.

Modern genetic research may begin to give us answers to some of our most perplexing questions:

Why do affluent and well-educated black men and women have a soaring incidence of hypertension and heart disease?

Why does lupus, a condition in which the immune system goes awry, inexplicably afflict 1 in 245 black women, but only 1 in 750 white women?

What is behind the "salt sensitivity" that causes many blacks to *retain* salt under stress rather than excrete it as most people do?

- Cultural beliefs, folklore, and home cures, along with the well-documented negative approach of health professionals to black Americans, that influence the way we seek, find, and use medical help.

I believe we are entering a new era of awareness and that we are much more willing to take charge of our own health. Many of these battles we have fought before, but now we have some powerful allies even in the top ranks of the Department of Health and Human Services.

I am particularly pleased by one example: Dr. Louis J. Sullivan, former Secretary of Health and Human Services, forced RJR Nabisco to cancel a campaign to launch its new Uptown cigarette into the black community. A few days before the tobacco company planned to distribute free packs of cigarettes in black neighborhoods, Dr. Sullivan spoke at the University of Pennsylvania and said, "Let this be the beginning of an all-out effort to resist the tobacco merchants' attempts to earn profits at the expense of the health and well-being of our poor and minority citizens. Enough! No more!"

Dr. Sullivan's speech made headlines across the nation. Within twenty-four hours, the tobacco company withdrew the brand from the market.

Soon after, Harlem community groups whitewashed billboards that advertised alcohol. Barbers in Baltimore's black neighborhoods began training themselves to check blood pressure and started referring their hypertensive patrons to medical clinics. In Washington, D.C., the Shiloh Baptist Church started a Family Life Center that provides an indoor track and offers counseling on drug abuse and teenage pregnancy. And these are just a few examples of new programs.

Across the country, increasing numbers of studies are under way, and—most important—more grass-roots organizations are getting on the good health bandwagon. And more ideas—which I will talk about throughout this book—are being initiated so that we can find our own personal way out of our health crisis. But it is still up to each one of us as individuals.

Part One

FROM THE PAST

1

AFRICAN CHRONICLES

Why do all the studies show that black Africans in this century (at least before the terrible present famine) seem to be healthier than African Americans? The truth is complicated, for there are many kinds of black Africans, each with different histories. Furthermore, they also experience health problems when their environment and lifestyles change. In a Kenyan study, it was found that the Masai who move from the countryside into towns gain weight and develop hypertension along with their change in diet.

I realized that to understand African-American health issues, I had to know more about our history. I read hundreds of anthropological journals that reprinted diaries from long-dead European traders; documents from clergymen, ships' captains, plantation owners, and overseers; and oral histories of American slaves themselves. It's a fascinating saga, this health story, and it begins in Africa.

The earliest inhabitants of Africa were skilled hunters and gatherers. Long before other ancient civilizations, Africans planted seeds, worshiped gods, and fashioned shapely tools from iron. The beauty they perceived, they expressed in masks, painting, pottery, wood carvings, and gold figurines. Their art and religion permeated and reflected every aspect of life.

Africans believed in a supreme god whose energy was present in all things—humans, animals, plants, and minerals. They also believed that spiritual energy continued to exist even after death. Spirit possession is said to thrive in the shouting and ecstasy complex of some black American churches today.

The Africans spoke many tongues, although with a common linguistic bond. Their music reflected the everyday ebb and flow of life—grounded in many rhythms played simultaneously, dominated by drums, with perfectly synchronized dance accompaniment. Leaders called and people chanted the response. Men and women danced for religious and social purpose, and because, to them, dancing was life itself.

In physical appearance, Africans varied greatly even in regional West Africa, the origin of most of our ancestors. They were short and tall; broad- and narrow-nosed. Some had short hair, others long and thickly straight. As Maya Angelou describes it, their skin color ranged from dark plummy blue to palest cream.

West Africa bulges out distinctively into the Atlantic Ocean. Prehistoric hardwood forests and tropical savannas lie between desert and ocean. After village life developed, around 2500 B.C., cities gradually grew, eventually becoming empires.

People traded gold, ivory, spices, seeds, and tools from village to village, state to state, and continent to continent. Between the ninth and eleventh centuries, powerful states emerged in the western Sudan, near trade routes established by the Egyptians. The first of these great ruling empires was ancient Ghana, a fabulously wealthy kingdom that supplied gold to North Africa and Europe. When Ghana fell to Muslim zealots, the nearby state of Mali took its place in power and prestige, followed by Songhai. Each of these fabled and gold-rich empires was a center of commerce and intellectual life. African traders were respected as far away as China, India, and Europe.

Despite this commerce and trade, African tribal villages were largely agricultural. The land belonged to the community. Religious worship focused on the fertility of crops and people.

Individuals saw themselves in relation to the group and its needs. Through bad times and bad weather, available food was shared. Always, the old, sick, and infirm were cared for. The worst fate to befall an individual was to become separated from his or her tribal group. This idea of kinship, which defined the societies of West Africa, has survived hundreds of years of violent oppression and colonialism, and exists in some form today everywhere people of African descent live.

West African foods also survive and in some regions of the United States even dominate African-American cuisine. Watermelon, black-eyed peas, okra, sesame, and taro were all native West African foods. Cowpeas of many varieties (black-eyed peas are one) were often combined with regional staples and eaten as a substitute for meat.

The staple used varied according to the region. Corn, millet, and rice were common in the coastal areas and Sierra Leone. Yams were popular in Nigeria, where they were traditionally boiled and pounded into a paste called *fufu*. In the more southern areas of the Congo and Angola, cassava and plantains were standards.

Cassava, along with chilis, peanuts, pumpkins, eggplant, and tomatoes had been introduced to West Africa through early trade routes. The enormous cassava tubers, although far less nutritious than native grains, were easy to grow even in poor soil and bad weather. Cassava could be roasted, boiled, or sun-dried and made into a powdery white flour. The dark green leaves were used as a vegetable, even as they are today, and were a valuable source of vitamins and minerals.

The most frequently eaten fruits were akee apples, baobab fruit, guava, lemon, papaya (papaw), pineapple, and watermelon. Many dishes included coconut milk.

Africa was a significant part of the international spice trade. The exotic images still evoked by place names such as Zanzibar, Marrakesh, and Timbuktu originate from their days as exchange points for spices. Similarly, many varieties of peppers, although not native to Africa, were adopted enthusiastically and incorporated into African cooking.

The tribes of the more arid savanna region that bordered the Sahara Desert raised camels, sheep, goats, and cattle for food. In other regions, local fish and game were eaten. Chickens were also raised, but they were usually reserved for special occasions. Eggs, although used for trade, were often taboo in the village of origin. Eating eggs was said to cause difficult childbirth and made children misbehave. These taboos, which may have developed to ensure future chicken flocks, still exist in some parts of Africa, and chicken itself is still considered a prestigious meat among many modern African peoples.

Peanuts, which originated in Brazil, were a popular legume (rather than a true nut) and were eaten raw, boiled, roasted, or ground into meal, flour, or paste. (Agricultural scientist George Washington Carver was credited with the creation of peanut oil and peanut butter, but both had been made in West Africa for centuries before he developed them in the United States.)

Africans used many kinds of nuts and seeds to flavor and thicken sauces. Cashews, agobono (or apon) seeds, watermelon seeds (egusi, usually dried and ground), kola nuts, and sesame seeds were popular.

Cooking methods throughout West Africa were similar. Ovens didn't exist and most foods were boiled or fried. Palm oil was the usual cooking fat, but peanut oil, shea oil (from the nuts of the shea tree), and occasionally coconut oil were used in different regions. African stews—flavored with tomatoes, onions, and hot peppers; spicy, thick, and made sticky with okra—were a forerunner of Louisiana gumbo.

Two meals a day were typical in West Africa, one late in the morning and one in the evening, although it was also usual to eat small amounts throughout the day. Everyone ate together except for formal occasions, when the men would eat first, followed by the boys, then the girls, and finally the women.

The culture from which our ancestors came had much to offer, not only to its people then but to us now. The parts of this diet that we would consider negative today were offset by its benefits. For example, nuts, particularly peanuts, supplied valuable fat, protein, and B vitamins often missing from the African diet. Likewise, frying in vegetable oils supplied most of the little fat received from any source. The main portion of the African diet came from whole grains, fruits, and vegetables, seen today as the hallmark of a healthy diet. It pays to remember history.

Slavery was an entrenched feature of the Old World. In most countries of the world, white, brown, and black peoples were bought and sold, mostly as spoils of war, with little attention paid to race. Almost anyone could become a slave. For several decades before the European exploration of Africa, the Muslims had been dragging captives across the Sahara into Arabia. However, all

Muslims, whatever their color or condition of freedom, were brothers in faith.

In the Middle Ages, Christians and Muslims began to capture and enslave one another for religious reasons. As climatic changes enlarged the Sahara to the south, large sections of Africa became isolated from the main centers of empire. The Africans were without modern weaponry, and this fact would eventually force the great kingdoms to their knees, the victims of the continuing and endless wars between Muslims and Christians.

In 1444, Henry the Navigator, seeking gold and spreading Christianity for Portugal, first explored the African coast. He captured a sleeping village and carried its people back to Portugal in chains. Within ten years, Portugal was importing one thousand African slaves a year.

At the same time, a flourishing trade in many types of goods soon developed between Europeans and Africans. The Europeans named each section of the African coast after its leading export: the Grain Coast; Ivory Coast; Gold Coast. From the Volta River to the Niger delta was the Slave Coast.

New vistas began to open up for future commerce between Europeans and Africans. But the opening of the New World— and Europe's passion for a new food—put an end to that bright prospect. The hunger for sugar forged a chain that eventually linked all the countries of Europe to Africa and the New World. And with sugar, almost all other trade was forgotten, except one: slaves.

2

AMERICA IN SLAVERY

It is said that a black man sailed with Columbus on his first voyage to the New World—and that black men were there to greet them. Certainly, Africans sailed with Columbus on his second and third voyages. Black men—descendants of the first Africans captured by the Portuguese in 1444—later accompanied Spanish and Portuguese adventurers across the mainland of the Americas. In 1513, Balboa's men included thirty Africans who hacked their way through the thick vegetation of Panama to the Pacific. Africans accompanied Cortés; they were with Ponce de León in Florida and Pizarro in Peru. Some (called maroons or runaways) broke their chains and fled into the wilderness to join the native Indians and form their own settlements.

It's important to note that the first African immigrants to the North American colonies were not slaves.

In the summer of 1619, twenty Africans stepped ashore in Jamestown, Virginia, one year before the celebrated *Mayflower* landed at Plymouth Rock. Legend has it that somewhere on the high seas pirates hijacked the Africans from a Spanish slave vessel bound for the West Indies. The pirate ship eventually put in at Jamestown, where her desperate captain exchanged the Africans for food. Since slavery did not exist in North America, the Africans joined the ranks of white indentured servants. Four years later, in the same Virginia colony, the first black American was born. The census of 1624–1625 recorded twenty-three black settlers—eleven men, ten women, and two children.

Hundreds of Africans eventually made the journey to America as indentured servants or freemen. Some came through England, others from Spain, Portugal, and the West Indies. At that point, the Virginia colony was equally oppressive to both black and white servants, who were assigned similar tasks and held in equal contempt. The prejudice against indentured servants—who were mostly debtors, religious dissenters, and criminals who had been forced to the colonies—was extreme, but historians believe it was freely displayed without regard to race or color. No laws connecting servitude to color existed. Black and white servants worked together in the same fields and shared the same huts. They ran away together, married, and raised families.

Most of the early African Americans worked out their terms of servitude and eventually, like their white counterparts, were freed. As free men and women, they purchased land and worked it, and generally were equal colonial citizens. Some even owned other black servants, and there is evidence that a few imported white indentured servants.

Historians believe that this early New World was not color-conscious. Why did an economic system based on slavery develop? And why were blacks, and only blacks, designated as slaves? Their story unfolds in the deadly swamps of the West Indies.

The development of large-scale sugar planting, first on the islands off the coast of Africa and later in the Caribbean, created a demand for laborers that casual kidnapping couldn't supply. Europeans had an insatiable sweet tooth: The more sugar supplied, the greater the demand. New planting methods were developed based on gang labor.

Sugar planters did not care where their workers came from or what color they were. But they did care about profit. Therefore, from the beginning, they looked to see who could be forced to carry out the work without pay. They tried to enslave the native Indian population, but the Indians died of smallpox and other diseases transmitted by Europeans. They considered enslaving white servants but hesitated; white slaves could appeal to white public opinion, as well as foreign governments, for protection; they could also more easily escape and hide in the larger community.

By a process of elimination, Africans were selected to become a permanent enslaved work force. Africans had many advantages for the planters. First, they were strong. Slave traders said that since Africans came from tropical climates, they could work in extreme heat for long hours without succumbing to heat exhaustion. Second, runaway blacks could not blend easily into the larger community. Third, Africa offered a seemingly inexhaustible supply of new labor. Finally, there was no one of influence anywhere in the world to speak for them.

There was one more important reason why Africans were chosen: They were largely immune to malaria and other great tropical fevers, which killed Europeans and Indians by the thousands—for reasons that only became known in our century.

Thus, in 1517, West Africans were officially, and solely, nominated for slave labor on the sugar plantations of Brazil by famed missionary bishop Bartolomé Las Casas. From that fateful decision, human slavery based on color became the foundation on which the New World's economic system would thrive.

Now, the old African-European trade partnership became dominated by Europe and focused almost exclusively on trade in human beings. Within a few years, hundreds of thousands of slaves were crossing the Atlantic each year, the soil of Africa and America drenched in their blood.

As the years went by, the slave trade boomed as sugar planting spread rapidly through the Caribbean. As the British, French, and Dutch broke the monopolies of Spain and Portugal, the demand for slaves to work the new settlements grew even greater. From 1502, when the first records of Spanish colonials were kept, until the 1860s, more than 11 million Africans were brought to the New World in chains. Brazil, the world's leading supplier of sugar and gold, was by far the largest single trafficker in slaves; British and French colonies in the Caribbean and the far-flung Spanish-American empire were next. Slavery grew more gradually in the American colonies, where tobacco and cotton were the main crops.

Many African leaders tried to end the trade by forbidding their subjects to participate in it. Europeans were impervious to such pleas, however, and continued to take slaves from a thousand villages and towns, often in collusion with African slave merchants. Some slaves were captured in wars; others were kidnapped. Some were sold into slavery for infractions of African laws. The strong and the weak, warriors and merchants, priests and princes—all might become slaves.

They were chained two by two, left leg to right leg. Forced marches of five hundred miles to the coast were common. At coastal trading stations, slaves were shackled in irons and imprisoned in underground pits. Fevers spread rapidly through these dungeons. The Africans treated many of their tropical diseases with lime juice, malagueta pepper, cardamom, herbs and roots, and the branches and gums of trees. Europeans were amazed by these cures and some tried using them to keep their captives alive. However, the Europeans scoffed when Africans told them that yellow fever was caused by mosquitoes. Everyone knew, they said, that "miasma," the rotting vegetation of the swamps—not mosquitoes—caused yellow fever.

Despite attempts to contain disease, many died at the trading stations before setting foot on a ship. Many more died during the awful passage to the Americas. Chained in pairs, man to man, woman to woman, they were stacked on platforms secured in the holds of the ships. The slavers knew that overcrowding caused death, but they thought it worth the financial risk based on a potentially larger number to sell at the end of the journey. It was common for slave ships to arrive in harbor with one-fourth or more of their captives dead and more dying.

To keep captives alive, traders tried feeding them their customary West African foods. Corn or another staple, yams, malagueta pepper, and palm oil made up the shipboard diet, along with some European foods. Hot peppers were added to help prevent dysentery. Even so, the quantity and the quality of the food was poor and many ships ran out of provisions before reaching port.

The hold of a slaver was a perfect environment for disease. Smallpox, measles, and dysentery, caused by contaminated food and water, could spread quickly among people tied together. Death also came in other ways. Many were killed as they fought to liberate themselves. Others resisted by refusing to eat. Hunger strikes led to whippings and forced feeding. Suicide was a way out for some. Profound despair often led to death as impassive and motionless men and women refused all food and drink.

Those who survived the slave ships endured every assault on body and spirit. They were tough and they were courageous. In Africa, they had fought death from the stings and bites of a thousand varieties of murderous disease-carrying insects. Only those who had very specific resistance to certain diseases survived. Soon, these same biological advantages would be turned against them.

The slave trade in the colonies was relatively small compared with that in Brazil and the Caribbean. Initially, slavery in North America was justified by the clergy, who said that Africans had to be enslaved in order to be saved by Christianity. It followed that once a slave was baptized, he or she would be freed. The colonials needed a way out of that particular conundrum. To exploit the slave-based economy to its fullest, the colonies also had to increase the slave population without the continual expense of importing new slaves from Africa. As Lerone Bennett, Jr., writes in his superb historical account *Before the Mayflower,* beginning in 1667, Virginia, followed by the other colonies, enacted a series of laws to strip "black slaves of all rights of personality and make color a badge of servitude." Enslavement would continue even after death: Children of slaves would also be slaves.

In 1710, the number of slaves in the colonies was fifty thousand. Over the next 150 years, the economic success of southern planters ensured that the slave trade grew steadily. Eventually, 425,000 slaves would be captured and sent to North America; as slavery was handed down from mother to child, the numbers swelled to millions. By 1825, the United States had become the largest slave power in the Western world and the most resistant to abolition.

Once baptism had been put aside as a rationale for enslavement, the colonials had to look elsewhere for authoritative support for the "peculiar institution." Many years later, Frederick Douglass would write that "the oppressor ever finds, in the characters of the oppressed, a full justification for his oppression." In North America, those who found such justification were southern physicians. It is here, in the scientific journals of southern medical institutions, that racism was born and the real story of our health in America begins.

The blade of medical reason conveniently cut two ways: First, Africans were healthier. The Africans' well-known resistance to certain deadly diseases helped convince doctors that blacks were somehow immune to the effects of extreme, debilitating heat. One physician wrote, "In our swamps and under our sun the Negro thrives, but the white man dies." His conclusion was that God had created Africans to labor for whites.

Experimenting on the bodies of dead slaves, physicians claimed that the livers, kidneys, and "glands" of blacks were larger, and their skin able to throw heat off more rapidly. Thus, the bigger and tougher Africans could labor eighteen hours a day in the sweltering climate of the South.

The blade cut in the other direction when physicians cited anatomical "facts" that made blacks inferior. The doctors said that the hearts and brains of blacks were smaller, and their nervous systems less well developed, which protected them from fevers and also accounted for their childlike behavior and absolute dependence on whites. Believing this, it followed that Africans were stupid and didn't feel pain as intensely as other races.

Doctors also claimed that the lungs of blacks were smaller than those of whites and blamed the high incidence of pneumonia and tuberculosis among slaves on "weak lungs."

These physicians, who had no accurate knowledge of how diseases were contracted and spread, drew a scientific portrait of blacks as sluggish, dull in mind, weak in will. It was a portrait so deadly, and so economically useful, that it survives even to this day.

Historians Kenneth and Virginia Kiple, writing in *Phylon, The Atlanta University Review of Race and Culture,* in 1980, believe that by the beginning of the nineteenth century the truth about disease immunities and susceptibilities had become so twisted that whites felt completely justified in enslaving Africans and subjecting them to harsh working conditions. Slaves had by now paid twice for their disease experience: enslaved because they were strong and resistant to disease; kept enslaved because they were physically inferior.

What was the truth? Let's look at a few of the health facts put forth by these early doctors: resistance to malaria and resistance to heat exhaustion; susceptibility to cold and respiratory diseases.

Like all populations, Africans had certain resistances to disease and certain susceptibilities. (With two exceptions, skin color has nothing to do with either.)

When we speak of resistance and susceptibility, we are talking about how millions of genes, handed down through generations, help individuals survive in a particular environment. Thus, Africans whose blood contained certain factors were able to survive malaria in a malarious environment.

Africans were genetically adapted in at least three ways to resist malaria. Technically speaking, red blood cells that are Duffy group–negative, meaning that they lack a specific antigen, are resistant to invasion by *Plasmodium vivax,* one of the four strains of malaria. Nearly 100 percent of West Africans are Duffy group–negative.

West Africans were also resistant to the even more deadly *Plasmodium falciparum.* People who carry a single gene for sickle-cell trait are resistant to this type of malaria. So are those who are deficient in a red-cell enzyme called G-6-PD. It's estimated that half of the West Africans had one or both of these protective genes against this strain of malaria.

What about heat? Despite their resistance to malaria, Africans could not tolerate heat any better than anyone else. In general, slaves probably suffered an even greater heat load because deeply pigmented skin absorbs heat; their intense labor would have increased that burden even further.

It's possible that some groups who have lived in tropical climates over many generations may develop a genetic adaptation to extreme heat, but with time, all humans adapt to heat stress in the same way. Modern studies have shown that when blacks and other races are equally active in the same environment over a period of time, there is little difference in heat tolerance.

In slavery, blacks may have shown a higher initial tolerance for extreme humid heat because they were more accustomed to working in that kind of environment. But other laborers probably adjusted to the heat and fared just as well.

One physiological difference, perhaps a rapid evolutionary adaptation that occurred during the slave trade, might have helped slaves survive heat better—an inherent ability to retain vital body salts. Conservation of salts may have helped protect slaves against dehydration, heat prostration, and heatstroke. Later, we'll see how this factor may have come to affect us adversely—even today.

Just as blacks were said to tolerate heat, they were, conversely, believed to suffer especially from cold. This seemed logical. But, in fact, modern studies of American soldiers have shown that while blacks may at first be more susceptible to cold injury, over time they become acclimated like everyone else.

As far as "small lungs" and respiratory diseases are concerned, our lungs are no smaller or larger than anyone else's. Yet even today there is some confusion regarding our susceptibility to pulmonary infections. In early America, pneumonia and tuberculosis ravaged both slaves and planters. The incidence was higher among Africans because they had never been exposed to respiratory infections and thus were extremely vulnerable to them. Although these diseases eventually decreased among blacks, they always remained relatively high. There are several possible reasons.

Slaves worked outdoors in all seasons and in all weathers, and their drafty cabins, while cramped, did not afford much protection from dampness and cold. Airborne infections spread rapidly through people living closely together. Finally, poor nutrition leads to lowered immunity, which makes people more susceptible to infections. Some of these same factors may account for the rising incidence of respiratory illnesses among African Americans today.

Finally, what about those "small brains" and "big glands"? There was no such thing as comparative anatomy in those days. Dissections were carried out on black corpses; in no recorded instance were their organs systematically compared with those of whites. Modern anatomists agree that once the very thin protective layer of skin is gently separated and lifted from a cadaver, there is virtually no difference whatsoever among the bodies of varying races. The greater susceptibility of Africans to certain diseases was largely due to environmental and living conditions, not to their anatomy. And with the exception of resistance to malaria, none of the racial suppositions made by these doctors proved to be true.

In fact, they missed the two ailments that actually do involve skin color. Dark skin protects against sun damage. Lighter skin, heavily exposed to sun, grows cancers. The second exception: Because dark skin does not absorb sun rays very well, it cannot make much vitamin D, which probably accounted for the high incidence of rickets in black children. Neither of these two skin color–related ailments was recognized by southern physicians.

It's important to say, however, that pigmentation varies in all races. Light-skinned African Americans are as vulnerable to sun exposure as light-skinned European Americans.

Racism was let loose upon the new land like a slow, hot wind, blowing far and wide. The erroneous medical notions spawned seeds of ignorance that would float from place to place, easily take root in fresh soil, and grow into a garden of weeds—weeds of misinformation.

One other aspect of medicine developed during slavery that would have far-reaching effects on our lives, troubling (as we'll see) even today: the medical care slaves received.

On most plantations, slaves were expected to report an illness quickly, before it became incapacitating or infected the white master and his family, as well as other workers. Treatment was usually provided by the planters, overseers, midwives, herbologists, dentists, and barbers. Only if these ministrations failed to cure might a physician be called.

What diseases did slaves contract and how were they treated? Everyone living in the southern colonies suffered from infections and diseases of all types, especially fevers, respiratory diseases, and parasites of the gastrointestinal tract.

Slave children were especially vulnerable, dying frequently of diphtheria and whooping cough. Gastrointestinal parasites and rickets were unfortunately part of a slave child's life. Some children suffered severe joint pains, chronic leg ulcers, and abdominal pains, overt symptoms of sickle-cell disease. Other reported causes of death were "teething, convulsions, seizures, and fits." We now know that these were probably due to malnutrition, particularly to a lack of calcium, vitamin D, and magnesium in the diet of the youngest slaves.

Many black children died in infancy. Infants were born too small, much as our black infants are today, and their low birth weight was largely responsible for their high mortality rate. One cause of infant death occurring almost exclusively among slaves was "smothering" or "suffocation." Planters said mothers rolled over on their infants in the night or pressed them so tightly that air was cut off. But some planters, and many blacks, too, believed that mothers deliberately suffocated their babies rather than have them raised in slavery. Some cases of smothering may have been sudden infant death syndrome, or crib death, which even today, for unexplained reasons, is higher among black infants.

The southern physician relied on excessive use of purging drugs, leeches, and lancets, which depleted the body of blood and nourishment and exhausted the already-weakened patient. Slaves got even sicker from their treatments, probably because they were already undernourished and anemic from such parasites as hookworm.

Slaves often resisted white remedies. When symptoms of illness appeared, instead of reporting to the overseer, they turned to older relatives for medical advice or sought care from herb and root doctors among the slave population. This was in keeping with their traditional ways of seeking cures in Africa.

Forbidden to treat themselves with these home cures, African remedies circulated secretly through the slave quarters and were passed down privately from generation to generation. Occasionally, whites would learn of a particularly effective medicine and adopt it. Milkweed (*Asclepias syriaca*), an ancient black folk remedy almost as effective as quinine for fevers, was reported by Dr. Richard Cauthorn in the white medical journal *Stethoscope* in 1857.

Among the slaves were conjure doctors, African healers who used "magic" plants, spells, and suggestion to heal. These doctors were far ahead of Europeans in their appreciation of the power of the mind over the body. They used the beliefs and superstitions of their patients, and their powers of persuasion often healed illnesses that white doctors could not cure. They could also work their powers of suggestion in reverse, casting spells to bring sicknesses to a well person. Hexes were administered with certain foods and potions, and some of these recipes persist today, particularly in remote rural areas of the southern United States and the Caribbean.

The desire to treat themselves, or at least choose their own practitioners, brought slaves into direct conflict with their masters. Slave owners complained that blacks tended to report sickness only after the disease had progressed to a serious stage. Thus, the dilemma for the slaves was whether to treat at home, risking reprisal, or to surrender the body to white medicine. To use his own treatment, a sick slave would have to conceal the illness or pass it off to the master as less serious than it actually was. I believe this historical tendency to hide illnesses and resist professional medical treatment from white physicians, understandable in the past, persists and plays a part in our present dismal health statistics. (See Chapter 19 and Chapter 20.)

The slaves' self-help medicine shows that African traditions survived in the colonies. Yet most American blacks today, myself included, grew up believing that no genuine African culture had lasted—because our culture had been stamped out.

Orlando Patterson, writing in *Slavery and Social Death,* has said three elements were essential to make slavery work. The first was violence. Slavery wasn't a one-time-only pact: The slave could be killed at any time for even minor disobedience. The second was dishonor, a state that Frederick Douglass said fell to anyone without power. And the third, which was most rigorously enforced by the slaveholders, Patterson calls "natal alienation"—the deliberate separation of an individual from his cultural past. This last has been the basis of controversy for generations of historians and anthropologists. And it is extremely important when it comes to understanding—and changing—our health story.

Over half the American slaves came from the coastal areas of what are now Angola and Nigeria. Others came from the regions that are today Senegal, Gambia, Sierra Leone, Liberia, Togo, Ghana, Benin, Gabon, and Zaire.

Some came by way of Europe or the West Indies; others came directly from Africa. They belonged to different kinship groups —the Mandingo, Hausa, Efiks, Fantins, Ashanti, Bambara, Fulani, Ibo, Malinke, or Yoruba—and spoke different, though related, languages. Most were ordinary people, but some were warriors and some were from the highest ranks of African society. At home, each had identified closely with his or her own tribal group. In America, slave owners, seeking to dominate the slave population quickly, were determined to stamp out all vestiges of the African past. Relatives and members of the same tribe were separated. New slaves from many different villages and nations were housed together, usually in small groups of eight to thirty. Without kinship or even a common language, they learned English from white or Native American indentured servants. To make separation complete, masters assigned new names to slaves, allotted clothing, and cut hair. To survive, slaves were forced to adapt totally to the colonial American culture.

Unable to claim their own past, they had none to pass on to their children. The total cleaving of an individual from his society meant that only the master stood between him and death. Planters reasoned that when Africa was left behind, the old ways of independence and self-pride would soon be forgotten.

Generations of African Americans grew up believing that they were the only Americans without a past. Their cultural patterns seemed identical to those of European Americans, shaped only by the particular region of the United States in which they were born and grew up. At the beginning of this century, scholars of black history generally believed that there was no surviving African culture in the United States.

Then, in the 1920s, cultural anthropologist Melville J. Herskovits set that notion on its ear. Herskovits, who eventually dedicated his life to tracing cultural influences from Africa, was the first to propose that even though slaves came from different villages and spoke many different dialects, they shared many things in common.

By firsthand observation of modern Africans, Herskovits discovered that certain "Africanisms" survived in American life. They survived in the way we use certain foods, in knowledge of herbs and their medicinal value, and in our view of the world and our perception of life and death. The way we sing and walk and dance is African. These traits are not carried in genes; they are cultural. Africanisms survive in family life, religious practices, and music.

Herskovits and many of the anthropological scholars who followed him believed that the slave system that had been designed to erase memory had actually forced that culture first to submerge, only to be recreated in the New World. Enslaved people, powerless and stripped of their identity, separated from their nearest kin, kept their traditional practices hidden—religious worship, myths, stories, music, dance. These, they shared with one another and handed down to their children and to others who would come later.

Melville Herskovits published his classic work *The Myth of the Negro Past* in 1941. In the fifty years following its publication, many scholars have taken up his themes, although not everyone has agreed with every opinion he held. Sidney W. Mintz and Richard Price, Lawrence Levine and Sterling Stuckey, Charles Joyner and Mechal Sobel are only a few of the hundreds of black authors and scholars who were deeply affected by Herskovits's ideas. As they looked closer at African-American culture, they discovered a rich heritage. Linguists, for example, found a large number of ancient African word formations and intonations present in modern America: *goober, gumbo, ninny, tote,* and *yam* are all African words.

Africa permeates American music: playing between the beat (syncopation), improvisation, several contrasting rhythms occurring simultaneously (polymeter), a percussion-heavy beat, the unity of song and dance, highly emotional and deeply felt performance, vocal harmony, the call-and-response style of singing and chanting, until an almost trancelike state is induced.

Africa also exists in the concept of the family. Despite laws against marriage, and the practice of selling children away from their parents and separating the mothers and fathers, a strong sense of family grew up among slaves. "Weddings," performed by the slaves or sometimes by the owner of the plantation, were days of rejoicing and feasts.

As the slave population increased, family structure began to imitate the white nuclear family—with one crucial difference: Slave families could be torn apart by the sale or loan of a parent or child. The extended family—a memory of ancient kinships in Africa—reached out and cared for dislocated parents and children. Today, extended family ties, respect for elders, and respect for mothers are a continuation of that kinship system that developed in Africa.

Our African heritage is also visible in our contemporary food traditions, even though there's still controversy about nutrition among slaves. Their basic diet was corn and fatback, or bacon, distributed in weekly rations. Some slave owners provided rice instead of corn. Some added molasses and occasionally salted fish to the weekly rations. (Molasses formed one point on the slave-trading triangle. Molasses is the liquid that remains when sugar has been crystallized from sugarcane; molasses was shipped from the Caribbean to New England and distilled into rum; rum was shipped to Africa and exchanged for slaves; and slaves were shipped to the West Indies to work in the sugarcane fields.)

During the hog-slaughtering season in the fall, lesser pork cuts such as chitlins (intestines), maws (stomach lining), and hocks would sometimes be given to slaves. Some slaves were encouraged to raise hogs and chickens, which might be sold by the slave for cash or taken by the slave owner.

On all plantations, the hours of labor were long, as long as eighteen hours a day during the planting and harvesting seasons. Field hands often ate their meals while they worked, mixing corn-meal with water and baking small cakes on the backs of their hoes. On some of the large coastal plantations, community cooks fed everyone. On smaller plantations, slaves prepared their own meals from rations, usually given out on Fridays. Children apparently were generally fed from a common feeding trough, where they ate the worst available food.

Meals prepared after a full day of labor were usually simple, one-dish vegetable stews that could be made to last an entire week. (Iron from the cast-iron pots would have provided an unintended dietary supplement.) Some of these stew inventions are still eaten in the south today—stews combining rice, salt meat, fish or game, and vegetables, and Hoppin' John, a one-pot meal of rice and black-eyed peas. Sunday was the traditional day of rest and Sunday dinner became an important family occasion.

Was the monotonous core diet of corn and fatback ever supplemented? Travelers in the South told stories about slaves who hunted wild game and fish. We also know from plantation records that slaves somehow managed to introduce black-eyed peas, okra, peanuts, and sesame—all African staples—to the colonies. These vegetables may have been part of the shipboard provisions, or the Africans may have managed to smuggle in seeds. On small plots allotted by some plantation owners, slaves grew these vegetables, along with cabbage, collard and mustard greens, sweet potatoes, and turnips. This historical evidence suggests that slaves ate from a wide variety of foods with good nutritional value. The trouble with such evidence is that it comes from occasional visitors to the South and records kept by slave owners and overseers on many different kinds of farms across a large region.

The question is whether or not slaves were able to *routinely* supplement their food rations. Modern archaeological evidence suggests that there were huge differences in the way slaves fared in their daily diets. In the spring of 1980, in an extensive analysis published in *Medical Anthropology,* Dr. Tyson Gibbs, then an instructor in the Department of Preventive Medicine and Community Health at the University of South Carolina School of Medicine, and his colleagues from the departments of anthropology at the University of Miami and the University of Georgia examined new archaeological information from four major plantation sites. The new evidence showed that only along the seaboard coast of South Carolina, Georgia, and northern Florida were slaves able to fully supplement their food rations. Here, with a rich abundance of wild foods available year round, they gathered herbs and set overnight traps to catch small game such as opossums, rabbits, raccoons, and squirrels. Shellfish were plentiful along the shore, and freshwater fish were thick in the inlets.

Away from the coastal plantations, nutrition was poor and hunger was common. Due to the corn-heavy diet, slaves suffered from pellagra, a disease caused by a deficiency of niacin. Symptoms began with diarrhea and vomiting; the individual would become disoriented and begin to hallucinate, then finally die.

Beriberi and "sore-mouth" were also common among the slaves, caused by deficiencies in vitamin A and many of the B vitamins. Calcium was lacking in the basic diet. Many Africans, then as now, were lactose-intolerant, meaning that they were unable to digest milk sugar. Lactose intolerance often prevented them from consuming milk when it was available. Fish and vegetables were only occasionally available.

Whatever their circumstances, slaves clearly adapted their West African cooking methods to whatever foods they had. Now lard, instead of palm oil, was used to fry or flavor everything. Corn kernels were dried and boiled (hominy) or coarsely ground and prepared as grits.

Household workers received more varied diets than did field hands. To local recipes, they added their own West African cooking methods. The result was a purely American southern cuisine. They fried chicken and fish, roasted sweet potatoes, boiled green leafy vegetables with pork fat, and invented vegetable-based stews thickened with okra or file powder ground from sassafras.

Ultimately, a new culture was forged as the African and colonial cultures worked on each other, took root, and grew in the New World. As we have seen, cultural traditions in languages, music, arts, and cuisine brought from Africa were treasured and protected by our ancestors, who eventually passed these into the larger culture. Ralph Ellison has said that the new culture was neither black nor white, but uniquely all-American. But first the United States had to go through the first modern war, fought largely over the issue of black freedom.

Many of the northern states had banned slavery since the beginning of the American Revolution. In 1808, it became illegal to import slaves. By the 1830s, there were 300,000 "free persons of color" living in the United States, most of them in the North.

In the South, slavery remained entrenched. More than 2 million slaves labored on the cotton plantations of the South, supporting an economy largely based on a single important crop. Although new slaves could no longer be brought into the country, the slave population continued to grow.

In most of South America and the Caribbean countries, slavery ended without bloodshed. But in North America, tensions between the states that supported slavery and those that opposed it led to the Civil War in 1861.

By the end of that war, the 4 million blacks were second-, third-, fourth-, or fifth-generation Americans. Their parents, grandparents, and great-grandparents had been born into slavery on American soil. Now their children were free.

3

THE TWENTIETH CENTURY

Some blacks left the South immediately, searching for relatives and a better life in the North. However, with emancipation, most African Americans remained in the South. Many lacked skills and few could read and write. Former slave owners continued to exploit black labor through tenant farming and sharecropping. Under this system, the black farmer was perpetually in debt to the white landowner.

Food was often scarce during and immediately after the war and people experimented with wild vegetables such as dockweed, dandelion greens, lamb's quarter, marsh marigold leaves, milkweed, pokeweed, and purslane. Pork variety cuts and salt pork remained the primary meats. The phrase "living high on the hog" comes from the postwar period, meaning that a family was wealthy enough to eat the best pork cuts, such as chops and ham.

Health among African Americans continued to deteriorate. The death rate was so high, particularly in urban areas, that many predicted that blacks were doomed to extinction. In the cities, two more diseases—syphilis and tuberculosis—overwhelmed the black community. Children continued to die of fits and seizures, convulsions, and tetanus. Rickets was so common that many thought it was a normal stage of development for black children.

The runaway diseases provided more ammunition for racists: Some scientists said it was too dangerous to wait for blacks to die out naturally. To protect whites from catching these deadly diseases, they said, all black males should be quickly sterilized, which amounted to advocating genocide.

Even such liberal publications as the *Atlantic Monthly, Harper's Weekly,* and *The Nation* carried scientific articles claiming that blacks were innately inferior and incapable of participating in white civilization. (In 1984, Alphonso Pinkney looked back at this period in *The Myth of Black Progress* and gave the medical charges leveled against blacks a name: "scientific racism.")

As the century turned, depressed conditions in the South prompted over 750,000 black Americans to move north and west to seek industrial jobs. Most were young men who moved to the large metropolitan areas of New York, Boston, Chicago, and Philadelphia.

Whites, as well as the small number of middle-class blacks who had already made a place for themselves, resented the influx of southern blacks. New segregation laws were hastily put on city books, creating large inner-city black ghettos. Blacks were systematically locked out of unions. Segregation, official and de facto, remained an integral part of American life through the first half of the twentieth century.

But also with the new century came advances in medical science. The virulent racism of the medical profession faded as old diseases that had ravaged all groups were brought under control. Death rates fell for both blacks and whites, although the mortality rate from tuberculosis and pneumonia remained higher for blacks, just as it does today.

As the Great Depression of the 1930s swept across the country, the northward migration of southern blacks slowed to a trickle. During World War II, the flow picked up again, and in the next thirty years over 4 million African Americans left the South to settle in other regions of the country, primarily the cities. The move north meant a change from the slower-paced rural lifestyle to a harder, more intense urban existence.

To the cities, southern blacks carried old medical myths, transformed by centuries of slavery and rural poverty. "High blood," they said, was caused by excess blood migrating to one part of the body, usually the head. Perhaps they referred to what we now call high blood pressure. High blood was attributed to eating too many rich foods or red-colored foods such as beets, carrots, grape juice, red wine, and red meat. "Low blood," or anemia, was believed to be caused by eating too much garlic and such acidic foods as vinegar and pickles, and not enough red meat.

Some believed that they could eliminate ringworm by eating figs and honey and cure stomach infections by drinking a mixture of goat's milk and cabbage juice. Some mothers believed eggs and milk were bad for sick children.

One of the more unusual African traits that survived the journey north was the ancient practice of eating clay and other nonfood substances, which is now called pica. In West Africa, clay eating was common because it was said to alleviate hunger and soothe irritation caused by intestinal parasites. Some anthropologists suggest that clay eating may have been part of religious rituals. Looking back, it's possible that clay eating may have added calcium, iron, and phosphorus to diets otherwise low in minerals.

Clay eating survived during slavery, even though planters despised it, and it is still fairly common in some parts of the South and in northern cities, especially among pregnant women, who say they crave nonfood substances. In rural regions, the substance ingested is usually clay. In urban areas, laundry starch is often the first choice, although some women eat milk of magnesia, coffee grounds, plaster, and paraffin. Some say that clay prevents birthmarks or that starch makes the skin of the baby lighter and helps the baby to slip out during delivery. Pica seems to be taught from mother to daughter. For example, a woman may think of laundry starch or cornstarch as a comfort food and develop an almost continual craving for it.

Whether pica is harmful is uncertain. Possible problems include weight gain from consuming large amounts of laundry starch and aggravated hypertension from the sodium in clay. Pica may also interfere with nutrition, blocking the absorption of vitamins and minerals and reducing the amount of real food people eat.

In the 1950s, the movement against "separate but equal" laws gained momentum. Eventually, the Civil Rights Act of 1964 and the Voting Rights Act of 1965 reversed legal segregation and legal discrimination.

During this period of growth and renewal, soul food, the traditional southern black cuisine, became a symbol of ethnic solidarity everywhere. In the South today, soul food still reigns. Pork, corn, and greens are staples. Onions and green peppers added to a roux of butter and flour form the basis for many thick stews and gumbos, made sticky with okra, filé powder, or flour and served with rice. Meats, poultry, and fish are coated with cornmeal or flour and deep-fried in lard. Corn bread, fried hominy, or biscuits with butter or gravy accompany almost every meal. Dumplings are sometimes added to stews and greens.

In rural areas, small game such as rabbits and squirrels, opossum, and raccoon is still caught and eaten. Catfish, crab, and crawfish, and in some areas frog's legs and turtle, are popular. Seafood, when available, is commonly added to soups and stews, sometimes with meat and chicken.

In the many regions of the country where African Americans have settled, sharing food that is lovingly prepared continues to bind family and friends. Sunday dinner is still the highlight of the week. The menu may include fried chicken, spareribs, chitlins, and pig's feet (or ears or tail). The most common vegetables are greens boiled with salt pork, fatback, bacon, or ham, plus hot peppers and lemon. The intensely flavored broth, called pot likker, is served along with the greens and sprinkled with hot sauce at the table. Black-eyed peas, okra, peas, and tomatoes appear in every combination. Squash and sweet potatoes may be used as vegetables or, sweetened with molasses, as dessert pies. Bread pudding and fruit cobblers are all traditional southern desserts.

In many parts of the country, however, old traditions have given way to a faster pace. Today, half of all black Americans still live in the South, but only a small percentage live in rural areas. The other half live in the urban areas of the Northeast and Midwest. Less than 1 percent of American blacks are of Caribbean descent, and even fewer are recent immigrants from Africa.

Wherever they live, African Americans continue to suffer from discrimination. Their unemployment rate is more than double that of whites; both average income and educational level are substantially lower. In 1985, nearly one-third of black families lived below the poverty line.

Our health statistics reflect this dismal picture. From the time record keeping began at the turn of the century, life expectancy has generally improved for everyone, although blacks were always behind. For example, in 1900 a white infant could expect to live 47.6 years and a nonwhite infant could expect to live about 33 years. In each decade, the numbers continued to increase in parallel fashion, until 1984, when the figures were 75.3 for whites and 69.7 for blacks.

Over the next four years, in the crunch of increased unemployment and poverty, the parallel march of progress stopped. While life expectancy for whites continued forward, blacks began to fall behind. By 1988, life expectancy for whites had improved to 75.6, but that for blacks had fallen to 69.2. The life expectancy for black men was lower than for any other group in the United States— 64.9.

Most researchers believe that in one way or another poverty is at the base of most of our health problems, pointing out that there's more to poverty than low income. Poor diet, poor housing, overcrowded clinic facilities, and inadequate information about health and nutrition form the larger picture.

Some studies show that blacks living near poverty level receive less than half the calcium and iron whites do, and their diets are often low in vitamins A and C, magnesium, vitamin B complex, and protein. Even when income increases, blacks tend to choose meat and other protein foods over fresh fruits, vegetables, and whole-grain products. Sodium intake is high, particularly for those who rely on processed, packaged, or convenience foods.

Certain vitamin deficiencies affect blacks at every income level. No matter how rich we are, we may not get enough vitamin D and calcium. Because of our skin pigmentation, we receive one-third less ultraviolet light, which triggers the body's production of vitamin D. Vitamin D is needed to help the body use calcium and magnesium, minerals already low in our diet. Most Americans get extra vitamin D from milk—but blacks, who are often lactose-intolerant, tend to avoid fresh milk and milk products.

Another health problem that affects blacks at every income level is salt sensitivity. In the 1970s, researchers first discovered that people differ in their tolerance for salt. Most people release excess sodium through sweat and urine. But many blacks do the reverse: Their kidneys retain salt. Retaining salt helps the body conserve fluids. This may have been a beneficial mutation that occurred thousands of years ago among people who survived the torrid African climate. Or it may have occurred in a period of rapid evolutionary adaptation that took place during the slave trade: Those Africans who could conserve fluids survived the arduous journey to America. (See Chapter 26.)

But when people with extremely high salt sensitivity began to eat more salt, as surely they did and continue to do in the United States today, the helpful mechanism became a disadvantage. The incidence of hypertension among blacks is about twice as high as among whites. And our particular form of hypertension, in the majority of cases, is salt-sensitive: *Reduce salt intake and blood pressure falls.*

Obesity is another common problem for black Americans. Our incidence of diabetes is two to three times higher than the rate for the population as a whole, almost surely connected to obesity.

Why are we fatter than other Americans? Although most blacks and whites with similar income and education, living in the same region, usually eat much the same foods, there are still some differences in our eating habits. Like most Americans, blacks throughout the country are now eating lighter breakfasts, and sandwiches at lunch. Dinner is eaten after work, and it has become the biggest meal of the day. However, we still seem to snack more than other groups throughout the day. In many families, meal schedules are irregular and family members eat when it is convenient.

There are other important differences. We still fry foods. Next to frying, we like to boil and bake foods. We choose cookies or candy as snacks.

Among poorer blacks, the biggest change in diet, particularly in the city, is our dependence on quick-service restaurants and convenience stores for meals.

As a result, even when we're poor, we're not necessarily hungry. Jesse Jackson has said that "low-income Americans, with a certain desperation that there might not be any more food tomorrow, are eating themselves to death." Many residents of the inner city are seriously overweight, their hunger fed by a diet loaded with sugar, salt, and fat.

Critics say that fast-food chains may feed into the crisis of poor nutrition. Although these restaurants are offering more choices and many foods are prepared in a healthful manner, company officials say that their customers still prefer the saltier, fattier selections and larger portions. In the inner city, people eat to survive; they try to get the biggest sandwich with the most calories in order to stay full longer.

There is more than food involved in our attraction to quick-service restaurants. The restaurants are safe, clean, well-lighted oases in a wasteland of poor housing and dangerous streets. Officials speaking for McDonald's, Burger King, and Kentucky Fried Chicken, among the most visible chains in the inner city, say that their food is nutritious and getting more so, and that they offer people not only affordable food but jobs and a safe haven.

In the home, many people seem unaware of new nutrition information. For example, out of long-standing tradition, many continue to prepare food with lard (animal fat). Some people eat unhealthfully simply because they can't afford better. Marketing in poor neighborhoods is a nutritionist's nightmare. Fresh produce is scarce and what is available is sky-high.

On the shelves in Harlem, it's rare to find low-cholesterol mayonnaise, whole-wheat bread, skim milk, and fresh vegetables. In the stores of most poor neighborhoods, there are *no* non-fat and no-salt products and only a few low-fat and low-salt items. When more healthful alternatives are available, such as low-salt soups, they cost more than the regular brands. As one woman shopping for cereal said, "For the stuff that has fiber and is good for you, you pay twice as much. They kick your butt." The story gets replayed in every food section. White bread, sugary snack cakes, liquor, and cigarettes are aggressively marketed, but, for a variety of reasons, food manufacturers don't even try to sell healthful foods in low-income neighborhoods.

Store owners say they can't sell healthy products to customers who don't want them. To change customers' eating habits, owners say, stores need the help of major food manufacturers, nutritionists, and advertisers. (Fortunately, you don't have to rely on the local market for fresh fruits and expensive brand-name grains and cereals. For smart shopping tips, see Chapter 9; for more information about increasing grains, fruits, and vegetables in your diet, see Chapter 14.)

Most inner-city residents believe that nutrition information is for rich white people. They don't see themselves portrayed on television and billboards consuming healthful products. Because of this poor image building, most African Americans have never received the information that can help us save our own lives.

All of these problems make good health and nutrition harder for blacks to achieve, but not impossible. For centuries so-called racial differences have been twisted to try to prove that we are somehow physically inferior. We are not. Despite the social and physical handicaps, the stamina of black Americans for survival has been miraculous. The oldest American on record was a former slave, Charlie Smith, who the Social Security Administration believed to be 137 years old when he died in 1979. In 1980, the Senate invited a group of healthy Americans over the age of one hundred to testify at a hearing on aging—nearly one-third were blacks. *We are a vigorous people and I believe we can overcome our worst health statistics by drawing on our past for strength and knowledge, and by learning how the foods we eat and the way we live today affect our bodies.*

We could also use some help from the scientific community. More research is needed on the precise links between diet and health, particularly when broken down along racial and economic lines. But there's a big problem here, too. History tells us that studies based on race are potentially dangerous. As recently as 1969, educational psychologist Arthur Jensen revived scientific racism by arguing that blacks perform less well than whites on IQ tests because they are genetically less intelligent. Jensen's theory caused so much controversy that the National Academy of Science called for extensive research into the way IQ tests are prepared. Jensen's ideas were thoroughly discredited by Jean Piaget, who believed that intelligence is not determined genetically at birth but is a continuous, dynamic process developed over time and shared by all, despite their culture. Since then, many educators and psychologists—including Jensen himself—have observed that environment plays a strong role in academic achievement. Yet Jensen's racist legacy, like that of the southern physicians of the eighteenth century, lingers. More recently, despite many studies showing that black children given the same benefits as white children do equally well on IQ tests, Nobel Prize winner

William Shockley still argues that people of African origin are less "evolved" and less intelligent than other groups.

This cloud of racism hanging over the scientific community causes legitimate researchers to avoid conducting medical studies along racial lines; it's too easy to draw erroneous conclusions and unwittingly provide ammunition for hate mongers.

To objective scientists, *race* is largely a label of convenience. All human beings belong to the same species, *Homo sapiens*. Most scholars hold that there has been a common evolution—that we are all descended from the same Eve—and that our various environmental adaptations occurred relatively late in human history. As different groups of humans moved and merged, individual genes were carried and melded into thousands of generations living in many different environments. Races, as we think of them, arose as a result of spontaneous mutations. Mutations that were beneficial in a particular environment survived and were passed on.

At the DNA level, there are literally millions of differences between any two human beings, unless they are identical twins. Two people similar in skin color will differ in height, blood type, and features. To classify groups on skin color assigns primary importance to that one gene, ignoring millions of others. Nevertheless, strictly for convenience, anthropologists—by differentiating on the basis of skin color, hair color and texture, eye color and shape, stature, and shape of head—grouped humans into three groups: Caucasoid, Mongoloid, and Negroid.

A discrete package of gene differences has never been identified among these groups. The diversity between individuals within these three groups is far greater than the diversity among the groups themselves. Nor can race be equated with any mental characteristics, such as intelligence, personality, or character. Variations in intelligence, from very intelligent to very slow, occur in all groups.

Thus, when we say *African,* we do not mean a race, but a population that originated in Africa. Similarly, *European* signifies a population that originated on the continent of Europe. Each could be divided into further geographic components—West Africans, Nordics, Mediterraneans, Britons, and so on.

The human body is an evolutionary compromise, an amalgam of trade-offs. Studying various groups can reveal how humans and other animals adapt biologically to their environments. For within every group, there are susceptibilities and resistances to certain diseases.

Studying genetics—the way in which genes are passed from parent to child—is extremely important because diseases are connected to genes. Although you don't have to be black to carry the sickle-cell gene, that particular mutation probably arose in Africa because it was protective against malaria. The gene for diabetes may have been protective in extremely cold climates with scarce food supply because it altered metabolism. Lighter skin became protective when populations migrated to the far north because it could soak up the small amounts of available sunlight to manufacture vitamin D. A little baby Swede wrapped from head to toe in a snowsuit can still soak up enough vitamin D from his cheeks alone to keep him from getting rickets. Almost anywhere else, light skin is a drawback because it is so vulnerable to cancer.

Gene mapping, the frontier of biological science, may help us understand some of the most intractable diseases that plague human beings today, particularly some of the more perplexing problems of black health—specifically, the extraordinarily high incidence of low-birth-weight babies, hypertension, and diabetes. I believe it is possible to study genetics without a political agenda. We cannot let the past, however grim, overwhelm the future.

OUR MORTALITY RATE

As we have seen, our health problems are complicated. For a host of different reasons, African Americans have a higher risk for disease and premature death than any other group living in the United States.

Other groups tend to have excess risks only in regard to certain diseases. For example, Latino Americans have a higher than average risk of some cancers (stomach and pancreatic cancer), diabetes, and obesity. But their risk of heart disease and stroke is lower. Native Americans have a higher than average risk of stomach cancer, diabetes, and obesity. But their risk of other cancers, heart disease, and stroke is lower.

By contrast, African Americans have a significantly higher risk for almost every condition. And we are much more likely to die of these diseases than other groups.

In 1988, the National Center for Health Statistics calculated the percentage by which the black death rate exceeded the white death rate for some leading causes of death:

Accidents	*24% higher*
Cancer	*32% higher*
Heart disease	*38% higher*
Cirrhosis/liver disease	*77% higher*
Stroke	*82% higher*
Diabetes	*132% higher*
Kidney failure	*176% higher*
AIDS	*250% higher*
Homicide	*500% higher*

TEN BLACK RISK FACTORS

When the American Heart Association speaks of risk factors, they mean conditions that lead to heart disease. For example, people with high blood pressure or diabetes are more likely than others to develop heart disease. So are people who smoke.

But when we speak of our risk factors, we're talking about conditions that cut across a huge variety of illnesses, not only heart disease. Unfortunately, we don't understand our risk factors very well because they've never been broken down specifically for us. Also, health information leaks slowly into the black community. By the time the information reaches us, it is so stale that it doesn't capture much attention. For example, in a recent survey, only 2 percent of pregnant black women knew that smoking was a risk factor that contributes to low-birth-weight babies. That description doesn't carry much impact and certainly doesn't sound very dangerous. But our ears would certainly perk up if someone said, "If you smoke while pregnant, your baby may be too small to survive."

TEN BLACK RISK FACTORS

We need to look at our risk factors in a new way. What we want to think about are *controllable* risk factors—the ones we may be able to do something about by ourselves.

Here are the ten controllable risk factors that are most likely to cause illness and death in African Americans:

Obesity	*Lack of physical exercise*
Smoking	*Stress*
Drinking	*Salt*
Drug use	*Untreated high blood pressure*
Fatty diet (high in saturated fats and cholesterol)	*Uncontrolled diabetes*

Each risk factor can lead to a range of devastating health problems; two or more together compounds the risk. And each one is within our control.

Dr. Louis J. Sullivan believes that more than 35,000 black Americans could save their own lives each year if they could make appropriate changes in these risk factors. There may be an even greater benefit: By reducing "environmental" risk factors such as smoking cigarettes, eating diets rich in fats and sodium, and drinking alcohol, some genetically determined diseases we suffer from would remain safely dormant.

To help us reduce those risk factors, Dr. Sullivan says that we need equal health opportunity, "including the good health information that will help every American make the right choices for healthy and productive lives."

That's what you're going to find in the following chapters. We're going to explore how our culture, genetics, nutrition and lifestyle practices, and stress impact on our health. Then we'll see, in the Sankofa Program, how each of us can begin to put healthful changes to work for us.

You don't have to become ill or die young simply because your parents did. Thanks to new, constantly evolving information, you can discover what risks you personally face and take matters into your own hands to lower those risks.

Part Two

Improving
Our Lifestyle

4

BLACK STRESS:
THE SECRET KILLER

Tension and anxiety, worry and fear—these are all conditions of stress that may have dangerous, and sometimes fatal, consequences. Back in the late 1960s, Dr. Thomas H. Holmes and Dr. Richard H. Rake, psychiatrists at the University of Washington Medical School, drew the first clear picture of the link between stress and disease. The researchers interviewed nearly four hundred people of various ages and backgrounds, asking each one to give a series of everyday life events a stress number between one and one hundred. The doctors said that the average stress event was marriage, which was assigned fifty points. Volunteers were then asked to assign points to the doctors' list of other life events: Did they have a stress number higher or lower than marriage? At the top of everyone's list, with the highest stress impact, one hundred points, was the death of a spouse. Divorce was second. At the bottom of the list, but still considered stressful, were the Christmas holidays and minor violations of law, such as a traffic ticket.

When the doctors compared the stress scale with health statistics, they learned that many widows and widowers die soon after losing their spouses. And divorced people are twelve times more likely to become ill with a major disease after a divorce. Later, Dr. Holmes and Dr. Minoru Masuda studied eighty-eight patients with major illnesses. *Ninety-three percent* of the patients could associate their illness with the accumulation of stressful life changes.

Holmes and his colleagues defined stress as a *change* from the expected and felt that all life changes, good and bad, could create stress. Stress, then, came to be seen not as a particular event in itself but as the product of change. Getting married or divorced, changing jobs, even to a better one, or losing a job, coping with the holidays, suffering injury or illness, worrying about children—all are examples of stress.

HOW STRESS AFFECTS THE BODY

Stress can be physical or emotional. Shoveling snow or laboring too long in the hot sun produces physical stress. Major life traumas such as a death in the family produce emotional stress. Your body responds by increasing its production of certain hormones, such as epinephrine and cortisol, which have become known as "stress hormones." These are hormones that can increase your heart rate, blood pressure, and metabolism.

Stress is experienced by everyone, yet everyone does not respond to it in the same way. Some people genuinely seem to thrive on stress, while others may fall apart under the very same strain. Some of us are more affected by stress and some are more susceptible to stress-related health problems. It is not the stress itself that does the damage but the way we handle it.

One crucial finding of a 1960 study was that the effects of stress events are cumulative. If enough events are clustered together at one time, they leave some people especially vulnerable to illness. In the same way, if you must live in a relentlessly stressful situation over which you have little control, your body simply may not have the resources to cope with it. This is a critical finding when it comes to what is known as black stress.

Stress poses a profound difficulty for us. More black men die from heart attacks associated with stress than any other ethnic group in the United States. Only black women over the age of fifty-five are second in their likelihood of dying from a stress-related heart attack. Why is our stress level so high? What is the unique impact of stress on our minds and bodies? Is there anything we can do about it?

STRESS AND YOUR HEALTH

Stress may affect both emotional and physical health. On the emotional side, stress has been linked to:

- *Anxiety*
- *Depression*
- *Drug and alcohol abuse*
- *Inability to concentrate*
- *Irritability*
- *Low self-esteem*

- *Overeating*
- *Poor memory*
- *Poor management of work*
- *Poor self-control*
- *Smoking*

On the physical side, stress has been associated with:

- *Acne, hives, and other skin conditions*
- *Cancer*
- *Cold hands, flushed face*
- *Constant sighing*
- *Dyspepsia*
- *Elevated cholesterol*
- *Heart attacks*
- *Heart disease*
- *Hypertension*

- *Irritable bowel syndrome (spastic colon)*
- *Kidney disease*
- *Muscular aches and pains*
- *Palpitations*
- *Rapid, shallow breathing*
- *Shortness of breath*
- *Stroke*
- *Ulcers*
- *Weight problems*

THE DAILY HASSLES OF LIFE CAN KILL YOU

New research has added an important dimension to the original stress scale devised by Holmes and Rake. Experts now believe that the ordinary daily hassles that many black Americans must live with cause more stress than major life events. Things like waiting for a check to come in the mail or not being able to pay the rent on time can loom as terribly stressful when these occur every day, month after month.

The everyday struggle of dealing with prejudice also contributes to the deadly level of stress in the black community. While events such as the death of a spouse cause enormous stress for

STRESS CHECKLIST—
LIFE HASSLES THAT LEAD TO STRESS
In the 1980s, A. D. Kanner and colleagues came up with a new list of 117 life hassles that are believed to create stress and may lead to illness. From this original list, in 1990, Patrick S. Romano and his associates from the Institute for Health Policy Studies of the University of California, San Francisco, derived a ten-item hassle index. Here it is:

- *Being out of work for a month or longer*
- *Having a serious illness or accident*
- *Not having enough money for food, clothing, housing, or other necessities of life*
- *Being concerned with getting credit*
- *Having a problem with getting things repaired around the house*
- *Having a check arrive late or lost in the mail*
- *Having something stolen or having the house or car broken into*
- *Having a violent argument with a friend or relative*
- *Having some other kind of trouble with family members*
- *Being concerned about living in an unsafe area*

Add one more to the list:

- *Living with racism*

everyone, ordinary life for a black man or woman in America produces a steady, suppressed anger that many scientists believe is the reason for the explosive rate of hypertension among us.

THE STRESS OF PREJUDICE

Stress has a different resonance for black people for one simple reason: As racism persists, black rage seethes and grows. Studies have shown that people who have the most control over their lives experience the least stress. Thus, the president of a car company suffers less stress than the assembly-line worker, and not just for obvious financial reasons. The more control you have over your life and its circumstances, the less stress you feel. And racism deprives people of control. Encountering the day-to-day slights—the cab that passes you by, the low-end job where you receive less respect than coworkers, the salesperson who waits on a white person when you were in the store first, the waiter who is rude or ignores your presence—all make you feel powerless. A burning anger slowly grows in you. Every black person has experienced this, and you and I all know what it means.

Scientists have always intuitively felt that anger is linked to the unusually high rates of hypertension and other diseases in blacks. In the last few years, new studies have emerged to support this hypothesis. People, black or white, who suppress their anger have higher than average blood pressure. Since black people must cope daily with the insults of racism, large and small, they are likely to have more anger to suppress than whites. This swallowed anger is thought to be a major reason for stress-related diseases among blacks.

FREE-FLOATING ANGER

There is yet another kind of anger in the African-American community. Slow rage has only minor consequences compared with the "free-floating anger" first described by psychologist Louis Ramey at the 1980 conference "Homicide Among Black Males," sponsored by the Alcohol, Drug Abuse and Mental Health Administration.

Dr. Ramey connected homicide, the leading cause of death among young black men, to the generalized anger that grows in young black people at a system that is slowly strangling them. While blacks are 12 percent of the U.S. population, 50 percent of all homicide victims are black! The volatile combination of poverty and racism in some black communities creates a deadly domino effect: Stress leads to anger and anger leads to violence.

It's not hard to understand how free-floating anger, an anger so pervasive that it has no one recognizable target, is linked to death. Poverty begins early for many of us. To grow and develop into healthy adults, all young people need to feel they have an open future with opportunity to achieve their goals. But black adolescents are often deprived of any such promise. Before a black youngster reaches adulthood—if he or she lives that long—poor health habits and stress have piled up.

In their in-depth study of adolescent violence, *Deadly Consequences,* Dr. Deborah Prothrow-Stith and Michaele Weissman describe how stress and frustration build up in young black men trapped in poverty and assaulted daily with the stings of racism. It doesn't take much to set off violence among these walking time bombs—and the victim is usually someone just like themselves, another casualty of a problematic social equation: poverty plus racism equal stress equals anger equals violence.

DANGEROUS CONSEQUENCES OF STRESS

Did your boss just unfairly reprimand you? Is there more work on your desk than you can get to? Or, conversely, do you have no job at all? Are there too many bills to pay and not enough money to go around? When things like this happen, do you want to have a couple of drinks and a deep drag of a cigarette? (According to a November 1991 study in the *American Journal of Public Health,* smoking is one way we cope with living in a stressful environment, which dramatically increases our risk of lung cancer and other life-threatening diseases.)

Stress can propel us to start drinking too much, or even to turn to drugs. None of these are effective coping strategies. The insidious long-term effects can be devastating, leading to a vicious cycle of more stress, poor health, addiction, and an increased risk of contracting—and possibly dying from—stress-related diseases. Believe me, there are safer, healthier ways to cope with stress.

WHAT TO DO WITH STRESS

Some studies suggest that it is *suppressed* anger that causes health problems. But suppose you let it all out? You tell off the uncooperative cabdriver, confront the inattentive salesperson, yell at the rude waiter. What happens then?

Unfortunately, nothing good. Even though you may be right, anger is not an effective way of dealing with stress for anyone. When stress is converted into anger, a new set of health problems can develop.

A study at the University of California Medical School in San Francisco, published in the August 1992 issue of the *American Journal of Cardiology,* found that hostile people are more likely to develop severe heart disease, and at a younger age, than their peers. The director of the study, psychiatrist Gail Ironson, also reported that anger is especially bad for people who already have heart disease. While Dr. Ironson and her colleagues did not discount other causes of heart disease—poor diet, lack of exercise, and genetic predisposition—they definitively concluded that anger can impair heart function. Later studies have disputed the direct connection between anger and heart disease, but much of the debate centers around how researchers define hostility. Clearly, something is going on here.

Obviously, we need to find other ways to release underlying rage. Stress is real. And the racism and poverty that often lie beneath it are real. But if suppressing rage or getting angry doesn't help, what *can* you do with stress?

WAYS TO REDUCE STRESS

Spend your time on situations over which you have the most control, and try to steer clear of those over which you lack control. For example, don't accept responsibilities or obligations that you know you cannot deliver on.

Ask yourself, What is it about a particular situation that makes it stressful? Can you imagine different ways in which you could change that situation?

If you are angry at someone, don't suppress that anger—but also try not to get into a shouting match. No one ever "wins" in these situations, which simply multiply feelings of tension. Instead, try to talk it out rationally. Explain to the person why you feel angry, and talk about positive actions you can take to avoid repeating this stressful situation.

If your anger is out of control, try to blow off steam through exercise (see page 47).

If money is a constant worry, think about how you might change your life to improve your financial situation. Whom can you turn to for advice? A family member? A job counselor? Your minister?

Look for small yet specific ways to reduce the daily pressures and demands in your life and to add pleasure to it. One very talented black novelist has a message on her telephone machine: "When you hear the tone, you will feel calm and relaxed." She recognized the stress everyone feels and reached out to her friends —a fabulous idea!

Do something for the pure joy of it. I recently went to a gospel breakfast at a church in Harlem. Everyone felt it was a terrific experience, whether they were religious or not. You might want to convert, or maybe just relax and have fun.

Turn your frustration into helping promote positive action in the African-American community. If you have extra time on your hands, or even if you don't, join an organization such as the National Urban League, Jack and Jill, 100 Black Men/Women. You may think you already have too much to do, but sometimes adding activities that you enjoy and that make you feel productive can reduce your stress load.

Talk to a friend—your spouse, a friend, a minister—anyone with whom you feel comfortable. Many of us have close ties to our churches; when you're in trouble, you might turn to prayer or speak with a member of the clergy. Speaking of the stress that black women are especially vulnerable to, Opal Palmer Adisa writes in *The Black Women's Health Book*, "The best doctor, best medicine, best antidote for what ails us is the mirror reflection of ourselves: our friendships, our bonds, the comfort we seek and the support we receive from each other. If truth be told, black women would cease to exist if we didn't have each other."

Is the stress you feel an accumulation of small stressors? A cluster of small stresses can be as troublesome as a single big event, and it may be even harder to turn around. It helps to break them apart and look at each separately.

Are you stuck in a relationship which is bad news? If you know it's not going to change, make up your mind to move on—and do it.

Learn to recognize your own personal quirks that lead to stress. Are you oversensitive to criticism? Do you see racial slurs in every situation? Do you panic if someone doesn't like you? Sometimes it helps just to identify the behavior in yourself that leads to stress. Just naming things, even if you can't change them, is in itself a step toward change.

Look on the funny side. Sometimes seeing the humor in a predicament can release tension all around. Laughter is the best stress medicine in the world. When you're feeling down, tell a joke; put a comedy video on the VCR. There have always been black comedians on the stage, films, and television. Richard Pryor revolutionized comedy when he first came on the scene in the 1960s, and a legion of modern black comics have followed in his steps— Whoopi Goldberg, Sinbad, Marcia Davenport, and Eddie Murphy are only a few. Let your favorites give you a stress break.

Try to find a relaxation technique that works for you. A hot bath, a run, reading a good book, listening to your favorite music —all can reduce stress.

There are also formal relaxation techniques. Some people use meditation to reduce feelings of anxiety (see below). Others may try yoga or deep-breathing exercises. You can practice these techniques on your own by using videotapes or books as your guide, or you can participate in programs offered at school, the Y, or a health club.

In every stressful situation, there is usually some small step you can take to ease the tension. For example, if your job is boring you, or overwhelming you, talk to your boss about it, if you can. You don't need to get yourself in trouble—nobody needs that! But maybe there is something you can do to add responsibility and interest to your job or to reduce your work load. If not, think about changing your job. Sometimes just allowing yourself *to think about* change, about what you might like to be doing with your life, can lead you toward positive action, even in a poor economy.

Meditate Your Way to Health

Meditation is a fourth major state of consciousness, completely different from waking, sleeping, and dreaming. Meditators are deeply relaxed but also wide awake.

When you meditate, your heart rate immediately starts to fall,

STRESS BUSTERS

- *Breathing exercises*
- *A healthy diet*
- *A hot bath*
- *A long walk daily*
- *Meditation*
- *Prayer*
- *Regular workouts*
- *Music*
- *Physical relaxation techniques*
- *Tackling harmful negatives in your life, such as smoking or drug addiction*
- *Talking it out*
- *Trying to see the humor in a situation*
- *Yoga*

and so does your blood pressure. Meditation also directly helps to lower muscle tension. Scientists believe meditation reduces the body's response to stress, in part by reducing levels of potentially dangerous body chemicals, those stress hormones we mentioned earlier. It doesn't matter what kind of meditation technique you use, the effect is the same.

Is meditation something that fits with black culture and lifestyle? Meditation is one of the oldest known religious practices. Some form of it has been practiced in virtually every religion in the world since time began. When we pray, we are performing a kind of meditation. When we chant rhythmically, we are meditating. Although no one has ever measured our physiological response to these particular meditation methods, I believe they generate the same positive effects as any standard meditation.

A new study from the West Oakland Health Center confirms that meditation works for blacks. Here, high blood pressure is more the norm than the exception. The study involved African-American seniors suffering from mild hypertension. Researchers compared the meditation group with another group that practiced

muscle relaxation and a third group that followed a diet and exercise plan. The meditators did best, and most lowered their blood
pressure dramatically.

Everyone has the capacity to meditate, and the method is so
simple that you can train yourself. Harvard cardiologist Dr. Herbert Benson, now based at Boston's Deaconess Hospital, was the
first scientist to measure the physiological effects of meditation.
He isolated four components needed to produce physiological
benefits. They are: a passive attitude, a quiet environment free
from distraction, a comfortable position, and a repetitive sound
or word.

So simply set aside a quiet time when you won't be disturbed.
Sit in a comfortable chair or lie down on the floor; then relax your
body from head to toe.

Breathe quietly in and out through your nose. Then on every
out breath repeat your word—to yourself or out loud. What's
your word? I don't know, because it's *yours*. If you have strong
religious convictions, there is probably a simple prayer or phrase
in your own religion that you might like to repeat. If not, try
choosing a neutral word that has no emotional content for you.
For example, Dr. Benson prefers the word *one*.

You may experience various feelings during and after meditation, including a sense of calm and well-being. If your mind wan-
ders while you're meditating, gently bring it back to your word.

Physical changes occur within the first three minutes of meditation. The best results seem to come if you meditate anywhere
from five to twenty-five minutes, twice a day.

Here's the good part: As long as you maintain a regular period
of daily meditation, the beneficial effects carry over into parts of
the day when you're not meditating.

If you can't seem to get started on your own, ask around and
see who is offering a stress-reduction class. Your doctor, local
hospital, neighborhood clinic, or YMCA may have information
for you. (If you have hypertension, make sure that you continue
to have your blood pressure monitored by your doctor and follow
his or her instructions about taking medication. See Chapter 21.)

Exercise Your Stress Away

Exercise seems to help relieve stress on several levels. It makes people feel good because it distracts them from their worries. Studies also show that the moods of depressed people dramatically improve when they adopt a regular exercise regime. Endorphins, natural chemicals released into the bloodstream during a workout, can produce an almost euphoric feeling of well-being (better than drugs and more long-lasting).

When you're physically fit, you have a lower heart rate and blood pressure. With a strengthened physical system, you can better tolerate stress.

Under stress, your muscles tense and your blood pressure and heart rate increase. This is sometimes called the "fight or flight" reaction because your body is prepared to take immediate action —either to stand and fight or run away. But when you can neither fight nor run, stress builds up in your body. *You can exercise your way out of this dilemma.* A brisk walk, for example, can relieve muscle tension and burn off the unhealthful stress hormones.

COPING WITH BLACK STRESS

It's fine to look at what's worked in the white community and try to use it for our own special needs. But there is something missing. "In order for us to become healthy, we have to take charge of the powers we have within ourselves. We can't change anyone else, but when we change ourselves, we change the way the world relates to us. We are in charge." Those are the inspirational words of Byllye Y. Avery, the founder and executive director of the national Black Women's Health Project in Atlanta. Individual empowerment is one stress-reduction technique that speaks directly to black stress. The main message? Turn your anger into a positive assertive response. I have learned to do so in my own life and I can tell you that it works for me. When stress is positively managed, it contributes to enhanced thinking and creativity and a higher energy level.

I was very proud to become a registered dietitian, thinking that it was a way to help people improve the quality of their health. I

WHEN TO SEEK MEDICAL HELP

There are times when stress is just too much to handle. If none of the methods you try help, you should seek professional counseling from a psychologist or other mental-health professional. Relentless, unrelieved stress can make you sick.

The symptoms of stress may be warning signs of an underlying disease. If the stress you feel is persistently accompanied by any of these symptoms, see a doctor:

- *Fainting or dizziness*
- *Overwhelming anxiety*
- *Severe headaches*
- *A chronic racing heartbeat or pulse*
- *Insomnia*
- *Irritability*
- *Change in eating habits, such as loss of appetite*
- *Chronic diarrhea*
- *Chronic neck or back pain*
- *Sweaty palms*
- *Trembling*
- *Skin rash*
- *Withdrawal from friends*
- *Loss of interest in sex*

---

had studied and worked long and hard. I was invited to appear on local television programs to speak about nutrition. Eventually, I became a regular broadcaster and extended my appearances to national television. I feel I have made many noteworthy accomplishments in my profession. And yet, along with many other African Americans in my field, I have received little recognition from my professional association, the American Dietetic Association (ADA). In fact, my credentials often were questioned by my peers: Why should I be selected as a television health reporter and consultant to major food manufacturers? I knew that no one would ever question the credentials of a white nutritionist in the same role. So I am very familiar with professional racism and it creates a lot of anger and stress for me. But I know I can't let it run my life. Here are the four steps I personally use to cope with stress, especially when that stress is permeated with racism:

1. Acknowledge the stress and identify its source. Just knowing where the stress is coming from helps. If the trigger is racism, acknowledge it to yourself.
2. Think about positive things rather than negative ones. What can you do to make a situation productive? None of us can alter other people's thoughts, but we can turn the stress into a productive response. My productive response was to concentrate on helping people instead of feeling upset about racial put-downs. I feel better because of the positive feedback I get from the people with whom I work.
3. Next, get active. Turn positive thinking into *positive action*. For me, action means being involved with people— writing this book, helping my patients, educating people about nutrition, talking to and working with children and young people. Someone else might use physical exercise as an active way to get rid of stress, and this is also a very good way to release tension and elevate mood.
4. Finally, and very important, reaffirm your positive thoughts and actions. Every time I'm confronted with racism from my colleagues, I reaffirm my reasons for doing what I'm doing in the first place; I try to turn my energy into positive, productive action.

RESOURCES

For stress-reducing suggestions and a list of books and articles, contact:

American Institute of Stress
124 Park Avenue
Yonkers, NY 10703

RECOMMENDED READING

White, Evelyn C., ed. *The Black Women's Health Book: Speaking for Ourselves.* Seattle: The Seal Press, 1990.

Christensen, Alice. *The American Yoga Association Beginner's Manual.* New York: Fireside Press, 1987. Easy-to-do techniques for relaxation.

Benson, Herbert, with Miriam Klipper. *The Relaxation Response.* New York: Avon Books, 1975.

National Institute of Mental Health
Public Inquiries
5600 Fishers Lane, Rm. 15C-05
Rockville, MD 20857
Free fact sheet: "Plain Talk About Handling Stress"

5

GIVING UP ADDICTIONS

Smoking, alcohol, and drug abuse all fall into the general category of addictions.

Are all addictive substances *all* bad? The answers to both questions are no. There do seem to be benefits to some substances, but the benefits run out quickly with overuse. Researchers say that drinking one or two glasses of wine each day may reduce stress and be good for the heart. However, drinking a bottle of wine each day is good for the owner of the liquor store—and bad for your health.

Smoking cigarettes may help control your appetite, but it will hurt you in so many other ways that your appetite will permanently disappear. Smoking marijuana can also calm tension, and it has the quality, too, of easing nausea caused by chemotherapy in some cancer patients. It also contains tar, like tobacco, and can cause emphysema and lung cancer. It's hard to stay calm when you can't breathe.

Heroin, too, will calm you down. Involvement with it also increases your chances for developing smaller problems, such as dental trouble and vision impairment, and larger problems, such as violent death. Cocaine will give you visions of grandeur and it will drive you crazy. Cocaine in the form of crack has no benefits to you, or to anyone else whatsoever, except maybe (and maybe not) the person selling it.

Even if you believe you personally have never been addicted to anything yourself—not sweets, not TV—the odds are that somebody you know has a problem with an addiction of some kind. Drugs of all kinds are available everywhere in the United States, from the ghetto to the backwoods: This is a land of opportunity for addictive behaviors. But it seems as if African Americans have been suffering longer and harder with the results of alcohol and drugs than other groups. It's hard to tell from current surveys just how prevalent substance use is among blacks and whether the incidence is going up or down.

The fact is that drugs still hurt us more than anyone else. The trade in illegal drugs, and the violence that goes along with it, is still centered in our communities. Legal drugs such as alcohol and cigarettes kill us at a rate far higher than they do whites: We're more likely to die from cirrhosis of the liver, and African-American men are ten times more likely to develop cancer of the esophagus; we suffer higher rates of lung cancer, heart disease, and stroke from smoking than do whites.

But you don't need a survey to know that prolonged drug use is unhealthy and dangerous. It's going to take you either to the emergency room or to an early grave, or both. We're all going to die someday, right? But for many African Americans, where the numbers really count—in disease and death rates—you can amend that statement to read: going to die someday . . . soon.

Though addictive substances have bedeviled our communities for a long time, according to statistical reports from the 1880s, blacks had the lowest mortality rate due to alcoholism of any ethnic group. Historians Frieda Brown and Joan Tooley, writing in *Alcoholism and Substance Abuse in Special Populations,* have said that chronic drunkenness among blacks was "so rare that they were considered immune." These statistics were reported during the period of Reconstruction following the Civil War, when we expected to have a role in determining our destiny. According to Brown and Tooley, blacks were active in the temperance movement until it was taken over by white supremacists and the temperance message was expanded to include black disenfranchisement. The myth of protecting white women from the so-called "drunken debauches of half-crazed black men" sprang from this message. Alleged sex crimes were said to be caused by alcohol. As a result, blacks turned their backs on the temperance movement as many moved north. Alcohol also moved north, and after 1900 rates of alcoholism and other problem drug use were about the same for every group in the country. But after World War II, disillusionment set in among black people. We'd been fighting in Europe for the freedom of others when we didn't have our own freedom at home. For some, this realization led to involvement in the civil rights movement. For others, it led to heavier drinking and more drug use.

Researchers continue to debate whether or not genetic factors lead to substance abuse among certain groups. Those who believe that a person can inherit a disposition for addictions base their conclusions on studies that show alcohol and tobacco use passed down from generation to generation, even when individuals had grown up in drug-free environments separated from their parents. This "disease theory" contends that addiction is an illness that the individual can control but cannot cure. Alcoholics Anonymous and similar groups subscribe to the disease theory.

People who believe the disease theory also say that if you can become enslaved by one drug, you can be enslaved by all. They point to people who graduate from one drug to another, like the stereotype of the person who smokes reefer and winds up shooting heroin. Indeed, statistics show that most current users of "hard" drugs used "softer" drugs at the beginning of their drug careers.

The other theory is called the "environmental/secondary theory," meaning that addictions stem from our life experience and the environment in which we live. It seems obvious that much of our history of self-destructive behaviors with alcohol and other substances has grown out of poverty, oppression, and history. Many of us sought comfort in addictive behaviors. Some of us succumbed to cigarette and alcohol advertisements targeting black people, buying the image that a Rémy in one hand and a Salem in the other defines the good life.

Part of our drug problem also comes from our own myths and practices. "Drinkin', hollerin', and raisin' hell" was a way of rebellion down south. In *Manchild in the Promised Land,* Claude Brown wrote that it was part of being "so bad, even Charlie wouldn't mess with [us]." Nothing can hurt you when you're high. As a people, we have acquired a high tolerance for pain. It's one of our legacies from slavery and we believe and perpetuate the mythology. We can stand a lot of pain, we tell ourselves. And because we *can* stand a lot, we tend to have trouble recognizing when we've become addicted to a drug, and even defining what addiction is.

The environmental/secondary theory says that a person can have a problem with one drug and no problem with another. You can be as hooked on cigarettes as a picture on a wall and still not have a problem with any other drug.

Both theories are just that—theories. The environmental theory seems to carry more weight for blacks. But in the end, maybe it really doesn't matter which you subscribe to. You can start out using a drug just once in a while, but once addicted, you can never take it casually again. Some people never get to that point, however. The social drinker remains just that, or a person who smokes marijuana every now and then may get bored with it and stop.

One fact: Studies clearly show that the more different kinds of drugs you use, the greater your chances of becoming drug-dependent. You smoke when you drink. You like drinking and smoking so much, you start doing cocaine so you can drink and smoke some more. But you get so wound up drinking, smoking, and doing cocaine, you smoke a little reefer to take the edge off. The drugs all seem to complement one another. You begin to feel like something's missing when you do one without the other. It becomes a ritual.

There are various flash points for every drug, and some have more "addictability" than others. There are some drugs that no one can use casually, ever. The decision to use heroin may be made casually, but it won't have a casual impact. Continued use sucks the pleasure out of everything else in life. For all the problems heroin causes, crack is worse. Smokers of crack cocaine say that they've gotten addicted the first time they ever put a pipe to their lips. The effect of the drug is so overpowering and ends so quickly that withdrawal is practically instantaneous. There's an overwhelming desire for another hit only minutes after the first. That's just one reason why crack is such a dangerous drug.

Frequently, it seems that when someone has been using a drug for a while, whatever the drug and in whatever situation, that person is the last one to admit when the drug has gotten the upper hand. Drug use is a problem if it's messing up your relations with others. But when you suddenly discover that you can't make it through the day without it, then it's a Problem with a capital *P*.

Generally, a problem drug user, the newer term for addict, is defined as someone who has "physical and psychological dependency and the need for increasing dosage to achieve effect." If you know somebody like that and even mention his or her dependency, you're taking a risk, but it's a risk worth taking. Such people may think they don't need to hear it, but they do.

And how can you tell whether that person is you? The signs vary depending on the substance, but each one gives you situational clues: You never smoke except when you drink. But you drink three nights every week, no matter what. You might have the beginnings of a problem with those two substances. You might think that smoking and drinking aren't too serious. But it's tobacco and alcohol, of all substances, that have the worst impact on African-American health.

The central question is, and always has been, Am I using the drug or is the drug using me? Don't let the drug answer for you. Get straight and define it yourself, or sooner or later someone else will do it for you.

TAKE THIS DRUG AND SHOVE IT: STRATEGIES FOR QUITTING

You know that getting cigarettes, alcohol, or other drugs out of your life is the best thing you ever will do for yourself, but if you've ever tried to quit any drug, you don't need me to tell you that breaking its hold can be hard to do. For some smokers, quitting cigarettes was the hardest thing they've ever done in their lives. Others have said it was pretty easy for them. Whatever habit you're trying to break, it will be a life-transforming experience. In the process, you have to get the drug out of your head before you can get it out of your body.

Surveys of smokers who quit say that 90 percent gave up cigarettes on their own—no clinic, no treatment program, just themselves and their desire to quit. However, of those 90 percent, over 75 percent returned to smoking within a year. They had a higher return rate than smokers who quit through stop-smoking programs or clinics, such as SmokEnders. Does that mean that the programs were more effective, or that the people who went to them were more motivated to quit in the first place? Probably a little bit of both.

Breaking an addictive behavior requires sustained individual motivation. Wherever that motivation comes from, whether you're doing it for yourself or because the behavior is hurting your family, the desire must come from you. No one can force or coerce someone who is chemically dependent to quit for good.

The substances we are concentrating on in this chapter are among the leading causes of disease and premature death for us. If you're using any of them heavily, you're headed for self-destruction unless you stop. First, we'll consider what these drugs do to you. Then we'll discuss what you can do to offset some of their worst effects. Finally, we'll talk about how to kick the habit successfully.

ABOUT SMOKING

We are starting with cigarettes because smoking is so prevalent and so addictive—and *because so many people have already successfully quit,* despite the fact that nicotine is one of the hardest habits to break. Smokers undergoing treatment for alcohol and hard drugs compared their experience with quitting cigarettes. Nearly three-quarters of them said quitting smoking was at least as difficult—and over half said it was harder. But quitting can literally save your life.

Tobacco causes:

> Emphysema
> Many kinds of cancer, particularly lung cancer and
>   esophageal cancer
> Heart disease
> Stroke
> Low-birth-weight babies
> Chronic bronchitis

The premature death rate from all diseases, particularly heart disease and lung cancer, is much higher among smokers than nonsmokers. According to statistics first released by the American Cancer Society more than twenty-five years ago, a person who smokes two packs of cigarettes a day has a premature death rate *ninety times higher* than that of a nonsmoker. The Environmental Protection Agency in 1993 says that 434,000 Americans die every year from diseases caused by or aggravated by cigarette smoking.

Much of the harm caused by tobacco smoke can be traced to what biochemists call oxidative damage: an attack by highly reactive oxygen that damages cell membranes, raises serum cholesterol, and increases the conversion of substances into carcinogens

Living with people who smoke doubles a person's risk of developing cancer. The risk goes up according to how many smokers a person lives with. The newest estimates from the EPA say that secondhand tobacco smoke causes lung cancer that kills an estimated three thousand nonsmokers a year and subjects hundreds of thousands of children to respiratory disease. Even *smokers* living with other smokers increase their risk of cancer beyond their own habit.

Women who smoke have even more problems. In addition to the higher risk of lung cancer, female smokers have a much higher risk of cancer of the cervix or the uterus. They tend to have more difficulties with pregnancies—more spontaneous abortions, still-births, and premature deliveries. Their babies are born smaller and at much higher risk than the babies of nonsmokers.

SMOKING AND NUTRITION

Tobacco may lead to malnutrition by depleting the body of essential vitamins and minerals. For example, smoking robs the body of calcium and may accelerate osteoporosis. Smoke also seriously depletes vitamin C. Smokers also tend to be careless about nutrition. Some smokers thoughtlessly overeat, thinking of food as something more to keep the mouth busy. Others don't eat much at all, using cigarettes as a substitute for food.

What You Can Do Until You're Tobacco-Free
What to Eat. To help counter the negative effects of tobacco smoke, the diet should be rich in a group of nutrients known as

antioxidants: vitamins C and E, beta carotene, and, to some extent, the trace element selenium. All fruits and vegetables, particularly fresh carrot juice, broccoli, brussels sprouts, cabbage, turnip greens, citrus fruits and juices, tomatoes, strawberries, cantaloupe, green peppers, and sweet potatoes are recommended.

Fish such as mackerel, salmon, bluefish, and sardines are recommended twice a week for everyone for their heart-protective oils; smokers should *double* that amount.

Selenium, a trace element needed in only tiny amounts, is found in seafood, whole grains, pasta, garlic, and milk. Selenium works hand in glove with vitamin E.

Take Your Vitamins. Adding a good multivitamin daily is a good idea. Your daily vitamin pill should include or be supplemented by:

- vitamin B complex family—100 mg. per day plus extra vitamin B_{12} and folic acid. These are important antioxidants that destroy free radicals produced in smoke.
- vitamin C—500 mg. per day
- beta carotene—25 mg. per day
- vitamin E—400 IU (international units) once or twice a day

Add Exercise. Smoking contributes to bone loss, or osteoporosis. To maintain strong bones, add weight-bearing exercise to your life—walking, running, weight training, and so on. Exercise will also give you a euphoric lift, which may help you quit smoking.

QUITTING SMOKING

It's hard to say what quitting method will work best for you, because different methods work for different people. But at least one will work if you're determined to succeed. Maybe you'll quit on your first try and maybe you will need to quit three, four, or more times. Don't give up until you've given them up. Here are some options recommended by the American Cancer Society:

Cold turkey. You pick a date, then don't pick up another cigarette. It takes strong motivation, but this option works for some individuals.

Cutting down gradually. You can do it yourself with a filter system available at any drugstore for a couple of dollars. Or join a self-help group such as SmokEnders or Fresh Start.

Nicotine chewing gum. It's expensive, but so are cigarettes. The chewing gum reduces your nicotine intake, and you eventually stop chewing the gum. Right now, it's available only by prescription. If you've got health insurance and a prescription card, you can get it cheaply. For instance, a box of ninety-six usually costs between thirty and forty dollars. With a card, the same box costs three dollars.

Caution: Don't drink coffee, cola, or even juice when you're chewing nicotine gum. Acidic drinks neutralize the gum and block its effectiveness. Water is okay. You can still drink coffee or other drinks if you have them fifteen minutes before or after the gum.

The patch. This is another method available only by prescription, but it could be the best yet. You put a nicotine patch on your arm and it gradually releases nicotine into your system. Each new patch contains less and less nicotine. After three months, your body doesn't need nicotine anymore. Someday, the patch method may be used to help people quit other drugs. The patch is expensive, but, just like nicotine gum, you can probably get it for less with a prescription card.

Caution: The patch comes in various dosages, depending on how many cigarettes you currently smoke each day. It releases a total day's nicotine slowly over twenty-four hours. If you smoke one cigarette while you're using the patch, it probably won't affect you much. But if you resume smoking at your regular level while wearing the patch, you will double your dose of nicotine; that can make you really ill, or even, in some cases, kill you.

Other quitting methods include replacing a cigarette with another activity—exercise, or chewing on something like carrots, cinnamon, or clove. These have the added bonus of helping to keep you from gaining weight when you stop smoking.

The Mind at Work

While nicotine substitutes such as the patch and nicotine gum can help to wean you off nicotine, they can't help you with the psychological part of quitting cigarettes. If you've been smoking for a long time, it's probably part of your self-image. For example, close your eyes and imagine you are waiting for a train or talking to someone at a party. Do you see yourself with a cigarette? If you've been using cigarettes as a prop—and almost all smokers do—it's important to change your image.

Try this exercise: Take a minute, close your eyes, and imagine yourself in a specific situation where you would normally smoke. In your mind's eye, see your hands without a cigarette. Imagine how you are sitting or standing, and what your hands are doing. Repeat this exercise. The next time you are in that exact situation, remember your imagery and try to carry it out in real life.

Ready to Quit

Regardless of which method you choose for quitting, there are certain steps recommended by the National Heart, Lung, and Blood Institute that have helped over 3 million Americans quit smoking each year.

The most important step is deciding to quit. It doesn't matter if you've tried before and started to smoke again. *In fact, the more times you try, the more likely you are to succeed.*

List the reasons you want to quit. Review the list every day. Add to it as you think of more reasons.

Think about each cigarette before you smoke it. Unless you really want it, put the pack away. Try telling yourself that you can wait a little while longer.

Set a quit date and mark it on your calendar.

Tell everyone your quit date so they can be ready to support your efforts.

Start looking for ways not to smoke. Avoid tempting situations. For example, don't reach for a cigarette after dinner. Try a brisk walk instead.

Make a list of activities you will do instead of smoking. You might include sipping water, chewing sugarless gum or ice, or eating fruit or light snacks. (Avoid sweets and high-fat foods.) To keep your hands busy, try playing with a coin, paper clip, or pen. Doodle while you're on the phone. You can also move around, talk to helpful friends, or breathe deeply. Choose activities that appeal to you and that you can do easily.

Postpone smoking some cigarettes each day for fifteen minutes.

Worried about gaining weight when you quit? Many smokers do gain weight, because the metabolism goes through a period of adjustment when it is nicotine-free. You also begin to enjoy the taste of food more than smokers do. Don't worry about it; you can lose the extra pounds after you've quit. Or you may avoid gaining weight if you switch to low-fat foods and add exercise to your daily routine before quitting.

The night before your Quit Day, throw out your cigarettes, lighters, and ashtrays.

It's the morning of Quit Day. You're a new nonsmoker. The American Cancer Society recommends that you give yourself a reward each of the first three days off smoking, then each week. Be good to yourself. It doesn't matter whether the reward is something you buy with the money you save from quitting or if it's just something like listening to music for an hour, calling a friend, or eating food you especially enjoy. If you quit, you deserve something good. Choose a gift and give it to yourself.

When you have the urge to smoke, use the stop, think, act approach. Stop yourself, then think of all the reasons you want to quit. Tell yourself you can wait out the urge. (The urge to smoke lasts only from three to five minutes.) Then immediately take one of your substitute actions (remember your list of activities).

If you start smoking again, regain control. Learn from the slip, then forget it. Keep trying and you will make it.

Withdrawal

The physical dependency on nicotine operates through your central nervous system, which means that when you stop smoking you may experience unpleasant withdrawal symptoms. You may feel irritable, depressed, and anxious; you may cough more, and may even have stomach cramps or headaches. The severity of withdrawal symptoms varies considerably, and most people say they get past them in two to three weeks. A gradual quitting plan reduces or avoids withdrawal symptoms.

ABOUT ALCOHOL AND DRUGS

Alcohol abuse causes:

Cirrhosis of the liver
Violent behavior
Damage to the brain, pancreas, duodenum, and central
    nervous system
Cancer, especially cancer of the stomach and esophagus
Weakened immune response
Low-birth-weight and malformed babies
Mentally impaired babies

In moderation, alcohol seems to have little harmful effect on most people, and some studies suggest that small amounts of alcohol protect the heart and relieve stress by relaxing tense muscles (see Chapter 25). But if a little alcohol is helpful, a lot can be devastating.

Ten percent of all deaths in the United States are linked to alcohol, including those caused by diseases, accidents, and homicide.

Because alcohol is processed by the liver, the toxic effect on this organ is very serious. The alcoholic will first experience a fatty degeneration of cells in the liver; next comes hepatitis, a condition in which liver cells become inflamed and die. Usually, the final stage is cirrhosis, or scarring, of the liver, followed by death. Complications from liver disease are the ninth-leading cause of death in the United States; and the mortality rate for black Americans is nearly twice that of white Americans. (See Chapter 23.)

Alcohol can also damage the entire length of the gastrointestinal (GI) tract. In a study of over eight thousand Japanese men living in Hawaii, those who consumed more than sixteen ounces of beer daily had an increased risk of colorectal cancer. Alcohol abuse creates other cancer risks as well, especially in parts of the GI tract that come in direct contact with the alcohol, such as the esophagus and stomach. And while alcohol probably doesn't cause ulcers, it certainly can make existing ulcers worse.

Women are especially sensitive to the toxic effects of alcohol because they have lower amounts of the enzyme that breaks down alcohol in their stomachs; therefore, their bodies absorb more alcohol. This may be the reason that female alcoholics suffer a greater degree of liver damage sooner than do males.

Pregnant women should avoid alcohol from the moment they conceive (and even before) because alcohol easily crosses the placenta and damages the fetus. Babies born to alcoholic women are at high risk for fetal alcohol syndrome (FAS), a cluster of severe physical and mental defects that account for half of all birth defects. Even women who drink a modest amount of alcohol during pregnancy, especially in the first three to four months, may increase their baby's risk of FAS. Since there are no known safe limits, pregnant women should avoid *all* alcohol. (See Chapter 29.)

NUTRITION AND ALCOHOL

Alcohol has a devastating effect on nutritional status. Even if alcoholics eat a healthy diet, which most do not, they still may suffer from malnutrition for several reasons:

Drinking inhibits the liver's production of digestive enzymes, which impairs the body's ability to absorb proteins and fats, as well as vitamins A, D, E, and K.

Once damaged, the liver may be unable to convert vitamins into substances that can be used by the body.

Alcohol can also injure the lining of the small intestine and pancreas and further interfere with the body's ability to absorb vital nutrients. Drinking on an empty stomach lowers blood sugar, which can lead to volatile emotions.

What You Can Do Until You Stop Drinking

All alcohol you ingest must be detoxified by the liver. So if you drink, it's important to drink in quantities small enough for the liver to handle, about one ounce of alcohol per hour. One ounce of hard liquor translates into one four-ounce glass of wine or twelve ounces of beer. If you drink more than that in one hour, the liver is overloaded.

What to Eat. Nutritionwise, it's important to include foods in your diet that are high in vitamin B complex and vitamin C: whole-grain breads and cereals, citrus fruits and vegetables, such as lemons, limes, oranges, broccoli, and tomatoes.

Take Your Vitamins. Vitamin supplements should include: thiamine (B_1), vitamin B complex, cyanocobalamin (vitamin B_{12}), folate (folic acid), niacin (B_3), magnesium, and vitamin C.

IF YOU USE DRUGS

All drugs weaken the immune system, making the body vulnerable to many degenerative diseases, including cancer and AIDS. Drug addiction of any kind—cocaine, heroin, crack, marijuana, or a host of other drugs—also produces a wide range of negative mental and emotional effects, including acute anxiety, followed by paranoia, poor concentration, frequent mood swings, and hallucinations. Those addicted to drugs typically lose their temper easily, experience crying spells, and have slow, slurred speech.

Different drugs produce various biological responses, none of them good. Here are two examples.

Cocaine causes:

Heart attack, coronary artery spasm, and life-threatening
   damage to the heart muscle
Respiratory problems
Loss of appetite
Violent behavior
Death

Marijuana causes:

Lung cancer
Increased heart rate
Impaired brain function
Bronchitis
Emphysema

What You Can Do Until You Stop Using

What to Eat. Drug users often suffer from malnutrition because they don't eat enough. It helps to add a high-protein drink to the daily diet. Sugar and foods low in nutritional value should be avoided, because although they are a quick source of energy, they are followed by a low feeling that may make some people turn back to drugs when they're trying to quit.

Take Your Vitamins. In addition to a multivitamin and mineral formula, add a B complex vitamin, vitamin B_{12}, vitamin C, calcium, and magnesium.

DRUGS AND AIDS

Drugs are believed to depress the immune system and leave it vulnerable to viruses that can kill. Beyond that, behaviors associated with drug use can directly cause HIV infection and AIDS—unprotected sex and using needles that are contaminated with the blood of a person with the AIDS virus. If you use drugs *or know someone who does,* read Chapter 21 carefully.

ALCOHOL- AND DRUG-TREATMENT PROGRAMS

Though they all have the same goal, treatment programs for chemical dependency vary in philosophy and outlook, in racial and economic makeup, and in success rates. The key to success, regardless of the program or type of addiction, is personal motivation. Wanting or needing to kick the habit makes the difference. Treatment programs, which can last up to two years, tend to work best for people who have something to lose if they don't quit—a job, status in the community, home, or family.

Dr. Al J. Mooney and Arlene and Howard Eisenberg, coauthors of *The Recovery Book,* a valuable resource, say that different treatments work for different people; which one will work for you depends on your own personality, the nature of your addiction, and your life experience.

Some people can choose a program by themselves, but many need a helping hand to help sort through the treatment options and get started. Ask someone to help you, perhaps a family member, a trusted friend, your doctor, or your minister (if he or she is savvy about drug problems). Perhaps you know someone who goes to AA or another self-help program. Here is a brief description of treatment options.

AA and Other Self-Help Programs

No matter which treatment option you choose, you will probably also be asked to attend AA meetings or a similar type of twelve-step or other self-help support group. (Twelve-step programs are named after the steps taken by the founders of AA as they turned away from alcohol; the term is used today by many other recovery groups to describe a similar method.) For many, probably most, people, attending a self-help group makes the difference in whether their treatment works.

AA looks upon addiction as a disease; it can be stopped but not cured. The heart of the program is lifetime abstinence from alcohol and other drugs—one day at a time.

The only requirement to join AA is a desire to stop drinking or using drugs. Many drug users are also alcoholics and attend AA meetings for both addictions. There are also AA offshoots that deal with specific addictions; these include Narcotics Anonymous, Pills Anonymous, Smokers Anonymous, and Cocaine Anonymous. However, cocaine users often prefer regular AA meetings, because a desire for this particular drug can be stimulated just by hearing about it: Sitting around for an hour talking about cocaine can be very hard on cocaine addicts.

AA meetings take place in many kinds of settings—church basements, cafeterias, hospitals, synagogues, meeting rooms at work, in people's homes—at all hours of the day and night, everywhere in the world. Many people have a meeting in their area that they attend regularly, but they also attend other meetings wherever they happen to be. You don't need an appointment to go to a meeting; all you have to do is show up. When first getting started, many alcoholics and drug users go to one or more meetings a day. There is no charge; a hat is passed for contributions to cover rent, coffee, and cookies. You drop in what you can.

At meetings, people talk about their past experiences with alcohol and drugs, and they talk about their fears and their hopes. In some miraculous way, listening to others and sharing your experiences help relieve the compulsion to drink or use drugs.

One of the twelve steps involves recognizing that there is a higher power that can help you overcome your addiction. This makes some people uncomfortable. But the programs don't require that every step be followed, and they don't ask for submission to any higher power in particular—it can be the power that created the universe or the power of love—so it's possible to fit the philosophy into your present religious practice, if you have one. Many nonbelievers do belong to AA.

Two alternative self-help groups bypass the spiritual approach: Rational Recovery (RR) and Secular Organizations for Sobriety (SOS).

SOS is compatible with the principles of AA and some SOS members also attend AA meetings. RR has a different viewpoint about addiction. While it also preaches total abstinence, RR does not adhere to the disease theory. Its abiding principle is that people need to feel good about themselves and build on their inner strengths. Independence is its theme, and "think yourself sober" is its motto. Meetings take place only twice a week, supervised by professional coordinators, and most people attend for about one year. If you're uncomfortable with AA, give SOS or RR a try if you can find a group where you live.

Blacks and Self-Help Programs. When you choose a self-help program, it's important to find a group with whom you feel comfortable. Although AA and other self-help programs began as mostly white organizations, this is changing as more urban chapters are being organized. One of AA's offspring, Narcotics Anonymous, has been multiracial from the start.

Still, color was never intended to be a factor in these programs. People in AA form their own special society and, no matter what their ethnic or economic background, have much in common. You are neither black nor white; everyone in the meeting shares a disease, has similar symptoms, and requires the same basic treatment. Individual differences fade next to that common bond. However, even people who believe in the disease theory—that we inherit our predisposition to addiction—understand that racial oppression can make recovery more difficult. As a result, cultural issues are beginning to be raised in AA meetings.

Even so, blacks and other minorities can feel out of place at recovery meetings. Actually, everyone, regardless of background, feels out of place at the first couple of meetings. It's weird to talk about experiences and feelings in front of others. But many blacks feel that other members cannot appreciate our particular cultural issues. And some of us aren't ready to trust our feelings to whites.

Although it's important to feel at home with the people you're with, you also want to be able to go to any AA meeting at any time, anywhere. The best advice is to start with an integrated meeting, or an all-black group, even if that means extra travel and effort.

If you still feel uncomfortable talking in front of the group, Dr. Mooney recommends getting together with a few black members of your group separately a few times, in addition to your regular meetings. Once you start to talk among friends, it's easier to do it in a larger group, even one that's predominantly white.

If there are no integrated meetings you can get to, experiment with various groups and choose the one that feels best to you for your regular meeting. (You can ask a couple of friends to go with you for additional support.)

If all else fails, think about starting your own group. People do it all the time. You and a few other members can begin informally and then register later with the Alcoholics Anonymous General Services Office. You may also find special help from your neighborhood church. More and more black churches are starting their own programs. These are usually similar to AA but also deal with black issues and community problems.

Whatever you do, don't use "it's too white" as an excuse not to go. The important thing about support groups is the opportunity to listen to what others say and to open yourself up and share your own experiences. Talking about your life is the way you get better. You don't have to ignore racial or cultural issues; talk openly about them in meetings.

Private Physicians

An experienced physician can help you get through withdrawal and work through your alcohol or drug problem. If you decide to go this route, make sure the doctor is certified by the American Society of Addiction Medicine (ASAM) or the American Academy of Psychiatrists in Alcoholism and Addiction (AAPAA). If you receive addiction therapy from a doctor, you will also be urged to go to a self-help support program such as AA.

Psychiatrists

Psychiatrists offer the same treatment services as physicians (see above) with the addition of psychotherapy to help build self-esteem and deal with depression, anxiety, anger, and other feelings that feed your addiction. Psychiatrists also should be certified by AAPAA or ASAM. You can ask for a recommendation from someone in AA or from an experienced addiction counselor.

Addiction Counselors

Many counselors and therapists treat chemically dependent people, but you should look for someone who puts the addiction issue first, the psychology second. Counselors should meet the standards for a certified addiction counselor or credentialed alcoholism counselor. Most use a similar approach, which usually includes individual and group therapy, as well as AA meetings.

Outpatient Treatment Programs

Outpatient treatment consists of regularly scheduled counseling sessions, including individual, group, and sometimes family therapy. It may also include evaluation interviews, a complete physical exam, periodic drug screening, and signed attendance at AA meetings. You can start treatment before withdrawal or after you are already clean and sober. Because quality is largely unrelated to cost, it's important to meet the staff before choosing a program. Again, you're not looking for it to be easy and comfortable—in fact, feeling *uncomfortable* is the route to recovery. But you do want to find people you can trust and listen to.

Inpatient Programs

Inpatient or residential programs are the same as outpatient programs except that you are spared the temptation of being out on the street after therapy. Some people start with an outpatient program, find they need something more intense, and later switch to an inpatient facility. Many do the reverse: start with an inpatient program, then after discharge continue with outpatient treatment.

Private inpatient programs offer drug users around-the-clock support, individual counseling and group sessions, and are the most expensive form of treatment. Private clinics treat their clients carefully, paying extra attention to health and nutrition. Some use drug therapy; that is, they wean the user off one drug by giving him another. Eventually, they wean the user off the substitute, too.

Private clinics are expensive. The poor have access to public treatment programs, but it's hard to know just how effective these are because, like other government-run programs, they are usually underfunded and understaffed. Waiting lists are long. Many users are there on court orders rather than from personal motivation. Despite these problems, some people attending public clinics successfully beat their addictions. And while such programs haven't eliminated heroin use, they have at least lowered it.

Methadone-maintenance clinics raise other questions. A common complaint is that maintenance trades one addictive drug for another. The only difference, critics say, is that methadone is legal. In other words, the prime reason for methadone maintenance is not treatment but lowering crime associated with the illegal drug trade.

Therapeutic Communities

Independent therapeutic communities like Phoenix House or Gateway are multiracial programs that have shown a lot of success in turning around the lives of both young and adult addicts. These communities, staffed mostly by former addicts and graduates of the program, stress a self-help approach. Their goal is to change all aspects of the drug user's life. They use encounter and confrontational therapy techniques based on peer pressure that help reinforce change. These programs also provide some job training. Treatment can last from three months to two years, though most people stay less than six months.

Once a user has joined a therapeutic community, he or she is always considered a member, even after graduation. Set up mostly for the hard-core user, independent communities are supported by private donations and public funding, so most are usually free.

Recovery strategies are evolving, and more community-based organizations are developing treatment programs. These range from counseling services offered by African-American organizations to halfway houses administered and run by blacks. If you want to be treated in an African-American setting, and if you live in or near a black community of any size, you probably have access to at least one of these programs.

If you're having trouble with drugs or alcohol, ask for help. There are people and organizations around who will help. Use them. If you want to find a self-help group or treatment center in your community, look in the Yellow Pages under the listings for city and state government. The Public Health Department should list such centers.

Going It Alone

It's true that you don't have to join a treatment program to overcome an addiction. But it can be dangerous to quit drugs and alcohol cold turkey, and this is the hardest of all roads. If you do decide to quit on your own, make sure you get in touch with a doctor first. At a minimum, you will need professional supervision while you go through a period of withdrawal.

To minimize symptoms, withdrawal from any substance should be done slowly and gradually over a period of four weeks or longer. This task should not be undertaken alone. A professional health-care worker can help you through the withdrawal process by giving you high doses of specific vitamins and minerals aimed to help detoxify your system and reduce your cravings. Certain herbal remedies may also help. For example, the herb valerian root has a calming effect. The herb silymarin (extract of the milk thistle weed) has been used to help to repair damage done to the liver from alcohol.

In some cases, your doctor may prescribe medications to help you cope with discomfort and to aid withdrawal. Generally, doctors avoid prescribing tranquilizers for recovering patients because there is a danger of substituting one drug addiction for another.

After you quit, you still have to learn how to cope with all the fallout from your past. And long-term users always have a lot of fallout, so it's important to get help from a support group.

RESOURCES

The Regional Alcohol and Drug Aware Resources (RADAR) is a network of state information centers. The RADAR office in your state should be able to get a list of all the treatment and counseling programs available in your area. You can also call your local health department for information, or the Office of Minority Health (see below).

FEDERAL GOVERNMENT AND NATIONAL ORGANIZATIONS

Office of Minority Health
  Resource Center
PO Box 37337
Washington, D.C. 20013-7337
(800) 444-6472

National Institute on Alcoholism
  and Drug Abuse (NIDA)
5600 Fishers Lane
Rockville, MD 20857
(301) 443-4373
(800) 662-4357

ACTION
Drug Prevention Program
1100 Vernon Avenue NW
Suite #8200
Washington, D.C. 20525
(202) 634-9759

National Clearinghouse for
  Alcohol and Drug
  Information
PO Box 2345
Rockville, MD 20852
(301) 468-2600

National Council on Alcoholism
12 West 21 Street
New York, NY 10010
(212) 206-6770

National Association of
  Alcoholism and Drug Abuse
  Counselors
3717 Columbia Pike, Suite #300
Arlington, VA 22204
(703) 920-4644

SELF-HELP ORGANIZATIONS

Alcoholics Anonymous
PO Box 459
Grand Central Station
New York, NY 10163
212-870-3400

Rational Recovery
(916) 621-4374

Secular Organizations for
  Sobriety (SOS)
Box 5
Buffalo, NY 14215-0005
(716) 834-2922

AL-ANON/AlaTeen Family
  Groups
PO Box 862
Midtown Station
New York, NY 10018
(212) 302-7240

Cocaine Anonymous (CA)
6125 Washington Boulevard,
  Suite 202
Los Angeles, CA 90230
Hotline: 1-800-COCAINE

Cocaine Baby Help Line
(800) 638-2229

Narcotics Anonymous (NA)
World Service Office
PO Box 9999
Van Nuys, CA 91409
(818) 780-3951
1-800-662-4357 for a referral in
your area

Northeast Drug/Alcohol
Referral and Tracking Station
1809 N. Broadway, Suite C
Wichita, KS 67214
(316) 265-8511

Institute on Black Chemical
Dependency
2614 Nicollet Avenue South
Minneapolis, MN 55408
(612) 871-7878

BOOKS, PAMPHLETS, AND OTHER READING MATERIALS

There are more than two hundred specialized recovery bookstores in the United States and many general bookstores are adding recovery books to their stock. Check your telephone directory under "Bookstores." If you can't locate a book you need, try ordering by mail from: Choices Recovery Bookstore, 220 East Seventy-eighth Street, New York, NY 10021. (212) 794-3858.

Hazelden Educational Materials
15251 Pleasant Valley Road
PO Box 176
Center City, MN 555012-0176
(800) 328-9000

Multicultural Training Resource
Center
1540 Market Street, Suite 320
San Francisco, CA 94102
(415) 861-2142

RECOMMENDED READING

Alcoholics Anonymous (also known as the "Big Book"; available at special recovery bookstores, some bookstore chains, and directly from AA)

Rational Recovery from Alcoholism: The Small Book (available at recovery bookstores and from Rational Recovery, 916-621-4374)

Allen, Chaney. *I'm Black and I'm Sober* (Minneapolis: CompCare, 1978). A minister's daughter's victory over alcoholism.

Bell, Peter. *Chemical Dependency and the African-American* (Center City, Minnesota: Hazelden, 1990)

Bell, Peter. *Black and Recovering* (Minneapolis; Johnson Institute, 1993). Pamphlet.

Mooney, Al J., M.D., Arlene Eisenberg, and Howard Eisenberg. *The Recovery Book*. (New York: Workman Publishing, 1992).

Rustin, TA., *Quit and Stay Quit* (Center City, Minnesota: Hazelden 1991). An effective personal program for kicking cigarettes.

6

WHAT TO DO
ABOUT YOUR WEIGHT

Tremendous health hazards are linked to excess weight, many of which are special risks for African Americans. Obese people at every age—even those just over the borderline—have higher death rates from life-threatening diseases than the non-obese.

Obese people are more likely to develop Type II diabetes (the most common form of diabetes), hypertension, stroke, and heart disease. If you already have any of these diseases, being overweight makes them worse. For black women between thirty and fifty-five, who typically gain weight at this age, death rates are two to three times higher than among white women the same age.

The most deadly of these diseases is heart disease. The more you weigh, the more blood vessels your body needs to fully circulate blood from head to toe. (Every pound of fat requires another mile of blood vessels.) Your heart must work harder to pump blood through so many extra miles. The heart grows larger, and blood pressure usually goes up.

There is a long list of other health problems associated with obesity. For example, respiratory problems include sleep apnea, an interruption of breathing that can occur for a few seconds or long enough to kill; shortness of breath; tightness in the chest; bronchial infections; and erythrocytosis, an excessive production of red blood cells that affects the body's ability to carry oxygen.

If you ever need surgery to help correct a medical problem, obesity increases the risk of surgical complications.

Obesity can alter hormone levels, which may cause impotence and low sperm counts in men and a host of reproductive problems in women, making pregnancies and childbirth hazardous for both mothers and their babies. Overweight girls often get their first periods sooner than leaner girls; this is significant because some studies show a link between early menarche and breast cancer.

Adult women who are obese are more likely to develop breast cancer, as well as cancer of the endometrium, cervix, ovaries, and gallbladder. Obese women are believed to produce a more potent form of estrogen, which overstimulates the lining of the uterus, leading to endometrial cancer. Current statistics suggest that women who are 30 percent overweight are twice as likely to die if they develop this highly curable form of cancer, regardless of their age or race. Those who are 40 percent overweight have *four times* the risk.

Men who are obese are more prone to cancer in the rectum, colon, esophagus, bladder, pancreas, stomach, and prostate.

Both men and women are more likely to develop arthritis, because carrying excess weight strains the joints. Obesity can lead to a fatty liver. Obesity also makes you six times more likely to develop gallstones. Other risks include varicose veins, high blood sugar, and elevated blood lipids, which may lead to clogged arteries and heart disease.

In short, excess weight has no benefit; it creates many serious health problems. Yo-yo dieters—those who gain, lose, and regain weight—have a greater risk of heart disease and early death than those who are simply overweight for a sustained period of time.

A SPECIAL PROBLEM FOR BLACK WOMEN

Roughly 26 percent of all Americans are overweight, and 12 percent of us are dangerously obese. Obesity is rising among all minorities, but one of the more mysterious health statistics to emerge from a decade's worth of research conducted at the Centers for Disease Control and Prevention shows that weight gain is most likely among black women between the ages of twenty-five and thirty-four. Indeed, at every age, black women are significantly more likely to be obese than any other group.

In our childbearing years (twenty to forty-four), 35 percent of us are overweight, versus under 25 percent of white women. By the time we reach age forty-five to fifty-five, fully 50 percent of us are overweight. Oddly, black men don't show the same tendency. In the age range from twenty to forty-four, only 10 percent of black men are overweight, compared with 16 percent of white men.

Statistics suggest that education and money are telling factors in weight gain. People with lower education and income levels—regardless of race—tend to be heavier than those who are more educated and earn more. Overall, rural and southern populations are more overweight than city people who live in the north and west. Here is another peculiar twist between men and women: Richer men may be slightly heavier, while poorer women are *significantly* more obese.

No one knows why black women tend to gain weight so readily in their prime years. Overall, researchers blame a diet high in fatty and fried foods and surmise that better education about nutrition might solve the problem. I believe that stress and cultural influences on African Americans play a role. Using quantities of fat for cooking everything from biscuits and fried fish to greens and fruit cobblers is such an entrenched cultural habit that we don't even think about it. This was certainly true in my own family.

People also eat certain foods for reasons that may have nothing to do with their knowledge about nutrition or their cultural upbringing. Those struggling to make ends meet every day may eat unwisely out of necessity, or they may do so in order to feel secure. For poor women, convenient, processed, and inexpensive carbohydrates—potatoes, beans, cakes, chips, candy, and fatty foods—seem to be comfort foods, promoting a good feeling that satisfies hunger. Anyone, rich or poor, who has suffered any form of deprivation or stress knows how soothing food can be when it comes to quieting dull emotional aches. For many of us, eating fills emptiness. And fullness satisfies cravings to feel safe. It's not only the quantity of food but the type of food that lend security. For example, a wealthy man may equate high-fat premium foods —butter, cream, bacon and eggs, roast beef and other red meats —with richness and well-being.

Low self-esteem, feelings of impotence, fear, anger, tension, stress—all can contribute to the urge to reach for food even when we're not physically hungry. Any weight-loss program for African Americans should take this need for comfort and security—the need for fullness—into account. This is a central issue in the Sankofa Program that we'll explore in Part Three.

There is one other significant piece to the obesity puzzle confounding black women—our cultural self-image. Many of my overweight African-American patients, as well as patients my husband sees in his internal medicine practice, do not feel their weight is a problem.

When I ask my female black patients what they would like to weigh, it's almost always ten to twenty or more pounds above healthy weight for their height and frame. They tell me their husbands don't want them to be skinny, saying, "No one wants a bone but a dog." Many black men say they prefer a woman with hips, large breasts, or big legs.

The Hollywood image for white women is often scrawny to our eyes, which in the long run may actually be a good thing. I know it sounds as if I'm contradicting myself here, but this is a complicated issue. We don't need or want to be skin and bones—because what society calls beautiful is a trap for women, particularly black women. For centuries, we've been made to feel that our hair isn't long enough or good enough, our skin not light enough, and our bodies not thin enough. We don't want to buy into that common negative thinking that makes women always dissatisfied with their appearance, no matter how beautiful they are. And women of color are notoriously beautiful—all the way from Cleopatra to Naomi Simms, one of the first black models with very dark skin. We've got to reach a middle ground. Though we don't need to be superthin, we also need to be realistic about weight. Excess weight is a serious health risk for blacks as well as whites, and it's important for us to tackle obesity to preserve our health.

WHY DIETS FAIL

If many people are overweight, it's not from lack of dieting. But the evidence is rolling in that diets simply don't work. Oprah

Winfrey, after regaining much of the weight she lost on a liquid diet program, said she would never diet again. Apparently, Oprah, like many of us, had spent years trying various diet programs; she did well initially, then later regained most or all of the weight she had lost. Oprah has said she will stop dieting to avoid the dangerous yo-yo results of losing and regaining weight. I think she has the right idea.

Many other celebrities, including Delta Burke, Nell Carter, Elizabeth Taylor, Jayne Kennedy, and Luther Vandross, have lost and regained weight before our very eyes. In an interview a few years ago, following one of his dramatic losses of weight, Mr. Vandross admitted his weight fluctuates based on his personal life. When a "special person" is in his life, he said, he tends to be more successful at keeping his weight down. (His example is by no means unusual, since stress can be associated with both weight loss and weight gain.)

Although people have come up with a huge variety of "foolproof" diets over the years, each guaranteed to provide rapid weight loss, we seem to be getting fatter and fatter.

Most diets fail because they disrupt ordinary life too much. They're too restrictive or too unrealistic. Here's a rundown on some of the nation's most famous kinds of diet and why they don't work.

Restrictive Macronutrients. In this kind of diet, one essential food group is eliminated or drastically reduced.

For example, some limit carbohydrate intake. The hazard in this is that the body may begin to burn protein for fuel, leading to a serious health threat known as ketosis.

By contrast, extremely low-fat diets—*less than* 20 percent of your total calories—present a different set of problems. Without any dietary fat, the body has trouble absorbing vitamins E and A. Extremely low-fat diets are invariably low in quality protein, which can lead to a deficiency in calcium, zinc, and iron.

Fad Diets. Fad diets emphasize one food or one food group (like eating only grapefruit or eggs) or certain foods eaten in strict combinations. These diets are not nutritionally balanced; as soon as you stop dieting, you quickly regain the lost weight.

Fad diets can put tremendous strain on your body due to the loss of minerals and vitamins. Though people lose weight rapidly, the loss is largely water and muscle, which can be dangerous.

Very Low-Calorie Diets. In the 1970s, very low-calorie (VLC) liquid diets of predigested protein first appeared on the market and proved very lucrative for their manufacturers—until dieters following the plan began getting sick. Doctors consider any diet under eight to nine hundred calories per day starvation level, and some of these liquid diets recommend levels of six hundred calories or less.

Though today's formulas are significantly more nutritious than those of the 1970s, VLC diets can still be dangerous, particularly when they are used without medical supervision. It's important on these diets to include the recommended "real" meal each day. Even so, the overall level of vitamins and minerals may be so low that health problems occur. The huge fluid loss on VLC diets depletes sodium and potassium from the body. Since the heart muscle especially depends on proper potassium levels, in the worst extreme these diets can lead to heart failure. They also leave dieters susceptible to other complaints, including sensitivity to cold, fatigue, light-headedness, dizziness, irritability, dry skin, anemia, menstrual irregularities, constipation, or diarrhea. Starvation also raises the level of uric acid in your blood, leaving you more likely to develop gout and kidney stones.

Perhaps the worst side effect of these diets is that 95 percent of those who follow them ultimately regain all (and sometimes more) of their weight when they resume eating. The effects of losing and regaining weight are devastating to body and mind.

These diets are recommended—and then guardedly—only for the severely obese who use them *under medical supervision.*

Diet Pills. Diet pills can also be dangerous and ultimately ineffective. Amphetamines, for instance, reduce appetite and speed metabolism, but once you stop taking the pills, both appetite and metabolism return to normal and you regain the weight. Even worse, amphetamines are highly addictive and produce an array of dangerous side effects, including blurred vision, palpitations, hypertension, dizziness, irritability, nausea and vomiting, and constipation and/or diarrhea.

Diet pills sold over the counter without a prescription generally contain an ingredient called phenylpropanolamine (PPA), which is linked to such side effects as anxiety, dizziness, and increased blood pressure. These pills should *not* be taken by anyone with diabetes, high blood pressure, or heart, thyroid, or kidney diseases.

Diuretics and Laxatives. A lot of people take "water" pills, or diuretics, to shed pounds quickly. Continual use of these pills may ultimately damage the heart because the careful balance of body salts and minerals may be destroyed, placing stress on your heart.

Laxatives also destroy this delicate balance and have virtually no effect on weight. Most of the calories you eat are absorbed by your body *before* the laxative does its work. (Laxatives also bloat you, so you won't even look any thinner.) Prolonged laxative use also creates a dependency, and after a while your colon loses its ability to contract and cannot function without drugs or enemas. Constant use of laxatives, called laxative purging, is even more dangerous than the vomiting associated with the eating disorder bulimia because of the damage done to the gastrointestinal tract.

A new study has found that laxatives and diuretics are a popular form of attempted weight control for young African-American women. Nutritional anthropologist Dr. Lillian Emmons analyzed self-administered questionnaires from 1,269 high school students. Her findings, published in the March 1992 issue of *Journal of the American Dietetic Association,* reports that 41 percent of the black boys and 42 percent of the white boys dieted, mostly by simply reducing their food intake. But the story was different among the girls, who tended to use more extreme methods: 61 percent of the black girls and 77 percent of the white girls dieted. A significant number of black girls purged with laxatives and diuretics, while a significant number of white girls purged by vomiting.

The study supports other evidence that teenagers—especially girls—feel intense pressure to conform to certain physical standards, no matter what toll it may take on their health. Why white girls and black girls choose such distinctively different ways of trying to control their weight is a mystery, but it may be rooted in cultural habits. This is pure speculation on my part, but I hear many of my black patients say that their mothers and grandmothers recommended "cleaning the system" from time to time. My own mother used to insist that we use mineral oil or castor oil several times a year for this purpose. Laxatives fit right in with this idea. Laxatives are also less weird and less distasteful to us than vomiting, which is associated with illness. Diuretics are also familiar to most of us because many of our parents take them to get rid of excess fluid associated with high blood pressure.

We need to educate our daughters about the dangers of using laxatives and diuretics. We also need to get them started young on paying positive attention to their weight by improving their nutrition. Along with this good information, we can help build their self-esteem and provide an awareness of realistic body weight.

WHAT DOES WORK

The year I completed my dietetic internship, after being constantly exposed to a wide variety and quantity of foods, I found myself forty pounds overweight. As an occupational hazard, my predicament was not unusual, because part of the job was tasting different foods and testing recipes. There was so much tempting food available that I was constantly eating!

After seeing my graduation picture, I was determined to do something about my weight. How could I set an example for my patients and be an advocate for health if I was overweight myself? More important, given my family's poor health background, I knew I was courting early death by carrying so much excess weight. My family history put me at risk for high blood pressure, stroke, and premature death.

Since my goal was to lose weight, at first I chose speed over sound nutritional practices. I thoroughly analyzed every morsel I ate. I chastised myself if I ate even one cookie. Periodically, I fasted. I lost the excess weight fairly quickly, but six months later I was back where I'd started. I was miserable, always worrying about my weight. I dieted again, lost weight, then gained it back. I know now that such fearful dieting leads to many of the eating disorders we see today.

After a few frustrating cycles of losing and regaining weight, I backed off and began to explore nontraditional, or alternative, styles of nutrition and weight loss and began to pay attention to *what* I was eating rather than to how much. One of the first nontraditional diet books that influenced me was *Cooking with*

Mother Nature by comedian and political activist Dick Gregory. (Later, Gregory developed his liquid diet for those overweight by at least one hundred pounds.)

Herbal and holistic medicine soon took their place in my overall approach. I learned that nontraditional medicine and nutrition had a healthy place alongside traditional modern approaches. I also began to exercise. I discovered that exercise improved my energy level and increased weight loss. The more regularly I exercised, the better I felt. I chose running as a preferred exercise and began reading about the experiences of other runners. I was skeptical when I heard that a Russian runner had given up red meat to improve his performance (I had always associated meat with endurance and stamina and thought it enhanced physical performance). Nevertheless, I followed his example and was surprised to find that the less red meat I ate, the more energy I had.

Eventually, I developed a nutritional and exercise plan I've been able to live with for the last fifteen years. I eat a variety of foods in moderate amounts. In addition, I watch the amount of fat, sugar, salt, and high-calorie foods I eat. If I start to gain, I cut back my portion size and drink more water; I also increase my level of exercise.

I believe the same approach works for most people. I also believe that deprivation and constant self-denial are the dieter's downfall. Even people with serious medical problems—extreme obesity, hypertension, diabetes—will find that *moderate* changes in diet and regular exercise bring the best long-lasting results. In Part Three of this book, I'll show you a simple, enjoyable nondieting program designed to revolutionize your eating *for the rest of your life.*

But before you start on any attempt at weight loss, it will help enormously if you understand what you're dealing with. You can circumvent much of the endless aggravation and unhappiness associated with dieting if you understand how your body is fighting back against weight loss.

WHY SOME PEOPLE ARE OVERWEIGHT

Why do some people become fat while others remain lean? For most, weight gain is caused by the combined forces of genetics

BEHAVIOR MODIFICATION
Behavior modification is an integral tool for any long-term change. There are three stages to altering a behavior pattern:

1. *Motivation: You have to want to change—not for any superficial reason, such as an upcoming wedding, but for internal reasons, such as the desire always to look and feel better.*
2. *Action: Make the change!*
3. *Maintenance: This is the most important part, sustaining change over time. You have to find ways to fill your life with plenty of positive reinforcement, daily motivators, and rewards.*

What kind of new behaviors should you adopt if you want to lose weight? Try some of these:

• *Plan the day's food in advance and stick to this menu.*

• *Try eating several small meals daily to keep metabolism working at a higher speed (eating actually triggers metabolism). Individuals who eat three or four meals per day tend to weigh less than those eating the same number of calories divided into two meals.*

• *Dish up individual servings in the kitchen so excess food isn't on the table to tempt.*

• *Use small plates so portions seem bigger.*

• *When you eat, just eat. Don't also read or watch TV. Concentrate on the food and your enjoyment.*

• *Make food attractive with colorful vegetable garnishes and tasty with herbs and spices, but not salt.*

• *Don't feel compelled to clean your plate.*

• *Eat slowly. Take at least twenty minutes to eat your meals. Put your fork down between mouthfuls.*

• *Never eat standing up or lying down in bed.*

and lifestyle—the weight package we're born with and the kind of life we lead, including physical activity, the amount and kinds of foods we eat, and our ethnic traditions. (Only a few people become overweight because of glandular problems. A small minority may gain because of illnesses or medications that cause fluid retention or slow down metabolism.)

Let's start with basics. Obesity comes from having too many fat cells in your body (called hyperplastic obesity) or from having extra-large fat cells (called hypertrophic obesity).

Everyone is born with a certain number of fat cells. These are the only cells in your body that can expand to hold more fat—up to 62 percent, versus the 20 percent found in other body cells. The number of fat cells you are born with multiplies during peak periods of growth: generally, late infancy, early childhood, adolescence, and during pregnancy. If you overeat during any of these periods, fat cells can multiply as many as five times. (Therefore, it's especially important that foods eaten in these periods of peak growth are nutritional rather than poor in quality and high in calories.) Fat cells can also multiply during any period when you gain a lot of weight.

Your birth weight does not determine your future weight. Large infants don't necessarily become overweight adults. Yet obesity may begin in early childhood, as early as age two in girls and age three in boys. Children who are overweight may have lifelong weight problems; when fat cells multiply at an early age, it is virtually impossible to reduce their number later in life.

Fat cells can *enlarge* at any time in life, but this most often happens when people gain weight as adults. (If you periodically gain a lot of weight and lose it, you have both hyperplastic and hypertrophic fat cells.)

How can you know what kind of fat cells you have? You probably can't, unless you're a scientist. By drawing samples of fat tissue through a needle, then examining the tissue under a microscope, scientists can count the number of fat cells they see.

Does it matter what kind of obesity you have? It might. Everyone can lose weight by following similar regimens, but those who have the normal number of fat cells appear more successful at keeping it off.

Looking at this new information, it's obvious that there are many reasons for obesity. Your weight and body type are determined primarily by the genes you inherited from your parents, and any adjustments made up or down are more or less limited by your biological heritage.

For example, when identical twins are raised in separate families with adoptive parents, their weight patterns and body shape consistently match those of their biological parents. Dr. Theodore B. VanItallie, Professor of Medicine Emeritus, St. Luke's–Roosevelt Hospital Center in New York City, refers to this predisposition to obesity as "metabolic vulnerability." But Dr. VanItallie also says that metabolic vulnerability is a *tendency* to retain fat or increase the number of fat cells, particularly if the diet is high in fat. If the same individual ate fewer high-fat foods and exercised more, he or she wouldn't be overweight, in spite of this inherited tendency.

Different people also burn calories at different rates. One large study of over six thousand adults found that overweight people in the study ate the same amounts as their normal-weight peers, and their exercise levels were also comparable. Their metabolism was simply slower. Interestingly, obese people who lose weight continue to have a slower metabolic rate than people who have never been fat.

Every person has a preprogrammed metabolic rate. Some scientists believe that your body has a particular weight it would like to be; no matter what you do, it will strive to maintain that weight by adjusting its metabolic rate. This is called "set point" theory. According to this theory, when you restrict calories, your body will fight to hold on to its weight by lowering its metabolic rate and increasing its hunger drive. The harder you cut the calories, the less weight you lose and the hungrier you feel.

Set point explains a lot about why dieters, black or white, can't keep off the weight they lose. Ninety-five percent of overweight people who lose weight regain it within a year, plus a few extra pounds for good measure.

Set point is part of the marvelous evolutionary advantage of being human. It has allowed us to survive periods of starvation and poor nutrition. However, assuming that the set point theory is valid, it still does not mean that you are powerless to change it.

CHANGING YOUR SET POINT

Research indicates that the set point can be reset by *very gradual* calorie reduction and increased physical activity. If you decrease your caloric intake gradually—by no more than a few hundred calories per day—your metabolism seems not to detect the decrease and doesn't slow down. Secondly, adding one hour of good walking at least six times a week seems to rev up the metabolism for the whole day and can result in a thirty-pound weight loss in one year.

So we aren't doomed to be fat if our parents gave us fat genes. Only your weight *potential*—not your actual weight—is predetermined. Anyone can become obese if they make unwise food choices for a long time, and anyone can lose weight and maintain the loss. If you have a tougher time than someone else, it's not your fault. It's just the way the cards were dealt. You might take a little longer to get a beneficial result, but you *can* get it. People may gain weight for many different reasons, but how to lose it is the same for everyone, regardless of color or anything else: Lasting weight loss results not from a diet you go on temporarily but from a permanent eating and exercise-management plan.

HOW MUCH WEIGHT IS TOO MUCH?

Most doctors judge obesity by total weight: If you're 10 to 20 percent above "ideal" weight on health-insurance charts, you're overweight. Twenty percent or more over ideal weight is considered obese. Morbid obesity describes anyone more than one hundred pounds over ideal weight.

The problem with these definitions is that they don't evaluate the percentage of fat in the body. It's too much fat—not weight per se—that poses health risks.

You can be overweight according to the charts and still not too fat—like many professional athletes whose heavy bodies ripple with muscles. That extra weight, in the shape of lean body mass, poses no health risk for such people. Lean muscle weighs more than fat because it is denser. That's why two women weighing 120 pounds may wear different dress sizes. I have a friend who joined a jazz exercise class a few months ago, going three times a week. She was surprised to find she didn't lose weight (exercise by itself is not a very efficient weight-loss tool), but the size of her waist and hips decreased. She was losing body fat and replacing it with denser, leaner muscle, which takes up less space.

Conversely, you might be the "correct" weight according to charts yet still be too fat for good health. Therefore, measuring percentage of body fat is a more accurate way to judge whether or not you're overweight. For women aged eighteen, average body fat is 20 to 25 percent; for men the same age, it's 10 to 15 percent. Percentages of fat greater than average are deemed obese.

Unfortunately, measuring body fat is not always easy or convenient. Methods range from the skin-fold caliper "pinch test" and bioelectrical impedance to water-buoyancy tests. Knowing the exact percentage can be helpful to athletes working toward a peak performance and for certain medical conditions where nutritional status is in doubt. If you want to know your fat percentage, ask your family doctor, a specialist in physical medicine, or a registered dietitian or nutritionist to measure it for you, using one of several body-fat testing methods.

But knowing this figure probably isn't important for most people. In truth most of us know if we're too fat. (You can do a simple pinch test yourself: Pinch a fold of skin on the back of your upper arm, midway up the back of your thigh, and to one side of your navel. More than an inch at any point? Too much.)

ARE YOU AN APPLE?

Even total weight and fat percentage isn't the whole story. The biggest news is that how much you weigh is less important than *where* you carry your fat. Scientists have determined two body types, nicknamed the apple (extra weight above the belt) and the pear (below the belt). The apple shape is associated with an increased risk of cardiovascular disease, especially heart attacks, stroke, hypertension, diabetes, gallbladder diseases, and dangerously elevated cholesterol. In other words, a big gut is far more dangerous to your health than big thighs. In some studies, pear-shaped women could carry as much as sixty excess pounds without endangering their health, because that extra weight was carried in the hips and thighs.

The reason may be that fat cells above the waist are loosely stored and easily freed for quick energy. Loose fat cells can circulate through the bloodstream and travel to the liver, clogging that organ to the point where it cannot function properly, particularly when it comes to processing insulin. If the liver cannot handle insulin, a chain reaction may lead to high blood pressure, diabetes, and heart trouble.

By contrast, fat deposited in the hips, thighs, and breasts produces more lipase, an enzyme that adheres to fat. Theoretically, holding fat securely means a woman's body can use it during pregnancy.

In general, white women tend to carry extra fat below the waist and around the hips and thighs. White men tend to carry excess weight above the waist and have a much higher rate of cardiovascular disease. However, blacks of both sexes carry more fat deposits on their upper bodies. Black women are more likely to gain weight in their upper body than white women, which may account for their high rate of cardiovascular diseases.

In addition, women past menopause—regardless of their skin color or previous shape—tend to gain more upper-body fat than younger women. This may be another reason why the incidence of heart disease in women rises sharply as we age.

Since you get body shape from your genes, what can you do about it? Lucky for apples, fat around the waist comes off easier and faster than the more stubborn fat deposited on hips and thighs.

YOUR IDEAL WEIGHT

In their 1990 revised dietary guidelines, the U.S. Department of Agriculture suggests Americans "maintain a healthy weight." They admit, however, that there is no single "right" weight. The typical life-insurance charts offer ranges of weight for every height and try to account for differences in an individual's build.

The charts don't account for lean-to-fat ratios. Nor do they consider age. Most people are naturally heavier as they age.

Here is a further problem for blacks: These charts don't accurately reflect *our* average body frame and size. (Life-insurance formulas were drawn from people who could afford life insurance—predominantly white middle-class males, mostly young or middle-aged.)

In general, we have greater bone density than whites. When I see black patients who look healthy and seem to have a good lean-to-fat ratio, I automatically allow an additional four to six extra pounds above "ideal" if they have a medium frame—and maybe a little less for a small frame or a little bit more for a large frame. In other words, there's more that I look at than height and weight tables in judging whether someone is overweight. I like to consider the person, not the chart.

Here's a simple formula for African Americans to use to determine their ideal weight:

> *Women:* Count 104 pounds for your first 5 feet of height, then add five pounds for each additional inch.
> *Men:* Count 110 pounds for your first 5 feet, then add six pounds per additional inch.
> If you're small-framed, subtract 10 percent from the total; if you're large-framed, add 10 percent.

Some doctors feel that overweight individuals who have no other risk factors (no family history of high blood pressure or heart disease, and normal blood counts for sugar and fats) and who also exercise regularly and maintain a healthy lifestyle do not have to diet.

If you already have medical problems or are at high risk for medical problems, losing 10 to 15 percent of your starting weight may significantly reduce your health risk, even if you are still considerably above your so-called ideal weight. Many people who suffer from these health problems are able to stop taking medications (under their doctor's supervision) when they take weight off and keep it off.

More and more, I've come to agree with obesity specialists who believe that seeking your "natural" weight is better than trying to pursue a goal weight based on a chart. In general, a natural weight is what results when you eat normally (about 1,800 calories a day for an adult woman and 2,200 calories a day for an adult man) and do the exercise equivalent of a brisk one-hour walk each day.

So how does all this information help us? I think it shows us how important it is to put our weight problems into context. Before embarking on any weight-loss program, ask yourself these questions:

1. *When did you become overweight?* If you've been overweight since adolescence, you have a higher risk of weight-related health problems. Make sure that you have your blood pressure, electrocardiogram, and other laboratory tests taken before you start. If you have a long history of yo-yo dieting, you will have to expect to go slower and be more persistent with your weight-loss goals.

2. *What do members of your family weigh?* If you have a strong family history of obesity, set a healthy and realistic weight-loss goal. Make sure you tell your doctor about obesity in your family, particularly if other members of your family have suffered from heart disease, diabetes, hypertension, or gallbladder disease.

3. *What are your eating habits?* What you eat, when, and how much are all part of the picture. Observe your own habits and take notes: Do you always take second or third helpings? Eat heavily before going to bed? Snack constantly? Are you in love with desserts and high-fat foods?

4. *How much physical activity do you get each day?* Think about your activity level. If you are sedentary, what can you do to change to a more active lifestyle?

All four factors are significant in your attempt to lose weight. Consider each of them. Think about them. Get a realistic overview of your weight picture. Then you can begin to put a total plan into place.

HOW TO LOSE WEIGHT

There are a lot of poor ways to lose weight! But there's only one good way: Gradually reduce calories and fat and increase exercise.

A safe, effective diet meets five criteria:

- It satisfies all your nutritional needs.
- It minimizes hunger and fatigue.

- It complements your food preferences and includes some foods you enjoy.
- It creates a long-term healthful change in your eating patterns.
- It uses ordinary food that's easy to purchase and prepare (no special canned formulas or prepackaged food available only through a diet service).

KEYS TO SUCCESSFUL WEIGHT LOSS

- *Set realistic goals that take into account your lifestyle, personality, and genetics.*
- *Exercise to burn calories, build muscle, and maintain good mental health.*
- *Abolish the all-or-nothing perfectionist mentality.*
- *Concentrate on health and the benefits you'll gain.*
- *Find menus that let you eat well without feeling deprived.*
- *Avoid drastic measures.*
- *Make a lifetime commitment to yourself.*
- *Tap into support systems—family members, self-help groups, or anyone who offers emotional aid.*

Abandon the word *diet*. You're not embarking on a short-term, numbers-oriented way of eating. In Part Three, you will be able to follow a twenty-four-week program for transforming your eating patterns into healthful lifetime habits. You'll discover how to get the most benefit from foods without sacrificing great taste, variety, or pleasure.

If you want to lose weight, simply follow the plan, but gradually reduce your normal calorie intake by about five hundred calories a day. Also make sure to read the information on keeping a food diary in Chapter 10. This is a great idea that has helped many people lose weight—even when they do nothing else! Some people lose a pound a week just by faithfully keeping a food journal.

Pay special attention to the amount of fat you're eating. High-fat foods are high in calories. (Fat is by far the most concentrated source of calories you can eat. One gram of fat contains nine calories—more than twice the calories of one gram of protein or carbohydrate.) More important, dietary fat is easily stored in cells and turned into body fat. For many people trying to lose weight, simply counting fat grams in foods you eat does the job. The government experts say we should derive no more than 30 percent of our total daily calories from fats. I personally find this number too high, especially if you're trying to lose weight. Instead, aim for 20 to 25 percent of total daily calories from fat. (For a simple way to count fat grams, see Chapter 11.)

Overall, the Sankofa Program features lots of complex carbohydrates—whole grains, cereals, vegetables, and fruit—that offer many vitamins, minerals, and nutrients while speeding food through the body. Carbohydrates also make us feel fuller faster. This kind of diet is closer to our eating patterns in Africa, which were far more beneficial than those we've adopted here in the United States. The rural African diet is still based on grains, fruits, and vegetables, with a minimum of sugar and salt.

Gradual and consistent weight loss is better than losing large amounts all at once. Your short- and long-term weight goals should reflect this approach. It's realistic to aim for a twenty-five-pound loss over six months. This averages out to about one pound per week. Keep in mind that some weeks you'll lose a whole pound, sometimes a little more, sometimes a little less.

Don't despair. Slow weight loss gives you time to adjust your eating habits and gives your body time to adjust to the change in weight, which means you are much more likely to keep the weight off!

Do consult your family doctor, a nutritionist, or registered dietitian for help if you are more than twenty pounds above your ideal weight or have a medical problem that must be monitored as you slim down.

As you make gradual changes in your eating style, you may decide to trim down further by reducing your calories. Strictly speaking, how many calories you *need* daily depends on how active you are. Overweight people who are sedentary but don't eat much may find that merely adding exercise enables them to trim down. But most people will have to combine calorie reduction with increased physical activity.

Here are some guidelines:

If you're extremely inactive, you need about twelve calories per pound to sustain your current weight.

If you're lightly active, the number is fifteen calories per pound.

For the moderately active, the number is twenty calories per pound.

The highly active require roughly twenty-five calories per pound to maintain their weight.

Therefore, if you are moderately active and now weigh 150 pounds, you'll need to consume three thousand calories a day to maintain your present weight (20 × 150). To lose one pound a week, all you have to do is cut your calories by five hundred each day.

Generally speaking, it's estimated that an inactive male needs about 1,200 to 1,500 calories per day to lose weight at a rate of one pound per week. For inactive women, the number is 1,000 to 1,300 calories daily.

EAT WHEN YOU ARE ACTIVE

Breakfast	*Lunch*	*Dinner*
25 percent	*50 percent*	*25 percent*
(early activities)	*(active)*	*(less active)*
reading	*working,*	*watching TV,*
newspaper, getting	*walking,*	*reading, preparing*
ready for work	*housework*	*dinner*

THE IMPORTANCE OF EXERCISE

No diet offers permanent effects on its own; you *must* exercise to keep your metabolism purring and your bodily systems in good working order. Studies prove that people who combine exercise with healthy food choices maintain the greatest weight loss over the longest period of time. *Frequent exercise may also help curb your cravings for fatty foods.* The following chapter describes the importance of exercise not only to weight loss but to maintaining overall good health.

RESOURCES

In some special cases where nothing else works, your doctor may suggest joining a specific weight-loss program or clinic. Some of these programs can be expensive and usually require insurance or cash payments. What they do offer is additional support—the kind you get from other participants. If your doctor feels this is right for you, he or she may recommend a program.

I know many people who go to a self-help group, such as Weight Watchers, after they've lost weight in order to help them maintain the loss or who return for meetings if they start to regain weight.

Weight Watchers and TOPS are examples of self-help programs that advocate moderate calorie restriction and behavior modification. If you think you would like to try one of these groups, look in the Yellow Pages under "Weight Control Services" for the Weight Watchers or TOPS chapter near you.

Some chapters of the American Heart Association also have weight-loss programs. For information and educational materials, write to:

The American Heart Association
7272 Greenville Avenue
Dallas, TX 75231-4596
(214) 373-6300

7

LET'S GET MOVING: EXERCISE

I don't have to tell you how much we appreciate the importance of physical activity and athletics. Just ask any black youth. Kids admire Michael Jordan, Magic Johnson, Riddick Bowe, Dave Stewart, Carl Lewis, Jackie-Joyner Kersee, and Debbie Thomas to the point of adulation. We need only remember the triumphs of black Olympians to see the exceptional athletic talent blacks possess throughout the world. Dancers and choreographers like Judith Jameson, Gregory Hines, and Arthur Mitchell are legendary.

What we see in these athletes and performers is their beauty and excellence. I always have felt that black people are especially comfortable and in tune with their bodies. We walk tall and carry ourselves gracefully. We seem naturally able to express emotion and ideas through movement, a hallmark of our ancient African culture. That ease of physical expression is a cultural trait, unconsciously passed down to each new generation. A lot of people say that's nonsense, that black folks are just *born* with better muscle development and coordination. In fact, just like any other group, we are enormously varied in build, musculature, and coordination. Believe it or not, some black people are klutzes and some have no muscle definition to speak of.

Nevertheless, we tend to take beautiful bodies for granted. When we look at great black athletes and dancers, we don't see the years of hard work and the daily effort it takes to condition and train their bodies in order to master flawless performance.

Physical excellence for African Americans usually begins in junior high school, encouraged in youth fitness programs and neighborhood games. But the average youngster tends to stop exercising and stop participating in regular sports upon reaching adulthood. African Americans seem not to have caught the fitness fever sweeping through the adult white community. (Actually, many whites don't routinely engage in exercise, either. Even today, exercise is largely confined to the richer, better-educated Americans, regardless of color.)

Does everyone need to exercise? Yes. Studies consistently prove that those who exercise regularly are much more likely to lead healthier, more vital lives into old age. On an average, they also live two years longer.

Even if you have a good set of muscles, even if you look perfect from head to toe, exercise can improve your stamina, coordination, heart and lungs, and control your weight. And if you don't have muscles, exercise can help you get some. So you've got nothing to lose when you exercise, and everything to win. It's never too late to start rebuilding the body.* Let's look at some of the ways exercise helps you.

- *It improves stamina* by increasing the work capacity of your heart and lungs.
- *It boosts the immune system,* making your body more resistant to disease and infection.
- *It helps prevent obesity.* If there were only one positive benefit to exercise, this would be it. Exercise, combined with a heart-healthy diet, is the most effective way to help you reach and maintain your ideal body weight. (See Chapter 6.)
- *It reduces the risk of heart disease.* Studies show that regular exercise increases the amount of "good," or HDL, cholesterol, which protects against fat deposits accumulating in the arteries.
- *It acts as a natural tranquilizer* (by producing endorphins) to help relieve stress, anxiety, and depression.

---

* Before beginning any exercise program, consult with your doctor, especially if you've been inactive for a long time or have health problems or concerns (like diabetes, heart disease, asthma, arthritis, obesity). Always remember, safety first. Pain while exercising is a sign that something is wrong. Slow down or stop.

- *It helps you stop drinking and using drugs.* When you exercise, you get a natural high.
- *It helps lubricate joints,* thus easing aches and pains associated with arthritis.
- *It helps build stronger, denser bones and decreases the risk of crippling osteoporosis.*
- *It increases the size and strength of muscles,* which protects against unexpected strains.
- *It staves off, or improves, many of the common disorders typically associated with aging*—weak muscles, frail bones, clogged arteries, memory loss, waning sex drive.
- *It promotes an active life.* Once you're in the habit of exercising regularly, you'll find you've got more energy for everything.

WHAT KIND OF EXERCISE IS BEST

The best exercise program combines both aerobic and anaerobic exercise on a regular basis. What's the difference between these two types of activity?

The body has two main systems of producing energy: Aerobic means in the presence of oxygen; anaerobic means without oxygen.

During aerobic exercise the body burns a combination of glucose and oxygen for energy, which causes the body to burn its fat stores. Thus, aerobic exercises are ideal for losing excess fat. The most common aerobic activities—walking, running, swimming, cycling, rowing, cross-country skiing, and aerobic dance—all use large muscle groups in a repetitive fashion.

Anaerobic exercise, on the other hand, is primarily fueled by carbohydrates. Anaerobic activities such as weight lifting build and tone muscles but don't burn fat from your frame. Both forms of exercise can produce important health benefits.

IS EXERCISE ALWAYS EXPENSIVE?

Dancing is a fabulous exercise and so enjoyable that you can do it for hours every day and never get bored. One of the most exuberant exercises I've seen in years is the new (actually, very old) African tribal dancing. Ask around to see whether there's a tribal dance group in your community.

(In fact, music adds dimension to every kind of exercise. Hip-hop is fabulous to exercise to. I make my own tapes from songs and artists I love most and listen to it while I work out.)

If you have a VCR, invest in some inexpensive workout tapes (or rent them from a video store) or borrow them from the local to guide you through aerobics, dancing, yoga, stretching, or light weight training. There are a large variety of tapes for every level. You can make your own tape by recording an early-morning exercise program on television and using it at your convenience.

A minitrampoline can be inexpensive, running roughly thirty-five dollars.

Jumping rope is inexpensive and a perfect way to keep aerobically fit even if the weather's rotten. Get a rope that's a good length—the handles should come to your armpits if you're standing on the rope's midpoint. You can make your own out of a clothesline and it's a great portable option when you're traveling.

An aerobic step costs anywhere from fifty to one hundred dollars, but if you're handy, you can make one from wood blocks.

Rubber tubing cut in strips is inexpensive and offers a great isometric workout. The tubes go around your arms and legs during calisthenics to provide resistance.

If you like walking or running, you don't have to join a health club to find a suitable track. Your local high school may have a track you can use during the school year, or tennis courts you can use when the team's not in training. If you are not sure that the general public is allowed to use these facilities, ask at the school office first.

Thinking about joining a health club? It doesn't necessarily have to be expensive, depending on options in your community. Clubs vary in cost, depending on what's offered, and range from bare-bones bodybuilding gyms to high-tech clubs outfitted with spas, indoor/outdoor pools, racquetball courts, aerobics rooms, juice bars, and more. Some cities have free gyms. (You have to look in the phone book and may have to make a lot of phone calls, but it is possible.) YMCAs are located in most cities and some have low-cost memberships for the entire family.

MATCH THE EXERCISE WITH YOUR GOALS

- *For flexibility try yoga, ballet, modern dance, or water calisthenics.*
- *For strength and bone building, try jogging, weight lifting, tennis, or calisthenics.*
- *For weight loss, opt for prolonged low-level aerobic exercise (even just walking) for forty-five to sixty minutes five or six times a week.*
- *To stay heart-healthy, choose aerobic exercise (brisk walking, jazz dancing, jogging, cycling, swimming, jumping rope, and so on) three times weekly for at least thirty minutes each session.*
- *For toning the upper body, try swimming, cross-country skiing, rowing, using Versa Climber equipment and stationary bikes with moving arm pieces, boxing, and racquet sports.*
- *For toning the lower body, try cycling, climbing stairs, jogging, walking, running, skating, and downhill skiing.*

EXERCISE AND WEIGHT LOSS

One reason it is so hard to lose weight after age thirty-five is that metabolism—the rate at which our bodies burn calories—begins to slow down. The less you eat, the more it slows down, because your body automatically adjusts its metabolism downward. The more strenuously you diet, the less weight you lose. That's when most people give up or begin to experiment with starvation diets, dangerous medications, or quick-loss cures in an effort to move the scales. As soon as you resume a normal eating pattern, you regain all the weight you lost. Exercise is the one element that can change the dismal picture of yo-yo dieting.

When you exercise, your metabolism is forced to work faster. The booster effect continues for several hours after you stop. This means even when you're resting, your metabolism continues to work at the higher rate. However, your body cannot sustain this effect indefinitely, which is why exercise must be consistent.

When you use exercise to help lose weight, you still have to cut calories. Start by measuring your daily calories. Cutting five hundred calories a day means you'll lose one pound a week if you exercise properly and eat properly.

To burn fat and lose weight, you need to work out frequently, slowly, and for a long period of time. The body doesn't begin drawing from fat stores until the twenty-minute mark, so aim for thirty to forty-five minutes of low-intensity aerobic exercise as often as possible—up to five or even six days a week.

How *long* you exercise and how *frequently* is more important than what you actually do. Choose an exercise that you can do for a long time, such as walking or cycling. If you're more than thirty pounds overweight, avoid such activities as weight lifting, running, or high-impact aerobics that put stress on your frame. Instead, choose walking, swimming, yoga, and light calisthenics. After you've lost weight and prepared your body through regular exercise, you can move on to greater weight-bearing activities if you choose.

EXERCISE AND THE HEART

Inactive people are almost twice as likely to develop coronary heart disease as those who exercise regularly, a risk similar to smoking a pack of cigarettes a day. Exercise is the best prevention against heart disease. (If you already have heart disease, exercise can help prevent further deterioration. Your doctor will advise on the best type of exercise for your condition—probably walking, swimming, or cycling.)

As you begin regular aerobic exercise, your pulse rate will lower, blood pressure should drop slightly, and your red blood cell count will increase.

All aerobic activities work the heart muscle, but some are more challenging than others. Climbing stairs, boxing, running, jumping rope, and cross-country skiing are excellent heart workouts. Start slowly and gradually lengthen your training time until you're exercising for at least thirty minutes a session three times a week. Aim to burn three hundred calories per session—about three miles walking or jogging, twelve miles on a bicycle, or one mile of swimming.

GOING BY THE NUMBERS

If you want to be scientific about your training, you can learn to measure your heart's response to exercise. You need to know three numbers: your resting heart rate, your target heart rate, and your recovery rate.

Resting Heart Rate. Take your pulse while you're resting. The easiest way is to feel at the artery on one wrist with the fingertips (never the thumb) of your other hand. Look at your watch and count the number of beats you feel for fifteen seconds. Multiply by four to get the number of beats per minute (sixty seconds). For example, if your heart beats nineteen times in fifteen seconds when you're sitting calmly, your resting heart rate is seventy-six beats per minute.

Target Heart Rate. The target heart rate is a percentage of what your heart can handle at its peak performance, a number which decreases with age. To calculate your target heart rate, subtract your age from 220 to get your maximum heart rate. For example, if you are fifty-five, your maximum heart rate is 165 beats per minute. Then multiply this number by .6, .7, or .8. This is your target heart rate. (Beginning exercisers should multiply by .6, intermediates by .7, and advanced trainers by .8.)

If you're a beginner with a maximum heart rate of 165, multiply by .6 to get a target heart rate of 99.

Anywhere between seventy-six (resting heart rate) and ninety-nine (target heart rate) is now your training zone. The idea is to work your way from seventy-six to ninety-nine while you're exercising. Count your pulse at intervals during your workout to make sure you do not go above ninety-nine. (If you do, ease up.) If you're new to exercise, take your pulse in the first three minutes of your program and again every five minutes.

As you become more fit, you will be able to exercise for longer periods of time without going above your target heart rate. Also, as you become more fit, you can increase your target heart rate by changing the percentage to .7 or .8.

Recovery Heart Rate. The length of time it takes your heart to return to its normal resting heart rate after you stop exercising is called your recovery heart rate. This helps determine your level of cardiopulmonary fitness. Start taking your pulse thirty seconds after you stop exercising (count it for fifteen seconds and multiply by four).

Here's a sample scale:

Women:

Age	Excellent	Good	Fair	Poor
20–29	86	88–92	93–110	112 +
30–39	86	88–94	95–112	114 +
40–49	88	90–94	96–114	116 +
Over 50	90	92–98	100–116	118 +

Men:

Age	Excellent	Good	Fair	Poor
20–29	74	76–84	86–100	102 +
30–39	78	80–86	88–100	102 +
40–49	80	82–88	90–104	106 +
Over 50	83	84–90	92–104	106 +

EXERCISE AND YOUR BONES

Exercise can help prevent osteoporosis, a major cause of bone fractures later in life. As we grow from childhood into maturity, our bones continue to develop until peak bone density is reached around age thirty-five. About ten years later, bone mass begins to decline gradually.

Bone loss occurs in both women and men, but women are *eight times more likely to develop the severe bone thinning that characterizes osteoporosis.* Female bone loss is believed to be most severe in the first five or six years of menopause, when the body loses large amounts of estrogen. Although bone loss appears to slow after age sixty-five, by age seventy a woman may have lost one-third of her bone mass.

Osteoporosis is painful and disfiguring. As the bones become brittle and weaken, fractures of the wrists and hips can occur with even minor stress. The spine may collapse into a hump, and a woman may lose several inches of height from her upper body.

Although most experts find osteoporosis is less common in black women, it still can be a problem for some small-boned sisters. Aging, the loss of sex hormones at menopause, and family history are cited as chief causes. If your mother, sister, grandmother, or aunt had osteoporosis, you have a higher risk. Other contributing factors are:

Slender build
Delicate bone structure
Underweight
Early menopause—either natural or surgical hysterectomy
Low intake of calcium (dairy products) throughout life
Inactive lifestyle
Excessive alcohol consumption
Cigarette smoking

Osteoporosis also occurs more often in people who have chronic lung disorders such as bronchitis and emphysema, although doctors don't know why, except that these conditions are frequently associated with smoking. Additionally, women who have never had children are more likely to develop osteoporosis.

Women who carry extra weight are *less* likely to develop osteoporosis—because even after menopause estrogen continues to be produced in the body's fat layer.

Although black women have a lower risk of developing osteoporosis, race alone will not protect you. Consider *all of* the risk factors; if you see obvious ways to improve your risk profile, make the appropriate changes in your lifestyle. Remember, once bone loss occurs, it cannot be easily replaced.

If you are at risk, you must stop smoking and reduce or eliminate alcohol and caffeine. These are things you should do, anyway. Add calcium—either dairy foods or calcium supplements—to your diet. And start regular *weight-bearing exercises,* which builds bone mass by placing stress on the bones. Many common drugs also leach calcium from your bones, which is another reason for walking and exercise.

Weight-bearing exercise doesn't only mean lifting weights. For example, you bear the weight of your own body when you walk. Light weight training, running, or climbing stairs are all better for bones than swimming, where the water—not your skeleton—bears the weight of your body.

Estrogen-replacement therapy may also be prescribed by your doctor if you have had a hysterectomy or are past menopause.

Estrogen has been shown to help bones retain density. However, hormone replacement is controversial and may not be good for everyone. (See Chapter 25 for more information about estrogen therapy.)

GETTING STARTED

What activities are best for you and how hard should you train? First of all, if you are in poor health, if you are extremely overweight, or if you are older than age fifty and have not engaged in any regular exercise for years, it's absolutely essential that you check with a doctor before starting any exercise program. Your doctor may want to test your fitness level before recommending a start-up program for you. Fitness testing determines whether it's safe for you to exercise or if you're at risk—particularly from heart attack. Fitness testing also measures muscle performance and heart/lung capacity.

The Fitness Test. Your heart's electrical activity is measured by an electrocardiogram (EKG) taken at rest and during exercise. Your doctor will also take your blood pressure in both situations. You will be asked to walk a treadmill or ride a stationary bike. You may be asked to rapidly step up and down off a block of wood or low step for several minutes while your heart rate and breathing are monitored. These measurements help gauge fitness levels and calculate your risk for heart problems. A full test usually includes a physical, complete with height, weight, and possibly body-fat measurements, plus blood and urine analysis to screen for disease and to determine cholesterol/triglyceride levels.

Based on your health profile and fitness level, your doctor will suggest the type and amount of activity best for you.

Obviously, not everyone needs a fitness test, and not everyone who needs one can afford it. But if you have any doubts about your capacity to exercise, at least *call a doctor* or other health professional and describe your condition.

Most people who are in general good health can safely start to exercise *as long as they begin slowly*. Here are some easy ways to raise your activity level before you commit to a full-scale exercise routine.

Park the car a few blocks from your destination and walk the rest of the way.

We don't all live in the suburbs, so get off the bus or subway a stop or two before your destination and walk the rest of the way.

Take the stairs instead of the elevator.

Walk to your neighbor's barbecue instead of driving.

Swim or participate in other activities at the beach instead of just lying in the sun.

Take the dog for a long romp.

Get out into the garden and weed. If you have a lawn, use an old-fashioned lawn mower that's pushed instead of one you ride. If you're a city dweller without a garden of your own, join a community garden or vacant-lot program.

All over the country, people are getting into "mall walking": Drive to the mall, park your car, and hoof it for a few laps—you can window-shop at the same time, as long as you don't stop!

DON'T SKIP THE STRETCH

Every exercise session should begin and end with a good stretch of your arms and legs, neck, and back to guard against injury and keep you limber. But you should never stretch a cold muscle hard. First, spend five minutes hopping or jogging gently in place, riding a stationary bike, or walking. Then stretch gently for a few minutes. *After* your workout, you can stretch further without getting sore, but don't bounce while you're stretching; you'll only tear your muscles.

FIND YOUR PERSONAL EXERCISE STYLE

To reap the benefits of exercise, you need to participate consistently. (Working out in spurts doesn't tone the heart, but it does leave you wide open for injury. And running ten miles every other week actually defeats the purpose.) But for many people, consistency is simply another word for *boredom,* and roughly two-thirds of all those who start an exercise routine quit within six months. One way to maintain your enthusiasm is to find activities that appeal to you and also suit your body's natural ability. In this way, your comfort level will be high. So along with your specific health goals, also consider your build and your personality.

For example, if you're a loner, try sports such as walking or jogging (use a Walkman-type radio or tape while you go), weight lifting, cycling, swimming, yoga, or aerobics on video in the privacy of your living room. For extroverts, team and group activities are perfect. Try basketball, volleyball, soccer, aerobics, or dance class.

Would you rather exercise indoors or outside? If nature's your thing, try running, mountain biking, golf, rowing, or even scuba diving. Those who prefer the great indoors can choose from boxing, gymnastics, racquetball, swimming, fencing, or circuit training (alternating between aerobic activity and weight training), to name just a few options.

Consider yourself awkward? Try sports that don't rely on co-ordination for success. Hiking, rowing, jogging, and rebounding on a trampoline are good options you can do at your own rhythm. You may find as your body becomes more conditioned that those sports requiring hand-eye coordination, such as handball, racquetball, or gymnastics aren't out of the question, after all!

One overlooked sport is bowling, which is my personal favorite. Bowling is challenging and fun, although it's not aerobic because the activity is stop and go. Nevertheless, it's a great sport for all ages and encourages you to get out of the house and meet friends. If you join a league, as I did, your teammates help keep you motivated.

Other options include *isometric exercises,* which make muscles move against resistance. You can use your own body—pressing hands palm-to-palm and increasing the pressure—or work with giant rubber bands.

Isotonic exercise means working isolated muscle groups at different speeds against constant resistance. Weight lifting is isotonic. So are sit-ups.

Isokinetic exercise uses muscles at a constant speed against varying degrees of resistance. This strengthens and tones the body. An example is training on Nautilus machines.

Interval training involves short bursts of high-level exertion coupled with periods of rest or low-level activity. As the period of intense activity increases, you gain greater aerobic effects. You might want to experiment with various kinds of exercise and sports to see what most appeals to you.

FAMILY FUN

Since children learn by example, make exercise a shared family time. Exercise is a wonderful way to help toddlers develop their coordination and motor skills. You'll also help your child avoid juvenile obesity—currently plaguing some 25 percent of children in the United States. Obese kids have higher blood pressure and higher levels of fat (lipids) in their blood, which leads to severe health problems as they age. Exercise is also a healthy alternative to hours of TV watching, which contributes to childhood and adult obesity.

If your child is already heavy, she or he may feel uncomfortable about working out. Start off with activities that are fun, even if they're not aerobic, to get kids excited about the idea of moving around. Remember, they may feel awkward if others see them exercising, so help your child find a private place to get started.

MIX IT UP: CROSS-TRAINING

It's always a good idea to combine various types of exercise or to change them from time to time. Cross-training keeps you from getting bored and also avoids any sprains or strains associated with doing the same exercise repeatedly. Even professional athletes do different sports and exercises to stay in overall top condition.

Cross-training simply means varying your activities so your body doesn't get lazy doing the same thing day after day. You can do one exercise for a day or a week or even a month, then switch to another.

The routine that works best for me involves jogging three times a week, alternated with weight training and work on the fitness machines at the gym on the two days in between. On weekends,

I give myself the option to take a break or go to a dance class with a friend. Think about how you might mix and match activities.

Mixing up various exercises and altering your routine from time to time will not only keep you motivated but will give you a fuller total-body workout. Whichever exercises you choose, here are some tips that will help you stick with it.

- Establish realistic goals and create a written plan.
- Choose durable equipment.
- Set aside a time and place for exercise.
- Get family and friends to be your support network.
- Vary your routine. Choose activities that you enjoy and that accommodate your life and pocketbook.
- Keep a log charting your progress.
- Avoid injuries. If you hurt yourself and have to temporarily stop your routine, it's hard to get started again.
- Find new places to exercise, such as new bike or hiking trails, different walking and running routes, and so on.
- Reward yourself—but not with food!
- Upgrade your goals as your fitness level improves.
- Have patience. Good results don't happen overnight.
- Have fun.

Part Three

THE SANKOFA
PROGRAM

8

WE CAN DO IT

It's been proven beyond question that self-help nutritional changes can save lives. In the last fifteen years in the general population, heart disease fell 33 percent and stroke was cut in half —thanks largely to public education campaigns that encouraged people to stop smoking and reduce fat intake.

But the wealth of good information circulating in the media has largely bypassed African Americans. It certainly bypassed Harold Washington, Chicago's first black mayor, who died of a sudden heart attack in his early fifties. Washington, overweight and under pressure, knew he had high blood pressure, but his hectic political life kept him from following his doctor's advice to take his medication and lose weight.

True, at public dinners the mayor nibbled delicately on broiled chicken and steamed vegetables, but they say that later at night he would order in three large sausage pizzas. The foods he loved most, and ate in secret, were loaded with salt, fat, and calories, comfort foods that made him feel good—so good that they killed him.

Here's the point: *Learning* about healthy eating is only step one. Actually putting that information to work in your life is a whole different ball game. Only you can make the commitment to change, and change is challenging for everyone.

Motivation is the key to making the Sankofa Program work for you. Maybe you want to protect yourself against a disease that runs in your family. Or maybe you want to lose weight to look and feel better. I was motivated by both of these factors. When I weigh too much, I feel sluggish physically and mentally. I am disappointed with myself. The excess weight also prevents me from achieving peak performance when I exercise.

What's *your* motivation? You may already have been diagnosed with a particular ailment, such as high blood pressure, diabetes, or heart disease, and you want to maximize your nutritional base to help treat these problems. You may be pregnant or thinking about becoming pregnant and want to ensure that your baby develops normally and gets off to a healthy start in life.

Your motivation is entirely your own. Think about it. What could motivate you enough to make you turn away from damaging eating habits that are familiar, easy, and in their own way comforting? What difference might good nutrition make in your life?

While I can't answer for you, personally, I do know that each of us can take control of our own health behavior and make a difference in the outcome of our own lives. Given the proven links between nutrition, obesity, chronic illnesses, and death, this is one area in which we can make changes ourselves, both in the foods we eat and the way we prepare them. Not only will we become healthier as a result, but in the process we will strengthen our families and our community as a whole.

This section will introduce you to the program I call Sankofa, which is an African proverb meaning "learning from the past, building the future." The Sankofa Program is a self-help nutrition and lifestyle plan. It is grounded in what is best about our African-American past and all the healthful nutritional practices that are compatible with our culture. It also incorporates all the modern knowledge about the effects of nutrition on African-American health.

It's never too early—or too late—to begin eating right. Children who eat healthful diets become healthier adults. An added bonus to an early start is that good nutrition is more likely to become a lifelong habit rather than something your child will have to struggle to achieve after the damage is done. But you can get positive results no matter where you start, no matter what your age or physical condition. *You can't be reborn, but you can redesign yourself and your health.*

I believe that variety is the key to good nutrition. All foods can be enjoyed in moderation—though a moderate amount of one kind of food—say, fat—may be a smaller quantity than a moderate amount of fruit or grains.

I also believe in gradual change, not instant makeovers. Instant makeovers can be traumatizing and are virtually impossible to sustain, especially if your diet has been full of excess to begin with. It's easy to boomerang back to the old eating habits because your body and your head don't have enough time to absorb the change. It's a scientific fact that it can take a year to turn a new behavior into a habit.

So, we're going to take it easy and approach the Sankofa Program over a period of twenty-four weeks. You can take even more time if you want to, as long as you stay on the basic track toward change.

Overall, you're going to add foods that help you fight disease while they also increase your feelings of satisfaction and comfort. You will learn how to reduce the foods that make you fat, clog your arteries, raise your blood pressure, and create a host of other health problems.

The plan is laid out in weekly steps (see Chapter 17). You don't need to be perfect. The idea is to have a sensible goal and to stay flexible. You can add and subtract foods, making allowances for your personal preferences, your schedule, and seasonal availability of different foods where you live.

Keep things simple, and introduce small changes one at a time. As you move from week to week, and month to month, maintain the terrific changes you've already made. The process is cumulative and the goal is always balance.

Read the next eight chapters carefully to prepare yourself for the Sankofa Program. You'll learn a lot about food and what keeps us functioning like the amazing creatures we truly are.

9

WHAT EVERYONE SHOULD
KNOW ABOUT NUTRITION

All Americans—regardless of race—need to come to a diet centered largely on three important food groups: whole grains, vegetables, and fruits. Mounting evidence points to these three types of foods as the prime promoters of that maximum state of well-being defined as good health. A diet founded on these foods will do more than help us avoid or alleviate some of the ills that seem to strike us with greater frequency and intensity than others. It will also provide protection against a host of other ailments.

This information on good health has at last been recognized officially by the United States government. Gone (forever, I hope) are the old four food groups. The new food pyramid lists foods in ascending order, stressing variety, balance, and moderation. Foods at the bottom should be eaten most frequently and those at the top only sparingly.

At the pyramid's base—and the basis of a healthy diet—are all the complex carbohydrates: breads, cereals, rice, and pasta.

The next level contains vegetables and fruits.

The meat, poultry, and fish group, which also contains dry beans, eggs, and nuts, comes next.

Dairy products—milk, yogurt, and cheese—come in at the same level.

And finally, at the very top of the pyramid, come fats, oils, and sweets, which should be consumed in absolutely minimum amounts.

WHAT FOOD CONSISTS OF

Nutrients in food are broken down into three types. Macronutrients—which include carbohydrates, protein, and fats—are those needed in large amounts. Micronutrients—the vitamins and minerals—are present in much smaller quantities (see Chapter 16). Water, though normally not thought of as a nutrient, is a basic component of all foods and is essential to life (see Chapter 15).

Every nutrient depends on the others to carry out its functions. The macronutrients provide energy and help maintain and repair the body. Vitamins and minerals regulate the chemical processes that take place in the body. Minerals also play an important role in forming new tissue, including bones, teeth, and blood. Water provides a fluid medium for all chemical reactions in the body and for the circulation of blood and removal of waste.

THE MACRONUTRIENTS

Carbohydrates are an important source of energy. They also help the body preserve protein and burn fats. Anything sweet or starchy is a carbohydrate—fruits, vegetables, bread, grains, and cereals are all examples. So are candy, cookies, cake, and anything else that has a sugary base. The typical American diet provides an abundance of sugars or simple carbohydrates, but it falls short in complex carbohydrates such as whole-grain cereals.

Carbohydrates are much bulkier than fats and protein, so it's possible to eat a large amount of carbohydrate and get the same number of calories that you would from a comparatively small amount of protein and fat (see Chapter 14).

Proteins help all body cells and tissues grow or regenerate. Protein can come from animal or vegetable foods.

Animal-derived proteins, which include meat, fish, eggs, and dairy products, are often called high-quality protein because they contain all the essential amino acids needed to keep you healthy. But animal protein is inevitably accompanied by high quantities of saturated fat.

Vegetable proteins, which have no saturated fat, are not usually complete proteins. But in certain combinations, such as rice and beans, vegetables can add up to high-quality protein.

Many people believe that protein is less fattening than starchy foods like potatoes and rice. This isn't true: Gram for gram, protein and carbohydrates contain the same number of calories: four per gram. The difference is that animal protein is dense, so it doesn't take much to add up to a lot of calories and you can easily eat more than you actually need. Once we hit adulthood, our need for protein decreases, and the excess we consume is stored in the body as fat.

Fats in small amounts are essential for body repair and growth of tissues. Fats are found in animal foods and also in vegetable oils. But excess fat causes weight gain and elevated cholesterol, both of which contribute to disease (see Chapter 11).

SHOULD YOU SEE A NUTRITIONIST?

Anyone who wants to improve his or her diet, especially those with an existing health problem, can benefit from a consultation with a nutritionist to learn how diet may effect health. People who are overweight or underweight, those who have asthma or allergies, ulcers, and other digestive problems, heart disease, diabetes, or high blood pressure can all benefit from professional nutritional advice.

If you suffer from indigestion, loss of appetite, stress, nail problems, chronic anemia, fatigue, hair loss, chronic skin problems, and/or constipation, you might consider having your nutritional status checked by a professional.

No nutritionist on earth can "cure" you of a health problem or guarantee a result, but a reputable professional can work with you and your doctor to help you develop better eating habits.

But how can you find a qualified, reputable nutritionist, not a quack? Only about half the states regulate nutritionists and require them to be licensed. If dietitians or nutritionists are licensed in your state, they would have the professional designations L.D. or L.D.N. after their names, signifying that they have met the educational criteria required to practice nutrition in that state.

It's important to look for someone who has a solid educational background in nutrition, which usually means they are registered dietitians. (Registered dietitians, R.D.s, have graduated from an accredited college or university with a specialty in nutrition and have completed an internship in a hospital or clinical environment or had three years of specialized employment with an R.D. They may also have advanced degrees such as a master's or a doctorate. An R.D. must pass an exam and continue to keep abreast of changes through continuing education programs.)

Interview a dietitian or nutritionist as you would anyone you'd hire to do a job for you. Do you like the way the nutritionist talks to you? Does he or she seem well versed in the latest findings? Or are his recommendations wildly unorthodox or peculiar? Is she pushing only vitamin and mineral supplements, with less emphasis on a balanced, varied diet? Does he advocate a fad diet? If you answer yes to any of these, this is probably not the person to give you sound nutritional help. Avoid those who make grandiose claims and tell stories of astounding case histories. I'd also avoid anyone who's selling a product—a food product, expensive vitamin supplements, publications without scientific support, or hair analysis or other diagnostic tests, while avoiding traditional lab tests recommended by physicians. (If you're not sure about someone's credentials, you can call the ADA or the Better Business Bureau in your area for more information.)

For the names of registered dietitians in your area, contact the local Dietetic Association listed in the Yellow Pages, or call the American Dietetic Association in Chicago at 312-280-5000. Your family doctor, local hospital, or clinic may also be able to give you the name of someone reputable.

The American Society for Clinical Nutrition at 9650 Rockville Pike, Bethesda, MD 20014 can provide you with the names of nutritionists with Ph.D.s.

IS GOOD NUTRITION TOO EXPENSIVE?

Quality nutrition doesn't have to be expensive, although many people feel eating healthfully is for the rich only. It's true that breast of chicken costs more than beef bologna. A "lite" frozen dinner costs more than an ordinary frozen dinner. Part-skim mozzarella is more expensive than American cheese. And brand-name low-fat, low-salt spaghetti sauce is more expensive than the regular supermarket variety. Obviously, you could spend a lot more money on exotic imported fruits and vegetables.

Fortunately, there are plenty of examples of healthful foods that are cheaper. Plain yogurt is cheaper than sugar-filled yogurt. Five pounds of canned or dried beans, full of fiber and protein and minus any fat, are much cheaper than any meat. Plain or flavored seltzer, which has no sodium or sugar, is cheaper than any soft drink. Fresh peaches in season are cheaper than a bag of corn chips. Bananas are half the price of canned onion rings or potato chips and make a far healthier snack.

Inexpensive produce bought in season and grown close to home is just as nutritious and you can save more money if you cook from scratch and use mainly plant foods, such as grains and vegetables, rather than animal foods.

Where you live can also affect how much you pay for food. Generally, shoppers in poor areas pay higher prices. If you live in the inner city, you are paying more for your food than someone who lives uptown or near an affluent suburb. So in many cases, the less money you have, the more expensive the food.

Still, there are ways to save money on food, no matter where you live. Buy rice, beans, and pasta from the bulk bins at health-food stores. If you have a car, drive out to a local farm and pick up produce of all kinds. Even in the cities, farmer's markets are springing up, and food there is often cheaper and fresher than in the supermarket.

Another shopping trick is to seek out markets that sell foods in volume and start your own shopping club. For example, if one person in your apartment building or neighborhood has a car, offer to share gas and suggest that a group of you pool resources. You can try buying foods in bulk, then splitting them up at home.

Coupon clipping from newspapers is another way to save money. The money you save on your grocery bills more than makes up for the price of the newspaper. Most supermarket chains also put out their own weekly shopping guide, available at the store, which is full of money-saving coupons. And don't forget to save the extra-value coupons included in or on the packages of many foods.

READING LABELS

For many years now, nutritionists and consumer groups have felt the current system of listing nutritional information on food packages is inadequate and confusing. For example, percentage labels, such as "96% fat-free," suggest the product is low in fat but does not actually tell how much fat it contains. After years of debate, a new format has emerged that conveys nutritional information in a way that people can easily understand and use.

Products with more helpful food labels will appear in stores soon. The new labels, called "Nutrition Facts," include basic information on calories per serving and the percentage of calories derived from fat, as well as the total amount of fat and saturated fat in the product. Other mandatory information includes the amount of cholesterol, sodium, carbohydrates, and protein, as well as information on vitamins A and C, calcium, and iron. The labels also include the assigned limits of fat, saturated fat, cholesterol, and sodium, based on 2,000- and 2,500-calorie needs.

Not every product will carry the new labels; small businesses that sell less than $50,000 worth of food a year are exempt from the new regulations.

MAKING SENSE OF FOOD LABELS

Foods are listed in order of weight, so avoid those with fats or sugar listed first.

Pay attention to serving sizes. Nutritional information alters according to the serving size. When comparing products, always start with the portion size. If portion size is small, calories will seem low.

A product may emphasize one good claim, ignoring a negative one. For example, peanut butter has no cholesterol (and never did), but it may be loaded with fat and sugar. Yet some brands proudly claim "no cholesterol" on their labels but make no mention of the fat or sugar content.

Foods claiming to be high in vitamins and minerals are generally fortified. You may pay more for this feature. The word *enriched* or *fortified* means nutrients have been added, often the same nutrients that were lost by processing—not extra nutrients above and beyond what the food would naturally possess. Therefore, natural whole-grain cereals may have even more nutrients than those that are fortified.

When buying bread, don't be fooled by the color. Some very dark brown breads may not contain whole grains at all, just molasses for coloring. Check the label for ingredients: the word *wheat* is meaningless; all bread, including plain white bread, is made from wheat. Look for the words *whole wheat* and *whole grain* on the label.

Watch out for the word *dietetic*. For example, some dietetic cookies may be low in sugar or use an artificial sweetener like saccharin or NutraSweet but may contain a lot of fat.

MORE LABELING INFORMATION

Labels also carry additional information that can help you choose fresh, safe products.

Dates

Several dates may appear on a label. "Packed on" tells you the date the food was placed in the container. "Sell by" indicates the last date it should be sold. "Best if used by" tells you when to prepare this food to ensure optimum quality.

A product should not be purchased or used after the expiration date. This date most often appears on foods that spoil, such as yeast and milk.

Recommended Daily Allowances

Many labels state that their product offers a day's worth of recommended daily allowances (RDA) of certain vitamins and minerals. But RDAs are not carved in stone. So, while this information is interesting, you can't count on it to figure your total day's requirement. (For further discussion, see Chapter 16.)

Light or Lite

The word *light* or *lite* appears on many food labels and its true meaning varies from product to product. Such products may contain fewer calories, less fat, or lower sodium. They may also be lighter in color. It may mean your wallet is lighter, since these products often cost more than their "heavy" counterparts, without any appreciable nutritional benefit. Read the labels carefully and pay special attention to the size of the serving.

Low-Fat
The FDA says foods labeled low-fat must contain no more than 2 grams of fat per serving. So the only foods that qualify are automatically 99 to 100 percent fat-free.

Low-Calorie
"Low-calorie" means the food contains no more than 40 calories per serving and no more than 0.4 calories per gram.

"Reduced calorie" means the product has at least one-third fewer calories than a similar food. However, it must be equal nutritionally to the food it is a substitute for. Being lower in calories doesn't necessarily make it lower in fat, cholesterol, and sodium.

"No sugar added" or "no added sugar" means the item has been sweetened with fruit juice or fruits, or not sweetened at all.

Dietetic
"Dietetic" may mean the item has fewer calories, or it may mean that it is lower in sugar or salt than the regular product.

Grades of Meat and Poultry
Beef is graded according to the amount of fat it contains—the higher the grade, the more fat, calories, and cost per pound. In descending order, beef is categorized as USDA prime; USDA choice; USDA select; and USDA standard. Poultry comes in grades A through C.

Natural
The USDA says the word *natural* can be used only on products without artificial flavor, coloring, chemical preservatives, or other synthetic ingredients. The product can have undergone only minimal processing, generally for safety or preservation. Not all products graded by the USDA are actually inspected and labeled by them, however, meaning there's no strict supervision of terminology.

No Preservatives

The USDA says this designation can be used only on foods that would normally contain preservatives. This is not the same as "no food additives."

USDA GUIDELINES

The USDA has issued a brief list of healthy guidelines to go with its new food pyramid. The Sankofa Program incorporates the guidelines into its own framework, but for your information, this is what the government recommends to all Americans regarding nutrition.

- Eat a variety of foods.
- Maintain healthy weight.
- Choose a diet low in fat, saturated fat, and cholesterol.
- Choose a diet with plenty of vegetables, fruits, and grains.
- Use sugar, salt, and sodium only in moderation.
- If you drink alcohol, do so in moderation (one drink a day for women, two for men).

RESOURCES

Two federal agencies supply a wide variety of printed materials about food safety and nutrition to the public.

The Food and Drug Administration
5600 Fishers Lane
Rockville, MD 20857

Human Nutrition Information Service
U.S. Department of Agriculture
6505 Belcrest Road
Hyattsville, MD 20782

The FDA has a monthly publication called *FDA Consumer* (HFW-40), which describes frauds and dubious products and activities and offers tips on good health. A similar newsletter published bimonthly by the National Council Against Health Fraud can be ordered from P.O. Box 1276/Loma Linda, CA 92354.

10

A SELF-CHECK

A good way to get motivated is to take stock of your present eating habits. How? By recording what you eat and drink each day in a small notebook or desk diary. That isn't as daunting as it sounds.

Get a notebook or a three-ring binder to which you can add pages. Start by recording your vital statistics—height and weight, as well as bust/chest, waist, hip, thigh, and upper-arm measurements.

Measuring yourself is wise, because, as we discussed in Chapter 6, weight alone doesn't tell you everything you need to know about body composition. Many people who follow the Sankofa Program will find initially that their weight stays about the same, but their body configuration changes for the better.

Here's how to measure yourself: Measure your abdomen one inch above your belly button; your thighs just below the buttocks; your calf at its widest point; your upper arm at its widest point. Measure your bustline/chest and buttocks across their widest point.

Unless you're already in peak physical condition, chances are these numbers will diminish as you make dietary changes. With this basic information in place, the next step is simply to record what you eat each day. This will be your project for the first month you're following the Sankofa Program. For now, we're just going to *talk* about it. You don't actually have to do anything. Here's how a food diary works.

KEEPING A FOOD DIARY

There are countless ways to set up a food diary. Start out with the day and date. After each meal, jot down in your notebook the foods and beverages you've consumed and how much. Record the time of day and where you ate—at home, a restaurant (include the name), or a friend's house. If you eat something with several ingredients, such as a casserole, salad, or stew, try to determine which are the dominant ingredients. If eating lasagna, for instance, note whether it's mostly noodles, cheese, or meat.

Record any snacks you eat throughout the day.

Do your best to keep an honest record. The purpose of the food diary is not to launch a guilt trip but to determine what you *really* eat, and how much, on a daily basis. *You don't need to show your diary to anyone.*

SAMPLE DAILY ENTRY

7 A.M. 1 ounce of cornflakes with 1 ounce of whole milk, 1 teaspoon sugar, and 1 medium banana
2 slices of white toast with 1 ounce of margarine and 1 tablespoon grape jelly
2 8-ounce mugs coffee with 1 teaspoon of sugar and 1 ounce of whole milk per mug

10:00 A.M. 1 jelly doughnut (about 3 ounces)
12 ounces of diet cola

1:00 P.M. Egg-salad sandwich (about 6 ounces) on 2 slices of rye bread
4 ounces of corn chips
3 ounces of soft ice cream
12 ounces of diet cola

6:00 P.M. 9-ounce steak with mushrooms (about 2 ounces)
6-ounce baked potato with 2 ounces of sour cream
½ cup peas with pat of butter
8 ounces of coffee with 1 ounce of whole milk and 1 teaspoon of sugar
1 slice (about ⅛ pie) of blueberry pie

USING THE FOOD DIARY FOR WEIGHT LOSS

If you are trying to lose weight, be sure to include *everything*— the three potato chips your friend offered at lunch, that handful of nuts, or the leftovers nibbled while clearing the table. You'll be surprised at how the calories pile up when you're not looking!

You can also use the food diary to help you get a handle on the psychological component of your eating habits. Many overweight people have lost touch with their biological hunger cues; instead, they eat in response to emotional triggers such as tension, boredom, excitement, or depression.

Therefore, in your food diary, keep track of how hungry you are when you eat. Rate your hunger pangs on a numeric scale: 1 for not at all, all the way up to 5 for truly hungry. Also note how you felt, where you ate, and what you did while you were eating (e.g., talked to a friend, read a book, watched television).

After you've kept the food diary for a week, look it over and see whether you identify when you eat without being really hungry. Can you identify any emotional triggers? For example, do you eat whenever someone is mad at you? When you're depressed or lonely? Most cravings start in the brain. Pinpointing their origins is the first step toward mastery.

If you want your food diary to be really useful, once you've gotten used to keeping it, try to include nutritional breakdowns for the food you eat—whether that's grams of fat, sodium, cholesterol, or just calories. Manufacturers' labels can give you this information, but since you'll be eating fewer processed foods, it's good to educate yourself about the nutritional components of fresh foods. Get yourself a basic nutrition counter. Such counters come in small pocket sizes so they are easy to carry around. (See Resources on page 127.)

Keeping track of grams and calories is especially important for weight loss because you can see where you're spending your calories. Some experts say that just by keeping an *honest* food diary, you can lose a pound a week!

A QUICK SELF-CHECK

Some people don't want to keep a food diary. They think it's too much trouble. If you're among them, here's a quick and easy way to get started. All you have to do is read down the columns and check off the answers that best describe your eating habits.

The more checks you have in the column on the far right, the better your nutritional profile is. Be honest. At the end of the six-month Sankofa Program, you can repeat this checklist* and see how your food habits have changed.

MEATS

Beef, pork, lamb, veal, spareribs, sausage, hot dogs, bacon	Very often (twice a day or more)	Often (once a day)	Occasionally (twice a week or less)
Organ meats such as liver, brains, kidney, heart	Often	Occasionally	Rarely or never
Fish and seafood	Rarely or never	Occasionally (1 serving or less a week)	Often (2 or more servings a week)
Cold cuts	Often (several times a week)	Occasionally (once a week)	Seldom
Dried beans such as kidney, lima, chick-peas, black-eyed peas, lentils, split peas	Rarely or never	Occasionally (at least twice a month)	Often
Eggs, whole, with yolk	Often (7 or more a week)	Occasionally (5–6 a week)	Seldom (4 or less a week)

DAIRY PRODUCTS

Milk, whole	Use daily for drinking alone or with cereal and coffee	Use sparingly for coffee or tea only	Never use
Milk, 2% fat	Use daily for drinking alone or with cereal and coffee	Use sparingly for coffee or tea only	Never use
Milk, 1% fat	Use daily for drinking alone or with cereal and coffee	Use sparingly for coffee or tea only	Never use

* Adapted from Rate Your Plate®, Memorial Hospital of RI, Pawtucket, RI 02860.

	DAIRY PRODUCTS (cont'd)		
Skim milk	Never use	Use for drinking only	Use daily for drinking alone or with cereal, coffee, and tea
Cheese, whole-milk, such as American, cheddar, Swiss	Often (twice a week or more)	Occasionally (once a week)	Rarely
Ice cream or other frozen dairy desserts	Often	Occasionally	Rarely
Nonfat ice cream, yogurt, or sorbet	Rarely	Occasionally	Often

	BREAD, CEREALS, PASTA		
Bread, white	Often	Occasionally	Seldom
Bread, whole-wheat	Rarely	Occasionally	Often
Rice, white	Often	Occasionally	Seldom
Rice, brown	Rarely	Occasionally	Often
Oatmeal and other high-fiber cereals	Rarely	Occasionally	Often
Pasta	Rarely	Occasionally	Often

	FRUITS AND VEGETABLES		
Fresh fruit	Rarely (once a week or less)	Often (once a day)	Often (twice a day or more)
Dark green, leafy vegetables	Rarely	Occasionally	Often (twice a day or more)
Dark orange and bright yellow vegetables	Rarely	Occasionally	Often
Citrus fruits	Rarely	Occasionally	Often

	FATS AND OILS		
To sauté vegetables and meats	Very often (twice a day or more)	Occasionally (three or four times a week)	Rarely (once a week or less)
To fry meat, fish, fritters	Very often (once a day)	Often (once a week)	Occasionally (twice a month)

| As a spread for bread | Very often (every day) | Often (three times a week) | Occasionally (once a week) |
| As a topping for vegetables, potatoes, popcorn | Very often | Often | Occasionally |

SNACKS

| Chips, nuts, crackers | Often (once a day or more) | Occasionally (once a week) | Rarely (twice a month or less) |
| Cookies, cake, cupcakes, candy, sweet rolls | Often (once a day or more) | Occasionally (once a week) | Rarely (twice a month or less) |

SOME RESOURCES FOR NUTRITION COUNTERS

At your bookstore, you will find many new nutrition counters and they all provide a lot of detailed information in a small package. They will all do the job; here are a few examples:

Becker, Gail L. *The Antioxidant Pocket Counter.* New York: Times Books/Random House, 1993.

Franz, Marion J. *Fast Food Facts.* Wellness and Nutrition Library. Wayzata, MN: DC Publishers, 1990.

Heller, Richard F. and Rachel F. Heller. *The Carbohydrate Addicts' Gram Counter.* New York: Signet Books/Penguin, 1993.

The Long Life Guide Series (The Fiber Counter; Sodium Counter; Cholesterol, Fat, Calorie and Gram Counter) from the Human Nutrition Service, USDA. Available from Bart Books, 155 East Thirty-fourth Street, New York, NY, 1989.

Pope-Cordle, Jamie and Martin Katahn. *T-Factor Fat Gram Counter.* New York: W.W. Norton, 1991.

Webb, Denise, Ph.D, R.D. *The Complete "Lite" Foods Calorie, Fat, Cholesterol and Sodium Counter.* New York: Bantam Books.

11

ABOUT FAT AND CHOLESTEROL

Your body needs a certain amount of dietary fat for good health. Small quantities help your body use important vitamins and minerals for repair and growth of tissues. Fat deposits provide energy for the muscles, including your heart muscle. They support and buffer our internal organs against jarring. Body fat supplies oils to your skin and hair follicles, giving you a beautiful complexion and shiny hair. The layer of fat under your skin insulates against extreme heat and cold. Fat also produces prostaglandins, a hormonelike compound that the body uses to regulate cholesterol and keep cell membranes and blood vessels in good repair. And some body fat is needed to regulate a woman's sex hormones and menstrual cycle. Women athletes who overtrain may have so little fat that they cease menstruating; young female athletes who begin hard training before puberty may have delayed sexual development.

The problem is that it doesn't take much dietary fat to maintain good health—a mere tablespoon a day. Yet the average American adult consumes six to eight tablespoons of fat a day.

Too much fat makes you overweight and clogs your arteries. Fat is the most caloric food you can eat: nine calories for every gram. Even worse, it's only a short trip from dietary fat to body fat, so people who eat too much fat over a period of time *get fat*. This is a serious problem for African Americans, because our high rate of obesity is tied to high blood pressure, adult-onset diabetes, heart disease, and several forms of cancer. In other words, reducing fat in your diet could save your life.

On the plus side, the less fat you eat, the more heart-healthy grains, vegetables, fruits, and foods bursting with vitamins and minerals you'll be eating.

FAT AND CANCER

It took a long time to recognize fat as a cancer-causing agent because there didn't seem to be a direct cause and effect. Now, new studies of large populations around the world have uncovered a kind of chain reaction that is triggered by high-fat diets: Fat stimulates the production of other substances which in turn may cause cancers. For example, fat stimulates the liver and gallbladder to produce and release bile acids; these acids are more readily converted to a carcinogen, or cancer-causing substance. In the colon, these bile acids may also injure healthy tissue, making the colon more susceptible to cancer. Dietary fat may also stimulate the production of certain hormones that in turn promote the growth of malignant tumors. Thus, high-fat diets are thought to increase the risk of breast and uterine cancer in women, prostate cancer in men, and colon cancer in both men and women. (See Chapter 22.)

As a result of this new information, a high-fat diet has been identified as an important risk factor for several cancers.

FAT AND HEART DISEASE

High levels of dietary fat increase the levels of cholesterol in the blood, which puts one at major risk for heart disease. Although the human body naturally produces about one thousand milligrams of cholesterol each day, we also consume more cholesterol in food, especially animal products. The body needs cholesterol to make bile, vitamin D, and sex hormones. But if we get too much, the body must try to manage the excess. When there's too much, for example, the body cuts back on its own production or moves the excess to the liver to be excreted. The extra cholesterol may also move into the bloodstream, where it is deposited like hard paste along the inside of the arteries. As a result, the interior channels of the arteries become so narrow that blood cannot flow through easily; the risk of heart disease and premature death go up when this occurs.

You probably know about "bad" LDL cholesterol and "good" HDL cholesterol. Both types of cholesterol contribute to your total cholesterol value; however, LDL cholesterol damages artery walls. The molecule that carries the cholesterol through the bloodstream determines its effect.

LDL molecules are quite fragile. As they transport cholesterol through the arteries, they frequently smash into one another and get stuck; mashed-together molecules form a kind of paste, or plaque, that builds up on arterial walls. LDL usually accounts for 60 to 70 percent of total blood-serum cholesterol readings. A desirable LDL level is below 130 mg/dl. (Cholesterol is measured in milligrams of cholesterol per deciliter of blood plasma, or mg/dl.)

HDL molecules are much hardier and less likely to break down. Women, nonsmokers, and people who exercise regularly usually have higher levels of HDL. Even if your total cholesterol reading is normal, if HDL levels are low (less than 35 mg/dl), you may still be at risk for heart disease. Desirable HDL levels for men: 42 to 50 mg/dl; for women: 50 to 60 mg/dl.

The idea behind cholesterol management is to reduce the number of LDL molecules while maintaining or increasing the number of HDL molecules.

Can cholesterol be too low? Several recent studies reveal a curiously sinister side to especially low levels—160 units and under —of cholesterol in the blood. People with such readings are far less likely to die of heart disease, but it turns out they are far more likely to die from a variety of other causes, including stroke, liver cancer, and lung disease, as well as from alcoholism and suicide.

One study published in July of 1992 in *The Archives of Internal Medicine* involved 350,000 healthy middle-aged men. At the outset, the authors of the study, Dr. James Neaton and his colleagues at the University of Minnesota, observed that 6 percent of the men had very low total cholesterol levels. Twelve years later, that 6 percent had hardly a trace of heart disease. But they were twice as likely to have a stroke or die of lung disease; twice as likely to kill themselves; three times as likely to have liver cancer; and five times as likely to die of alcoholism. Similar findings come from

Dr. David Jacobs, an epidemiologist at the University of Michigan. He and his colleagues studied 170,000 men and 120,000 women in various countries, and their conclusions were published in a watershed paper in the September 1992 issue of *Circulation*. It sounds as if you're damned if you do and damned if you don't. But this is not necessarily so. Low cholesterol may not cause all of these deaths. Alcoholics, for instance, are apt to have very low cholesterol levels, but their alcoholism—not their cholesterol levels—is more likely to account for their high rate of homicide and suicide, as well as liver disease.

While scientists continue to ponder cholesterol, it's certain that people with high cholesterol run a high risk of dying of heart disease. If your cholesterol is elevated, it's vital for you to try to lower it. Is there a point below which cholesterol should not fall? The new data shows that problems occur when cholesterol levels drop below 160. Dr. Jacobs's paper showed that *cholesterol levels from 180 to 200 or 220 seemed ideal for total health.*

ARE YOU AT RISK FOR HIGH CHOLESTEROL?

Before 1960, blacks had significantly lower cholesterol levels than whites. By 1980, the total cholesterol values were similar in black and white populations, and heart disease among blacks had risen significantly. Recently, a few small studies have shown that black men tend to have more of the beneficial HDL cholesterol than white men (although the same advantage hasn't been consistently shown among black women). But the death rates from heart disease are still higher among blacks. Why? The study that originally revealed the higher HDL cholesterol profile for blacks may have been flawed—the men studied were wealthier than average and probably had a better diet and better nutritional profiles than most people. (For other reasons why blacks have a higher death rate from heart disease, see Chapter 25.)

Most cholesterol comes from high-fat foods. But for unknown reasons, not everyone who eats a high-fat diet has elevated cholesterol. And, conversely, some who have a low-fat diet do have elevated blood cholesterol.

The answer to this mysterious paradox may lie in genetics: Some people use cholesterol more efficiently than others. Since high blood cholesterol can develop at an early age, if you have a strong family history of early heart attack or high cholesterol, it's smart to have your children's blood cholesterol screened.

For now, we have to assume that high blood cholesterol is a problem for everybody and that everyone should look for ways to reduce their intake of dietary cholesterol. Today, about 25 percent of all Americans between the ages of twenty and seventy-four have high total blood cholesterol, which translates into at least 40 million people.

How High Is High?

The Expert Panel of the National Cholesterol Education Program has classified total blood cholesterol above 240 mg/dl as high blood cholesterol, from 200 to 239 as borderline high, and below 200 as within normal range. The panel advises that everyone over age twenty should have their total cholesterol measured at least once every five years.

Cholesterol Recommendations for African Americans

Because of the somewhat different LDL-HDL cholesterol profile among blacks, Dr. Jackson T. Wright, Jr., and his colleagues from the departments of medicine and pharmacology of the Medical College of Virginia Commonwealth University in Richmond recommend a different set of guidelines for African Americans. These researchers suggest treatment for African Americans be determined by LDL cholesterol levels, *plus the number of additional risk factors an individual has for heart disease* (see page 133). Here are their guidelines:

Using diet alone, make a serious effort to reduce cholesterol if:

1. your LDL is between 130 and 160 mg/dl and you have two or more additional risk factors or a history of heart disease;
2. your LDL is between 160 and 190 mg/dl (even if you have no additional risk factors).

Add cholesterol-lowering drug therapy to your diet if:

1. your LDL is between 160 and 190 mg/dl and you have two or more risk factors;
2. your LDL is above 190 mg/dl.

Here are the risk factors for coronary heart disease:

• Male sex
• Family history of coronary heart disease
• Cigarette smoking
• Hypertension
• Diabetes
• Obesity
• Low level of HDL cholesterol (less than 35 mg/dl)

MORE FAT LANGUAGE

Triglycerides are a compound made up of three fatty acids. They are made from carbohydrates but are stored in fat tissue. (For you chemists, triglycerides consist of strips of carbon atoms linked in threes to a glycerol molecule.) High levels of triglycerides in the blood usually correspond to high cholesterol levels and are linked to increased risk of coronary heart disease, diabetes, and chronic renal (kidney) disease.

VLDLs (very low-density lipoproteins) consist mainly of triglycerides.

DIET TO LOWER CHOLESTEROL

It's not only how much cholesterol you eat that counts *but how much saturated fat.* Saturated fat increases the cholesterol level in your blood and is derived mostly from animal products but also from coconuts, avocados, and palm-kernel oils. (All other vegetables are free of both cholesterol and saturated fat.)

HARMFUL FATS VERSUS BETTER FATS

All fats are high in calories and are used slowly by the body, but some fats are more harmful than others.

Fats are either saturated or unsaturated. Both have the same number of calories and both are easily converted to body fat. However, generally speaking, *saturated* fats are more harmful because they can elevate blood cholesterol; *unsaturated* fats are a better choice because they do not. The trouble with these labels is that fat can change from one form to another. How can you tell the good guys from the bad guys? Here's a rundown.

HARMFUL FATS

Saturated Fats. These fats are found mostly in animal products—especially red meat, milk, cheese, butter, and other dairy products. They are usually solid at room temperature. Saturated fats are so named because their chemical structures are literally saturated with hydrogen atoms. For the most part, saturated fats are easy to identify. But some vegetable oils known as tropical oils are also saturated.

Tropical Vegetable Oils. These oils (coconut, palm, and palm-kernel) are highly saturated and promote cholesterol in the blood. Products containing them include nondairy creamers, cookies, and other bakery products and snack foods. These foods may actually claim they contain no cholesterol. Technically, they're correct—but saturated fat promotes the body's production of LDL cholesterol.

Trans Fats. Manufacturers who claim to have eliminated tropical oils from their products may replace them with partially hydrogenated oils, called *trans fatty acids;* these may be just as harmful as saturated fat and tropical oils when it comes to raising LDL cholesterol levels.

How can you tell whether a product contains trans fats? Any product that lists partially hydrogenated oil on its label contains trans fats. Likely products include crackers, cookies, pastries, cakes, doughnuts, french fries, potato chips, puddings, and graham crackers.

Some researchers believe that trans fats are not harmful unless consumed in large quantities. By following a reasonably low-fat diet, you should be able to keep trans fats in check.

Margarine and Solid Shortenings. Margarine and other solid vegetable shortenings are produced when liquid vegetable oils are hardened, or hydrogenated. In this process, some fatty acids in vegetable oil become more saturated. New studies suggest that solid margarine has the same effect as butter when it comes to clogging arteries.

BETTER FATS

Unsaturated fats are found only in vegetable oils. There are two kinds of vegetable oil that are considered "heart-healthy"—the polyunsaturates and the monounsaturates.

Liquid Polyunsaturated Vegetable Oils. For more than two decades now, polyunsaturated vegetable oils such as corn oil, sunflower oil, and safflower oil have been recognized as heart-healthy alternatives to butter and other fats derived from animal products. They're credited with lowering cholesterol. These fatty acids are missing more than one pair of hydrogen atoms.

However, as we've said, these good fats, which are liquid at room temperature, can be made more saturated by adding hydrogen to them: Thus, hardened hydrogenated vegetable oil that comes in cans (the stuff we love to fry chicken and fish in) is a saturated fat. So is stick margarine. The harder a vegetable oil is, the more saturated. Thus, stick margarine is more saturated than tub margarine, and tub margarine is more saturated than liquid oil.

Monounsaturates. Monounsaturated fat has become the "fat of choice." Like the polyunsaturates, monounsaturates lower *total* cholesterol in your blood, but they do it by selectively reducing LDL. Some may even boost HDL levels. Monounsaturated fats are also liquid at room temperature. Olive oil, avocados, and some nuts are monounsaturates. These oils have an added advantage: They are believed to boost HDL, the "good" cholesterol. This is a fat missing one pair of hydrogen atoms.

Olive oil is a good choice because more than three-quarters of its fat is monounsaturated. *Canola oil* is even higher in monounsaturates than olive oil and is now often used in margarines. Peanut oil and avocado oil, although monounsaturates, are neutral—they aren't harmful, but they don't provide the same benefit as olive oil or canola oil.

Omega-3 Fatty Acids. These are found in fish oils and benefit the body in several ways. They appear to slow tumor growth in cancer patients. Omega-3 fatty acids are also heart-healthy and reduce clotting of the blood, which helps prevent the progression of coronary artery disease. Salmon, tuna, mackerel, herring, sardines, halibut, and trout are all high in omega-3 fatty acids.

WHICH FATS ARE WHICH?

Monounsaturated	Polyunsaturated	Saturated
Olive oil	Safflower oil	Butter
Canola oil	Sunflower oil	Meat fat
Peanut oil	Corn oil	Lard (pork fat)
Avocados	Soybean oil	Hydrogenated (solid)
Olives	Cottonseed oil	vegetable oils
Peanuts	Margarines	Cream
Peanut butter,	Sesame oil	Cheese
natural	Mayonnaise	Whole milk
Cashews	Walnuts	Coconut oil
Almonds		Palm kernel oil
Pecans		Palm oil
		Peanut butter,
		commercial

Note that natural peanut butter that you grind yourself or have ground at the health food store contains monounsaturated fat. Since the oil rises to the top, all you have to do is pour it off before eating. Commercial peanut butter that you buy at the supermarket has been hydrogenated, that is, put through a process where it is made more saturated.

Also, when choosing a margarine look for a *liquid oil* as the first ingredient on the label. If the first ingredient listed is a hydrogenated or partially hydrogenated vegetable oil, the product is relatively high in saturated fat. Generally the softer the margarine, the less saturated.

FOODS HIGH IN CHOLESTEROL

Certain low-fat foods also contain large amounts of cholesterol. For example, egg yolks, organ meats such as liver and kidney, caviar, fish roe, and shellfish all contain cholesterol, but they may have less impact on your blood cholesterol levels than foods high in saturated fat.

One thing we know for sure: If you reduce *all fats* in your diet, particularly animal fats and tropical oils, you automatically reduce cholesterol. You can further cut cholesterol by adding fiber to your diet in the form of oat bran, whole oats, and dried beans, which act like sponges to mop up excess cholesterol and transport it out of the bloodstream. (For more information on fiber, see Chapter 14.)

It's interesting that cholesterol levels may increase with stress. Stress releases adrenaline and cortisol, which in turn release glucose, fat, and cholesterol into the blood. Reducing stress, particularly by adding exercise, may help lower cholesterol. (See Chapter 4 for information about reducing stress.)

SPECIAL TIPS TO REDUCE CHOLESTEROL FURTHER

Follow all the low-fat recommendations in the Sankofa Program, Chapter 17. Don't smoke. Limit alcohol intake. Exercise regularly. Get to your healthiest weight.

It's okay to eat seafood such as shrimp, lobster, scallops, oysters, squid in moderation (crabs and clams less so). Although high in cholesterol, shellfish are lower in fat and calories and nutritionally valuable, providing iron, protein, potassium, zinc, and selenium. Most shellfish also contain omega-3 fatty acids. So, enjoy these cholesterol-dense foods in moderation or, if your cholesterol levels are very high, as directed by your doctor.

Any food you substitute for saturated fat helps lower cholesterol levels, but only if you eat this food *instead* of the fat, not along with it! So beans and rice are great, but they won't help much if you eat sausages with them.

Adding oat bran and other fiber-rich foods will help lower cholesterol. For more about how this works, see Chapter 14.

Niacin has been recommended by some health experts to lower cholesterol. However, don't try megadosing on niacin (vitamin

B_3). In very large doses, niacin acts as a drug, not a vitamin. Niacin causes flushing and tingling skin and can aggravate gout, diabetes, ulcers, and liver problems. It is also important to note that recent reports suggest time-released niacin can cause abnormal liver function, so your doctor is likely to advise certain laboratory tests on a regular basis to keep your overall health in check while you're using niacin. *Consult with your doctor before taking niacin supplements.*

QUICK RESULTS

We always thought that it took years to get results from reducing fat in the diet, but now it seems you can get results immediately. New studies show that eating fatty meals clogs arteries within a few hours. And eating low-fat meals quickly reverses the process.

Studies of 170 men between the ages of forty and fifty-nine conducted by Dr. George J. Miller of the Medical Research Council in London showed that fatty meals activate a substance called factor VII, which sets off an explosion of blood-clotting chemicals in the blood within six or seven hours, sharply raising the danger of blood clots forming in the arteries feeding the heart. Another study, from the University of Chicago, showed a similar effect in women. When twenty-four women were switched from high-fat diets to low-fat diets their factor VII activity dropped by 11 percent.

Scientists have always known that most heart attacks occur in the early-morning hours, and one reason could be that high-fat dinners put the blood in a hypercoagulation state by the following morning.

Good advice: Reduce fats in your overall diet throughout the day, particularly in your evening meal.

DRUGS TO LOWER CHOLESTEROL

If dietary changes fail to do the job, cholesterol-lowering drugs are now available. People who have very high levels of cholesterol to begin with are the most likely candidates for drug therapy. But all drugs have some side effects, so most doctors will ask you to try first to lower cholesterol with diet alone for about six months. If your cholesterol level doesn't drop to within normal range, drug therapy is usually recommended. The main drugs used to lower cholesterol are niacin (nicotinic acid), lovastatin (Mevacor), gemfibrozil (Lopid), cholestyramine (Questran), and probucol (Lorelco).

Some doctors feel *low doses* of fish-oil supplements containing omega-3 fatty acids also may be useful to lower cholesterol. The idea comes from an early study in Greenland, which showed that Inuits, despite a diet high in fat and cholesterol, had a low incidence of heart disease. A number of follow-up studies showed that while their total cholesterol was indeed high, it was largely comprised of good HDL cholesterol. Further, triglycerides, another heart-damaging blood fat, were low. This beneficial cholesterol profile was then traced to the large amounts of omega-3 fatty acids in the fish and other marine animals that Inuits lived on. Fish-oil supplements should be taken only under medical supervision, because they contain high levels of vitamin A, which in excess can be toxic.

For all of these important health reasons—heart disease, obesity and its many concomitant diseases, and cancer—it's crucial to reduce fats in your diet.

Do you really have to do it? You bet. Will it be harder for you as an African American to reduce fats in your diet? It might be, depending on where you live, the traditions you grew up with, and your socioeconomic status. The truth is, it's hard for most people, regardless of race, to change eating habits. But thanks to new low-fat products available in most stores in most parts of the country, it's a lot easier than it used to be. The Sankofa Program gives you a full month just to pay attention to lowering fats in your diet.

12

ABOUT SALT

Does eating salty foods actually cause high blood pressure? Do all African Americans need to reduce salt—or just people who already have high blood pressure, fluid retention, and kidney or heart disease? Unfortunately, these two tricky questions about salt don't have clear-cut answers.

As far as African Americans are concerned, numerous studies have shown that many, and perhaps most, of us *are* salt-sensitive, making us particularly vulnerable to any action salt may have on blood volume. Further, we tend to enjoy salty foods to the extreme. We also fail to get enough potassium to counteract our typically high-sodium diet. It's this imbalance between the two minerals that may be linked to hypertension. Therefore, while the salt controversy continues in the scientific community, it seems imperative that we African Americans—who suffer the highest rates of hypertension and death from stroke and heart attack in the world—go all out to reduce the salt in our diets. It can save our lives and the lives of our children.

High blood pressure was never a problem for us in Africa, where the traditional diet was naturally low in sodium and high in potassium. Our African ancestors were not as overweight as we are, and they also performed more manual labor than we do, which meant they could release more excess sodium through perspiration. They may also have had a different salt-using profile than most American blacks (see Chapter 26). In the United States, the situation is reversed. Our high-salt diet and lack of activity, plus a genetic predisposition to retain salt, promote the expression of hypertension.

I think there's enough evidence now to show that we can all benefit from reducing the amount of salt we eat.

WHAT IS SODIUM?

Table salt is 60 percent chloride and 40 percent sodium. Sodium is a mineral needed to balance body fluids, control acid-alkaline balances, transmit nerve impulses, and contract muscles, including the heart. Sodium also removes carbon dioxide from the bloodstream and dissolves other blood minerals. Therefore, some sodium is essential to good health. Since our bodies don't make sodium, we need to replace it in our diet every day.

The body is designed to use the sodium it needs and get rid of the excess. Safety mechanisms are built into the body's systems to filter excess sodium through the kidneys and dump it out of the body via urine. If this system fails, as it apparently does in many African Americans, the kidneys hold on to the excess sodium. As a result, the sodium attracts and retains water, which dilutes blood, and makes blood volume rise. With more blood on the move, heart rate and blood pressure increase. Fluid retention has other negative effects on the body. It can restrict your activity, promote blood clots, and even adversely affect your mood. If excess water builds up around the heart, it can cause congestive heart failure.

SODIUM OR CHLORIDE: WHAT DOES THE DAMAGE?

Everyone has always assumed that salt-sensitive hypertension was caused by the sodium in salt. But some researchers now believe that chloride may actually induce hypertension.

One study measured blood pressure in rats known to be salt-sensitive. After five weeks of being loaded with sodium chloride, the rats showed an increase in blood pressure; but when the chloride portion was replaced with bicarbonate, blood pressure remained normal. In a small study in humans, sodium chloride increased blood pressure in five hypertensive men; when sodium *citrate* was substituted, the blood pressure returned to previous levels.

ARE YOU SALT-SENSITIVE?

In the general population, about 50 percent of hypertensives are salt-sensitive. Proportionally, many more African Americans are salt-sensitive, although the exact percentage remains unknown.

So far, the only way to tell whether you're salt-sensitive is to reduce salt and measure your blood pressure to see whether it goes down. If blood pressure doesn't fall, then you may not be sensitive to salt.

However, some researchers believe that even people whose bodies handle salt properly may benefit from reducing the amount of salt in their diets. Even if they don't get the dramatic initial lowering that salt-sensitive hypertensives do when they reduce salt, over the long run of many years, *all* hypertensives seem to have better results if they reduce salt.

Everyone's blood pressure naturally goes up as they get older, along with their taste for salt. (The older you are, the more salt you're likely to use.) If you don't have high blood pressure, reducing salt now may prevent the hypertension from ever developing. This is vital information for African Americans because we are so vulnerable to this devastating disease. Studies of infants, children, and adults with normal blood pressure have shown that blood pressure drops in response to salt reduction. These results have led researchers to conclude that people who reduce salt intake while young will be less likely to have elevated blood pressure later in life.

POTASSIUM

In addition to reducing salt, you may be able to help your blood-pressure profile by adding potassium—another important mineral necessary to normal body functions—to your diet. Seventy years ago, researchers first observed that potassium appeared to lower blood pressure in hypertensives. Then, in the 1980s, researchers studying a group of hypertensives in Evans County, Georgia, found that hypertensive black adults consumed less potassium than whites with normal blood pressure, suggesting that increasing potassium may be especially helpful.

Whether potassium benefits blood pressure may depend on your family history. For example, if you have a family history of hypertension, reducing sodium and adding potassium to your diet may lower your blood pressure. If you don't have such a family history, the low sodium/high potassium approach probably won't work. Longer-lasting studies are still needed to examine the sodium/potassium/family history connection, so stay alert for news in the media about this interesting treatment approach.

S A L T   A L E R T
Here are some of the foods that have a high sodium content.

Cheese	*pizza*
anchovies	*relishes*
bacon	*salad dressing (dry and bottled)*
baking powder	*salted chips, nuts, popcorn, pretzels*
baking soda	*sauerkraut*
barbecue sauce	*sausages*
bouillon cubes	*seasoned salt (garlic, onion, or*
catsup	*lemon pepper seasonings)*
chili sauce	*soup or sauce mixes (dry or canned)*
cocoa mixes	*soy sauce*
commercial horseradish	*table salt*
mayonnaise	*teriyaki sauce*
MSG (monosodium glutamate)	*tomato sauce (regular)*
mustard (prepared)	*vegetables, canned*
olives (green)	*Worcestershire sauce*
pickles	

GETTING MOTIVATED

Reducing salt is easier said than done, because humans develop a taste for salt early in life—as soon as four months of age. And salt is added to many of our favorite foods, including sausages, bacon, corned beef, frankfurters, ham, processed cheeses, margarine and butter, olives, and most snack foods such as potato and corn chips. In addition, there's natural sodium in foods.

For many years, I thought food had no taste at all unless it had salt added. When I was growing up, my mother added salt to foods before, during, and often after cooking. She always said that salt brought out the flavor in foods.

However, after my mother developed hypertension and later suffered a series of strokes, I was really motivated to eliminate most of the salt from my food. Still, if you have no apparent health risks, this can be hard to do. Unlike other nutritional changes you'll be making on the Sankofa Program, you may not see any obvious benefit to reducing salt. For example, if you reduce fat and sugar, you usually lose weight, which is a pretty good motivation. But reducing salt doesn't always show, unless you retain fluid when you eat salty foods. (In that case, as soon as you reduce your salt intake, swelling and bloating from fluid retention begin to disappear.)

But let me tell you, reducing salt does have a big payoff! It may prevent the emergence of high blood pressure, especially in salt-sensitive people, and can help control it for those who already have established hypertension. Reducing salt will cut down on the medication you have to take and may reduce your doctor visits. Reducing salt can literally save your life. It may also save the lives of your children by preventing high blood pressure before it gets started. That's pretty good motivation.

If you still hate the idea of giving up salt, let me assure you it's not as hard as you think. In fact, once you get used to them, low-salt foods taste much better.

I didn't realize just how salty my favorite foods were until I stopped using salt. At first, I thought everything tasted bland. But soon I started tasting the real food instead of the salt. I began to realize how much taste food had by itself. Salt hadn't brought out the flavor, as my mom said, it had covered it up. It took several weeks for my salt taste buds to subside, but eventually they did. Now I eat almost no salt at all and enjoy the difference of savoring fresh foods.

DO YOU KNOW HOW MUCH SALT YOU EAT?

About one-third of the salt we consume is present in natural, unprocessed food. Another third is contained in packaged or

SALT SUBSTITUTES

Herbs, onions, garlic, and liquids such as lemon juice or wine make flavorful substitutes for salt in dishes you cook. Retrain your taste buds and try the following alternatives to salt:

allspice	mint
basil	mustard (dry)
bay leaf	nutmeg
caraway seeds	onion (juice, fresh, dry, flakes, or
chili powder (no salt added)	powder)
chives	oregano
cinnamon	paprika
cloves	parsley
cocoa (dry, not instant or Dutch	pepper
process)	pimiento
cranberries	rosemary
curry powder (no salt added)	sage
dill	Tabasco
garlic (fresh or dry, pure	tarragon
powder)	thyme
ginger (fresh or dry)	tomato (fresh or canned without
lemon and lemon juice	salt)
mace	vanilla
marjoram	vinegar

canned foods. And we add another third during cooking or at the table. Salt is the second-most-common additive in foods (sugar is first), so pervasive that it's hard to keep track of how much we're getting.

Many people eat as much as seven thousand milligrams of sodium a day (about 3 teaspoons of salt). But we need only a fraction of this amount—250 to 500 milligrams—to meet daily health needs.

Until more evidence is in, it's still the sodium content in salt that you're concerned with.

To reduce sodium, it's almost essential to get familiar with the ingredients of the foods you eat on a daily basis. This means becoming aware of foods that have a high sodium content and getting in the habit of reading labels on packaged foods.

SALT LABELS
The FDA regulates sodium content labeling as follows:

Label Says:	Meaning:
Sodium-free	Fewer than 5 mg. per serving
Very low sodium	35 mg. or fewer per serving
Low sodium	140 mg. or fewer per serving
Reduced sodium	Processed to reduce the usual level of sodium by 75 percent
Unsalted, or no salt added	Processed without added salt
Lite	Processed with less than the usual amount of salt (it does not mean no salt was added during processing)

13

ABOUT SUGAR

What's all this fuss about sugar? We love it and our body needs some form of sugar. All sugar contains glucose, which is the body's primary source of energy. Whether you eat a protein, fat, or carbohydrate, the body breaks food down into its basic components, one being glucose. Glucose then circulates through the body, where it is used by cells for energy. Any excess is stored as fat. Since our bodies survive on the glucose extracted from all foods in the small intestine, we don't need it in the form of refined sugar.

And yet sugar makes food taste better, adds texture to baked goods, and acts as a preservative. It also helps baked products retain moisture. In fact, if you buy processed foods, you may be getting more sugar than you realize: All ingredients ending in *ose* —sucrose, lactose, dextrose, glucose, and fructose—are sugar. So are corn syrup, molasses, and honey.

All forms of sugar are basically metabolized the same way and none is intrinsically better, or worse, than another.

According to figures from the American Dietetic Association, Americans overall consume about 125 pounds of sugar per person a year and a whopping 20 pounds of artificial sweetener. This amounts to more than half a cup a day—from beverages, baked goods, candy, and other foods. A twelve-ounce can of soda pop contains the equivalent of nine or ten teaspoons of sugar.

Sugar has been blamed for causing problems ranging from obesity and high blood pressure to diabetes and volatile mood swings. But is it really *that* bad? Years of research have shown that moderate sugar consumption poses no health risks for most people.

For example, sugar does not cause diabetes, although it can make the disease worse once it exists. (See Chapter 24.) Nor is sugar itself the culprit in causing other medical problems such as heart disease and obesity, but it is guilty by association. Too often sugary foods are also calorie-dense, high in fat and cholesterol. To fill up, you eat more and more. Thus, sugary foods are a problem for the obese, and obesity does cause health problems.

If you must watch the number of calories you eat each day (and who doesn't?) in order to control your weight, you probably don't want to spend many on sugar. America's favorite food additive is not very nutritious. Table sugar, or sucrose—which comes either from sugarcane or beets—has almost no macronutrients. Sucrose has roughly fifteen calories per teaspoon, contains no fat, protein, cholesterol, or fiber. Honey has some potassium, calcium, and phosphorus; molasses has traces of calcium, iron, potassium, and B vitamins.

Some researchers say table sugar interferes with the absorption of important vitamins such as magnesium, zinc, and chromium and can prevent the body from using the B vitamins.

The less sugar you eat, the more places you can spend those calories enjoying foods with better nutritional value. For instance, two ounces of chocolate has the same calorie value as three bananas, but bananas are fat-free and pack a terrific nutritional wallop, plus giving you fiber.

If sugar has no nutritional value, why do human beings seem to have such a natural craving for it? Most researchers feel that the taste for sweetness is inborn in humans. Photographs of newborns show them making unhappy faces when they taste bitter foods. This may be linked to biological survival mechanisms, which tell us instinctively to shy away from bitter-tasting foods. Sweeter foods are also immediately uplifting and provide quick energy.

Nevertheless, overindulgence in the sweet stuff is an acquired habit and has not been found to be a genetic given. Taste preferences, like preferences for clothes and music, are influenced by family and friends. While children don't necessarily like foods because their parents do, as they grow up, their food choices become strikingly similar. Brothers and sisters have very similar food preferences.

Television also influences food tastes. Not only are we bombarded with nonstop images of food but advertisements carry messages that certain foods are "cooler" than others. Discovering that Bart Simpson loves Butterfinger candy bars may be enough to convince a child to love them, as well.

As we age, our taste buds change. Our threshold for sweetness rises after age fifty. Elderly people may need three times the amount of sweetener to get the same sensation a younger person experiences.

While everyone may have a sweet tooth to some degree, African Americans are particularly susceptible to its attractions because of our particular environmental conditioning.

Sugarcane originated in Papua, New Guinea, about eight to nine thousand years ago. The crop gradually moved west over thousands of years, arriving in the Caribbean shortly after Columbus. The slave trade between Africa and the Caribbean began with the need for labor in sugarcane fields. Cultivation of sugarcane spread to Central America, and today sugarcane plantations around the world account for annual harvests of millions of tons.

African slaves practically *breathed* sugar as they cut cane from dawn to dark every day of the year. At first, slaves were allowed to eat only molasses, the by-product of refined sugar. Molasses quickly became a popular addition to poor and tedious slave rations and later, along with cane syrup, was incorporated into traditional southern black cooking. Today, syrup, molasses, and sugars are still considered staples in many of our homes.

Sugar is one of those foods that conjure up pleasant associations, causing us to reach for them when our emotions cry for comfort, even if we're not hungry.

TOOTH DECAY

As far as we know, the only disease sugar actually causes is tooth decay. In ancient Greece, Aristotle noticed that people who ate soft figs developed rotten teeth. In the fifteenth century, Arculanus wrote that those wishing to keep their teeth should shun sweet and sticky foods. Since then, the damaging role of sugar in causing tooth decay (dental caries) has been well documented.

Despite this knowledge, I can remember looking forward to visiting the dentist or doctor when I was a young child—because I was given a piece of candy if I was good. I think a lot of kids grow up the same way, indulged with sweets for good behavior, conditioned to think of sugar as something especially good.

Caries-producing bacteria love simple sugars like glucose, fructose, and lactose. They turn sugar into acids, which drill a hole in the tooth enamel, in which other bacteria then create decay.

Cavities develop in direct response to the amount of time sugar is in contact with the tooth surface. The longer food remains in your mouth, the easier for tooth decay to begin. (That's why it's important to brush within fifteen minutes of eating.)

Slippery sweets that pass through the mouth quickly are less dangerous—from a dental perspective—than eating solid sugars. So ice cream, fruit juice, and soda pop are "safer" options than raisins and chocolates, which cling to teeth longer.

FLUORIDE

In the United States, tooth decay has been diminished by adding fluoride to the water supply. The benefits of fluoride were first observed in the 1930s and 1940s, when large population surveys discovered that people who lived near sources of naturally fluoridated water didn't seem to develop cavities. In 1945, fluoride was first added to the water supply of Grand Rapids, Michigan. After fifteen years, children age twelve to fourteen years old had about 55 percent fewer cavities than children of the same age growing up before fluoridation.

If you live in an area where there are inadequate concentrations of fluoride in the water, your dentist may recommend fluoride supplements to make up for the difference.

If you use bottled water because you are worried about toxins in your area's water supply, you can provide some protection against cavities by using a fluoridated toothpaste. Some mouth rinses, soft drinks, and other foods also contain fluoride. Check with your dentist first before using these products. There is such a thing as too much fluoride for children, which leads to mottling of the tooth surface in developing teeth, a condition called fluorosis.

Despite the improvement provided by fluoride, tooth decay and gum disease remain serious problems. Of the thirteen leading health costs in America, dental problems rank second ($21.3 billion in 1985).

SPECIAL CAUTION FOR AFRICAN AMERICANS

In childhood, dental problems probably affect African Americans in about the same proportion as the rest of the population. As adults, however, we tend to have fewer decayed, missing, and filled teeth. On the other hand, we have *more* gum and bone disease. My dentist likes to say, "You might never have a cavity and still lose every tooth in your head because of gum and bone disease."

Therefore, it's especially important for us to pay attention to cleaning and flossing our teeth. Removing plaque is the ultimate goal. (A buildup of plaque can cause your gums to become so inflamed that you begin to lose your teeth.) When you brush, scrub both gums and gumline. Floss your teeth twice a day. And twice a year have your teeth cleaned by a dentist or dental hygienist.

Unfortunately, because few people have dental insurance, the cost of going to the dentist comes directly out of your pocket. Some dental schools, such as the New York University Dental College, offer dental services at reduced fees. Check in your community.

Although nothing can replace the professional cleaning provided by a dental hygienist, you can go a long way toward protecting your own teeth and gums if you reduce the amount of sugary foods you eat and brush and floss after meals or *at least twice a day.*

READING SUGAR LABELS

Trying to avoid sugar isn't always easy. Manufacturers can use various forms of sugar in their products without having to list the word *sugar* on the nutrition label. Nutritionwise, no form is better, or worse, than another, although they may taste slightly different to your palate.

Galactose and lactose are milk sugars. Maltose, or malt sugar, comes from starches. Mannose comes from legumes. Fructose, one of the most commonly used sweeteners, comes from honey, corn syrup, and fruits. Fructose is 70 percent sweeter than sucrose. Since a little goes a long way, it's a popular additive with food manufacturers and is frequently found in processed foods and soft drinks. These products may be labeled "reduced-calorie," although they are not sugar-free. You'll see fructose listed as "high-fructose corn syrup." Some people feel that fructose is better for you than sucrose because it takes a little longer to enter the bloodstream, thereby avoiding a sudden increase in blood sugar.

SUGAR RUSH

Does sugar really give us a quick burst of energy, followed by an equally fast letdown? This widespread belief in a sugar rush is being reexamined. The amount of sugar present in your blood normally stays relatively stable throughout the day. About thirty to sixty minutes after you eat *any* food, the blood-sugar levels rise. This signals the pancreas to produce more insulin, which stabilizes blood-sugar levels again by helping glucose enter cells. This is an automatic response in healthy people.

Still, scientists recognize that different foods affect blood-sugar levels at somewhat varying rates. For instance, potatoes raise blood sugar faster than pasta. Bananas and raisins raise blood sugar faster than table sugar. Shredded wheat acts faster than kidney beans. Oatmeal works faster than all-bran cereal, whole-wheat bread faster than white bread.

However, trouble arises only when insulin doesn't properly handle the sugar present in the blood. Too little insulin (as in diabetes), and you get sugar overload in the blood. Too much insulin, and blood sugar can drop too low, a condition known as hypoglycemia.

HYPOGLYCEMIA

Hypoglycemics have low levels of sugar in their blood, meaning their bodies aren't getting enough fuel to function at peak performance. Their pancreas produces too much insulin (the reverse of diabetes), causing the blood-sugar levels to drop sharply.

The symptoms of hypoglycemia are episodic, usually occurring in response to certain kinds of foods and when they are eaten. Fatigue and weakness in the legs are the most immediate and common symptoms, followed by swollen feet, tightness of the chest, constant hunger, aching eyes, migraine, insomnia, random body pains, nervousness, and mental distress that can appear as confusion or even a kind of derangement.

In reactive hypoglycemia, victims experience drastic plunges in blood sugar after eating sugary foods. If a hypoglycemic eats sugar between meals, the effects can be devastating. A cup of sugar-sweetened tea, coffee, or soda in midafternoon could lead to severe fatigue, sweaty palms, heart palpitations, dizziness, or light-headedness a few hours later. A hypoglycemic will experience crippling fatigue and severe mental fuzziness, often to the point of falling asleep or actually fainting.

Hypoglycemia usually improves if the individual avoids sugar and other simple carbohydrates and eats more complex carbohydrates such as grains, cereals, and legumes. It also helps to eat five or six smaller meals instead of two or three big ones. This keeps your blood sugar on a more even keel, rather than dipping and rising dramatically. Finally, hypoglycemics should avoid alcohol, coffee, and cigarettes.

Few people have true clinical hypoglycemia. However, it is a bona fide disease, one that seems to affect more blacks than whites.

Diagnosing Hypoglycemia

Many people have mild symptoms of hypoglycemia when they go without eating for several hours and then eat something especially sweet. But that doesn't make them hypoglycemic. How can you find out whether you're a true hypoglycemic? If you frequently have any of the symptoms associated with hypoglycemia, you should ask your doctor to check you out.

The diagnosis requires a laboratory test to measure the amount of glucose in your blood. There are two ways to perform this test, either early in the morning after you have fasted for twelve to fourteen hours, or exactly two hours after you have eaten. It is also possible to measure glucose randomly.

Another test is called a glucose-tolerance test, which measures your body's response to a highly concentrated large dose of sugar.

In this test, a special glucose beverage (with a measured quantity of glucose) is given to you and your blood is drawn several times during the next five to six hours to determine sugar levels. This test is usually used only if the standard glucose test is inconclusive or borderline.

If your blood contains less than the normal amount of glucose (below 60 mg/dl) it may mean hypoglycemia. Greater than normal amounts may be caused by diabetes (above 160–180mg/dl). If low blood sugar is a problem, you may be able to monitor your blood sugar using a home testing kit prescribed by your doctor.

SUGAR SUBSTITUTES

Sugar substitutes are either nutritive or nonnutritive. Nutritive sweeteners are as sweet as sugar and have at least 2 percent of the calories of table sugar. The FDA allows "sugarless" gums and products for diabetics to be sweetened with sorbitol, manitol, or xylitol, sugar alcohols containing the same number of calories as table sugar but that are more slowly absorbed by the body. Products sweetened with sorbitol often contain more fat to dissolve the sorbitol. That means "sugarless" products can be equal to or even higher in calories than regular versions.

Nonnutritive substitutes have few or no calories and cannot be converted by your body to energy or fat. Nonnutritive sweeteners include Aspartame (Nutrasweet, Equal), saccharin (Sweet'n Low, Sugar Twin) and acesulfame k (Sunette). Nonnutritive additives are commonplace in diet sodas, chewing gums, and such desserts as gelatin and pudding.

It's an odd fact that the national consumption of sugar substitutes continues to rise while our consumption of sugar itself remains steady. Many nutritionists, myself included, believe that sugar substitutes cause an even greater craving for very sweet foods.

Artificial sweeteners may actually stimulate the appetite by suppressing the brain's satiety response. Instead of feeling satisfied after you eat something sweet, you feel hungrier and crave even more sweets. Studies seem to indicate that people using these sweeteners gain rather than lose weight. I've seen it happen in my own practice. I once had an overweight client who drank a six-pack of diet soda every day. When I convinced her to stop drinking diet soda, she lost weight. Why? I believe the diet soda increased her cravings for sugar-rich carbohydrates—cookies, cakes, pies, and bread. When she eliminated the diet sodas and allowed herself occasional sweet treats, her cravings stopped. As a result, she consumed fewer calories, and lost weight more easily.

ARE ARTIFICIAL SWEETENERS SAFE?

The Center for Science in the Public Interest (CSPI) feels that unless you have diabetes or hypoglycemia, ordinary sugar is better than artificial sweeteners. However, another consumer group, the American Council on Science and Health (ACSH), deems all sweeteners, sugar included, harmless unless consumed in excess.

The American Medical Association also considers artificial sweeteners safe, although there have been cancer scares. Saccharin was nearly banned in 1969 because lab animals given large doses developed bladder tumors. Congress overrode the ban in 1977 and saccharin is used in foods at levels considered to be safe. Cyclamates remain banned.

Some people—about one in fifteen thousand—have a disease called phenylketonuria (PKU), which is adversely affected by the amino acid phenylalanine in Aspartame. Some research suggests that in developing fetuses and infants, too much phenylalanine can impair brian function. Additional adverse side effects, such as headaches and rashes, have been found to occur in some sensitive individuals. Other possible side effects for adults include allergic reactions, mood changes, and irritability. However, a 1984 report from the Centers for Disease Control and Prevention evaluated consumer complaints about Aspartame and concluded that allergic reactions were low and human consumption safe. Nevertheless, the FDA does require that products containing Aspartame carry warning labels about the presence of phenylalanine.

According to the American Dietetic Association, a moderate, safe level of Aspartame for a person weighing at least 130 pounds is eighteen packets a day, the amount found in three cans of diet soda. In general, parents are advised not to let children use artificial sweeteners.

(If you have diabetes, see Chapter 24 for more information about sugar substitutes in your diet.)

SUGAR ADDICTIONS

There is no scientific evidence that sugar is addictive. You don't have to keep increasing your sugar intake over time to satisfy a craving, nor do you suffer withdrawal side effects when you stop eating it. However, it is true that people often become passionate about foods they particularly like—whether chocolate cake or popcorn—so in a sense there may be psychological pleasure addiction. Food passions seem to occur most often with regard to carbohydrates.

Dr. Judith Wurthman has done several studies showing that sweets and starches increase the release of serotonin, a brain chemical that causes a calm, relaxed feeling and decreases our sensitivity to pain. Thus, a desire for carbohydrate-rich snacks seems linked to a physiological need to increase serotonin levels. This desire can't be satisfied by other foods. But it can be satisfied by eating complex carbohydrates rather than simple sugars. In other words, brown rice can be as satisfying as a candy bar—even better, because the good effect lasts longer.

So, if you seem to be hooked on foods that provide energy and a feel-good high, give your body what it really wants: complex carbohydrates. The glucose you get will be accompanied by fiber and important vitamins and minerals. African-American diets have always been traditionally high in complex carbohydrates, beans, legumes, rice, and other grains. Because of the link to serotonin, these also tend to be calming foods. In the next chapter, we'll see what healthful foods we can *add* to our regimen.

14

FOODS THAT FIGHT DISEASE

Lest you feel this program is all about cutting back, it's time to look at the countless terrific foods in the form of complex carbohydrates that you can *add* to your daily diet. There are many more positive foods to add to your diet than you will ever have to take away. And here, African Americans have a distinct advantage because many of our best-loved traditional foods—greens, rice, beans, corn bread, and black-eyed peas—are good for us, as long as they are prepared in a healthful way. *Retrieving our traditional foods from the past is a major part of the Sankofa Program.*

COMPLEX CARBOHYDRATES

Vegetables and fruits, whole grains and cereals are all complex carbohydrates, providing protein and lots of B vitamins. They're virtually fat-free and very high in fiber. Complex carbohydrates can and should be eaten together to form the centerpiece of every meal. The Sankofa Program uses a wide variety of complex carbohydrates daily to add color and variety to recipes and to help keep you feeling full and satisfied.

Complex carbohydrates have two important disease-fighting properties. The first is fiber, the second, antioxidant vitamins and minerals.

FIBER

Although fiber itself has little nutritional value, it has a miraculous effect on the digestive tract. Here are a few of its best-known benefits: High-fiber foods help control weight, reduce blood cholesterol, and avert, or at least soften the severity of, diabetes. Fiber relieves constipation and also stops diarrhea. Fiber helps to relieve hemorrhoids and prevent diverticulosis. Fiber provides some protection against the formation of gallstones and helps prevent colon cancer. Fiber can also help heal and prevent ulcers.

In Africa, where high-fiber foods are a dietary mainstay, people rarely suffer from such illnesses, nor do they suffer much from appendicitis, varicose veins, or hernias, ailments common to Westerners of all races.

The benefits of fiber in the African diet were first brought to light in the 1950s by Dr. Denis P. Burkitt, a British physician who went to live and work in Kenya in 1946 and remained there for more than twenty years. Dr. Burkitt traveled tens of thousands of miles and plotted detailed maps that pointed to vast differences in the kinds of diseases affecting poor Africans and the affluent Western world. He observed that low-fiber diets in his own country seemed to be associated with an increased incidence of many diseases, particularly appendicitis, colon cancer, diverticulosis, and hiatal hernia. These ailments were almost unknown in Africa, where people consumed large quantities of natural fiber in the form of whole grains, seeds, and nuts. Dr. Burkitt was convinced that this high-fiber diet protected people against illness—because it resulted in a bulky stool that was rapidly eliminated from the digestive tract.

In the 1970s, Dr. Burkitt and his colleague Dr. Hugh Trowell expounded the dietary-fiber hypothesis in scientific journals and several books. Additional research done by many different scientists supported their contention and confirmed the role of a high-fiber diet in maintaining good health.

In another unusual animal study, rats were fed small amounts of three potentially harmful food additives. When they ate one additive at a time, they remained healthy. When they ate two additives together, the animals experienced hair loss, scruffy fur, diarrhea, and poor weight gain. When they ate three food additives all at once, all the rats died within two weeks. Yet when a control group of animals ate all three additives *plus* a high-fiber diet, all survived unharmed.

Today, the role of fiber in preventing illness and disease is fully acknowledged. A diet high in fiber is now recommended by the National Cancer Institute, the Food and Nutrition Board, the National Academy of Sciences, and the USDA.

What Is Fiber?

Fiber is plant-cell material that's only partially broken down during digestion. When we eat high-fiber foods such as whole-grain breads, cereal, or brown rice, the small intestine absorbs the nutrients from the food, then passes the bulky fiber only. In the large intestine, the fiber absorbs water and ultimately is expelled. This process protects health in several ways.

First, high-fiber foods tend to be chewy, which means it usually takes longer to eat them, giving the stomach more time to signal the brain that it's full.

Since high-fiber foods make you feel full longer, they satisfy your comfort zone. At the same time, high-fiber foods tend to be low in calories, which allows you to eat a lot without worrying about one of our biggest health pitfalls—weight gain. These facts —fullness, satisfaction, and low calories—are enough to make high-fiber foods the preferred choice for all African Americans. But there's more.

As high-fiber foods pass through the bowel, they absorb toxins and carry them out of the body. And because waste passes through the colon so rapidly, cancer-causing agents do not have time to form.

By contrast, low-fiber foods such as meat and white bread pass through the bowel slowly, allowing more time for carcinogens present in stool to come in contact with the colon wall (one reason that colon cancer is associated with low-fiber diets). The sluggish movement also causes diverticulosis, a condition that affects about 30 percent of all Americans over the age of sixty. (Diverticula are little pouches inside the colon. Most of the time, they cause no discomfort, but if they become infected or perforated, they can cause bleeding and pain—all conditions associated with low-fiber diets.)

What Kind of Fiber?

There are two main categories of fiber: water-insoluble and water-soluble. Both are found together in the same foods, although the ratio varies. Each kind of fiber has different health benefits.

Insoluble fiber, such as the tough outer husk of brown rice or whole wheat, absorbs water, bulks up, and speeds wastes through your system, acting as a natural laxative and lessening the risk of colon cancer. It also prevents diverticulitis and helps relieve irritable bowel syndrome and hemorrhoids. Some insoluble fibers also decrease the amount of bile acids in the stomach, which makes it an ideal treatment for ulcers. Insoluble fiber also helps control weight because it makes you feel full.

Soluble fiber dissolves in water. Its greatest benefit is to help decrease cholesterol levels by washing bile acids from the intestinal tract, a boon in preventing heart disease.

Soluble fiber also slows down food transit from the stomach to the small intestine, helping to control appetite. Soluble fiber helps regulate blood-sugar levels by slowing absorption of carbohydrates into the blood, which helps protect against both hypoglycemia and diabetes.

Insoluble	*Soluble Fibers*
Wheat bran	*Oat bran*
Corn bran	*Whole oats*
Rice bran	*Dried beans*
Whole grains	*Chick-peas, black-eyed peas*
Dried beans and peas	*Lentils*
Popcorn	*Sesame seeds*
Seeds and nuts	*Fruits and vegetables, especially*
Most fruit and vegetables, especially	*citrus, apples, pears, sweet*
carrots, white potatoes, sweet	*potatoes, carrots, okra, cauliflower,*
potatoes, artichokes, broccoli,	*corn*
leeks, parsnips	

About Bran

Bran, the outer shell of wheat, oats, rice, and other whole grains, can be separated from foods and purchased separately. But when your diet emphasizes fiber-rich foods, you don't need to consume concentrated straight bran. Cooked oat-bran cereal is fine if you like it, but a bowl of oatmeal is just as good. If you wish, however, you may add small quantities of straight bran to your own recipes.

If you do, remember that soluble bran (such as oat bran) seems to work best when it's cooked. Insoluble bran (such as wheat bran) can be used either cooked or uncooked. Coarsely ground wheat bran also appears to work better than finely ground bran, though chemically the two are identical.

Add Fiber Gradually

When you start adding high-fiber foods to your diet, do it a little bit at a time. The best way is to try a variety of foods. If you find that one kind of high-fiber food makes you feel bloated, switch to another. For example, if beans make you gassy, eat oatmeal instead, or more fruit and vegetables. (Note: you can reduce the gas-forming property of beans by using the "quick soak" method of preparation. See page 162).

It's important to drink plenty of water when you increase your fiber intake so you won't become constipated. Older people, especially, should add fiber slowly, because their bowels may have slowed down. Too much too soon could create a blockage. Always add fiber over the course of a day, not all at once.

Grains

Choose white, rye, pumpernickel, and wheat breads, low-fat crackers, hot and cold cereals made without extra sugar, and rice. Potatoes are another terrific choice. A three-ounce potato has just one hundred calories, and provides protein, vitamins B$_6$ and C, iron, iodine, calcium, zinc, copper, magnesium, folacin, niacin, and phosphorus.

Market shelves are bursting with variously priced new grains—new to us, although our ancestors grew them hundreds of years ago. Quinoa and amaranth are two of the new/old arrivals. There's also been a resurgence in popularity of standards such as barley, kasha, buckwheat, and millet. Oats have been good food since time began—long before the oat-bran excitement—providing seven B vitamins, protein, vitamin E, iron, calcium, and fiber.

And there's no question that oat bran reduces blood cholesterol. Research shows that three to four pure oat bran muffins per day produce significant reductions in cholesterol without the side effects of medications. That sounds like a lot of muffins, but they're small, delicious, and easy to eat.

Storing Grains. Store flours and crackers at room temperature unless it's very hot. Cereals should be kept in dark, airtight containers at room temperature. Breads made with yeast should be covered by foil or plastic and stored in a cool, dry place, unless it's very hot, when they should be refrigerated.

About Excessive Gas

Suddenly eating large quantities of grains and bran can cause gas. Many people also believe that beans and cruciferous vegetables such as cabbage cause gas and flatulence. The answer is to add these foods to your diet in small quantities. *Begin gradually, several times a week, and build to several times a day.*

You can reduce the gas production of beans by using the quicksoak method: Bring the dried beans to a boil for two minutes, then turn off the heat and let them stand for one hour. Drain the water. Add fresh water, then cook the beans as usual. This method reduces gas production by about 20 percent.

Another way to reduce that gassy feeling is to add yogurt to your diet. "Friendly" bacteria (acidophilus) found in yogurt and other fermented food helps digest gas-forming foods before "unfriendly" bacteria have a chance to multiply.

If you have a particular problem with excessive gas, here are some further steps you can take, recommended by Dr. Steven Peiken, director of Gastrointestinal Nutrition at Jefferson Medical College, Thomas Jefferson University.

- Eat slowly.
- Chew your food well.
- Avoid eating when you feel tense or upset.
- Don't overload your stomach.
- Keep meal sizes moderate.
- Limit fluids with meals.
- Avoid constipation.
- Limit carbonated beverages.
- Exercise.
- Eliminate gum chewing, smoking, sucking on hard candies, drinking through straws or from bottles, and gulping large quantities of fluid: These activities encourage air swallowing, which leads to gas buildup.

ADDING FRUITS AND VEGETABLES

All fruits and vegetables are excellent sources of fiber, as well as vitamins and minerals. Fruits are also a great source of natural sugar if you need an occasional sweet treat.

Cancer-Fighting Vegetables

It's better to eat fruits at the start of a meal rather than at the end to reduce bacteria that grow in the presence of undigested sugar on your teeth. At the start of the meal, an abundance of digestive enzymes are on hand to cope with all the sugars present in the meal. So have a fresh fruit as an appetizer instead of a dessert.

Vegetables are potent sources of a group of vitamins and minerals known as antioxidants: vitamins C, E, and beta carotene. Antioxidants protect healthy cells from damaging molecules known as free radicals, present in our environment—for example, air pollution—and food additives. These unstable molecules travel through the body, oxidizing everything they touch and causing mutations in cells and damage to DNA. The damage leaves the body vulnerable to cancer. Antioxidants sweep up these free radicals and protect cells from damage. They protect mucous linings of the body and are believed to help prevent many kinds of cancers.

These fabulous vitamins and minerals are present in many vegetables and fruits, particularly those known as *carotenoids,* which contain large quantities of beta carotene. Anything yellow, orange, or dark green fills the bill, including broccoli, carrots, pumpkin, mangoes, tomatoes, winter squash, and spinach. The more intense the green or yellow-orange color, the more beta carotene it contains.

The cabbage family of vegetables, called cruciferous, also contains cancer-fighting substances: cabbage, brussels sprouts, broccoli, cauliflower, kale, and turnip greens. Vegetables rich in vitamin C, such as asparagus, sweet potatoes, cabbage (yes, again our fine friend), and red peppers are also potent antioxidants.

All of these vegetables and fruits also contain many other important vitamins and minerals. (For more about disease-fighting vitamins, see Chapter 16.)

Storing Fruits and Vegetables. Store produce in the vegetable crisper of your refrigerator or in unsealed plastic bags in the main part of the refrigerator to retain the maximum amount of vitamins and minerals.

Don't wash produce (except for lettuce and leafy greens) until you're ready to use it, or it may spoil faster. To preserve nutrients, try not to cut up your vegetables and fruits too far in advance of use.

Potatoes lose vitamins when exposed to light and high temperature. Keep them in a moist, dark, cool spot (do *not* store potatoes in the refrigerator, because their starch will turn to sugar).

Fruit will ripen at room temperature; once ripe, they should be refrigerated.

15

WHAT TO DRINK

Most people don't think of water as food, but when it comes to maintaining life, water is just as important as food. In fact, a person can live several weeks without food but only days without water.

Every single cell in the body needs water to maintain itself. Water forms the basis of most bodily fluids, including lymph, blood, and urine. It regulates our internal thermostat and replaces liquid lost through perspiration. Water is critical to digestion and elimination, cleansing and lubricating our systems.

And, believe it or not, water is also the best weapon against water retention, which can cause uncomfortable bloating. Drinking water actually encourages your body to *release* fluids. When you don't drink water, your urinary system shuts down and tries to conserve fluids to protect the body. So don't worry that you'll feel heavy and bloated if you drink more water.

Most weight-loss programs encourage you to drink plenty of water because water fills you up and makes you feel less hungry as you cut down on the amount of foods you eat.

HOW MUCH WATER TO DRINK

Each day, we need to replace two to three quarts of water. We derive a good deal of water from food, especially fruits and vegetables. We also consume large amounts in the form of coffee, tea, soft drinks, milk, and other liquids. *But the best source of water is water.*

Since fiber absorbs considerable amounts of water, it is important to drink plenty of water when following the Sankofa Program. If you consume an average of two thousand calories a day, you should drink six to eight eight-ounce glasses of straight water daily—more if your activity level is high or if you live in a hot climate.

WHAT KIND OF WATER?

Most American tap water is examined by local authorities on a regular basis, but in some areas there are concerns regarding pesticides, industrial waste, sewage, and other toxins getting into the water supply. The problem is that contaminated water may look, taste, and smell normal, so you might not know there's a problem. Obviously, if you suspect any abnormalities in your drinking water, you are advised to contact local health authorities.

CHECKING WATER SAFETY

If you are concerned about your drinking water, contact the Environmental Protection Agency's (EPA) Safe Drinking Water Hotline at 800-426-4791. Their free booklet, "Is Your Drinking Water Safe?" is available by writing to: EPA Office of Drinking Water, WH-550, 401 M Street SW, Washington, D.C. 20460.

Those who draw their water from private wells must take their own precautions against toxins that may seep in from the groundwater. Contact your local or state health department for help and information. If you decide to hire a testing agency, make sure that it's certified by the state or the EPA. Two opinions are better than one, so don't hesitate to get a second opinion.

BOTTLED WATER

Bottled waters come from wells and springs, or they may simply be ordinary tap water that has been processed. If the labels read "spring fresh," "spring type," or "spring pure," rather than "spring water," it's probably tap or well water that has been processed by filtering water through carbon granules or sterilizing by ozonization. Bottled waters aren't necessarily purer than your local water supply, but they may taste better, depending on where you live.

If you don't like the taste of your tap water or are worried about impurities in your municipal water supply, bottled water may be just the ticket. The mineral content of springwater varies depending on where it comes from. A good choice is water taken from a spring located far from industrial pollutants and bottled directly at the site.

Some bottled waters are still. Others are naturally carbonated or given a shot of carbon dioxide to create bubbles. *Naturally sparkling* or *naturally effervescent* means the carbonation comes courtesy of Mother Nature. By contrast, club soda is heavily carbonated processed tap water. Many brands contain sodium. Seltzer is also regular tap water that's been filtered three times and carbonated. It has no salt, preservatives, or sugar.

Most bottled waters lack fluoride, so they do not help protect against tooth decay. (If your children are drinking bottled water instead of fluoridated tap water, let your dentist or pediatrician know so that he or she may recommend a fluoride supplement if necessary.)

Distilled water is regular tap water that has been turned into steam and recondensed, a process that removes chemicals and minerals. Natural springwater is a better choice than distilled water, which lacks naturally occurring minerals.

SOFT DRINKS

Most soft drinks are high in sugar and have no nutritional benefits. Many, especially colas, are also high in caffeine. Given relative body weights, a child drinking a can of regular cola may get the same jolt of caffeine as an adult drinking four cups of coffee. Diet soft drinks contain artificial sweeteners, which may cause problems for some people. Many sodas are also high in phosphorus, which can disrupt the calcium-phosphorus balance in your body and cause calcium loss, a particular problem for African Americans, who tend not to get enough calcium to begin with.

Overall, soft drinks offer no nutritional pluses, and many minuses. Almost any nonalcoholic beverage is a better choice.

COFFEE AND TEA

Millions of Americans start their day with coffee and continue drinking it throughout the day. Currently, Americans drink an average of three to four cups of coffee daily, and somewhat less tea. Coffee and tea contain many different acids—which can cause various problems for some people—and the most well known is caffeine.

CAFFEINE

Caffeine is a drug that mimics the chemical structure of adenosine, a natural tranquilizer that reduces brain-cell activity. Normally, when we're overexcited, adenosine soothes brain cells. Caffeine, its chemical look-alike, fills up the receptor sites in the brain cells and prevents the real adenosine from entering. Without natural tranquilizers, the individual may feel even more wired than before.

Caffeine appears beneficial when used in moderation. When you drink a cup of coffee, your body absorbs the caffeine immediately. The brain is stimulated and blood flow is increased to the heart; the heart muscle is stimulated and pumps more efficiently. This direct effect picks you up when you feel tired. Caffeine also raises the basal metabolic rate so you burn calories faster.

But caffeine becomes ugly when used in excess. All of its beneficial reactions go haywire. Instead of feeling energetic, you feel jittery. Instead of burning calories faster, you feel extremely hungry. Instead of a steadily beating heart, the rhythm of your heart becomes rapid and ragged.

The muscles of the digestive tract and blood vessels relax and the kidneys increase urinary output. Thus, large amounts of caffeine can dehydrate body cells and cause diarrhea.

Caffeine causes problems for people who have digestive difficulties. For example, because caffeine relaxes the sphincter muscle between the stomach and esophagus, stomach acids can freely back up, causing heartburn. By promoting secretions in the stomach, caffeine also aggravates ulcers.

While caffeine by itself is known to cause these problems, new studies suggest that other elements present in coffee and tea may be equally problematic. One well-designed study conducted at Ohio State University showed that both *regular and decaffeinated* coffee can stimulate acid secretion in the stomach, possibly due to the large variety of other acids in coffee, including tannic, acetic, nicotinic, formic, and citric. For this reason, ulcer patients are advised to avoid all forms of coffee. Tea also contains acids, especially tannic acid, that can irritate the digestive tract. Tannins may cause constipation, though their effects can be countered by adding milk to the tea.

Caffeine also exacerbates the symptoms of premenstrual tension in the stomach and esophagus.

If you have a cold or the flu, tea or coffee is a poor choice because the caffeine can raise body temperatures and block the fever-reducing properties of aspirin.

Some people get headaches from caffeine; others find it alleviates the pain. This double-edged effect is because caffeine is both a vasoconstrictor (tightens blood vessels) and a vasodilator (widens blood vessels). For those who suffer migraines—severe, crippling headaches thought to be caused by a sudden rush of blood through vessels around the brain—caffeine is often helpful.

The good news is that caffeine in moderate amounts has been cleared of its most serious health charges:

Cancer. The first wave of research found an association between coffee drinking and cancer, specifically cancer of the bladder and pancreas. The American Cancer Society's current advice tells us that there is no indication that caffeine is a risk factor in human cancer. Nor has caffeine been conclusively found to lead to fibrocystic disease (benign lumps in the breast), as was once believed.

Caffeine and Heart Disease. Studies in the 1970s showed that drinking one to five cups of coffee daily increased a man's chances of developing heart disease by 50 percent; six or more cups raised the ante by 120 percent. However, the studies are inconclusive because the scientists didn't separate out fatty diets, sedentary lifestyle, or cigarette smoking.

In one study, six or more cups of coffee per day was found to increase serum-cholesterol levels. Yet other studies have not found any association.

Oddly enough, decaffeinated coffee may pose a greater heart risk by raising LDL cholesterol. The elevated LDL may be due to the additional oils found in decaffeinated beans or the solvents, such as methylene cholide, that are used in the decaffeinating process.

With or without caffeine, coffee that's boiled or percolated results in an oilier brew; therefore, it's better to filter coffee through paper (drip) to remove cholesterol-raising oils.

Recently, researchers associated with the Framingham Heart Study have said there is no evidence to support a connection between coffee and heart disease.

However, some health issues surrounding caffeine consumption still remain worrisome.

Calcium. Caffeine can contribute to a calcium deficiency because it increases calcium excretion. This may be dangerous for African Americans who already have low quantities of calcium in the diet, especially postmenopausal women who are at risk for osteoporosis. Drinking milk in your coffee will *not* counteract this effect.

Iron. Coffee also interferes with the body's ability to absorb iron. The culprits are polyphenols, chemicals present in coffee that bind iron in the digestive tract and keep it from entering the bloodstream. Since African Americans tend to be iron poor to begin with, that's another good reason to limit caffeine.

Pregnancy. In 1980, the FDA issued a warning, based on animal studies, about caffeine use during pregnancy. In these studies, rats who were force-fed high doses of caffeine gave birth to offspring with birth defects. The FDA subsequently issued a warning about caffeine use during pregnancy based on these results. However, later studies in which rats sipped caffeinated beverages did not show the birth defects.

Few studies have been done on humans. In February of 1993, Dr. James L. Mills, a researcher at the National Institute of Child Health and Human Development, and his colleagues studied 431 pregnant women and found that moderate consumption of caffeine—three or fewer eight-ounce cups of coffee a day, for example—did not increase the risk of miscarriage, retard fetal growth, or reduce head circumference. The FDA has given moderate caffeine intake an okay for pregnant women.

My own feeling is that the Institute's study didn't go far enough. For example, the study does not tell us if there are any long-lasting effects on the baby's brain development. Caffeine is known to have powerful effects on the central nervous system.

This is particularly of concern to black Americans because one of our greatest health problems is the unexplained incidence of low-birth-weight babies and early infant death. The relationship between caffeine and low-birth-weight newborns is uncertain. So while most doctors will advise limiting caffeine intake to two or three cups of coffee during pregnancy, I believe there's good reason for African Americans to take greater precautions. I recommend giving up caffeine even before becoming pregnant, to make sure that a new pregnancy gets off to a good start. If you are already pregnant, give it up now.

Should Everyone Give Up Caffeine?

Most researchers believe that in moderate quantities caffeine poses no problem for most people. The question, of course, is what is moderate? Most experts say that fewer than three eight-ounce cups a day or three hundred milligrams of caffeine is moderate. The problem is you can swiftly develop a tolerance toward caffeine and may not even notice that you're steadily drinking more and more coffee.

A more complicated question is caffeine addiction. As little as two or three cups of coffee daily can produce an addiction. How can you tell if you're addicted? Try going without caffeine (from all sources) for a day and see what happens. If you feel sick to your stomach, headachy, groggy, and generally miserable, you've got a caffeine addiction. Should you break it?

If you're taking in more than five to six hundred milligrams of caffeine each day (from beverages, food, and medications), or if you consume less but feel the symptoms of "coffee nerves," consider cutting down. If you are pregnant or thinking about becoming pregnant, definitely cut down or, even better, eliminate caffeine completely. If your cholesterol is high, you may also wish to reduce caffeine, and also decaf coffee.

Breaking the Caffeine Habit

The way to break a caffeine habit without suffering withdrawal symptoms is to do it gradually. Reduce your coffee, tea, or soda consumption by one or two cups a day for a week at a time until you're totally off caffeine. You may feel a little groggy at first, or you may not experience any withdrawal symptoms at all. Any symptoms you do have will pass quickly. By the way, people who give up caffeine are just as alert and function just as well as those who consume it.

Decaf coffee still contains some caffeine. Although drinking decaf alleviates the most potent effects of caffeine, it can still be a problem for people with delicate stomachs or high levels of cholesterol in their blood. Coffee substitutes (products made from various grains, including barley, rye, and chicory root), should be all right for people with digestive problems. However, excessive consumption of grain-based products may have a laxative effect or cause flatulence.

HERBAL TEAS

In the past few years, we have seen a rise in the popularity of herbal teas. People feel that they are relaxing and comforting, and many contain no caffeine. Herbal teas are an old part of our tradition, and your grandmother or great-grandmother may have been expert in brewing various dried plants and roots. The catch is that herbal teas are not innocuous and some can even be quite toxic. For example, comfrey in large quantities causes liver damage; it has been banned in Canada. Lobelia can induce vomiting. Woodruff, tonka beans, and melitot are all anticoagulants, thinning the blood, not on doctor's orders. Sassafras root has been seen to cause cancer in lab animals and has been banned from all foods.

In other words, you can't brew up just any plant you find growing in the backyard and presume that it is safe to drink. Most of us today don't know much about the chemical properties of herbs and plants, and even if we do, we may have trouble identifying them in the wild.

HOW MUCH CAFFEINE DO YOU CONSUME?
Caffeine content varies considerably depending on the specific product and how it's prepared. For example, five ounces of perked coffee has about eighty milligrams. The same cup of coffee dripolated contains, on average, 115 milligrams of caffeine. Instant coffee has about half the caffeine of regular coffee.

The longer tea brews, the more caffeine the brew will contain. Tea brewed in bags has slightly more caffeine than loose tea, and in general, domestic brands have less caffeine than imported black teas.

Caffeine isn't found only in coffee and tea. Chocolate, cocoa, many soft drinks, and certain common over-the-counter drugs contain large quantities of caffeine. Some samples:

	Milligrams per Five-Ounce Cup (Approximately)
Coffee	
Instant	65
Percolated	80
Drip, automatic	115
Tea	
Brewed, U.S. brands	40
Brewed, imported	60
Cocoa Mix	
1-ounce packet	5
Soft Drinks *(12 ounces)*	
Colas, various	36
Some noncolas	54
Over-the-Counter Drugs *	
Stimulants	150
Weight-loss pills	200
Pain relievers	49
Diuretics	100
Cold remedies	30

* Different brands vary considerably in their caffeine content, and some do not contain any caffeine. Read the labels or ask your pharmacist for more specific information.

As for store-bought herbal teas, the FDA considers them a food, not a drug. Because most manufacturers make no overt health claims, these teas are not supervised or regulated by the government.

If you take a few simple precautions, drinking herbal tea is safe. But unless you are an expert, it's best to stick to products from reputable firms, such as Celestial Seasons or Lipton, which choose common herbs that scientists have studied for years.

The first time you try a new herbal tea, make a weak brew and see how you react. If nothing adverse occurs, experiment with longer steeping times and a stronger brew.

FRUIT AND VEGETABLE JUICES

I admit it, I'm a juicer. Fruit juices are big among African Americans and always have been—maybe because they're sweet; maybe because hot climates made fruit juice a particular pleasure. In any case, fruits and fruit juices of all kinds have been a mainstay of our diet for thousands of years. In Africa, it was the gourdlike baobob with its edible pulp, lemons, watermelon, guava, papaya, and pineapple. Many of the same fruits were grown in the Caribbean and in the American South.

Drinking fruit and vegetable juices is an excellent way to quench your thirst and get good nutritional value at the same time. Juicing, which is currently trendy, is an old practice among nutrition advocates. In her classic volume *Let's Eat Right to Keep Fit,* Adele Davis pointed out that fruit and vegetable juices were a great source of vitamin C. Tomato juice may supply thirty milligrams per six-ounce glass, and fresh strawberries and raw cabbage average thirty to fifty milligrams per serving. Juices are also a great source of many other vitamins and minerals.

Juices contain similar amounts of nutrients as whole fruits and vegetables but require no chewing, which makes them especially good for the elderly or those with dental problems. Juices are also easy to digest and absorb. However, as with whole foods, excessive use of some juices may cause minor reversible reactions in some sensitive individuals. Juices with a high acid content may aggravate arthritis; too much carrot juice may cause the skin to turn slightly yellow from the abundance of beta-carotene in carrots.

If you love juice, consider investing in a juicer. If you don't have the time or the money to juice, buy sugar-free, unfiltered juices in your supermarket or health-food store.

One note of caution: Most juice sold in your local supermarket is pulp-free, meaning that it is minus the valuable fiber that may lower cholesterol and help prevent certain cancers. Some vitamins and minerals contained in fruits and vegetables are also bound to the fiber. So, while you enjoy drinking juices, don't forget to eat plenty of whole fruits and vegetables, too.

16

SUPERVITAMINS

Vitamins are organic substances the body needs but can't make. At the most basic level, vitamins are important in the normal functioning of our bodies.

Vitamins are either water- or fat-soluble. The water-soluble vitamins—C and B complex—must be consumed daily because they are rapidly absorbed and rapidly excreted through sweat and urine. The fat-soluble vitamins—A, E, D, K—can be stored in body fat if they are not used up. For this reason, fat-soluble vitamins can become toxic if you consume too much.

Vitamins also help the body absorb minerals. Minerals are inorganic substances derived from metals and salt found in soil and water. In minute amounts, minerals are essential for vital bodily functions. Those we need in the largest quantity are calcium, phosphorus, and magnesium. Trace minerals, required in smaller amounts, include iron, zinc, iodine, copper, manganese, fluoride, chromium, selenium, molybdenum, arsenic, boron, nickel, and silicon.

The body knows how to maintain its own mineral balances and most people simply excrete anything in excess of their needs. (An important exception for some people is sodium. See Chapter 12.)

People have a lot of misconceptions about vitamins and minerals. For instance, they do not give you energy and pep. Energy comes from the calories we consume in carbohydrates, protein, and fat. Since vitamins and minerals do not contain calories, they cannot provide energy.

Some doctors and nutritionists think that most well-fed Americans get all the vitamins and minerals they need from their everyday diets. Recently, however, vitamin research has taken on a new breath of life as scientists have gathered provocative new evidence that certain vitamins do more than just maintain the body; they may help forestall, or even reverse, many deadly diseases, including cancer, heart disease, osteoporosis, a flagging immune system, and other chronic disorders.

This new information is especially important for African Americans, whose lifetime nutritional status has a profound impact on the development of many chronic diseases.

There are two groups of vitamins we should pay particular attention to: those that may be lacking in our diets and those supervitamins that are now recognized as protective against two major diseases that afflict us more than other groups: cancer and heart disease.

THE VITAMINS WE MAY BE MISSING

For various reasons, many African Americans tend to lack some important vitamins and minerals in their diets, such as vitamin D, calcium, riboflavin, vitamin A, and iron. Other vitamins that are especially important for us are folic acid, vitamin K, and vitamin B_6.

VITAMIN D

This vitamin enables one to absorb and use calcium and phosphorus; thus, it is vital for building a healthy skeletal system. Vitamin D is found in fortified milk and is also produced internally when the body is exposed to sunshine. As we've learned in earlier chapters, heavily pigmented skin does not absorb much vitamin D from sunlight. But we need this valuable vitamin, which may also have a wealth of effects on organs other than bones and teeth.

Researchers are learning that vitamin D seems to act like a potent steroid hormone, igniting wide-scale gene activity in many types of tissue, including cells of the skin, pancreas, parathyroid gland, breast, and ovaries. Vitamin D is thought to be involved in the ability of the body to secrete insulin, which means it may play an important role in preventing diabetes, a disease that afflicts blacks in huge proportions.

A lack of vitamin D can cause irritability, muscle weakness, dental decay, rickets in youngsters, and bone softening in adults.

Vitamin D, which can be produced from ultraviolet rays of the sun through the skin, is the only vitamin that isn't derived solely from the diet. Dark-skinned people living in cold or very cloudy climates may not get enough of the sunshine vitamin, so they should eat foods rich in vitamin D, particularly fortified milk and dairy products. But for those African Americans and others who may be lactose-intolerant, it's important to eat nondairy foods containing vitamin D.

Food Sources. Good sources of vitamin D include margarine, tuna and other cold-water fatty fish such as cod and herring, cod liver oil, and fortified milk. Liver and egg yolks also contain vitamin D, but these foods are recommended only in small amounts on the Sankofa Program, particularly for those trying to lower their cholesterol intake.

Vitamin D is unaffected by storage, processing, or ordinary cooking methods.

CALCIUM

This is the most abundant mineral in the body and 99 percent of it is stored in bones and teeth. The small amount of calcium transported through soft tissues and body fluids ensures proper nerve and muscle function and blood clotting.

Keeping calcium in balance is tricky because the body needs so much and yet the mineral is easily depleted. Overconsumption of alcohol, caffeine, and refined sugars can decrease calcium absorption and contribute to bone loss. So can too much fiber or excessive protein intake.

Women need more calcium just before and during pregnancy and during menopause. Unfortunately, it's too common for women of every color and ethnic background to fail to get enough calcium throughout their lives.

Blacks, along with Asians and many other groups, tend to have low levels of lactase, which is what makes us allergic to milk products. As a result, we're less likely to consume enough dairy products to get our RDA of calcium. But we also have naturally greater bone mass than whites, so our risk of developing osteoporosis is less.

Magnesium is vital to help the body absorb calcium, so eating more magnesium-rich foods, along with calcium-rich foods, can boost calcium absorption. Magnesium is as valuable as calcium for bones and teeth, and it is also important for metabolism, smooth muscle action, and for a healthy nervous system.

Food Sources. Dairy products are excellent sources of calcium. So are canned sardines and salmon eaten with the bones. Tofu is good because it has both calcium and magnesium. In fact, many foods high in calcium are also high in magnesium, including dried beans and peas, kale and other dark green leafy vegetables, meat, nuts, seafood, whole grains, and, of course, milk and cheese. Other magnesium-rich foods include apricots and bananas.

VITAMIN K

Scientists are also finding new roles for an old nutritional acquaintance, vitamin K, which is known for its ability to help blood clot when the body is injured. New research indicates that vitamin K also assists in bone metabolism, apparently influencing the bone's ability to absorb calcium. Although African Americans are believed to have strong, dense bones, as we've seen, we don't get much calcium or vitamin D in our diets. Therefore, vitamin K may be particularly important for us because it seems to help maintain bone mass, especially in the elderly.

Deficiencies are uncommon, except in newborns, although certain diseases may cause shortages. For instance, a vitamin K deficiency may develop in celiac disease and sprue, which affect the absorbing surface of the small intestine. Other diseases that also cause diarrhea—such as ulcerative colitis—may lead to a deficiency. Too little vitamin K may result in excessive bleeding from injuries.

Food Sources. Good sources include beans and green leafy vegetables such as spinach, brussels sprouts and cabbage, cheese, potatoes, cereals, yogurt, kelp, oats, liver, and pork. This vitamin is unstable when exposed to light but stable when exposed to heat and air; little is lost in cooking.

IRON

Benefits. Iron is present in every cell and combines with protein and copper to create hemoglobin, an essential ingredient of blood. Bone marrow needs iron to form hemoglobin, which moves oxygen from the blood to lungs and tissues and helps us resist disease.

Iron is a trace mineral that we need in small amounts, but too much of it can be dangerous. (New studies have linked too much iron buildup in the blood to heart disease.) But it's also hard to obtain adequate iron from diet alone. In the United States, it's still possible to find people with iron-deficiency anemia, partly because the body doesn't fully absorb all of the iron we take in. Most at risk are women before menopause, particularly pregnant women, and anyone who has lost blood through an injury or illness. It's possible to have an iron deficiency without full-blown anemia.

On the other hand, about 10 percent of all African Americans carry a gene for thalassemia, which makes them susceptible to iron overload. This inherited disease is also common among Italians and other people who trace their ancestry to Mediterranean countries. If they take extra iron in the form of supplements, they risk developing a dangerous buildup of iron in the liver, pancreas, and heart.

So the trick is to get enough iron for good health but not so much that it causes problems. If you get your iron from natural foods, there's little danger of getting too much. Iron supplements should be taken only under the advice of a physician.

There are two categories of iron. Heme iron comes from animal products and is easily absorbed by the body. Nonheme iron comes from both vegetables and animal products. If meat and vegetables are eaten at the same time, the absorption of iron from vegetables doubles.

Iron Blockers. Many foods and drugs block or interfere with iron absorption. Blockers include antacids, antibiotics such as tetracycline, ulcer medicines such as Tagamet, and other drugs. Foods such as wheat bran and fiber, soy proteins, calcium phosphate salts, coffee, egg yolks, and tea inhibit the absorption of nonheme iron.

Iron Boosters. Vitamin C, shellfish, poultry, meat, and fish help the body absorb iron. You can also increase iron absorption by cooking acidic foods (tomato-based soups, stews, and sauces) in cast-iron pots.

Food Sources. Good food sources include liver, oysters, heart, lean meats, dandelion greens and other leafy green vegetables, whole grains, molasses, legumes, and dried fruits.

VITAMIN A

Benefits. Vitamin A may help fight infections by protecting mucous membranes and the linings of the digestive tract, kidneys, and bladder. It may also help prevent cancer of the lining of the organs. Vitamin A promotes growth and repair of tissues and maintenance of smooth, blemish-free skin. It's essential for the formulation of the light-sensitive pigments necessary for vision, especially night vision, and the formulation of healthy bones, blood, and teeth.

A lack of vitamin A can result in retarded growth and lowered resistance to infection. Skin dries, shrivels, thickens. Xerophthalmia, an eye disease, may occur. Other local infections are possible. In Third World countries, vitamin A deficiency is still common, most often resulting in childhood blindness. But since the body can store about a year's worth of vitamin A in the liver, deficiencies are rare in the United States.

Vitamin A occurs as retinol, retinoic acid, or retinyl esters. Retinol itself comes from animal sources, usually associated with fat—for instance, fish-liver oils. However, the major source of vitamin A in our diets, and the best way to consume this vitamin, is beta carotene, which comes from plant sources.

Vitamin A itself can be toxic when taken in large amounts, causing headache, nausea, vomiting, blurred vision, and even brain damage, which is why supplements are not recommended. This almost never occurs when vitamin A comes from food. Amounts above five thousand IU for adults should never be consumed. Certain vitamin A–based drugs, like Accutane, are contraindicated for pregnant women.

Food Sources. Good sources of vitamin A are chicken and beef liver, butter, egg yolks, crab, parsley, fortified margarine, red peppers, pink and red grapefruit, cantaloupe, and all yellow, orange, and dark green vegetables such as dandelion greens, carrots, corn, sweet potatoes, pumpkins, and squash.

Vitamin A is not destroyed by ordinary cooking temperatures and doesn't dissolve in cooking water. It will be destroyed by air and sunlight, so store fruits and vegetables in the refrigerator.

VITAMIN B₂—RIBOFLAVIN

Benefits. Riboflavin assists in antioxidation and energy production. It's also important for protein metabolism, healthy eyes, cell respiration, good skin, nails, and hair. It maintains mucous membranes and preserves the nervous system.

A lack of riboflavin results in impaired growth, lassitude and weakness, atrophy of skin, anemia, and cataracts.

Researchers believe that almost everyone gets enough vitamin B_2 in the daily diet, but some studies indicate that African Americans may be short of this particular vitamin. For this reason, I include vitamin B_2 here as one of the vitamins we should pay particular attention to in our diets.

Food Sources. Vitamin B_2 is not found in many foods, but the whole grains recommended in the Sankofa Program provide good amounts. Other food sources that you may wish to include in your diet in *small* amounts are tongue, liver, and other organ meats, brewer's yeast, eggs, and milk if you can tolerate it. Skim milk and egg substitutes contain the same amount of riboflavin as their fattier counterparts.

Riboflavin, like other water-soluble vitamins, is unstable in light. It's not destroyed by the heat in cooking, but it can be lost in the cooking water and by exposure to light if cooking in open pans. *Don't* cook vegetables with baking soda.

VITAMIN B₆

Benefits. It appears to enhance immune response in the elderly and may alleviate some signs of carpal tunnel syndrome, a condition in which the median nerves of the fingers are compressed by the transverse ligaments of the wrist, causing pain, numbness, and the inability to grasp small objects.

Also called pyridoxine, vitamin B_6 regulates nerve-cell activity, maintains good protein, carbohydrate, and fat metabolism, and helps make red blood cells. It also helps us absorb vitamin B_{12} and convert tryptophan—one of a chain of amino acids that form protein—to niacin. Also, vitamin B_6 helps maintain the sodium/potassium balance vital to cell health. Those in danger of not getting enough vitamin B_6 include pregnant women, alcoholics, dieters, nursing moms, and the elderly.

Lack of vitamin B_6 can result in irritated skin around the eyes and mouth, loss of appetite, vomiting, and possibly PMS.

Food Sources. Good sources of vitamin B_6 include kidney beans, sweet potatoes, brown rice, wheat germ, baked potatoes with skin, lentils, bananas, green leafy vegetables, green beans, fish, beef liver, nuts, lean pork, yeast, blackstrap molasses, butter, and eggs.

Vitamin B_6 hasn't been added to most foods labeled "enriched," so it's important to choose whole grains and unrefined grain and cereal products. Save cooking liquids and use them later for soup stocks or stews.

FOLIC ACID

Benefits. Folic acid (folate and folacin) is a key nutrient in blood production and cell growth and maturation. It works with vitamin B_{12} and is necessary for nearly every biochemical reaction within cells. It may help to prevent cervical cancer.

Alcohol consumption, oral contraceptives, and other drugs may interfere with absorption of folic acid.

Many low-income groups are deficient in folic acid. Low folic acid is a particular concern for pregnant women because it has been proved that this vitamin can help prevent devastating birth defects involving the neural tube (spina bifida), which occur very early in fetal development, often even before a woman knows she's pregnant. It's important that all women of childbearing age have an adequate intake of folic acid.

Food Sources. Fortunately, folic acid is available in many *uncooked* fresh vegetables, particularly spinach and other leafy greens. Other good sources are sunflower and pumpkin seeds, chick-peas, and pinto beans.

THE SUPERVITAMINS

The second group of important vitamins are those that fight cancer and heart disease: the antioxidants. (See Cancer-Fighting Vegetables on page 163.)

Researchers have suspected for years that certain antioxidants might help prevent cancer by scavenging free-radical molecules that damage a cell's fragile genetic material.

Free radicals are substances produced by chemical reactions caused by cigarette smoke, pollution, and sometimes even by the normal metabolism in the body. By disarming free radicals, certain vitamins help protect cells from damage.

The antioxidants also protect against heart disease. Apparently, cholesterol is harmless until made rancid by the addition of oxygen. Then it's virtually magnetic, accumulating sticky fat-forming cells into the arteries. The antioxidant vitamins prevent that oxidation process from taking place.

The antioxidants are vitamins E, C, and beta carotene. Each has now been studied separately and together. Dr. Gladys Block, formerly of the National Cancer Institute and now at the University of California at Berkeley, analyzed fifteen studies on the effect of vitamin C on cancer (reported in 1993). Overall, the people who were in the top one-fourth for eating foods rich in vitamin C had only one-half or one-third the rate of cancers of the esophagus and stomach found in those who were in the lowest quarter for vitamin C consumption. This is particularly important for us, because these two cancers are significantly higher among African Americans than other groups.

Other studies have shown a reduced risk for cancer of the pancreas, cervix, lung, and breast when high amounts of all three antioxidants are eaten. Vitamin C, a water-soluble vitamin, and vitamin E, a fat-soluble vitamin, appear to work together to prevent cancer.

Nearly 87,000 nurses at Brigham and Women's Hospital in Boston have been participating in an ongoing health questionnaire for the past decade. Those whose vitamin E intake was in the top 20 percent had a 35 percent lower risk of getting heart disease than those who took less. Similarly, nurses with beta carotene intakes in the top 20 percent were 22 percent less likely to get heart disease. (See Chapter 25.)

Dr. Scott Grundy, director of the Center for Human Nutrition at the University of Texas Southwestern Medical Center in Dallas, led another study in which men and women received about five hundred milligrams of vitamin E daily—roughly ten times the average intake. Blood tests showed that their cholesterol was immune to oxidation. The results from taking vitamin C and beta carotene were less dramatic, but both also hindered oxidation.

VITAMIN C
Benefits. It may reduce the risk of cancer of the mouth, esophagus, and stomach; it may reduce the risk of cataracts; it may protect the lungs against pollutants; it may ease the symptoms of the common cold and promote healing. Higher intake of vitamin C is associated with higher levels of beneficial HDL cholesterol and lower blood pressure.

This antioxidant, also known as ascorbic acid, helps produce collagen, a connective tissue linking cells. It maintains capillaries, cartilage, bones, and teeth, protects vitamins A and E from oxidization, and increases the body's ability to absorb iron.

Vitamin C is one of the most researched vitamins, beginning with Dr. Linus Pauling's studies that focused on this vitamin as a cure for the common cold. Vitamin C is linked with increased athletic performance and improved immune system functions. Smokers need more C, as do those undergoing stress or trauma.

A deficiency of vitamin C can lead to lowered resistance to infections, joint tenderness, susceptibility to gum disease and bleeding gums, anemia, and scurvy.

Food Sources. Good sources are sweet red peppers, broccoli, cantaloupe, cauliflower, parsley, tomatoes, strawberries, raspberries, blackberries, pineapple, watermelon, oranges, grapefruit, and other citrus fruits.

Vitamin C is delicate and easily destroyed if fruits and vegetables are overcooked, overhandled, or oversoaked. Do not prepare C-rich foods with baking soda. Serve immediately. Do not allow frozen vegetables to thaw before cooking.

VITAMIN E

Benefits. It may lower the risk of cardiovascular disease (hardening of the arteries, angina, heart attack, and stroke); it may enhance immune response in the elderly; it may prevent the toxicity of some drugs; it may reduce the risk of cancer.

Vitamin E is actually a group of fat-soluble substances called tocopherols. Vitamin E helps cells respirate so they use less oxygen and have more stamina. It also reduces the oxidation of LDL cholesterol, inhibits blood clotting, strengthens capillary walls, and protects red blood cells from destruction. Vitamin E also assists in resisting oxidation and is useful in preventing scars both internally and externally. This vitamin has been successfully used by gynecologists to prevent unpleasant menopausal symptoms; it's also used to ameliorate symptoms of major skin disorders. And, finally, vitamin E seems to clean out the lungs by some as-yet-unknown process. Since so many African Americans smoke, we need to promote this vitamin.

Food Sources. Good sources of vitamin E are polyunsaturated fats (like vegetable oils), wheat germ and wheat-germ oil, egg yolks, whole grains, dark green leafy vegetables, nuts, and legumes. A lot of vitamin E is lost during the processing, storage, packaging, and freezing of food.

BETA CAROTENE

Benefits. It may lower the risk of cancer of the lung, stomach, and mouth; it may lower the risk of cardiovascular disease. Beta carotene is one of a large group of substances known as carotenoids. The body converts beta carotene to vitamin A as it needs it. But beta carotene is also a potent antioxidant.

Vitamin A is toxic if you take too much, but beta carotene—even in relatively large amounts—doesn't seem to cause any negative reactions. In extreme and very rare cases, some yellowing of the skin may occur with massive beta carotene intake, but even this goes away when you stop consuming so much.

Food Sources. Good sources are spinach, carrots, sweet potatoes, kale, winter squash, broccoli, asparagus, brussels sprouts, cantaloupe, and apricots. The more intense the color, the more beta carotene the food contains.

SELENIUM

Benefits. This mineral is an antioxidant that works with vitamin E to promote immune response, normal growth, and fertility. It may delay oxidization of LDL cholesterol and other fatty acids. Large doses of selenium are toxic; therefore, the proper dose should also be the maximum: fifty micrograms (mcg) and *no* more.

Food Sources. Good sources are brewer's yeast, chicken, seafood, onions, whole-grain breads and cereals, egg yolks, mushrooms, and garlic.

RECOMMENDED DAILY ALLOWANCES

There are some forty essential vitamins and minerals that humans need to maintain health. The Food and Nutrition Board of the National Research Council has established recommended dietary allowances (RDAs) for each of them. RDAs represent levels that the NRC considers adequate to meet the nutritional needs of most healthy men, women, boys, and girls in different age groups. The committee, which is made up of scientists from many specialties, evaluates the current research on nutrition about every five years and revises the RDAs to include any new information about human nutrition.

RDAs either exceed recognized deficiency levels or are based on what's typically consumed by healthy people. They were never meant to account for those times in your life when your needs might be increased because of illness or stress. In fact, many dietitians and physicians think the RDA levels are too low for everyone, based on the needs of Americans today. Personally, I think we need tables that give RDAs for people who are not so healthy and for the times all of us might have increased needs.

The RDAs established by the NRC were developed to guide health-care professionals in working with patients. The RDAs you see on food labels are a different, simplified version, called U.S. recommended daily allowance, or U.S. RDA. Food labels give the highest RDA value for a nutrient for people age four and older; three other less commonly used U.S. RDAs are for infants, children from one to four years of age, and pregnant or breast-feeding women. Not all food labels carry RDAs. Nine nutrients and as many as twelve additional vitamins and minerals may be listed on the U.S. RDA.

SHOULD YOU TAKE VITAMIN PILLS?

The big question for everyone is, Can you get an adequate amount of these important vitamins from the food you eat or do you need to take supplements? Experts come down strongly on one side—and the other side, too. Today, with all the new information about the power of vitamins and minerals to fight disease, the trend seems to be toward supplements of some vitamins and minerals, particularly the antioxidants. Even many scientists who don't believe in supplements think it couldn't hurt to take these as insurance.

In the past, the standard rule among nutritionists has been that we get all the vitamins and minerals we need from food. But, as we've seen, this may not be true for everyone. Blacks may not get enough vitamin D or calcium; people of any color may not get enough vitamins if they are elderly, have a serious illness, smoke or drink, or live in an area where the air is polluted, as many of us do. Even if you ate a nutritionally sound diet every single day, environmental toxins, stress, and habits like smoking and drinking make it almost impossible to meet your nutritional needs. It's particularly difficult to get large quantities of those good antioxidants.

Further, many blacks have low incomes, which in itself may bring about nutritional problems. Although we may not have true vitamin deficiencies, consuming low levels of crucial vitamins over a lifetime makes a big dent in our health, particularly when it comes to such deadly diseases as cancer and heart disease.

I would never recommend supplements in place of a nutritionally sound diet. *But I do recommend them in addition to a quality diet.* Supplements are especially important for people who have poor or irregular eating habits and for people whose health is compromised by specific illness, smoking, alcohol, stress, or poor diet.

I personally take a multivitamin/multimineral supplement which includes the antioxidant vitamins C, E, selenium, and beta carotene every day. I concentrate on iron and calcium because I eat much less red meat today and don't drink milk or dairy products regularly because of lactose intolerance. In addition, I have a tremendously busy travel schedule, which means I occasionally find myself skipping meals. Yet I have high energy and am almost never ill, even with a cold. (As I've said, though, new research on heart disease may indict excess iron in men and postmenopausal women.)

SAFETY

An overdose of vitamins may occur fairly rapidly, though rarely. When toxic reactions do occur, they're usually related to overdoses of single-vitamin supplements.

If you're taking supplements of the antioxidants—vitamins C, E, and beta carotene—you generally do not have to worry about taking too much, even if you take more than the RDA. However, some vitamins at megadoses can cause problems.

A megadose is a dose of a nutrient ten or more times greater than the average adult RDA or U.S. RDA. While small to moderate doses of vitamins and mineral supplements support good health, megadoses can be toxic. The most likely culprits are vitamins A and D, which are fat-soluble vitamins that can accumulate in your body. (Stick to the RDA, which is ten micrograms for young adults, and five for those over age twenty-five.) Vitamin A becomes toxic after long-term daily use above fifty thousand international units. However, when you get your vitamin A by taking beta carotene instead, toxicity is seldom a problem. Too much beta carotene can turn the skin yellowish orange, but skin color returns to normal as soon as you reduce the dosage.

Vitamin E, another fat-soluble vitamin, does not appear to cause problems, even in daily doses forty times higher than the RDA. People who are taking blood thinners (anticoagulants) have to be careful about vitamin E dosage and should talk to their doctors before taking supplements.

All of the water-soluble vitamins—vitamin C and all the B vitamins—are generally safe because excess amounts are promptly excreted in the urine. It's a good idea to take all the B vitamins together in a single supplement to make sure you get a good balance, rather than taking just one or two.

Many people take large doses of vitamin C—two thousand milligrams a day or more—and certainly the RDA of sixty milligrams is way below what most of us consume and need on a daily basis. In a few cases, mainly in people with a blood disease called hemochromatosis, large doses of vitamin C have caused health problems, but generally vitamin C is believed safe. Here's a funny twist on vitamin C: Your body can become adjusted to high doses of vitamin C; if you stop taking the vitamin, or abruptly lower your dose, you can get a rebound reaction and actually begin to have symptoms of scurvy, a sign of extreme deficiency.

Other vitamins and minerals that can be toxic in megadoses are thiamine, pyridoxine, folic acid, calcium, phosphorus, chloride, magnesium, potassium, sodium, iron, copper, zinc, fluorine, manganese, molybdenum, and selenium.

Do You Need Supplements?

Your personal needs are based on several factors: your age, sex, the amount of stress you live with, whether you smoke or drink, how well you eat, and whether you are generally in good health. If you fall into any of these categories, you should be thinking about taking supplements:

- *Women on birth control pills:* B vitamins (thiamine, riboflavin, B_6, B_{12}, folic acid (folacin), and vitamin C
- *Pregnant and breast-feeding women:* all vitamins, especially vitamin D, vitamin E, calcium, iron, and folic acid (See Chapter 28)

- *Heavy smokers:* vitamins C and E
- *Heavy drinkers:* thiamine, niacin, B$_6$, and folic acid (folacin)
- *Users of certain medications:* Antibiotics can destroy healthy bacteria in the intestinal tract and interfere with absorption of vitamin K and several B vitamins
- *People with chronic health conditions:* may be unable to absorb enough vitamins from food. These include people with bile duct blockage; chronic diarrhea; chronic disorders of the stomach and intestines
- *Those who have had a heart attack:* vitamin E under physician's supervision
- *People undergoing surgery:* vitamin C for healing
- *The elderly:* B vitamins, thiamine, and vitamin C
- *People on very low-calorie diets for weight loss:* all vitamins and minerals
- *Vegetarians:* calcium, iron, zinc, vitamin B$_{12}$

Since virtually everyone has different needs, I don't want to tell you exactly which vitamin supplements to take—or how much— unless you're sitting across the table from me and we're talking about your nutrition, your overall health, and your environment. I do think a multivitamin/mineral is good insurance for everyone, and we've built these into the Sankofa Program. The Sankofa Program itself is chock-full of vitamins, minerals, and other nutrients you will be getting from food. Any additional vitamins or minerals you take should be based on your personal needs, and hopefully you will discuss this with a physician or qualified nutritionist. I realize most people don't have their own personal nutritionist, but at least do some research by reading health magazines and assess your own needs before plunging headlong into the health-food store.

BUYING VITAMINS AND MINERALS

If you are overwhelmed by the shelves full of special vitamins and minerals in the supermarket or health-food store, don't worry about it. Most people do just fine with a regular multivitamin with minerals. These usually contain ten to eleven vitamins (A, C, D, E, thiamine, riboflavin, pyridoxine, niacin, and sometimes

B_{12} and folic acid) in amounts close to the RDA. (The level of each vitamin can range from 25 to 100 percent of the RDA.) Minerals might include copper, magnesium, manganese, zinc, calcium, selenium, chromium, biotin, and molybdenum. Unless your doctor or nutritionist specifically recommends it, do not buy a vitamin/mineral supplement that contains iron.

Buying a multivitamin/mineral combination is much cheaper —and just as effective—as buying vitamins and minerals separately. In fact, I think the combined multiple formulas are better because nutrients work together, just as the foods you eat complement one another.

But even multivitamins/minerals can be expensive, depending on the brand you purchase and where you buy it, but there are ways to get around the high cost. Store brands, especially from large chains, are generally identical to the more expensive national brands. There are also some excellent discount vitamin and mineral mail-order catalogs, which ship by UPS. So shop for the best price.

But the vitamins you buy at the supermarket or through the mail are just as good as the ones you buy in the health-food store, so suit yourself. Also, supplements come in various forms—capsules, soft gels, and liquids. Choose the form that's easiest for you to take.

Supplements are regulated as foods, not drugs, so their safety and efficacy do not have to be proven before they go on the market.

Here are a few tips on choosing vitamins and minerals:

1. Don't worry about the word *natural*. *Natural* doesn't mean much when it comes to vitamins, except for vitamin E, which in its natural forms appears to be absorbed better by the body. (To find natural vitamin E, look for "d-alpha-tocopherol," not "dl," as the only type of vitamin E listed on the label.)

2. Look at the expiration date. While manufacturers can choose arbitrary expiration dates, it's best to buy a supplement within nine months of expiration, because it has probably been in the bottle for several years.

3. Keep your vitamins in a cool, dark, dry place, or store them in the refrigerator.
4. Choose a supplement high in beta carotene rather than one high in vitamin A. Beta carotene converts to vitamin A and is the desirable antioxidant. Large quantities of vitamin A can be toxic; beta carotene is safe.
5. Buy vitamin C separately, since multivitamins that contain large quantities of C are usually very expensive.
6. Make sure the multivitamin contains folic acid.
7. Make sure the supplement is free of additives (the label will tell you) and iron-free (unless your doctor specifically advises you otherwise).

17

THE SANKOFA PROGRAM: A
TWENTY-FOUR-WEEK SELF-HELP
NUTRITIONAL AND LIFESTYLE
PLAN FOR GOOD HEALTH

Sankofa is a self-help nutritional program that puts you in the driver's seat. It uses all of the best of our old traditions— healthful whole grains, beans, vegetables, and all the fruits that we love—plus everything new we know about nutrition today— less salt, sugar, and fat.

On the Sankofa Program there are no bad foods and no ulti- matums. I believe the more variety you have in your diet, the better. What we're looking to change—gradually—is the empha- sis. You're going to add fruits and vegetables that help fight dis- ease and also keep you feeling full and satisfied. At the same time, you're going to reduce foods that contribute to heart disease, high blood pressure, cancer, and a host of other problems. You'll be able to do this over a period of twenty-four weeks: no sudden makeovers here that will have you climbing the walls in two weeks. Let's keep it simple.

Basically, it's everything we've discussed in the preceding chap- ters about nutrition, food, vitamins, and exercise—all in the form of a *program for you:* You're getting rid of the excess salt, fat, and sugar in your diet, and adding a whole lot of vegetables and fruits, pasta and rice, potatoes and whole-grain cereal. You're going to make these changes one step at a time: Every four weeks, you'll tackle a different element of the program. At the end of twenty- four weeks, you will have accumulated all the nutritional changes necessary to improve your health profile, plus exercise and vitamins. And you will have adjusted to a new way of eating that you can live with and enjoy—for the rest of your long and healthy life.

GETTING STARTED

If life were perfect, you would begin the Sankofa Program with a thorough physical examination by your doctor. He or she would take your blood pressure, do a blood workup to check your cholesterol and fat levels, do a urinalysis, check your heart, and isolate any health issues that might affect your particular dietary needs. When you got the test results, you would record them in your notebook and would begin from there.

But it's unrealistic to think that each of us is going to get a complete physical workup unless we have financially planned for it or have insurance coverage. If you're young and in generally good health, it would be hard to convince you of the need for one. However, there are two important health markers that it is very important for you to know—your blood pressure and cholesterol level. Fortunately, it's often possible to get baseline measurements for both numbers through screening programs offered by local hospitals and community clinics. Sometimes, a YMCA or health club offers free screenings, or there may be a special health event at a hospital near you. Keep your eyes open for posters and announcements and take advantage of the next program you see advertised.

When you have any health exam or test, make sure you record the results in your diary, along with the date and any recommendation your doctor makes.

If you suffer from diabetes, hypertension, heart disease, obesity, or another chronic disease, the Sankofa Program should be good for you to follow. However, tell your physician or dietitian about the program, particularly if he or she has prescribed a personal diet for you. Chances are that the changes recommended in the Sankofa Program will fit with your doctor's recommendations, but it's good to make sure.

THE FIRST FOUR WEEKS: TAKING STOCK

In the first four weeks of the Sankofa Program, you're simply going to get in touch with your body and your health. Remember the food diary we discussed in Chapter 10? We're going to begin by asking you to keep the diary for the first four weeks. With a record of your eating habits, it will be much easier for you to see where changes can be made. Remember, the diary is just for you.

You should record your vital statistics on page one: height, weight, measurements, blood pressure, and total blood-cholesterol level, including HDL and LDL if you know them.

If you are already following an exercise regimen, write down how much exercise you usually do, what kind, and how often. Also record whether you are now taking any vitamins. For the purposes of these instructions, we'll assume that you're not taking any vitamins and that you aren't paying much attention to drinking water. More probably, like most of us, you're just drinking water or other beverages when you're thirsty.

WEEK ONE

Begin keeping your food diary.

Drink at least one glass of plain water each day, in addition to any other liquids you consume.

Eat at least one fruit or fruit juice and one vegetable or vegetable juice each day.

Start taking a good multivitamin each day that includes the antioxidants, if you haven't been. (See Chapter 16 to learn if you need any other supplements.)

If you are not already exercising, find time to take at least a ten- or fifteen-minute brisk walk sometime during the day (see Chapter 7 for ideas). The walk should be all at once, no time out for window-shopping.

WEEK TWO

Continue your food diary.

Continue drinking one extra glass of water each day (assuming that you are presently drinking fewer than six to eight glasses).

Continue with at least one fruit and one vegetable each day.

Continue your multivitamin.

Continue the fifteen-minute walks.

Switch from white bread to whole-wheat bread. This is a permanent change.

WEEK THREE

Continue your food diary.

Continue your multivitamin.

Eat at least two fruits (or juices) and two vegetables (or juices) each day.

Add one more glass of water each day so that you are now drinking two extra glasses a day.

Extend your walk to twenty minutes each day (all at one time, not two ten-minute walks).

Start reading the ingredients labels on the foods you buy.

Switch from sugary cereals to whole-grain cereals without added sugar or salt. This is a permanent change.

WEEK FOUR

Continue drinking two extra glasses of water each day.

Continue taking your multivitamin each day. This is your baseline vitamin and you will continue taking it through (and beyond) the Sankofa Program. This is a permanent change.

Continue your twenty-minute walk.

Continue getting at least two fruits (or juices) and two vegetables (or juices) a day.

Record the fourth week in your food diary. From now on, you will write in your diary every fourth week to evaluate your progress.

Continue eating more fruits, vegetables, and whole-grain breads and cereals.

Pay attention to your stress levels. When you're feeling restless, angry, or anxious, get out and take your walk—or meditate for ten minutes; write in your journal; phone a friend; clean the house; take a bubble bath; read a book.

WEEKS FIVE THROUGH EIGHT: LOWER FAT AND CHOLESTEROL

The goal for the next four weeks is to reduce fat to no more than 30 percent of your daily caloric intake, the amount recommended by the USDA. I personally believe that 20 to 25 percent is a better goal for most people, both for good health and for weight control. Figuring out percentages is much easier than it sounds; all you have to do is count fat grams (see table on page 199).

Not only do you want to reduce the total amount of fat you eat; you also want to switch over to unsaturated fat, which is better for you.

The second goal for month two is to reduce your cholesterol intake to no more than three hundred milligrams daily, which should happen automatically as fat is reduced.

Here are the four big rules for reducing fat and cholesterol:

- Eat less animal protein.
- Avoid deep-fat frying.
- Use low-fat and nonfat dairy products.
- Shun greasy foods. (Try putting the food on a paper towel or paper bag—you'll be able to see how greasy it is.)

COUNTING FAT GRAMS

We've said you want to reduce your fat intake to between 20 and 30 percent of your daily calories. Also, you want to make sure that most of the fat you do eat is of the unsaturated variety. There are all kinds of mathematical formulas to figure out what 20 to 30 percent is, but the easiest way is simply to count fat grams. All you have to know is the number of calories you want to be eating each day, then follow the table on page 199.

Many food labels list the number of fat grams a product contains in each serving. (If a label doesn't list fat grams, it's probably got too much fat. Don't buy it.)

Ordinary natural foods, such as an egg, have a basic number of fat grams (5). One tablespoon of butter has 11.5 fat grams. One tablespoon of cream has 6. One bagel has 2.5. When you have looked up your everyday foods in a fat-gram counter a few times, you'll get to know them by heart. (You'll also find a quick list of fat grams in common foods discussed in Chapter 11.)

This table makes it simple. Here are the number of fat grams you should consume if you adhere to the 20 to 30 percent formula. (If you want to lose weight, or simply want a better fat-gram profile, go for the lowest number. It's the one I use myself.) Most of these fat grams should come from unsaturated fats, although a small amount can come from saturated fats.

Daily Calories	Total Fat Grams	Saturated Fat Grams (no more than)
1,200	27–40	12–13
1,500	33–50	12–17
1,800	40–60	14–20
2,100	47–70	16–23
2,400	53–80	19–27
2,700	60–90	21–30

When you are completely familiar with the Sankofa Program, you can probably stop counting fat grams, because you're concentrating on natural foods and cooking without much added fat; therefore, your whole diet is automatically low-fat. I pay particular attention to fat grams only when I'm trying to lose a few pounds—and it works for me.

How to Reduce Fat Intake

Lowering fat isn't an all-or-nothing proposition. The 20 to 30 percent figure is for the entire day. Therefore, if you eat an ice cream cone, you can balance it against a dish with much less fat. If you plunge into hot dogs at the ball game or at a major Sunday-afternoon barbecue or eat a wicked dessert, just plan ahead and make sure that the rest of the food you eat that day is low-fat.

Although an occasional serving of a high-fat food won't harm you, strive to cut down across the board. Supermarket shelves are filled with many new low-fat foods and many restaurants are offering low-fat dishes on their menus. Adjusting your cooking methods will also help reduce fats.

FOR YOUR CHILD

Scientists have proven that conditions leading to adult heart disease begin in childhood and are directly tied to a high-fat, low-fiber diet. Before age two, babies need a substantial amount of fat in order to develop. After they reach two, children can begin to follow the same dietary guidelines for fat and cholesterol as adults.

WEEK FIVE

How many glasses of water are you drinking each day? Unless you're already drinking six or eight, add one more now. You should be drinking at least three glasses of water each day now. Continue for the rest of the month.

Continue your multivitamin.

Continue your present level of exercise for the next four weeks.

Continue eating at least two servings a day of fruits and two of vegetables, or their juices.

Continue eating whole-wheat bread and whole-grain cereals.

Begin to experiment with some of the following:

Don't add extra oil, butter, margarine, or mayonnaise to vegetables or breads.

Don't eat any hamburgers, hot dogs, pizza, or french fries, all high in saturated fat.

Don't eat tropical oils.

Don't eat olives, which are 96 percent fat. You might as well be eating butter.

Don't eat processed meats such as bologna, salami, and other cold cuts, and no canned "potted" meats or meat spreads.

Start using soft or liquid margarine made from polyunsaturated fats such as corn, soybean, or canola oil. Diet margarines have fewer calories because they contain water. They are good to use for sautéing and as spreads but cannot be used for frying (you don't want to fry foods, anyway).

Stay away from solid vegetable shortenings and hydrogenated vegetable fats. Instead, start using canola or olive oil, both high in monounsaturated fat.

Begin to stock a low-fat pantry with zesty products such as mustards (for low salt, make it yourself from dry mustard), flavored vinegars, onions, garlic, fresh and dried herbs, lemons and limes, ginger, evaporated skim milk, cooking sprays, and nonfat yogurt.

Remove the skin from poultry *before* cooking.

Trim visible fat from meats (although this does remove about one-half the fat, it doesn't lower cholesterol, which is contained in the marbleized fat in the meat itself).

Scientists at the University of Minnesota successfully lowered the fat in ground meat from 27 percent to 7 percent by cooking it as follows: Brown meat in a nonstick pan (without any additional oil), drain off fat, pour hot water over the meat, and drain again. Ground meat prepared this way doesn't make great hamburgers, but it's fine for chili, spaghetti sauce, and casseroles. The same method works with sausages.

Read labels carefully! Some foods seem to be low-fat foods (like melba toast) but contain large amounts of saturated fat.

Start using a fat-gram counter to check on the everyday foods you eat. A fat-gram counter will give you a quick accounting on everything from a bagel to a glass of milk. In just a few days, you'll know by heart the fat content of the foods you routinely eat.

WEEK SIX

Buy nonstick cookware. This comes in all price ranges. Generally, the coated surfaces of less expensive cookware wear out sooner and the cookware has to be replaced more often—but it still works. You can buy nonstick cookware everywhere, including Walmart, Woolworth's, K mart, and even most big supermarkets. It's important to get started with at least one nonstick skillet and one nonstick three-quart pot. This is an investment that pays off in the long run.

Using nonstick cookware, sauté foods by using cooking sprays, defatted broth, wine, or low-sodium soy sauce. (You have to be a little more patient with these methods: Cover the pans and let food sauté slowly to cook through without burning.)

Eat fish at least once a week or more often (but don't fry it).

Choose low-fat dairy products—if you can tolerate milk. (See Chapter 18 for help about lactose intolerance.) Better still, choose nonfat! Two percent milk gets about 35 percent of its calories from fat. One percent milk gets 23 percent of its calories from fat. Skim milk is still the best bet, with only 5 percent of calories from fat. Look for a new "super skim" milk, which is being marketed in some states: It's a kind of double skim milk, which is thicker than regular skim milk but still nonfat.

Make sauces with evaporated skim milk instead of cream; low-fat or nonfat yogurt instead of sour cream.

Make egg-white-only omelets. (Many restaurants now prepare omelets this way on request.) One whole egg has five fat grams; one egg white has none. If you can't stand the idea of throwing away egg yolks (nobody likes to waste food), you can limit yourself to two whole eggs a week. Egg substitutes, which are made mostly from egg whites (Egg Beaters or Second Nature), also work well in place of whole eggs.

Top baked potatoes with nonfat yogurt instead of butter.

Skinned turkey breast is a good choice because it has less than 5 percent of its calories from fat. But ground turkey or processed turkey lunch meats are not necessarily low in fat. Read the labels.

Roast and bake meat on a rack so the fat drips off into a pan.

Cook fish covered in papillote (paper) or in a cooking bag. This gives it terrific flavor and keeps it moist without extra fat. Bags are available in supermarkets and gourmet shops.

Poach skinless poultry and fish in broth or vegetable juice.

Not all "lite" cheeses are really low-fat. If you need cheese in a recipe, try using *less* of a stronger-flavored cheese.

WEEK SEVEN

Eat beans instead of meat two or three times a week. Half a cup of cooked red beans equals one ounce of lean meat. Beans are a good source of protein *and* soluble fiber.

Choose leaner cuts of meat. For example, lean pork tenderloin gets just 26 percent of its calories from fat.

Choose snack products with three grams of fat or less per one hundred calories.

Snack the low-fat way: Air-popped popcorn without added butter is a terrific choice. So are raw veggies, fresh fruit, angel food cake, nonfat saltines, dried fruit, and rice cakes.

Top muffins with all-fruit jams or a thin smear of honey. Try a new nonfat cream cheese product.

Eat nuts sparingly. Although some nuts are high in unsaturated fats that appear to help lower cholesterol, they are high in total fat and often processed with a lot of sodium. So if you choose a few nuts as a snack (plain walnuts would be a good choice), make sure you cut back an equivalent number of calories in other foods. The exception is chestnuts, which get less than 5 percent of calories from fat.

Substitute unsweetened cocoa powder for chocolate whenever possible. Hot cocoa made with skim milk has less fat than a chocolate bar but just as much flavor.

Steam vegetables.

Eat more tofu, which is high in protein. People are confused about tofu because it gets half of its calories from fat, but the fat it contains is mostly mono- and polyunsaturated fat with no cholesterol. Tofu comes in different consistencies, from silky to solid, so experiment with types in your recipes. Also, tofu has no strong flavor of its own, so you can mix it up with your favorite spices and vegetables and it will pick up the dominant flavor. You can even turn tofu into a milk shake by blending it with fresh fruit and ice. Or use it as you would cheese to give body to a casserole.

WEEK EIGHT

Continue with all of the changes you have made up to now.

Maintain your vitamins.

Maintain or increase your exercise, if you feel ready.

This week, make sure you record your fat grams in your food diary. How are you doing? Is the daily figure no more than 30 percent, with 10 percent or less from saturated fat? If not, review Weeks Five Through Eight (see pages 200–203) and look for additional ways to trim fat from your life.

WEEKS NINE THROUGH TWELVE: REDUCE SALT

The goal by the end of twelve weeks is to reduce your sodium intake to no more than 2,000 to 2,500 milligrams per day, which comes to about 1¼ teaspoons of table salt.

¼ teaspoon salt = 500 milligrams sodium
½ teaspoon salt = 1,000 milligrams sodium
¾ teaspoon salt = 1,500 milligrams sodium
1 teaspoon salt = 2,000 milligrams sodium

How to Reduce Salt Intake

It's not necessary to go cold turkey in stopping salt use, unless your doctor recommends it to control your blood pressure. Most of us can start by cutting down gradually on the amount of salt we use. Our taste for salt is fostered by repeated exposure and we readily learn to tolerate larger and larger amounts. Studies at the University of California at Davis and the University of Minnesota suggest it takes about three months of sodium restriction for one's taste buds to change.

About one-third of the salt we eat occurs naturally in foods. Another third comes from salt-containing ingredients added to foods during processing. The rest is added during cooking or at the table.

The best approach is to cut back gradually over a period of one month, then allow yourself another two months to become completely comfortable with the new low level. Believe me, you will get used to it and a low-salt diet will seem natural to you.

Look at your food diary from month one. Choose several days at random and estimate the amount of sodium you consumed. This includes food prepared with salt or salted at the table, processed foods, as well as the natural sodium found in all foods.

Even if you cannot precisely calculate the amount of sodium, think about how much of what you eat each day contains high levels of sodium. Do you snack on chips frequently? Do you eat predominantly raw foods, like fresh vegetables, or processed foods, like canned vegetables and frozen dinners?

Week Nine

Maintain all of the changes you have made so far.

In addition, add one more glass of water so that you are now drinking four extra glasses of plain water each day.

To your daily walk or other exercise, add twenty minutes of aerobic exercise three times a week.

During this week, start eliminating some salt from your cooking. For now, halve the amount of salt you'd use in recipes. When you use canned foods, rinse them thoroughly to get rid of excess salt used in packaging. Don't add salt to your foods at the table, or do so very sparingly.

If you eat out frequently, try to pick a restaurant offering fresh choices that are low in sodium. If you go to quick-service restaurants, ask the manager for a nutrition reference guide, which gives the amount of sodium in the foods served.

Read labels. Choose products with lower sodium counts per serving. Hidden sodium includes baking powder and baking soda, monosodium glutamate (MSG), and any additive that has the word *sodium* in it. Also, soy sauce, whey solids, and brine have a high sodium content.

WEEK TEN

Remove the saltshaker from the table.

Cut back on salted snacks. Replace them with unsalted roasted sunflower and pumpkin seeds; air-popped popcorn with no added fat or salt; unsalted pretzels; carrot sticks; rice cakes; and so on. Flavor popcorn with chili, garlic, or onion powder instead of salt.

Low-salt vegetable juices add savory flavor to stews and soups.

Prepare homemade soup stock instead of relying on salty store-bought bouillon.

Grated lemon or orange peel adds zest to poultry or meat. Add apple or orange juice to skillet dishes for a rich, savory flavor. Low-sodium soy sauce mixed with orange juice is a terrific poultry marinade. Jelly or marmalade glazes are great basting sauces for pork, lamb, beef, and poultry. For fish, try lemon parsley and tarragon, or white wine.

Avoid prepared mustard, catsup, pickles, and olives, which are all high in sodium.

Buy salt substitutes, herbs, and fresh lemons and limes.

Invest in a good pepper grinder and fresh peppercorns; keep it displayed on the table where the saltshaker used to be.

Avoid over-the-counter drugs that contain sodium, such as antacids, laxatives, cough medicines, and some vitamins. Ask your pharmacist or doctor about substitutes—there are some.

WEEK ELEVEN

How much water are you drinking each day? If it's fewer than six to eight glasses, add another glass now. At this point, you should be drinking at least five glasses of plain water each day.

Start an herb garden on a windowsill, if you can.

Hide the salt container—it's good only for removing stains!

Buy fresh or frozen vegetables, not canned.

Cut back on cheese or purchase low-sodium varieties. Buy unsalted crackers, preferably those that are baked, not fried.

WEEK TWELVE

In your diary, record the total amount of sodium you consume each day. (Use your nutrition counter as a guide.)

You will find that even in nature some things have more sodium than others. For instance, celery is higher in sodium than cucumbers.

If you find your sodium intake is still more than 2,500 milligrams a day, further reduce the salt you add during cooking. If you have cut it in half, cut it in half again.

Collect low-sodium recipes and surprise your family with great-tasting foods.

Eat one or more servings of potassium-rich foods at least four times a week. These include potatoes, bananas, nonfat yogurt, oranges, broccoli, tomatoes, prunes, molasses, cantaloupe, watermelon, and raisins.

At the end of this week, *you will be halfway through the Sankofa Program*. Take a look at your progress:

Through your food diary, you've gotten a handle on your eating habits.

You are drinking at least five glasses of extra water each day.

You are exercising three times a week, plus your daily walk or other activity.

You're taking your vitamins every day.

You're eating fruits, vegetables, and whole grains daily.

You've cut way back on the fat in your diet.

And you've gone a long way toward reducing sodium intake.

There's something worth repeating at this point. You don't have to be perfect. If you've made all of these changes or only some of them, you've got a new way of looking at your health and your nutritional status. In other words, instead of just going along for the ride, letting whatever happens happen, you really have put yourself in the driver's seat and taken control of your own health.

WEEKS THIRTEEN THROUGH SIXTEEN: REDUCE SUGAR AND HIGH-CALORIE FOODS

The goal here is to decrease the amount of sugar in your diet by at least 50 percent. By the end of the next four weeks, you should be getting most of your sugar from natural sources—fruit and vegetables—and almost none from refined sugars. You also want to limit your use of sugar substitutes, since these may cause you to crave sweets.

WEEK THIRTEEN

Maintain all of the changes you've made so far.

If you're not yet drinking six to eight glasses of water each day, add another glass of water. You should now be drinking at least six glasses of water each day.

If you wish to increase your exercise, now is the time. If you are getting twenty minutes of aerobic exercise three times a week, extend the exercise period to forty-five minutes.

Begin this week by eliminating sugary soft drinks and excessive amounts of alcohol from your diet. (A twelve-ounce can of soda contains the equivalent of nine to ten teaspoons of sugar.)

Switch to flavored seltzers or sparkling waters. Make ice cubes from fruity herbal teas and drop them into your water. Try an ounce of orange or grapefruit juice in twelve ounces of water or seltzer. Try to keep your diet soda drinking to a minimum—diet sodas are usually full of caffeine and additives.

When you cook, halve the amount of sugar called for by the recipe.

Experiment with vanilla, unsweetened applesauce, all-fruit spreads, fruit slices or juices, or cinnamon in place of sugar. For example, top your breakfast cereal with fresh fruit; stir unsweetened applesauce into nonfat yogurt; drop a wedge of orange into your iced tea.

You can "frost" a cake with a light dusting of confectioner's sugar instead of high-fat, high-sugar frosting.

Don't use sugar on your cereal.

Do not add sugar to foods at the table.

WEEK FOURTEEN

Eat more fresh fruit. This is natural sugar combined with vitamins, minerals, and fiber! The riper the fruit, the higher its sugar content and the more satisfying to sugar lovers.

If you buy canned or frozen fruit, make sure it's packed in its own juice.

Try freezing whole bananas, with or without the peel; when slightly thawed and blended with a bit of skim milk or fruit juice, they taste like vanilla ice cream.

Frozen grapes taste like tiny round Popsicles. They're great in the summertime.

Cut back on sugary snacks.

Eliminate packaged foods with added sugars from your shopping cart.

Choose whole-grain cereals.

Read package labels carefully. Some foods are labeled dietetic because they contain sweeteners such as mannitol or sorbitol; these are still sugars.

Munch a bagel or low-fat whole-grain muffin instead of sweet, sticky breakfast Danishes and coffee cakes. Or try a toasted English muffin with a teaspoon of all-fruit spread.

WEEK FIFTEEN

When your energy flags, choose a high-carbohydrate snack without sugar. For example, instead of a glazed doughnut, try a rice cake with a thin smear of all-fruit spread. Some people think rice cakes taste like paper towels, but these high-fiber, low-calorie treats come in many different flavors, and some have no fat at all.

Prepare your own air-popped popcorn. Eat unsalted sunflower or pumpkin seeds instead of candy.

Eat smaller, more frequent meals. This will help you to maintain your energy level and also to fight the urge to reach for a candy bar midafternoon.

Include a baked potato or brown rice with your meals. Or finish meals with a small yam instead of a sugary dessert—it's sweet and loaded with beta carotene.

WEEK SIXTEEN

It's time to assess your progress. In your food diary this week, identify foods that you still sweeten with sugar. If your sugar intake still seems too high, can you think of natural alternatives such as whole fruits or juice?

An added reminder: Check your stress level. Your daily walk has probably helped reduce stress, but if you are feeling angry or overloaded, review Chapter 4 and think about incorporating additional stress reduction into your program. Ten minutes of meditation a day can do wonders for your head.

Don't be angry with yourself or disappointed if you fall back sometimes or find you weren't perfect. We all do this, and it isn't necessary to be 100 percent on target for the Sankofa Program to work. Even if you really screwed up one week, all your achievements from previous weeks still count in your favor and are still working for you. Just climb right back on the program and pick it back up.

WEEKS SEVENTEEN THROUGH TWENTY: ADD FOODS THAT FIGHT DISEASE

The goal by the end of the next four weeks is to adjust your diet fully so that your primary foods become high-fiber, high-vitamin grains, fruits, and vegetables.

Your first goal is to make sure you're getting thirty to forty grams of fiber each day.

Your second goal for the month is to be drinking six to eight glasses of water each day.

And your final goal is to bring your exercise routine up to the level you've chosen for yourself. If you have to stop your exercise routine from time to time—perhaps you've been sick or traveling and unable to exercise—just start back in again when you can. If you've been away from your regular routine for more than ten days, you'll have to start in slowly again to work your way back to your usual effort.

How to Increase Fiber Intake

In the previous sixteen weeks, you have already gone a long way toward adding high-fiber foods to your diet. Now you're simply going to ensure that you're eating a lot of fiber-rich foods every day.

You can do this by following these guidelines. Each day you want to eat:

- three to five servings of vegetables
- two to four servings of fruits
- six to eleven servings of whole-grain breads, cereals, rice, or pasta

This isn't as much food as you think, because servings are relatively small. For example:
One serving equals:

1 slice of bread	½ cup of cooked vegetable
½ cup of fruit	1 cup raw leafy vegetable
½ grapefruit	¼ cup dried fruit
¼ cantaloupe	1 piece medium-small fresh
¾ cup of juice	fruit

Week Seventeen

Add one more glass of water a day.

Start keeping track of your fiber intake by reading your nutrition counter.

Add at least one additional serving of unpeeled raw fruit or vegetable to your daily diet.

Keep a fresh fruit at your desk, in your purse, or on top of the kitchen counter for between-meal snacking.

Order an extra vegetable when you go to a restaurant.

In any dish you cook, use twice as many vegetables as usual.

Puree leftover vegetables with chicken stock or nonfat or low-fat buttermilk to make hearty soups.

Eat more main-meal salads filled with a variety of vegetables and rice or beans.

Cut back on meat. Eat animal protein in small portions, or substitute vegetable proteins such as beans.

Eat at least three servings of whole-grain products each day—whole-wheat bread, brown rice, oat bran or other grainy muffin, oatmeal, or any other whole-grain cereal.

For extra fiber, add fresh fruit or a small amount of dried fruit to whole-grain cereals.

WEEK EIGHTEEN

Add another helping of cooked vegetables to your daily diet, as well as another helping of whole grains, potato, or pasta.

Cook by color. By eating foods that are different colors (especially fresh vegetables and fruits), you are virtually guaranteed a variety of vitamins and minerals.

Eat more cornmeal products instead of regular flour products.

Experiment with wild rices, either on their own or mixed with brown rice. Wild rice comes in many flavors, from nutty to sweet, so you'll be less tempted to add butter and salt. Wild rices tend to be expensive, depending on what part of the country you live in, but you can use a small amount combined with plain brown rice for a similar nutlike effect. (Some prepackaged rice products combine wild rice with brown rice.) For more flavor, simmer rices in low-sodium broths.

Fill sandwiches with lettuce, cucumbers, peppers, tomatoes, or sprouts instead of extra meat or cheese.

Top plain pasta with herbed steamed vegetables.

Limit animal proteins to three meals a week. Learn to use meat as a garnish rather than the centerpiece of every meal. Introduce legumes such as lentils, black-eyed peas, black, pinto, kidney, and white beans. If time is short, buy canned beans but rinse them well to remove excess sodium.

WEEK NINETEEN

Go without red meat this week. Instead, eat poultry or fish for your three servings of animal protein.

Add another helping of vegetables and one more of complex carbohydrates to your daily fare.

If you have no time to prepare salads or dice vegetables, many quick-service restaurants and supermarkets offer salad bars or pre-pared bags of raw vegetables. Take advantage of these services.

Snack on vegetable pieces instead of chips.

Take a tip from the North Africans and try couscous, which is semolina, and top it with vegetables.

Eat a steamed or baked potato a day. Thinly sliced potatoes steam quickly for snacks—and steamed yams satisfy a craving for sweets.

For a great snack, try one or two pieces of dried fruit. Keep this to a minimum, however, because dried fruits, with their high sugar concentrations, are high in calories.

WEEK TWENTY

By now, you should be enjoying the tasty addition of a variety of breads and cereals and fruits and vegetables that are excellent sources of dietary fiber. This week, keep your diary and see how you're doing. Compare it with the goals you set for this month. Are you there? If you are, congratulations! Keep up the good work. If you're not, don't worry. Just give yourself more time and stick with the program.

WEEKS TWENTY-ONE THROUGH TWENTY-FOUR: EVALUATE YOUR PROGRESS

This is the fun part! All you have to do is keep on doing what you're doing.

Check how much water you're drinking. If it's between six and eight glasses a day, you're doing fine.

Maintain your vitamin schedule.

And keep up your exercise routine.

Your food diary is probably pretty full. Let's start a new one. Record everything you eat, just as before. Definitely keep track of calorie counts and other nutritional counts such as amounts of fat, salt, and fiber. After two weeks, compare your current food diary with your first month. What a difference!

How do you feel? And how do you look? What are your current measurements? Weight? Blood pressure? Cholesterol?

The Sankofa Program is meant to be a slow process, an "easy does it" program. But it always works, so don't try to be tricky and speed it up. Just follow along over the twenty-four weeks.

18

THE NEW SOUL FOODS

Even before I heard the words *soul food,* I knew the foods my mother prepared fed the soul and lifted the spirit. Her cooking made me feel so good! To say this food is tasty is an understatement. There's simply nothing like collard greens and corn bread, chicken smothered in brown gravy, black-eyed peas, okra, and tomatoes.

Back then, I assumed everybody ate the way we did, until I was old enough to spend the night at a friend's home and had to eat a breakfast of cream of wheat, toast, and eggs. I couldn't imagine breakfast without grits, smoked sausage, and biscuits. Eventually, I came to realize that most of the foods my family enjoyed were more popular in the South than the North, and even there they were not served in many of the homes of my Caucasian and Asian friends.

Most African Americans know what soul food is, no matter where we live or what foods were commonly served in our homes. We know that the spicy yellow mustard potato salad our mothers, grandmothers, and aunts prepared is different from the bland white potato salad served in local restaurants.

The great advantage soul food has is that even when you take out most of the salt, fat, and sugar, it's still fabulous! In fact, I hope you will eat lots of the new soul food, because it contains all of the good things that will help you make the Sankofa Program a part of your life.

Much of our soul-food tradition is southern-born, but some ingredients—as well as our cooking style—go back to Africa.

There, many cultures influenced cookery as people traveled from region to region, carrying with them family recipes and traditions. One thing is certain, African people used a lot of spices in cooking, particularly when meat was scarce or unavailable. Many African dishes were thick and full-bodied. Starches and a variety of vegetables were often the main ingredients of the family meal.

On their long journey to America, slaves managed to smuggle some spices, herbs, and plants into the colonies, possibly odds and ends left over from shipboard provisions, although we can never know how these were saved. Only a few plants survived, so vegetables native to this land were adopted by the Africans and seasoned with a variety of local spices.

The only foods regularly rationed to slaves were fatback, corn, or rice, and sometimes molasses and vegetables. Caribbean slaves had more spices and herbs at their disposal than did American blacks, which accounts for the exotic-tasting island dishes of today.

Creating soul-warming, pleasurable food out of virtually nothing was a significant part of our struggle to survive. Great cooking became an avenue of creativity for a people who were permitted almost no means of self-expression. Even the poorest kitchen was a place where imagination and skill could have free rein. With meager rations, black cooks developed a full-ranging cuisine. Two basic staples—corn and pork—evolved into a style of cooking that has survived for over four hundred years.

Spices and seasoning helped make an otherwise-bland meal tastier. Pork and fat were often accented with hot red peppers, vinegar, and onions to add lots of flavor to foods. Dusting meats in a seasoned flour mixture and frying them in lard covered up the otherwise-mild flavor of chicken and pork. Adding gravy or roux (flour and fat) to meat and vegetable dishes gave the foods more body and also enhanced the flavor. Soul food was inexpensive fare made to taste and smell good and intended to stick to the ribs.

When freed slaves began to leave the South, they took with them their cooking styles. Soul-food recipes are almost never written down—everything is prepared by memory, taste, or how the dish is supposed to look. As in early Africa, recipes are handed down from mother to daughter and enough food is prepared to feed family, friends, and neighbors.

Today, I can still prepare foods the way my mother did, even though in school I learned to follow written recipes and measure ingredients to guarantee the same results each time. The truth is, I still do a pretty good job just by relying on taste, appearance, and the aroma created with "a pinch of this," "more of that," and "maybe I'll add this, too."

Soul food, born in slavery, steeped in the African tradition, has now become a popular cuisine for even the most sophisticated palate. So, what's so wrong with it? Soul food tastes great and reminds us of good times—celebrations, holidays past, friends and family together, security and comfort.

Basically, there's nothing wrong with most of the ingredients themselves. It's what we do with them—how we prepare them and what we add to them—that causes problems. Traditional soul foods have generally been cooked too long and seasoned too much with salt, salt pork, and sugar. Foods such as rice, chicken, fish, red beans, yams, black-eyed peas, cornmeal, and collard greens have great nutritional value. But when we fry instead of bake, boil (too long) instead of steam, and add fatback and molasses, we gain fat and calories and lose nutritional value.

Traditional soul food is no problem if you eat it once in a while. But if fried chicken and gravy, biscuits slathered with butter, and bacon and ham hocks are the foundation of your regular diet, you're in trouble from a health point of view.

But believe me, it's a challenge to persuade African Americans—particularly those living in the South—to change old habits. These people are great cooks! They know how to turn out fabulous meals; they pride themselves on their traditions, reflected in the quality and quantity of food they lay out. They don't want to hear from me how they should change!

But luckily, if you're willing to keep an open mind, you can give your family recipes a make-over. It is possible to reduce the fat, salt, and sugar and still keep the great taste, the satisfaction, and the memories.

If you're a soul-food junkie—and who isn't?—this can be the transformation you need to help you manage your weight, lower cholesterol, and control diabetes and blood pressure. Trust me. If you take advantage of the abundance of spices and herbs available at your supermarket or specialty stores, taste doesn't have to suffer. Our cultural dishes are worth preserving, just as Italian, Mexican, and Asian specialties are in this country. All of these nutritious ethnic cuisines are also being transformed by creative cooks to reflect healthier methods of preparation. We can do the same make-over with African-American-inspired soul foods.

This chapter is designed to help you prepare great-tasting soul food in a healthier manner. I hope it inspires African-American chefs and restaurant owners to modify their dishes while striving to retain flavor and appeal. Black chefs are among the greatest cooks in the world. Wouldn't it be great to see fast-food African-American restaurants that specialize in heart-healthy entrées? They would need a dozen drive-up windows to keep customers satisfied and the soul food coming.

Let's get started on the new soul foods. The following recipes incorporate the principles of the Sankofa Program into everyday cooking. With a little experience, you will be able to adapt your own favorite recipes and even invent new ones.

SPICES AND HERBS

Spices and herbs were an important part of African cooking from the earliest days of trade. The exotic images evoked by such names as Zanzibar, Marrakesh, and Timbuktu arise from their importance as points of exchange for spices. In America, local spices and herbs were quickly incorporated into the new southern black cuisine.

Herbs and spices are important in re-creating your favorite soul-food recipes because they can compensate for using less fat, salt, and sugar. You can freely experiment with various combinations of spices and herbs. Here are some rules of thumb.

Herbs, either fresh or dried, are fragile plant leaves; to retain flavor they are usually added near the end of the cooking time. Add a little at a time, taste the result, and add more to please your own taste.

Spices, on the other hand, are berries or seeds and are much tougher; they are usually added at the beginning of the cooking time, and sometimes they are cooked together in the pan to mellow and blend their flavors before other ingredients are added.

For flavor, it's important to buy top quality. If possible, purchase herbs and spices in a busy shop with high product turnover
so you don't get packages that have been sitting on the shelf for
months. Bulk herbs and spices, which can be bought in many
ethnic stores, are almost always fresher and less expensive than
prepackaged varieties. Buy them in one-half-ounce or one-ounce
portions that you can easily store in your own glass jars with
tight-fitting lids. Write the date of purchase on the label, and plan
to replace them about every six months. Keep your spice jars in a
cool, dark cabinet. (Forget about the shelf above the stove, where
heat quickly destroys their flavor.)

Spices can be expensive, but they go a long way. Keep a ready
supply of both the basics and a few of the more exotic spices:
allspice, cardamom, cinnamon, cloves, coriander, cumin, ginger,
mace, nutmeg, marjoram, oregano, sage, tarragon, and thyme.
And don't forget plenty of garlic, onions, and hot peppers.

The more you experiment with herbs and spices, the easier it
will be for you to reduce fats, salt, and sugar in your cooking. I
hope you will try all of these spices and herbs in your favorite
recipes. Unless fresh herbs are specifically called for, I would
recommend dried herbs, which generally have a more intense
flavor.

GETTING READY TO COOK

There are two ways to reduce fat, calories, sugar, and salt in
your soul-food recipes: first by reducing or substituting for the
high-fat, high-salt, and sugary ingredients, and second by changing the way in which you cook the recipes.

When it comes to reducing cholesterol, fat, and calories, some
cooking methods are clearly better than others. Avoid all techniques that add fat or allow food to cook in its own fat. (Deep-fat
frying and panfrying are two common offenders.) Instead, try
these nutrition-conscious techniques:

Roasting. Always place a rack in the bottom of the roasting pan
so the meat or poultry doesn't sit in its own fat drippings. For
basting, use fat-free liquids such as wine, tomato juice, chicken or
beef broth, lemon or lime juice.

Baking. Poultry, fish, and meats can be baked in covered cookware with a little added fat-free liquid. The moisture from the liquid helps keep foods moist and juicy.

Grilling and Broiling. This is a tasty way to cook fish, meat, chicken, and vegetables. For extra flavor, marinate the food before putting it over the coals or under the broiler.

Braising or Stewing. This method uses a tiny amount of liquid added to meat, chicken, or vegetables. Food can be braised or stewed on top of the stove or in the oven, using a heavy pot with a close-fitting cover.

Poaching. Place fish or boneless chicken breast in a pan of simmering liquid, just enough to cover, on top of the stove. Do not overcook; when the fish or poultry is opaque, it is done.

Sautéing. Recipes that call for sautéing onions, garlic, vegetables, or fish and meats usually use a lot of butter or oil. You can avoid this heavy dose of fat by using nonstick pans, a light coating of vegetable spray, and a moderately high heat that will help keep food from sticking to the pan. If the pan is too dry, you can sauté by adding vermouth, wine, defatted broth, tomato juice, low-sodium soy sauce, fruit juice, or any other nonfat liquid.

Stir-Frying. The Chinese made stir-frying famous, but today everybody does it. This method uses relatively small amounts of oil. Foods are cooked at a high temperature and quickly so nutrients are retained; constant stirring keeps foods from sticking and burning. At high cooking temperatures, less oil is absorbed by food. You can stir-fry in a wok or a large cast-iron skillet. Try this method with various combinations of vegetables, seafood, and meats.

Microwave Cooking. This is a fast and easy cooking method that requires no added fat. Most microwave ovens come with a preparation manual that describes proper cooking containers for this oven (never use metal) and recommends cooking times and techniques for standard foods.

Steaming. Cooking vegetables in a basket over simmering water leaves the natural flavor, color, and nutritional value intact. Try adding herbs to the water or using broth instead of plain water to add even more flavor to the dish. Steamed vegetables should be brightly colored and crisp, never overcooked to the point where their colors begin to fade.

MAKE OVER ANY RECIPE
With only a few changes and additions, you can make a favorite recipe healthier—and even tastier—than before. Here's the basic formula:

• *Switch from high-fat cuts of meat to leaner varieties.*
• *Substitute fresh ground turkey breast or chicken for ground beef.*
• *Cut the usual amount of cooking oil by two-thirds.*
• *Use diet margarine. The softer the margarine, the better.*
• *Reduce the amount of sugar added by 80 percent (or substitute fruit, such as applesauce or a banana, in place of sugar in recipes).*
• *Use diet salad dressings as a marinade for meats and poultry.*
• *Remove the skin from chicken and poultry; you'll save nearly one-half the calories.*

ABOUT MILK INTOLERANCE

Milk intolerance, also called lactose intolerance, is seldom seen in infants or young children; it usually develops as people get older. About 60 to 75 percent of all adult African Americans cannot drink milk or eat dairy products because their bodies do not produce enough *lactase,* the enzyme necessary to digest lactose, a sugar present in all milk products. Milk intolerance is one of the world's most common complaints, one that we share with many other groups around the world.

Symptoms include intestinal gas, diarrhea, and abdominal pain. The symptoms are caused by the milk sugar, lactose, and not the milk itself or its fat content. Skim milk will cause as much trouble as whole milk.

Lactose intolerance is so common among blacks, it's become part of our culture to avoid dairy products. Actually, some experts believe that lactose intolerance is normal and that adults don't need dairy products at all. Pediatrician Dr. Frank Oski, author of *Don't Drink Your Milk,* takes a strong position against humans' drinking milk. Dr. Oski and a number of other physicians feel that cow's milk is intended for calves and human milk for humans. In 1965, a study conducted at Johns Hopkins School of Medicine first observed that 15 percent of all whites and 70 percent of all blacks tested were unable to digest lactose. Since then, surveys of the world's populations have revealed that the majority of people around the world are unable to digest lactose. Sometime between the age of one and a half and four years, individuals gradually lose the lactose activity in their intestines.

The problem is that dairy products are also a major source of calcium. Low calcium is our biggest mineral deficiency and always has been. It's true that people who are lactose-intolerant can usually eat some yogurt, aged cheese, buttermilk, and sour cream because some of the lactose in these fermented dairy products is predigested or broken down. However, with the exception of nonfat yogurt and nonfat buttermilk, these products are very high in fat.

So where does this leave us? There are two approaches. One is to avoid dairy products and concentrate on other foods that are high in calcium (canned sardines and salmon with the bones, tofu, dark green leafy vegetables, dried beans and peas, and whole grains). Second, even if you are extremely lactose-intolerant, there are some special dairy products that give you large amounts of calcium without fat or lactose.

Acidophilus milk is regular milk with active lactobacillus added to it—a culture that makes lactase, which in turn digests lactose. The catch is that acidophilus milk cannot be used in cooking or added to a hot drink, because heat kills the active culture. But it is okay for drinking. Acidophilus milk is not widely available, but if you find it at your health-food store you may want to give it a try. It tastes the same as regular milk.

Lactaid milk is milk that comes with lactase already in it. Therefore, it is heat-stable, meaning that you can cook with it. *You can buy skim or 1 percent low-fat Lactaid milk in your supermarket.* Because it is predigested, this milk tends to stay fresher and taste sweeter than regular milk.

Lactaid milk breaks down only about 70 percent of the lactose in milk, but most people can handle the excess. Some, however, are so lactose-intolerant that they require milk products that are 100 percent lactose-free. For these highly sensitive folks, the lactase enzyme itself—in the form of drops—can be added to milk products.

Adding lactase enzyme drops gives milk a sweet taste, although it actually contains no more sugar or calories than ordinary milk. Lactase enzyme drops are sold under various brand names at your health-food store or pharmacy. Instructions are given on the package label, but you will probably need to use more than the recommended amount to make the milk 100 percent lactose-free. After adding the drops to milk, allow the mixture to sit in the refrigerator for twenty-four hours before using it. You may then use the lactose-free milk for drinking or in any recipe that calls for milk.

An alternative to drops are lactase enzyme tablets, which you swallow whenever you drink ordinary milk, eat cheese, ice cream, or any products or dishes made with dairy products. Tablets also may be purchased over the counter in a drugstore or health-food store.

ADJUSTING LACTOSE IN YOUR DIET

Most people who are lactose-intolerant usually can consume some dairy products. Everyone's capacity is slightly different. To discover your limits, I recommend that you begin by using the drops or tablets with all milk products. Then gradually add small amounts of regular milk products to your diet while watching for symptoms of flatulence, diarrhea, or abdominal cramps. Try using regular milk in your coffee, or experiment with nonfat yogurt. If no symptoms occur, begin to use regular milk products in your recipes. When symptoms appear, back off. You've reached your limit.

RECIPES

I've selected a handful of traditional soul-food dishes and made them over so they contain less saturated fat, cholesterol, salt, and sugar. Feel free to experiment with these recipes in order to satisfy your own particular tastes and needs. If you adhere to the guidelines described above, you can't go wrong.

SOUTHERN OVEN-FRIED CHICKEN

Traditional southern fried chicken is heavily battered, then deep-fried in cooking oil. In this recipe, you bake the chicken instead to achieve the same crisp and crunchy texture as you enjoy from frying.

1 2½- TO 3-POUND CHICKEN (FRYER)

¼ TEASPOON SALT

½ TEASPOON GARLIC POWDER

¼ TEASPOON CURRY POWDER

¼ TEASPOON GROUND CUMIN

¼ TEASPOON PAPRIKA

¼ TEASPOON GROUND RED PEPPER (OPTIONAL)

¼ TEASPOON GROUND BLACK PEPPER

½ CUP ALL-PURPOSE FLOUR

¼ CUP YELLOW CORNMEAL

½ CUP LOW-FAT OR NONFAT BUTTERMILK

1 TABLESPOON LOW-SODIUM WORCESTERSHIRE SAUCE

1 TABLESPOON MUSTARD

NONSTICK BUTTER-FLAVORED VEGETABLE SPRAY

Preheat the oven to 350°F.

Remove the skin and fat from the chicken and discard. Cut the chicken into six or eight serving-size pieces, then debone the breast. (Reserve the wings, back, and bones from the breast to use for stock.)

In a small bowl, combine the next seven ingredients. Mix well and reserve ½ teaspoon of the seasoning mix; sprinkle the remaining seasoning over the chicken and set aside.

In a shallow baking dish, combine the flour, cornmeal, and the reserved seasoning; mix well and set aside.

In a medium bowl, beat together the milk, Worcestershire sauce, and mustard. Add the chicken and coat well, then roll into the flour mixture, covering well. Arrange the chicken pieces on a large baking sheet that has been lightly sprayed with butter-

flavored nonstick vegetable cooking spray. Lightly spray each
piece of chicken with the nonstick vegetable cooking spray; this
keeps the moisture in.

Bake for 30 minutes or until the chicken is golden brown, crisp,
and tender.

> Yield: 4 servings   Fat: 10 grams
>
> Calories: 353 per serving   Sodium: 304 milligrams
>
> Cholesterol: 130 milligrams

BROWN GRAVY

2 CUPS DEFATTED BEEF BROTH

2 TABLESPOONS CORNSTARCH

DASH PEPPER

Save the leftover meat broth and place in the refrigerator for several hours.

Skim the fat from the broth.

Place the defatted broth over low heat, then add 2 tablespoons
of cornstarch and stir until thickened. Season to taste.

> Yield: 2 tablespoons = 1 serving   Fat: 0 grams
>
> Calories: 2 per serving   Sodium: 55 milligrams
>
> Cholesterol: 0 milligrams

CHICKEN 'N' DUMPLINGS

I always remember eating this tender chicken dish with an extra bonus—biscuits. It was a great tummy filler, especially in the winter, and was especially handy for guests or family meals. (It still is—just double or quadruple the recipe to serve more people.) The downfall of this dish was the butter, milk, salt, and flour used for the fabulous sauce. Here it is, made over, with the same great taste and home-cooking memories.

3 POUNDS BONELESS, SKINLESS CHICKEN BREASTS AND THIGHS

1 ONION, SLICED

3 STALKS CELERY, CHOPPED

SALT (OPTIONAL) AND PEPPER (AS DESIRED)

2 BAY LEAVES

12 CUPS WATER

3 CARROTS, PEELED AND SLICED

½ POUND FRESH MUSHROOMS, QUARTERED

1 6-OUNCE PACKAGE FROZEN GREEN PEAS

2 TABLESPOONS FLOUR PLUS ¼ CUP WATER, IF NEEDED

Dumplings

1 CUP FLOUR

2 TEASPOONS BAKING POWDER

¼ TEASPOON SALT

½ CUP SKIM MILK

2 TABLESPOONS CANOLA OR CORN OIL

Place chicken, onion, celery, salt, pepper, bay leaves, and water in a large pot. Heat to boiling. Reduce the heat, cover, and simmer for 1½ hours. Strain the broth and reserve; cut chicken into smaller pieces and add to broth. (If you plan to prepare this dish ahead, the broth can be refrigerated at this point. Skim off fat accumulated at the top before proceeding. If broth has been refrigerated, heat again to boiling.)

Add the carrots to the broth and cook 10 minutes until tender. Add the mushrooms. While the soup is coming to the boil, prepare the dumpling batter. Combine all ingredients and stir until mixed. Add the dumpling batter to the simmering soup by large spoonfuls. Cover, return to boil, reduce heat, and simmer for 15 minutes (do not lift cover).

Add green peas, stirring carefully. If soup needs thickening, combine flour and water to make a smooth paste; quickly stir into broth. Serve in bowls.

Yield: 8 servings   Sodium: Less than 400
Calories: 329 per serving   milligrams (without
Cholesterol: 120 milligrams   additional salt)
Fat: 8.2 grams

SESAME OVEN-FRIED FISH

Catching fresh fish and frying them immediately was something my dad always enjoyed. There was something special about the way that fish smelled and tasted. Small fish, usually perch, were always tastier than large fish fillets. The problem was the huge quantity of oil used to deep-fry the fish. Here's a recipe that brings out the good taste of soul but keeps the fat out. Choose any fish you enjoy or one that's commonly found in the waters where you live.

1 POUND CATFISH OR OTHER FILLETS, FRESH OR FROZEN

¼ CUP SKIM MILK

½ CUP FINE DRY BREAD CRUMBS

¼ CUP YELLOW CORNMEAL

1 TABLESPOON TOASTED SESAME SEEDS

1 TABLESPOON MRS. DASH SEASONING

¼ TEASPOON DRY MUSTARD

Preheat oven to 450°F.

Thaw fish if frozen. Pour milk into a shallow dish. Combine the dry ingredients. Dip fish in milk, coat with the dry breadcrumb mixture. Spray baking pan with nonstick vegetable spray, place fish in pan, and bake until golden brown. Allow 4–6 minutes for each 2-inch thickness of fish.

Yield: *4 servings*   Fat: *4 grams*

Calories: *216 per serving*   Sodium: *114 milligrams*

Cholesterol: *4 milligrams*

ONION-SMOTHERED PORK TENDERLOINS

There have always been questions about including pork in healthful diets. Some religious groups such as Muslims and Seventh-Day Adventists forbid pork. Others worry that pork elevates blood pressure. Still, many African Americans continue to eat pork because of its good taste and traditional place in soul-food cooking. Fresh pork doesn't raise blood pressure, but cured pork products, with their high sodium content, do raise blood pressure in salt-sensitive hypertensives, the kind of high blood pressure that most blacks have.

Caloriewise, lean pork compares favorably with other lean meats. So if you wish to use fresh pork in your recipes, choose lean cuts and trim any visible fat before cooking.

2 PORK TENDERLOINS, ½ POUND EACH

NONSTICK VEGETABLE COOKING SPRAY

2 TEASPONS DIET MARGARINE, MELTED

2 CUPS DICED ONION

1 TEASPOON MRS. DASH SEASONING

¼ TEASPOON SALT

¼ TEASPOON PEPPER

Trim the fat from the tenderloins. Cut a lengthwise slit down the center of each tenderloin about two-thirds of the way through the meat.

Place a rack in a shallow roasting pan and lightly coat the rack with vegetable spray. Place the tenderloins in opposite directions, side by side on the rack.

Coat a large skillet with cooking spray, add the margarine, and place over medium heat until hot. Add the onion and sauté until tender, stirring frequently. Add the seasonings and stir well. Spread the onion mixture evenly over the tenderloins.

Bake at 400°F. for 40 minutes or until done.

Yield: 4 servings   *Fat: 6 grams*

Calories: 210 per serving   *Sodium: 221 milligrams*

Cholesterol: 84 milligrams

BARBECUED-LEMON CHICKEN

Whether you're using an open flame to grill or the oven right in your kitchen, barbecued chicken remains a popular summertime recipe. Top it off with baked beans and potato salad and you have a meal complete and satisfying in its flavors, colors, and textures. This recipe is finger-licking good in the true sense of the word. All cooks boast that they have the best recipe for barbecue sauce, but add this one to your list. It's spicy and tangy.

½ CUP FINELY CHOPPED ONION

2 TABLESPOONS LIGHT BROWN SUGAR

2 TABLESPOONS PREPARED MUSTARD

1 TABLESPOON CHILI POWDER

1 TEASPOON WORCESTERSHIRE SAUCE

1 LARGE CLOVE GARLIC, MINCED

½ CUP REDUCED-CALORIE KETCHUP

½ CUP LEMON JUICE

1 TEASPOON GRATED LEMON RIND

8 6-OUNCE SKINLESS CHICKEN BREAST HALVES OR THIGHS

Preheat the broiler.

Combine the first nine ingredients in a saucepan, stirring well. Bring the sauce to a boil over medium heat. Cover, reduce heat, and simmer for twenty minutes.

Place the chicken on a foil-lined broiler pan (or rack that has been sprayed lightly with vegetable oil spray). Lightly brush the chicken with the sauce mixture, and place under the broiler (or on the outdoor grill) for fifteen minutes. Brush with the barbecue sauce again, turn, and cook for 15 more minutes.

Yield: 8 servings   *Cholesterol: 73 milligrams*

Calories: 239 per serving   *Fat: 5.5 grams*

RED BEANS AND RICE

This is an all-time favorite. It's high in protein and an inexpensive meal that goes a long way in feeding a hungry family, but it's just as enjoyable for a couple who want a change from meat, poultry, and fish. Enjoy this easy recipe. It's pure soul.

1 POUND DRIED RED BEANS

1 POUND TURKEY SAUSAGE, SLICED

¼ CUP CHOPPED BELL PEPPER

¼ CUP CHOPPED ONION

¼ CUP CHOPPED CELERY

¼ TEASPOON GARLIC POWDER

¼ TEASPOON OREGANO

¼ TEASPOON RED PEPPER

¼ TEASPOON BLACK PEPPER

1 BAY LEAF

Place the red beans in a large pot with enough water to cover by two inches; soak overnight or for at least 8 hours. (I always drain and rinse the beans before starting to cook because it reduces the gas beans normally produce. Using the quick-soak method also reduces flatulence. Real soul-food cooks almost never use the quick-soak method, but if your mama says it's okay, it's okay with me.) Bring the dried beans to a rapid boil for 2 to 3 minutes, cover, and remove the pot from the heat and let it stand for about 1 hour. Then drain, rinse, and set aside.

Brown the sausage. Add the vegetables and cook for 2 to 3 minutes.

Stir in the dry seasonings and add all the ingredients to the red beans with 3 quarts of water. Bring to a simmer over medium heat.

Cover and cook for 30 minutes longer, or until beans are tender.

Remove the bay leaf. Serve over steamed brown or white rice. Garnish with sliced scallions and chopped parsley (optional).

HOPPIN' JOHN

Black-eyed peas and rice, just like other beans 'n' rice dishes, provide an excellent high-protein meal. Most people remember that eating Hoppin' John before noon on New Year's Day will ensure good fortune in the coming year. Hoppin' John was a traditional dish in which the beans and rice were cooked together; for this reason, Helen Mendes, author of The African Heritage Cookbook, *believes it may have originated in the West Indies, where beans and rice are always cooked together. The black-eyed pea is one of several pigeon peas brought from Africa that still flourish throughout the Caribbean and the American South. Today, the beans and rice are usually prepared separately.*

There are also various theories about how this dish came to be called Hoppin' John. Some say a certain John came a-hoppin' when his wife took the dish out of the stove; others remember children hopping around the table once before the dish was served; another says that it was named after a lively waiter.

Hoppin' John is a healthful dish almost by definition; in this recipe, its fat and salt profile is improved by substituting low-salt, reduced-fat cooked ham for the usual ham hocks.

½ POUND (1 CUP) DRIED BLACK-EYED PEAS

1½ QUARTS WATER

1 CUP FINELY CHOPPED ONIONS

1 CUP DICED CELERY, LEAVES INCLUDED

2 TABLESPOONS FINELY DICED GREEN BELL PEPPER

3 CLOVES GARLIC, MINCED

1 TEASPOON DRIED OREGANO

¼ TEASPOON HOT SAUCE OR ¼ TEASPOON CAYENNE PEPPER

1 BAY LEAF

½ TEASPOON SALT (OPTIONAL)

½ TEASPOON GROUND RED PEPPER

⅔ CUP DICED EXTRA LEAN (4 PERCENT FAT), LOW-SALT COOKED HAM
  (ABOUT 3 OUNCES)

2 CUPS LONG-GRAIN RICE, BROWN OR WHITE

Place the peas in a large saucepan and add enough water to cover. Soak for 8 hours or overnight. Drain and rinse.

Add the 1½ quarts of water to the peas and place over high heat; bring to a boil.

Reduce the heat to medium and add onions, celery, bell pepper, garlic, oregano, hot sauce, bay leaf, salt, and red pepper.

Cook uncovered for 45 minutes, stirring gently and frequently. If the peas begin to break up, you are cooking too fast. Turn down the heat.

Add the chopped ham and continue cooking for 15 minutes, until peas are tender.

Mash some of the peas with the back of a spoon to thicken the gravy. The gravy should be creamy but the peas intact. Cook the rice separately.

Some people mix the cooked rice right into the black-eyed peas at this point and stir it all together in the pot. I like to serve them separately, putting about one cup of each on every plate. You can also serve the peas alone as a side dish. Do it your way.

> *Yield: 6 1-cup servings of peas*
> *and 6 1-cup servings of rice*
> *Calories: 50 per serving*
> *Cholesterol: 0*
>
> *Fat: about 3 grams*
> *Sodium: 311 milligrams (less*
> *if salt is omitted)*

Note: The fat and salt content will increase if you use regular ham.

MUSTARDY POTATO SALAD

Potato salad is an honorable soul food, and no matter how hard you try, you'll never be able to make it like your mother does. None of us can. There is some disagreement about the best potato salad, but most of my friends agree that it should include chunky cubes of potato, crunchy vegetables, plenty of spices, a little pickle, hard-boiled eggs, and a touch of paprika—all combined in a mayonnaise dressing that makes it creamy. I bet you thought I forgot the mustard. No good potato salad should be without it. Despite all the fancy mustards you can buy, I still like to use the regular garden-variety yellow mustard we all grew up with. Its sharpness is perfect for potato salad. Here's a trimmed-down recipe that still has all the ingredients you remember.

6 MEDIUM POTATOES, COOKED

½ CUP GREEN ONION, CHOPPED

¼ CUP CELERY, CHOPPED

3 MEDIUM PIMIENTOS, CHOPPED

4 HARD-BOILED EGG WHITES (NOT YOLK)

¾ CUP FAT-FREE MAYONNAISE

1 TABLESPOON (OR MORE—TO YOUR LIKING) MUSTARD

¼ TEASPOON SALT (OPTIONAL)

PAPRIKA, PINCH

¼ CUP CHOPPED SWEET PICKLES OR PICKLE RELISH

Peel and cube the potatoes.

Mix the potatoes with the green onion, celery, pimientos, and the cubed egg whites.

Blend the mayonnaise, mustard, and salt.

Toss the vegetables with the sauce. Sprinkle with the paprika.

(Experiment further by using equal amounts of fat-free mayonnaise and fat-free yogurt in place of all mayonnaise.)

Yield: 16 ½-cup servings	Fat: 0
Calories: 96 per serving	Sodium: 143 milligrams
Cholesterol: less than	
1 milligram	

MACARONI AND CHEESE

If potato salad is not on the menu, you can believe macaroni and cheese is! This is a popular dish in all regions of the United States, but its big nutritional drawback is the loads of fat used in the sauce. This recipe does a good job of cutting down on those extras by substituting reduced-fat cheese, diet margarine, and skim milk for the butter and whole cheese usually called for. You still get the rich cheese taste and appeal of an old tradition.

2 TABLESPOONS DIET MARGARINE

1 12-OUNCE PACKAGE SMALL SHELL OR ELBOW PASTA

SALT (OPTIONAL)

PEPPER TO TASTE

1 8-OUNCE PACKAGE REDUCED-FAT CHEDDAR CHEESE, SHREDDED

5 CUPS SKIM MILK

½ CUP WATER

Preheat the oven to 350°F.

Melt the margarine in a two-quart casserole dish. Add the dry pasta, stirring to coat. Add salt and pepper to taste. Sprinkle the pasta with the cheese and pour the milk and water over all. Mix well. Bake for 1 to 1½ hours, until all liquids are absorbed.

Yield: 10 servings
Calories: 239 per serving
Cholesterol: 7 milligrams (will vary according to brand of cheese used)

Fat: 3.4 grams (will vary according to kind of cheese used)
Sodium: depends on sodium content of cheese and amount of salt added

SEASONED GREENS

Who says African Americans don't like vegetables? We love many vegetables, particularly greens. The problem is that we don't eat them often enough. Greens are high in nutritional value and fiber, but we tend to overcook them and season them with fatty, salty chunks of pork and ham. Fresh or frozen greens can be delicious without high-fat and sodium additions. As proof, here's a recipe that's a lighter alternative.

2 BUNCHES (10 OUNCES EACH) OF FRESH TURNIP, COLLARD, OR
    MUSTARD GREENS

NONSTICK VEGETABLE COOKING SPRAY

¼ CUP WATER

½ CUP FINELY CHOPPED ONIONS

½ TEASPOON MINCED GARLIC

⅛ TEASPOON SALT (OPTIONAL)

⅛ TEASPOON GROUND WHITE PEPPER

⅛ TEASPOON GROUND THYME

⅛ TEASPOON DRIED BASIL

In a large saucepan over high heat, bring two quarts of water and the greens to a boil. Boil for 20 minutes or until the greens are tender (yet still bright green).

Remove from heat, drain, and set aside.

Spray a large skillet with nonstick vegetable cooking spray and place over medium heat.

Add the greens, ¼ cup of water, and the onions. Cook for 5 minutes, stirring often.

Stir in all the remaining ingredients. Cook, stirring, for 10 to 15 minutes longer, or until liquid has evaporated. Serve hot.

Note: The water from the greens can be used as a base for vegetable soups or stews.

Yield: 2 servings	*Fat: trace*
Calories: 58 per serving	*Sodium: 182 milligrams*
Cholesterol: 0	

STEWED OKRA AND TOMATOES

Okra is good every which way. It was a staple in Africa, where its sticky sap was used to thicken many kinds of stews. Okra made the journey to America with the first African slaves; it was adapted into many kinds of southern dishes. Okra is just as good sliced and sautéed plain as it is in elaborate gumbos. This simple combination with tomatoes is a classic accompaniment to every kind of meal.

1 TEASPOON DIET MARGARINE OR VEGETABLE OIL

½ CUP CHOPPED GREEN BELL PEPPER

¼ CUP CHOPPED ONION

1 10-OUNCE PACKAGE FROZEN CUT OKRA

1 14½-OUNCE CAN NO-SALT-ADDED WHOLE TOMATOES, DRAINED
   AND CHOPPED

DASH SALT (OPTIONAL)

PEPPER TO TASTE

Heat the oil in a large saucepan over medium heat. Add the bell pepper and onion; sauté 3 minutes or until tender.

Add the okra, tomatoes, salt, and pepper. Lower heat and simmer, covered, about 15 to 20 minutes, until okra is tender.

Yield: 6 ½-cup servings   *Fat: 2 grams*

Calories: 54 per serving   *Sodium: approximately 200*

Cholesterol: 0 milligrams   *milligrams*

BAKED SWEET POTATOES WITH ORANGE

Because sweet potatoes flourished in the warm southern states, they became virtually a staple of black southern cooking. One of our oldest traditions is sweet potatoes with something sweet added—probably a holdover from the days when a dollop of molasses was a rare treat and was added to ordinary foods for a special occasion. For the record, sweet potatoes have yellowish flesh; the larger reddish potatoes are called yams. They are totally interchangeable in recipes.

Because they are both sweet and savory, sweet potatoes are extremely versatile. They can be used as a vegetable, for biscuits and breads, or in puddings and pies.

Sweet potatoes are one of the most healthful foods you can eat, an excellent source of dietary fiber, and high in vitamin A and beta caro-tene, both cancer fighters. Eat them anytime baked just like a regular white potato, straight out of the oven, or dress them up. But keep them healthy by adding spices instead of butter and sugar. Here's a sweet potato recipe that gives you an idea of how to do it.

1 POUND FRESH SWEET POTATOES OR YAMS

NONSTICK VEGETABLE COOKING SPRAY

¼ CUP SUGAR (OR 4 TEASPOONS SWEET'N LOW BROWN SUGAR)

¼ TEASPOON GROUND NUTMEG

¼ TEASPOON GROUND CINNAMON

1 MEDIUM ORANGE, PEELED AND HALVED

Preheat the oven to 425°F.

Scrub and clean the sweet potatoes and bake for 45 minutes to 1 hour, or until tender. Allow them to cool to the touch, then peel and cut into half-inch slices. Reduce the oven to 350°F.

Spray the inside of a nine-by-five-by-three-inch loaf pan with nonstick vegetable cooking spray. Arrange half of the potato slices in the pan, overlapping them slightly.

Combine the sugar (or sugar substitute), nutmeg, and cinna-mon and sprinkle half over the potatoes.

Cut one of the orange halves into thin slices and arrange on top of the potatoes. Follow with another layer of potatoes and sprinkle with the remaining sugar mixture. Squeeze the juice from the remaining orange half over the top of the potatoes and spray with nonstick vegetable cooking spray.

Cover with aluminum foil and bake for 15 minutes. Remove the foil and turn the potatoes in the pan. Cover and bake for an additional 15 minutes.

Cut into squares and serve hot.

Yield: 3 servings	*Fat: 0.3 grams*
Calories: 239 per serving	*Sodium: 16 milligrams*
Cholesterol: 0 milligrams	

PEACH COBBLER

When was the last time you had a piece of scrumptious, sinful peach cobbler? I always enjoyed this dessert when I visited my great-aunt and her extended family. Here's a way to enjoy this old-fashioned southern favorite without the calories and fat.

3 CUPS FRESH PEACHES (PEELED AND SLICED)

¼ CUP WATER

¼ TEASPOON NUTMEG

½ CUP WHOLE-WHEAT FLOUR

1½ TEASPOONS BAKING POWDER

⅓ CUP SUGAR

¼ CUP SKIM MILK

1 TABLESPOON CORN OIL OR CANOLA OIL

3 PACKETS SUGAR SUBSTITUTE

¼ TEASPOON CINNAMON

Preheat the oven to 400°F.

In a saucepan, combine the peaches, water, and nutmeg. Bring to a boil. Keep warm.

In a mixing bowl, combine the flour, baking powder, and sugar. Add the milk and oil; stir until mixture forms a ball. On a floured surface, pat the dough into an 8-inch circle and cut into 8 wedges.

Spoon the hot peach mixture into a 9-inch pie plate and top with cut pastry wedges. Combine the sugar substitute and cinnamon and sprinkle on top of pastry.

Bake for 25 to 30 minutes until pastry is brown.

Yield: 8 servings	*Fat: 3 grams*
Calories: 100 per serving	*Cholesterol: less than*
	1 milligram

RICE PUDDING SUPREME

Before bread pudding became popular in the South, rice—a plentiful grain with a long shelf life—was used to make a delicious dessert. Today, rice pudding is known around the country. The old-time pudding was a high-fat, sugary custard. Here's a made-over version that offers additional fiber, protein, and minerals. It's well worth returning to.

⅓ CUP RAW SHORT-GRAIN BROWN RICE

3¼ CUPS NONFAT MILK

½ CUP INSTANT POWDERED NONFAT MILK

½ CUP FROZEN UNSWEETENED APPLE JUICE CONCENTRATE

2 TEASPOONS PURE VANILLA EXTRACT

4 EGG WHITES, BEATEN UNTIL JUST FOAMY

1 RIPE BANANA, PUREED

⅔ CUP MUSCAT RAISINS, PLUMPED (15 MINUTES IN HOT WATER TO COVER)

1 TEASPOON GROUND CINNAMON

FRESHLY GROUND NUTMEG

1 CUP GRAPE-NUTS CEREAL

Preheat the oven to 350°F.

Cook the rice in 1 cup of boiling water for twenty-five minutes and then set aside. Mix together the nonfat and powdered milk and then scald (heat to just boiling).

Add the apple juice concentrate, vanilla, egg whites, and pureed banana to the milk mixture. Blend well.

Place the rice in a one-quart ovenproof casserole. Add the raisins and cover with the milk mixture.

Sprinkle with the cinnamon, freshly ground nutmeg, and Grape-Nuts.

Place the casserole in a baking dish with one inch of hot water and bake for 45 to 50 minutes. (The pudding is done when a sharp knife inserted into the custard comes out clean.)

Yield: 8 ⅔-cup servings

Calories: 174 per serving

Cholesterol: 1 milligram

Fat: 0.3 grams

Sodium: 56 milligrams

SOULFUL . . . BUT LIGHT CORN BREAD

What else tops off a good plate of soul food? Sometimes we ate corn bread in muffin or stick form, but I enjoyed it best cooked in an iron skillet and sliced while it was still warm and soft. The disadvantages of corn bread are the eggs, whole milk, and fat. Enjoy this lighter version. Because of its low-fat content, this corn bread will dry out if you bake it too long. The trick is to take it out when it's just right and eat it immediately.

¼ CUP CANOLA (OR OTHER VEGETABLE OIL)

1½ CUPS YELLOW CORNMEAL

1½ CUPS WHOLE-WHEAT FLOUR

½ CUP INSTANT POWDERED NONFAT MILK

½ TEASPOON SALT

1½ TABLESPOONS BAKING POWDER

3 TABLESPOONS SUGAR (OPTIONAL)

3 LARGE EGG WHITES

1½ CUPS SKIM MILK

Preheat the oven to 450°F.

Pour 1 tablespoon of the oil into a ten-and-a-half-inch cast-iron skillet or into a nine-by-eleven-inch glass baking dish. Set aside.

In a bowl, mix the cornmeal, flour, powdered milk, salt, baking powder, and sugar. Set aside.

In another bowl, beat the egg whites with a whisk until slightly frothy. Add the milk and the remaining oil and whisk again.

Pour the liquid ingredients into the dry ingredients and mix, but do not overmix (some lumps will remain).

Place the skillet or baking dish in the oven for 3 or 4 minutes to heat the oil. (Don't let it burn.)

Pour the batter into the hot skillet or baking dish. Bake for 20 minutes.

Immediately remove from the pan by turning onto a cutting board. Cut into twelve wedges or squares. Serve immediately.

Yield: 12 servings	*Fat: 5.1 grams*
Calories: 185 per serving	*Sodium: 236 milligrams*
Cholesterol: 0.9 milligrams	

These recipes are just a sample of what you can do to preserve taste and tradition in the soul foods you love. Use the guidelines in this chapter and in Chapter 17 to experiment with your favorite foods. You don't have to have a recipe (most of us don't cook from recipes, anyway). Just get in there and try it out. Invent your own healthy soul food!

Part Four

TACKLING HEALTH CARE

19

TAKING CHARGE OF
OUR HEALTH CARE

As the nation continues to grapple with health-care reform, African Americans are in a vulnerable spot: We are much more likely to need health care and much less likely to receive it.

Lack of access to primary health care remains the biggest barrier to improving our health. There are many reasons why we don't have access, but the most dominant is poverty. Many of us are simply too far outside the health-care system—too far from clinics and too poor or too discouraged to obtain proper care. In the poorest rural areas, just getting to a doctor may be all but impossible. Even those eligible for Medicaid—and many poor people are not—go to crowded public clinics where they must wait for hours, jeopardizing their jobs and often trying to manage small children while they wait. On these erratic visits, they see different doctors each time, which means that diseases that require continuous management and medication—high blood pressure, diabetes, heart disease, the leading causes of death among us—may be poorly treated. Yes, there are records, but even with the best of intentions, records are only records.

But it isn't only the poor who lack medical services. In May of 1990, the Council on Ethical and Judicial Affairs of the American Medical Association acknowledged that a range of studies and statistics showed that even when we can afford medical care, we are less likely than whites to receive the best treatment. When it comes to treating blacks and other minorities, some doctors tend to settle for Band-Aid treatment to relieve immediate symptoms.

In 1986, Dr. Robert J. Blendon, who is affiliated with the Department of Health Policy and Management at Harvard University's School of Public Health, led a study that surveyed 10,130 patients recently released from the hospital. A significant percentage of black patients said their doctors did not ask them about their pain, did not tell them how long it would take for a prescribed medicine to work, did not explain the seriousness of their illness or injury, and did not discuss the findings of their tests and examinations. They also felt they were discharged from the hospital too soon.

The study (reported in the *Journal of the American Medical Association* in January of 1989), also found that many doctors tend to spend more time with their wealthier, more assertive patients, believing that such patients are more likely to respond successfully to treatment.

All of this adds up to a picture of a flagging health-care system that does not begin to meet the needs of the minority black community. Doctors also are frustrated. "How can we help people," they ask, "when they won't change the behavior that makes them sick to begin with?" All health-care professionals know that prevention is the answer to many, and possibly most, medical problems. Yet the bitter irony is that we blacks are also cut out of the loop when it comes to prevention. Improved nutrition, healthy lifestyle changes, and exercise are largely promoted through job benefits or private health clubs available primarily to the middle and upper classes.

Thus, blacks are losing the health-care battle on three fronts: We have the highest rate of sickness, the lowest access to primary health care, and little or no access to prevention programs.

Many medical professionals say we ourselves are to blame: We wait too long to report symptoms, so that treatment is more difficult, sometimes even futile; we don't follow doctors' instructions properly; we are hostile to doctors and other health-care professionals who are trying to help us. Instead of seeing doctors on a regular basis, we mob the emergency rooms at hospitals when symptoms appear, overloading a system designed to care for people with serious emergency medical problems.

A white doctor from Oakland said to me recently, "Black people have so overburdened the emergency rooms in our city that the hospital services are in shambles. People who have acute emergencies can't get help. I don't understand it. They come in the

middle of the night with a cold or a cut finger and just sit there
for hours waiting for treatment."

He gave me a puzzled look, as if he thought there might be
something in our genes that made us behave this way. I couldn't
even feel indignant, because he was right. We *do* go to emergency
rooms for treatment. *Because most of us don't have anyplace else to
get help.* (Blacks are twice as likely as whites to seek care from
hospital emergency rooms and clinics.) And we do wait until the
middle of the night.

My husband has had the same experience in his private practice.
At 1:00 or 2:00 A.M., his phone starts ringing. People have been
nursing an ailment all day long, but only in the middle of the
night do they finally call him. Why? Because by habit most people, especially blacks, are symptom-driven—we don't go to doctors (or hospitals) until the symptom becomes too painful to
tolerate. This usually occurs in the middle of the night because
that's when pain is at its worst. What was bearable in daylight,
when other activities distract us, becomes unbearable at night,
when everything is quiet.

We know we need to change our approach to health care. We
want to change the way we seek medical help and give ourselves
new ways to deal with our doctors and other health-care professionals. We may not be able to change the whole medical system
overnight, but we can go a long way toward changing our own
attitude to care, taking advantage of what is there, however inadequate.

The white doctor who talked about overcrowded emergency
rooms was observing the situation as it exists right now. What
he didn't see was the despair of the people waiting for help. Nor
did he understand that many decades, even centuries, of medical abuse have fostered this attitude—because even when we can
afford the best medical care that money can buy, many of us
are wary of doctors. And there are good reasons for our resistance.

Dr. Mitchell Rice and Dr. Mylon Winn, writing in *The Journal
of the National Medical Association,* the publication of the premier
medical society for black physicians, identified three important
barriers between us and the medical system.

1. *We are reluctant to seek early help because care is provided by nonblacks.* We need more black doctors. Only about 3 percent of all physicians are African Americans. Despite a 1970 pledge by the American Association of Medical Colleges to increase black enrollment to 12 percent within ten years, only 6 percent of medical students today are black. By contrast, 17.7 percent of nurses are black, which is great. But we are overrepresented in other service-oriented health jobs—27.3 percent of all nursing aides, orderlies, and attendants are black. There's a clear pattern —as the pay scale and training requirements go down, the number of blacks in that profession goes up.

2. *Doctors are prejudiced against blacks.* Even when we can afford to go to private doctors, we don't *feel* cared for. We are kept waiting longer for appointments than are whites, especially if we are Medicaid or Medicare patients. We are often treated as if we weren't really there—doctors do not look into our eyes and *talk* to us. This is a recognized failing among doctors with all of their patients, but it is worse with minority patients. All patients, rich or poor, of whatever color, are anxious, even a little frightened, and most people don't know much about medicine. It's important that doctors recognize our anxieties. Prejudice just makes all of this worse.

3. *Doctors refuse to provide services in poor communities.* It's a fact that we see a doctor less often than do whites. Because many private doctors refuse Medicaid patients, and because many people do not even qualify for Medicaid, many blacks are never able to develop a relationship with a primary-care physician of their own. Blacks who live in southern and southwestern states, known to have the least generous Medicaid programs, have even less access to health care.

A HISTORY OF INADEQUATE CARE

Clearly, our problems with the medical profession didn't begin yesterday. Africa supplied 40 to 100 million souls to the slave trade. Less than half survived the journey to this continent. Once here, they were exposed to new diseases such as tuberculosis, syphilis, and measles, which quickly killed 15 to 50 percent of the survivors of the Middle Voyage. The rest were introduced to massive overwork, poor food, poor clothing, poor housing, inadequate sanitation, and overexposure to the elements.

On the cotton plantations, Africans received medical care from white planters, overseers, and physicians who prescribed bloodletting, induced vomiting, and other standard treatments of the day. These purgative treatments had harsh adverse effects on slaves, who were already debilitated by intestinal parasites and poor nutrition.

It's easy to understand how home remedies and self-care became important among slaves as they turned to one another for help. Some slaves developed their own healing arts based on African practices, a combination of spiritualism and herbal medicines. The most gifted healers were usually women who had been given permission by the planters to learn "white medicine" and minister to ailing slaves. Given some leeway, these black nurses experimented with their own home remedies, and many were revered among slaves for their healing abilities. Their recipes for cures circulated secretly through the slave quarters, were whispered from ear to ear, and passed down from parent to child.

Black conjure doctors operated even more secretly. The conjure doctors were said to heal by magic some illnesses that white doctors could not cure; they could also inflict sickness on any person they wished by casting spells. Planters detested the conjure doctors, probably because these healers, who had a long tradition in Africa and the West Indies, could readily influence other blacks.

A separate black system of health care developed in the slave era and operated within the very shadow cast by the white medical world. Meanwhile, medical exploitation of blacks spread beyond the plantation. Africans became a sort of training tool for southern physicians. Doctors thought of the Africans as subhuman carriers of disease, like mosquitoes. They advertised in newspapers for sick or injured slaves on whom they could conduct surgical demonstrations and experiments. Autopsies were never performed on whites in the South; almost all dissections were performed on black corpses. Blacks rightly feared the hospitals, expecting that they would be allowed to die in order to supply cadavers for medical research.

During the eighteenth century, America, following Europe's example, began to form a loose network of almshouses, poorhouses, and pesthouses as asylums for the "unworthy" poor. During this time, several tax-supported hospitals were established for blacks, both slave and free. Noteworthy were L'Hôpital des Pauvres de la Charité in New Orleans, founded in 1735 and later named Charity Hospital; Bellevue, founded in 1736 in New York City; the Washington Asylum, founded in 1896, which became the Gallinger Municipal Hospital and is known today as D.C. General Hospital; and Bay View Asylum, founded in 1776, which later became Baltimore City Hospitals.

Following abolition, mainstream health care remained inaccessible to blacks, and what was available was avoided. White physicians couldn't understand our resistance to the hospital system. Dr. L. C. Allen, addressing the American Public Health Association in Jacksonville, Florida, in December of 1914, observed: "Left to themselves they [Negroes] remain little better than savages. Their nature is such that benefits such as public charities provide, and have given them, are almost forced on them. It takes much persuasion to get one into a hospital."

While some mainstream care was offered, most was withheld. For example, although blacks were admitted to outpatient clinics in northern hospitals, they couldn't actually obtain beds in these hospitals. A 1930 study found one hospital bed available for every 139 white Americans and one bed for every 1,941 black Americans. Many of these beds were located in separate but dismally inferior all-black facilities that lacked money and qualified staff because black physicians were excluded from postgraduate training programs.

As the medical establishment systematically denied care to blacks, it continued to exploit them. The infamous Tuskegee study, in which four hundred black men with syphilis were left untreated for *forty years* so that researchers could observe the course of the disease, was a flagrant example of government-sponsored abuse, even more notorious because it took place in modern times, beginning in 1932 and continuing right through the great civil rights era of the 1960s. This was not benign neglect; it was a deliberate lie. Researchers told black patients they would receive free treatment for "bad blood" if they reported to the doctors yearly. The men were never told that they had syphilis, and the "medicine" they received was a placebo. The deception did not come out until 1972, when the *Washington Star* uncovered the story. Even then, it went almost unnoticed because of the headlines surrounding Watergate. But blacks noticed and remember.

Given this history of consistent abuse and neglect, it's not surprising that today some African Americans believe that the AIDS virus has been purposely unleashed from government laboratories to annihilate blacks and other minority populations. Even those who are less certain agree that it might be possible. Simply denying it doesn't address the abiding distrust many of us feel for the medical establishment based on our history. (See Chapter 21.)

For some, suspicion and distrust translates into hostility. I sometimes overhear doctors and nurses say, "Blacks come in with an attitude." I believe the prickly sensitivity of many urban blacks toward the medical profession is rooted in our past experience with it. Some African Americans, particularly in the more rural South, also feel unable to speak freely to their doctors. They assume a protective silence, asking few questions, which often means they fail to understand and comply with medical therapy.

Distrust and fear are part of the reason why we hesitate to seek early medical attention. Consequently, when an illness is finally diagnosed, it is harder to treat and may already be life-threatening.

The reason the past is so important is that it not only reveals the seeds of the present crisis but may also show a way out of it. Partly in response to mistreatment and partly based on our African traditions, an African-American culture grew up that emphasized sharing, family bonding, and the importance of spirituality —all of which generally conflicted with the mainstream white values of individualism, autonomy, and achievement. History and culture conspired to lead blacks away from physicians and other traditional medical help.

Today, when we are ill, many of us continue to follow the old practices adopted many years ago. Medical anthropologist Eric J. Bailey, who investigated the way Detroit blacks seek health care, agrees that distrust is a real and legitimate barrier to improving our health care. Bailey interviewed 203 black patients coming for blood pressure screening and asked them what treatment they sought when they were ill. He documented his findings for the World Health Organization. Dr. Bailey's most crucial observations: After illness appeared, people waited days or weeks before seeking help from the medical system. They asked advice from relatives, friends, or ministers. They tried home remedies steeped in lore and hand-me-down medical information. They hoped that the body would heal itself naturally or through prayer. Only when all else failed did they visit a clinic or see a doctor. And, yes, it was often in the middle of the night.

In this pattern may lie some of the answers to our health-care crisis. I think it's possible to use this heritage of self-reliance and self-healing inherent in our African past to our present advantage. Africans traditionally approached health from both a spiritual and a physical perspective, treating not only symptoms but the whole body and mind. Family and friends participated in caring for a sick individual. These were the hallmarks of health care in Africa —kinship, sharing, mental and spiritual healing, and nutritional and herbal remedies. Transplanted to the New World, this system helped slaves survive and it exists today wherever African Americans live.

I believe that by drawing on the powerful spirit of community and kinship that remain vital in our lives today, we can help reduce our appalling rate of disease and death. We still have to make changes as individuals. We need to understand when and under what circumstances it is vital to seek health care. And we need to find ways to use the available health care to our advantage.

OLD BELIEFS/NEW MEDICINE

Throughout our lives, we've all been offered advice about health cures by our relatives, friends, and ministers. Occasionally, that advice works against us. For example, a man may stop taking his blood pressure medicine because he's heard it will make him impotent. Or a young pregnant mother may satisfy cravings through eating starch because her mother or friends did the same, not realizing that doing so may interfere with the nutrition her baby needs.

On the other hand, some folk remedies have proved reliable over the long run. I can remember a neighbor who cooked up onions like crazy whenever she had a cold, boiling them away all day on the stove. We all ate warm chicken soup when we had colds, along with fruit juice and lots of other liquids, including lemon juice. We now know there's a medical reason why all of this really works. Warm liquids and steam help break up mucus, warm the body, and cause you to perspire. Liquids also prevent dehydration. Now researchers think there's actually something in chicken soup that fights infection.

Whether old beliefs help or hinder sometimes depends on how we visualize the ailment. In one study, Dr. Efrain Reisin and his colleagues at the Louisiana State University Medical Center in New Orleans examined the folk beliefs of fifty-four black women being treated for high blood pressure. His purpose was to discover why some women adhered to their medical regimen of three pills a day while others did not. The women most likely to stick with the doctor's regimen were those who understood that high blood pressure was caused by a biological malfunction.

By contrast, women who believed the problem was due to emotional excitement or excessive tension stopped taking their medication when they calmed down and emotional problems at home or work were solved.

Surprisingly, some who practiced home remedies also complied with the treatment, as long as they had some basic understanding of their illness. For example, even women who described their problem as "high blood," in which the blood was either "too hot, rich, or thick," still followed medical treatment because they saw the disease as something physical. They might try folk remedies such as drinking lemon juice, but they also took the antihypertension medicine prescribed by their doctors.

There seems to be room for old beliefs and modern medicine to work together.

HOW DOCTORS CAN HELP
IMPROVE CARE

One way for doctors to improve the health of their African-American patients is by involving family and friends in the treatment—by urging them to accompany the patient to an appointment so that they can help supervise dietary and lifestyle changes. Black patients are more likely to follow medical regimens, improve their nutrition, and join in exercise activities if they have caring support from "sisters" and "brothers."

Appreciating an individual's rich cultural heritage helps doctors talk more freely to patients; it also helps them tailor the treatment to each person. Simply *listening* gives doctors an opportunity to improve care. For example, hearing a patient's complaint that a particular drug produces side effects gives the doctor a chance to adjust the dosage or change the medication. Doctors can also listen for practical problems a patient may have—work schedules, child care, unemployment, transportation—that interfere with his or her medical regimen.

COPING WITH
OUR HEALTH-CARE PROBLEMS

The health-care problems of minorities are so vast that no single effort can solve them. Dr. Harold Freeman, director of surgery at New York City's Harlem Hospital, summed up the situation in *The New England Journal of Medicine:* "A major political and financial commitment will be needed to eradicate the root causes of this high mortality: vicious poverty and inadequate access to the basic health care that is the right of all Americans."

As we have seen, over the years not much help has been forthcoming from government agencies. Yet the money that does come from the government could be spent more effectively if it were targeted for prevention and long-term health rather than crisis intervention. Treating established illness is a much more expensive proposition than preventing it to begin with.

For example, chronic and acute disease could be dramatically reduced through better prenatal care, immunizations, and educational programs that promote healthier lifestyles. Yet we know that government-sponsored prevention programs are the first to be cut and the last to be funded. To change the government's approach requires clear direction from the top. That leadership may come, but in the meantime we don't have to stand by helplessly. Prevention is one area ripe for grass-roots community programs and individual activism.

COMMUNITY-BASED PROGRAMS

Here is where our efforts as a group can really pay off. Community-based programs offer African Americans—and other minorities—an opportunity to reach back to their rich cultural heritage and renew their holistic approach to health care. These programs involve working with everyone living in the neighborhood. They help build leaders and train local people to reach out into the community to identify their neighbors who are at the highest risk of becoming ill and make sure they get early help.

Dr. Marc Rivo of Washington's Commission of Public Health believes strongly that minorities respond better to health programs they develop and manage themselves. He and other proponents of community action don't mean that government agencies should step out of the picture; rather, they suggest that the money and efforts of these agencies be used to support programs designed and run by individuals in the black community.

There is room for programs of every kind and size; together, community empowerment programs can help close the health gap by replacing the old Band-Aid approach with one that emphasizes wellness and prevention. Dr. Ronald L. Braithwaite, who has devoted years of research to promoting community health, and Dr. Ngina Lythcott, writing in *The Journal of the National Medical Association* in January of 1989, liken community empowerment to a "sleeping giant—when it rises up, all will know that the historically disenfranchised will be more self-reliant and healthier."

There is one other important way that each of us can be instrumental in improving our own health care—through our individual behavior.

What You Can Do: Becoming an Active Patient

New research shows that active patients—people who regularly exercise their rights and responsibilities and act as partners with their health-care professionals—get better results than their passive counterparts.

Dr. James W. Pichert, a medical-education researcher who has videotaped hundreds of patient/doctor interviews, found that quiet, submissive patients within five minutes often forget half of the medical advice given them and either don't understand or disregard much of the rest. Some patients actually get worse instead of better. Active patients—those who speak up and ask questions—tend to remember more and follow treatment better.

If being active is so good, why are so many people passive? As we said, some people, especially African Americans, distrust the health-care system. Another big factor is fear: fear of the disease, the treatment, the costs, or the side effects. Fear often leads to denial—pretending problems don't exist.

At the heart of the problem is poor communication between doctors and patients. Many people are afraid they will appear ignorant if they ask questions. They hesitate to talk about sensitive issues such as sex and drugs; if they didn't perfectly follow a doctor's advice, they are embarrassed to admit it.

No question, the health-care system can be intimidating. Passive compliance is certainly the easiest way to cope, but not the healthiest. By becoming more active, you are more likely to receive the right diagnosis and treatment; you also remember more, carry out advice better, and get well more quickly.

Doctors can go a long way toward making African-American patients more comfortable by encouraging them to ask questions. But even if your doctor doesn't, you can still improve your own health care by becoming more actively involved in it. Researchers who have studied active patients offer this advice:

- Write down your questions and concerns before entering the doctor's office.
- Practice saying them out loud.

- Discuss them with your doctor on your next visit. (Either before or after the actual exam, you will have an opportunity to sit down with the doctor and discuss your condition.)
- Bring a notepad with you and take notes so you'll remember what your doctor says.
- Negotiate. You're the expert on yourself and your situation. By describing your lifestyle, you can help the health professional tailor treatment to your needs and circumstances. For example, a recommended diet can be adjusted to fit in with your food preferences, work schedule, and family obligations. If you find it hard to remember to take a medication prescribed three times a day, tell your doctor or nurse; he or she may have some creative solution to help you remember. Perhaps the drug can be changed to a once-a-day dosage.
- When you don't understand medical terms, ask for an explanation.
- Remain calm. When things seem rushed, gently but firmly remind the doctor of your questions and concerns. Make sure all your questions are answered to your satisfaction.

Some people think asking questions is an excuse to act hostile. Remember, your goal is to participate in your health care, not to accuse or challenge the doctor. Asking questions merely greases the conversational wheels in order to help you gain information. Always give the person a chance to respond before you plunge on. If the idea of asking questions makes you tense, or angry, take along a friend or relative when you visit the doctor.

QUESTIONS TO ASK YOUR DOCTOR
Try dividing your questions into three groups. Questions about:

1. *Tests and treatment*
2. *Medicines*
3. *Fees and insurance*

Tests and Treatment
What tests are being given?
Why?
Will there be any additional tests later?
How and when will you learn the results of the tests?

If the tests uncover a medical problem, what happens next?
Will the treatment be painful?
How long will the treatment last?
How much does treatment cost?

Medicines

Why is a particular drug being prescribed for you?
How and when should you take the medicine?
Should you take it with or without food?
What should you do if you miss a dose?
Are there any drugs or activities you should avoid while taking this drug?
Can you expect any side effects?
Can the doctor give you any written information about this drug?
What does this drug cost?
If it is too expensive, is there a less expensive alternative?
If you have side effects, is there a different medicine or a better way to take your current medication?

Fees and Insurance

How much does the doctor charge for the initial visit? What about follow-up visits?
If you have insurance, what portion of the fee will be covered by it?
Does the doctor's staff take care of the paperwork or do you have to do it yourself?
Is there a charge if medical information must be forwarded to your insurance company?
These are examples to give you an idea of some questions you might have. Every situation is different and you will have your own questions and concerns. Relax, think about it, and ask. If your doctor cuts you off or doesn't take your questions seriously, be persistent. If you still feel the doctor is disapproving or uninterested, you may want to change physicians, if you can.

GETTING THE MOST FROM YOUR DOCTOR VISITS

A positive and honest relationship between you and your doctor is your passport to good health. Communication needs to go both ways: You deserve to have a doctor who is open and responsive to you; in turn, you also need to be frank. The doctor needs to have a complete picture of what's going on with you.

DON'T

- *Get hostile.*
- *Feel guilty.*
- *Be intimidated.*
- *Assume the doctor is your enemy.*
- *Assume the doctor is God.*

DO

- *Feel free to ask questions.*
- *Prepare your questions ahead of time (the more coherent your questions, the more cooperative your doctor will be).*
- *Ask all your questions and feel free to add more.*
- *Write down what your doctor says.*
- *Tell your doctor if you're having any side effects from the medicines you're taking.*
- *Call your doctor between visits to report how you are doing and ask any questions that may arise.*
- *If your doctor is unavailable, seek assistance from other members of his or her health team, such as the nurse or dietitian.*
- *If you are unable to follow your doctor's instructions for any reason, say so.*
- *If you have a chronic disease, ask for a referral to a support group that deals with your illness.*
- *Make an appointment for your next visit before leaving the doctor's office.*
- *Be honest with your doctor.*
- *Be a partner with your doctor.*
- *Treat your doctor as a friend.*

RESOURCES

Watts Health Foundation
10300 S. Compton Avenue
Los Angeles, CA 90058
(213) 564-4331

African American Women for
   Wellness
PO Box 52378
St. Louis, MO 63136
(314) 385-2784

Health Promotion Resource
  Center
Morehouse School of Medicine
720 Westview Drive, SW
Harris Building 8C
Atlanta, GA 30310-1495
(404) 752-1622

National Black Women's Health
  Project
(National Office)
1237 Abernathy SW
Atlanta, GA 30310
(404) 758 9590

National Black Nurses'
  Association
PO Box 1823
Washington, D.C. 20012-1823
(202) 393-6870

New York Black Women's
  Health Project
PO Box 401037
Brooklyn, NY 11240-1037
(718) 596-6009

National Abortion Rights
  Action League (NARAL)
1101 14th Street NW
Washington, D.C. 20005
(202) 371-0779

20

FINDING HEALTH CARE

It is a hard fact that two separate health-care systems operate in this country—one for people with money and insurance and one for people who have neither. These two systems are radically different in the quality of health care they deliver and the way people choose to use it. Hopefully, we are moving toward health-care reform that will bring these two systems into alignment so that everyone has similar options and can make choices in the same way. In the meanwhile, we can only examine them as separate entities.

This chapter will describe the kind of medical care available. It will help you learn how to find a doctor and also learn when it is crucial to seek professional help. Do you need to see a doctor every year? Is it important to see the same doctor each time you go? If you don't feel sick, is there ever any reason to go to a doctor?

CHOOSING PRIMARY CARE

A primary-care doctor is the person you visit when you are sick or for a routine physical examination to determine your overall health. A primary-care physician may be a general practitioner, a family practitioner, or a doctor of internal medicine (an internist). Internists treat only adults over the age of sixteen, so if you have youngsters at home, you might prefer to choose a general practitioner or family doctor for your entire family's medical care. Or, separately, you may choose a pediatrician as the primary-care doctor for your children.

The half a million physicians in the United States practice in a variety of settings: alone, in a partnership or group, and in hospitals as well as community clinics. Whom you choose is to a great extent determined by what you can afford or which insurance plan you belong to.

FINDING A DOCTOR

Assuming that you have a choice, there are some very specific questions you should ask yourself before you choose any doctor.

Where do you want this doctor's office or clinic to be located? (Travel time can be important in your choice.)

What hospital do you prefer to go to should the need arise?

ABOUT THE DOCTOR

Is it important for you to go to a black doctor?

Do you prefer a woman or a man?

Do you want the doctor to be someone older, or a younger person?

Do you prefer someone who appears warm and friendly, someone personally concerned about you? Or would you prefer a recognized authority, regardless of his bedside manner?

Do you want someone who has the full approval of other doctors and medical organizations? Or do you prefer someone whose innovative approach sometimes draws criticism from the medical establishment?

Do you prefer someone who explores alternative medicine— holistic, herbal, acupuncture—in addition to accepted medical practices?

Do you want someone who is board-certified or board-eligible? Board certification means the physician has taken a national written test in the area of specialty. If you have to choose between them, are these qualifications more important to you than finding a doctor with whom you feel comfortable?

COLLECT NAMES

Start by collecting the names of doctors who might fill the bill. If your friends are pleased with their doctors, you can believe they will talk.

Call the American Medical Association (AMA) or the National Medical Association (NMA), the medical society to which many African-American doctors belong. You can also call your county or state medical association and ask for names. Many hospitals also provide the names of doctors on their staffs.

You can get more names by looking under "Physicians" in the Yellow Pages. Physicians are listed by specialty, so look under the headings for "General Practice," "Family Practice," or "Internal Medicine." Pick the doctors whose offices are convenient for you. Although the advertising in the Yellow Pages doesn't give you much information about the doctor, it at least provides some names to investigate.

After you have a list of names, ask friends and family again whether they've heard about any of the doctors. They might surprise you with additional information. Positive comments help to narrow the list further. You can confirm whether physicians are board-certified by calling the American Board of Medical Specialties (see Resources on page 270).

TELEPHONE CHECKS

With your list in hand, it's time to do a phone check. Here are a few questions you can ask over the phone:

Exactly where is this doctor's office (is it easy to get to)?

What hospitals does the doctor admit to?

Is the doctor board-certified or board-eligible?

What method of payment or insurance does the doctor accept? Will you have to do all the paperwork yourself? If so, are you willing to take on this chore?

Ask the receptionist or nurse how many years of medical training the physician has had. Where did he or she complete a residency? Ask if the doctor has some days when he sees patients after normal business hours. Does another physician cover the doctor's practice on days off?

From your original list of doctor names, circle the top two or three who meet most of your requirements. All you have to do now is choose the individual with whom you feel most comfortable.

The next time you have a medical problem or need a checkup, make an appointment with the physician who tops your list. You want to choose a physician who listens to your complaints and symptoms thoroughly before making a treatment recommendation. The doctor should be willing to spend enough time with you so that you do not feel rushed. An organized physician will take notes during the course of your conversation and review your medical history. If the doctor prescribes treatment, he or she should encourage you to call if the problem does not improve fully. Finally, your doctor should consult with other physicians if several treatment attempts fail or if your condition worsens.

It it turns out that you're uncomfortable with the doctor you've selected, you don't have to continue, even if the doctor suggests a follow-up visit. Although *you are not required to give any reason if you wish to change doctors,* you might want to let the doctor know. Some doctors appreciate knowing and sometimes the problem can be easily resolved. Let your feelings be known in a considerate yet firm manner. And be prepared to go to the second choice on your list the next time.

HEALTH-CARE OPTIONS

If you do not have private health insurance, you may have other sources of health care open to you. Most states offer public health services through regional, county, city, or town health departments. Community services and eligibility vary from state to state, but usually they include school health programs and screening, immunization and nutrition programs, maternal and child-health programs, primary-health clinics, and disease-management clinics.

The best way to locate these community clinics is to consult your telephone book: In most states, federal, state, and city listings appear separately at the end. Look under key headings such as "Clinics" and "Public Health." Here is a sample of what you may find in your area.

SCHOOL HEALTH PROGRAMS

In many communities, nurses and other health-care professionals are assigned to schools. Their services range from school nurses, who take temperatures, apply Band-Aids to scraped knees, and refer sick children to doctors, all the way to large-scale immunization programs and screening for dental, hearing, and vision problems. School programs also provide health instruction and nutrition education to administrators, teachers, and parents. These programs are especially valuable because they offer preventive services to all children.

SCREENING PROGRAMS

Screenings sponsored by city health departments are often given free or at minimum cost. Screening provides basic testing for widespread health problems, such as high blood pressure, diabetes, and some types of cancer. For children, there are programs available for early screening and diagnosis of many diseases. The purpose of screening is to detect a disease in its early stages; if a problem is detected, the individual is referred to a clinic or physician for follow-up treatment. Your local health department can usually provide information on screening programs in your area. These programs help fill the gap for those who cannot afford regular doctor visits and whose early-stage disease might otherwise go unnoticed.

NEIGHBORHOOD AND PRIMARY-HEALTH-CARE CENTERS

These clinics are important in underserved areas where there are not enough physicians to care for the local population. They are also found in inner cities and poor rural areas. The Migrant Health Program, established specifically to serve farm workers and their families, is sometimes combined with this type of health-care clinic.

There are fifteen hundred community health centers that serve 6 million low-income people. Health clinics offer a variety of services under one roof. They are a major source of prenatal care, deliver thousands of babies each year, and primarily serve areas with high rates of infant mortality.

Community health centers are a viable alternative to visiting hospital emergency rooms, which are designed for acute or emergency care. Unfortunately, such centers are underfunded and often understaffed. Enlarging this system could go a long way toward creating equal access to health care for everyone.

MATERNAL AND CHILD HEALTH

Maternal and child-care programs are available in many neighborhoods and communities, although, like other federally funded programs, they tend to be badly underfunded. The aim of such programs is to provide quality nutrition for pregnant women, new mothers, infants, and children up to the age of five whose weight is low for their age or who are anemic or almost anemic; they also offer instruction and counseling in prenatal care, infant care, nutrition, and family planning. To qualify, mothers and children have to be below a certain income level. But even when they qualify, they may not receive the service. For example, because of budget cuts and price increases for baby formula, the Women's, Infants', and Children's Supplement Nutrition Program (WIC) reaches less than half of the eligible population.

MENTAL HEALTH

Many cities offer mental-health clinics staffed with psychiatrists, psychologists, social workers, and other specially trained counselors. This type of clinic may receive funding from several sources, including federal, state, and private donations, which means that they accept various forms of payment, including private pay, private insurance, Medicare, and Medicaid.

Mental-health clinics provide a range of services, including individual and group therapy, as well as alcohol- and drug-abuse programs. Community mental-health programs also provide consultation and support for other programs, including detention centers, schools, rehab programs, churches, and volunteer organizations. Criteria for treatment varies from state to state. Mental-health clinics provide good services but are often overcrowded and underfunded. African Americans who have a crisis or break-down or who are suffering from stress-related drug and alcohol abuse are more likely to go to an emergency room or a doctor's office for help, and then be referred to a mental-health clinic.

OTHER MEMBERS OF
YOUR HEALTH-CARE TEAM

At various times, you may need the services of other health-care professionals: pharmacists, physical therapists, nurses, nutri-tionists and dietitians, and dentists. You can evaluate these sup-port people just as you would a physician. If you're not sure about their qualifications, you have every right to ask them to explain where they were trained and what professional organizations they belong to. Here are the people whose services you are likely to need on a more or less regular basis:

Nurses are the people with whom you have the most contact. Nurses can help you to understand the doctor's instructions and to make sure all of your needs are met. Whenever your doctor is unavailable to answer your questions, a nurse can provide tem-porary answers or solutions. Professional nurses include regis-tered nurses and licensed practical nurses. Registered nurses may also specialize, meaning they have months or years of additional training in a particular area of medicine. The critical-care nurse, nurse midwife, and emergency-medicine nurse are all specialists.

Pharmacists are trained to understand how medications act in the body. They can tell you how and when to take your medications, whether there are possible side effects you should be aware of, and whether food or other drugs might interact with your pre-scription. Having a good relationship with a pharmacist can be a great asset to your medical care, particularly if you are dealing with a chronic disease for which you take daily medication.

Physical therapists design proper exercises to help people regain or improve the use of impaired arms, legs, and joints. With a doctor's referral, physical therapy may be covered by health in-surance. Because most physical therapists require regularly scheduled sessions two, three, or more times a week, going to PT can provide a center of calm and well-being in an individual's life. If you ever need physical therapy, don't hesitate to give it a try. It is a recuperative and comforting form of medical care.

Registered dietitians and nutritionists are experts in the effects of food and nutrition on your health. If you are seriously overweight, have diabetes, ulcers, high blood cholesterol, kidney failure, or high blood pressure, a dietitian or nutritionist can help you to assess your present eating habits and can recommend changes that will help improve your particular medical condition. The dietitian or nutritionist also keeps track of your progress and lets your physician know how you're doing.

Dentists should be seen at least once a year, and twice is even better. Regular cleaning and early treatment of problems can prevent gum disease, tooth loss, and major dental work later on. Unfortunately, many people wait until gum disease or tooth problems occur before making an appointment. Dentists are expensive and it is not always easy to find money for preventive care. Most insurance carriers do not offer a dental package, which means the dentist's fee comes out of your pocket. (Some HMOs, however, do include dental visits as part of their services.) Dental schools often have clinics that offer services at reduced rates.

PAYING MEDICAL BILLS

Private insurance carriers such as Metropolitan, Aetna, or Blue Cross/Blue Shield permit you to select your own physician. Diagnostic tests and hospitalization are ordered directly by the physician at his or her discretion. The costs of the premiums vary depending upon the package, but they are generally extremely high for both individuals and groups. This type of health-care cost has edged many self-employed and unemployed Americans out of the health-care loop.

People who are self-employed or who work at jobs that do not provide health insurance must buy their own insurance, often prohibitively expensive, or pay doctors and hospitals directly from their own pockets.

HMOs and PPOs (preferred-provider organizations) have been the answer for many companies and individuals who must purchase their own insurance. These are the managed-care programs. Here's how it works: You select a primary-care physician from a list of participating member doctors; if you need a specialist, your primary-care physician refers you to another member in the HMO.

Some HMOs have their own centers, which are like large clinics, with various departments and attending physicians on the premises. The doctors are usually experienced and qualified physicians who join because of the simplicity of the program. However, because they receive set fees, the doctors tend to limit the time they spend with each patient. Otherwise, the quality of service is usually considered good.

Both HMOs and PPOs encourage members to see their primary-care physician regularly. Usually, screening tests and checkups designed for early detection of disease are included. The goal is to keep people healthy and reduce the need for specialists, excessive diagnostic tests, and hospitalization.

One drawback of these plans is that you may have to abandon your family physician if your doctor is not a member of the program. If you need to be hospitalized, the HMO or PPO must first approve both the procedure and the hospital.

If you do not have insurance, you may not be able to afford to go to a doctor or a hospital if you become seriously ill. An estimated 37 million Americans are uninsured. Another 70 million don't have enough insurance.

Medicaid—federal and state health insurance for the poor—has been the answer for some, although who is eligible for Medicaid varies widely from state to state. In most states, Medicaid recipients can now generally go to any doctor or hospital that will accept them. The doctors and hospitals are typically paid for each service or procedure they perform. But many doctors take only limited numbers of Medicaid patients because of the low reimbursement rate, and some doctors and private hospitals do not take any. As a result, many people must seek treatment at overcrowded state or federally supported clinics where treatment is on the basis of first come, first served.

The second national insurance program is Medicare, established for those over age sixty-five and those who are disabled because of serious illness or handicap. In this program, you pay a small monthly premium, which is deducted from your Social Security check. Under Medicare, fees are preset, regardless of the time the doctor spends or the quality of care he or she provides. In many cases, Medicare reimbursement for physicians is far less than customary charges for that specialty.

As a result, many physicians are turning away the needy elderly in favor of patients who can afford their services or who are privately insured. Some people who have Medicare coverage also buy a supplement, which takes care of some of the difference in costs. But supplemental insurance is expensive, and many people cannot afford it.

Our health care system is not the best it could be, but it isn't the worst. We have all the technologies available worldwide. We have fine doctors and clinics that are state-of-the-art. What we don't have is equal access to this system for all. Dr. Martin Luther King, Jr., said, "Of all the forms of inequality, injustice in health is the most shocking and the most inhuman."

We can all do our share to make access to health care for all a reality. The government can help by working to reduce costs and placing more emphasis on prevention. Doctors can offer suggestions for a better system that is fair to everyone, which means, among other things, offering their services to Medicare and Medicaid patients, as well as to those who have no insurance.

In a speech delivered to physicians at Morehouse School of Medicine in Atlanta in October of 1986, Dr. John O. Brown, past president of the National Medical Association, suggested that physicians could restore public confidence by "establishing with every patient a relationship based on honesty, compassion, concern, and good medical care. . . . Nothing can take the place of selfless, devoted, and dedicated patient care. That is the basis of our image, just as it is the basis of care itself." And beyond what the government can do and what physicians can do is what we ourselves can do.

HEALTH CHECKS

Early diagnosis and disease prevention are the answers to many of our health problems. Here are the kinds of health checks African Americans should have at different times of life, including those you can perform yourself.

Age	Self-Check or Community Screening	Doctor Visits
Children 1–13		Physical once a year
		Eye exam once a year
		Hearing tested once a year
		Dentist every six months
Teens 14–18	Check weight monthly	Physical once a year
	Follow balanced diet and exercise regimen	Eye exam as necessary
		Dentist every six months
Men 19–35	Blood pressure check annually (every six months if you have a family history of high blood pressure)	Physical exam every two years (once a year if you participate in sports), which should include a glucose test for diabetes, blood pressure check, an EKG, complete blood profile and urinalysis (for blood fats, anemia, liver function, kidney disease, diabetes, thyroid problems, infections, and problems of the immune system
	Check weight monthly	
	Follow balanced diet and exercise regimen	
		Dentist every six months

Women 19–35	*All of the above*	*All of the above*
	Breast self-exam every month	*Gynecological exam once a year, including Pap smear and breast examination*
Men 36–45	*Blood pressure check every six months*	*Physical exam once a year (as above), including lipid profile for cholesterol and other blood fats; prostate and rectal exam beginning at age 40; if you smoke or work in a hazardous environment, the exam should also include a chest X ray.*
	Check weight monthly	
	Follow balanced diet and exercise regimen	
		Eye exam as necessary
		Dentist every six months
Women 36–45	*All of the above, with special attention to weight checks*	*All of the above (without prostate exam)*
	Breast self-exam every month	*Gynecological exam once a year. (Inform your gynecologist of your menstrual status and symptoms associated with menopause)*
		Mammogram once a year
Men and Women 45 and older	*Continue all of the above*	*Continue all of the above*
		Yearly hearing and eye exams

RESOURCES

National Medical Association
1012 10th Street NW
Washington, D.C. 20001
(202) 347-1895

Black Women's Physicians
    Project
3300 Henry Avenue
Philadelphia, PA 19129
(215) 842-7124

American Medical Association
535 North Dearborn Street
Chicago, IL 60610

The American Board of Medical
    Specialties
1-800-776-2378

National Dental Association
5506 Connecticut Avenue NW
Suite 24-25
Washington, D.C. 20015
(202) 244-7555

Part Five

TAKING CARE
OF OUR
FUTURE HEALTH

21

AIDS

In January of 1993, the National Commission on AIDS said that being black or Hispanic was a risk factor for AIDS. African Americans and Latinos together total 21 percent of the population, but they account for 46 percent of the U.S. AIDS cases so far. This announcement was guaranteed to upset black leaders. Biologically speaking, blacks are no more likely than anyone else to contract HIV; black leaders worry that if whites begin to see the disease as a minority issue, concern about HIV and AIDS will wane. This lack of mainstream identification with AIDS is what got research off to such a slow start to begin with, because the general public believed AIDS affected only homosexuals.

Why are we running so far ahead of the rest of the U.S. population when it comes to the AIDS epidemic? Though you could almost hear the sigh from millions when, on November 7, 1991, Magic Johnson announced his retirement due to HIV infection, many African-American men and women still don't think that AIDS could be a problem for them.

It's true that the disease is spread most often through sexual contact and needles or syringes shared by drug abusers. But it's also true that anyone can get AIDS. AIDS does not discriminate and it does not make moral judgments. It doesn't care what color you are or whether you're gay or straight, male or female. There's nothing in us biologically that makes us more susceptible to HIV

274

and the opportunistic infections that accompany the v
not more vulnerable to AIDS—*unless we ignore and e*
known methods of transmission.

The question is, Why has it been so hard for us tc
message about AIDS? Some people simply won't face u, .u the
dangers of their behavior. For example, there is such a stigma
attached to homosexuality in the black community that one
mother told her friends that her HIV-positive son was a junkie,
even though he wasn't. When it comes to homosexuality in our
own families, many of us deny it. This attitude keeps many black
gays in the closet, which means if they discover they are HIV-
positive, they must confront their families with two explosive
issues at once: homosexuality and HIV infection. Some hide their
HIV status, worried that family members will reject them. Many
gay or bisexual black men marry to help disguise the fact that
they are homosexual, which means that their wives are unknowingly at risk for contracting HIV. (Lesbians, because they are less
visible, don't seem to draw the same kind of animosity from
family and friends as gay men; they are also at less risk for HIV
infection—though there *is* risk in any kind of sexual activity.)
Homophobia, like any other prejudice, serves no purpose and
only interferes with the prevention effort. And right now, prevention is the *only* road to conquering this disease.

The drug culture also impedes AIDS prevention. As drugs have
taken over our streets and schools, families and whole neighborhoods have been destroyed. When AIDS workers tell us that we
should provide sterile needles to drug addicts, many African
Americans are horrified, already convinced that the larger society
would like us to destroy ourselves through drug use. Asking
black people to distribute needles free of charge and teach addicts
how to clean their works is seen as just one more step toward
total death. If there's money for needle exchanges, many wonder,
why is there no money for drug treatment and education?

These are only some of the issues, complicating effective measures against AIDS in the black community, that we will discuss
later in this chapter. Unfortunately, there is still much we don't
know about HIV and AIDS. Here are some of the most common
questions about AIDS and the answers we have so far.

WHERE DID AIDS COME FROM?

This simple question is another sore point for us, because AIDS is presumed to have originated in Africa. We feel we are being blamed yet again for the spread of disease. On the other hand, some blacks are convinced that the virus was created by the U.S. government in a germ-warfare laboratory, then leaked to the general population, either accidentally or on purpose, to effect the genocide of blacks and other minority populations.

It's easy to see how some people might believe this rumor, because the medical establishment has been guilty of much abuse toward blacks in the past, including the infamous Tuskegee study. Based on current information, I don't personally believe that the government manufactured the AIDS virus. The earliest known sample of HIV was discovered in a blood sample taken in 1959 in what was then Leopoldville, the Belgian Congo (now Kinshasa, Zaire). As far as we know, scientists didn't learn how to engineer a virus until 1973, so it's unlikely that HIV could have been manufactured in a laboratory fourteen years earlier.

It's believed that AIDS originated in Africa sometime in the 1950s. Generally, new viruses arise spontaneously as one form rapidly mutates into another. For example, it is fairly common for a virus to exist in one form in animals, go through a mutation, and be transmitted to humans. It happens all the time with flu viruses. Theories have tied AIDS to green monkeys infected with SIV (simian immunodeficiency virus), which is almost identical to HIV-2, the strain infecting many Africans. There are several theories about how that particular virus might have been transmitted to humans. One plausible explanation is that it originated during trials of an experimental polio vaccine developed using kidneys from monkeys. It's possible that a single batch of vaccine was contaminated with HIV. That such a vaccine was administered in the same place and at the same time that HIV first appeared lends some credence to this theory.

The earliest evidence of HIV is from two blood samples taken in 1959. Seven mysterious deaths in the Belgian Congo in the 1960s were later attributed to AIDS. A 1972 outbreak in Uganda of virulent Kaposi's sarcoma is thought to have been AIDS-related. In 1976, a Norwegian sailor whose ship had put in at ports in West Africa died from an AIDS-like illness. Both his wife and daughter contracted the same illness; samples of their blood later tested positive for HIV.

Once established, the disease spread rapidly in Africa, possibly because of wide-scale immunization programs against measles and other diseases—in which it was common practice to use one hypodermic needle to inoculate an entire village.

Haiti was the next place AIDS showed up in great numbers, carried to that country by Haitian laborers who had been working in West Africa.

Theories vary as to when AIDS appeared in the United States. Some say 1978; others hypothesize that AIDS shipped over with the sailors who gathered from all over the world in New York for the bicentennial celebration in 1976. Some place its arrival further back, saying that AIDS might have made it to the United States as early as 1972. No one is certain.

In 1981, American physicians reported the unusual occurrence of *Pneumocystis carinii* pneumonia (PCP) and Kaposi's sarcoma in previously healthy homosexuals. Traced to a defective immune system, the underlying disorder was named GRID (gay-related immune deficiency). In 1982, after doctors realized that homosexuals weren't the only group of people getting the disease, the syndrome was renamed AIDS (acquired immune deficiency syndrome). Evidence of the same disorder was showing up in intravenous drug users of both sexes, in some of their babies, and in Haitians who were not homosexual. A doctor in Florida reported that one of his patients who had received blood products for hemophilia had died from similar symptoms.

Recognition of AIDS did not lead to much action. Proposals for funds to study the new disease, which at the time seemed to affect relatively few people, went unanswered by the Centers for Disease Control and Prevention (CDC) and other federally funded health organizations. American doctors and researchers wishing to study AIDS were on their own.

In 1983, AIDS transmission routes were figured out and in that same year the virus thought to cause AIDS was isolated by Luc Montagnier, a researcher at the Pasteur Institute in Paris, France. He named it LAV (for lymphadenopathy-associated virus). His findings were not presented in the United States until a year later.

In 1986, an international committee on viral nomenclature re-named the virus the human immunodeficiency virus (HIV). Not every scientist believes that HIV causes AIDS, but most world governments have accepted it as the official AIDS virus. In the remainder of this chapter, current information that has developed around this conclusion will be presented.

In Africa, the death rates soared unchecked. In 1961, international scientists were aware that Kaposi's sarcoma, one of the hallmark diseases associated with AIDS, was devastating the black male population of sub-Saharan Africa. By 1980, high rates were reported from Zaire, Rwanda, Uganda, Zambia, Zimbabwe, Kenya, and other central African countries. Today, according to the World Health Organization, more than half of the estimated 13 million HIV-infected people worldwide are Africans. By the year 2000, AIDS is expected to claim 5 million African lives. And according to researchers speaking at the 6th International Conference on AIDS held in December of 1991 in Dakar, Senegal, by the year 2010, at least 25 percent of the work force in Africa will have died from AIDS.

AIDS never picked on any particular group in Africa. From the start, the disease has infected men and women in equal numbers. This seems also to be true in Asia, the continent where AIDS is currently exploding the fastest.

In the United States, however, up until now, the overwhelming number of infected people have been homosexual men. But the American profile for HIV and AIDS is changing. The number of new HIV infections in women, particularly black women, is rising faster than for any other group.

HOW HIV DESTROYS THE IMMUNE SYSTEM

HIV invades CD4 cells (also called T cells) in our body. These cells normally fight off diseases and infections. The virus destroys these cells by turning them into "factories" that make more virus, which in turn enter and destroy more CD4 cells. This process continues unchecked until the individual has too few CD4 cells left to protect the body. The body's immune system becomes so badly damaged that it is easily overwhelmed by any of millions of bacteria, viruses, fungi, and protozoa that exist around us. Which diseases the body falls prey to depend largely on where and how the infected individual lives. For example, in big cities, tuberculosis is becoming a death threat to people infected with HIV. In rural areas, parasites of the gastrointestinal tract are more deadly. Once these infections begin, the immune system is known to be failing and the individual is said to have AIDS.

HOW YOU DON'T GET HIV

HIV is fragile and dies fairly quickly outside the body. You can't get HIV from a toilet seat. You can't get it from touching someone who has it. You can't catch it from a casual kiss. You can't catch it from a cough. You can't catch it from playing sports or holding hands. You can't get it from a glass or a washing machine, and it doesn't fly around in the air like the flu or bubonic plague. If you could get HIV from casual contact or by breathing the air, everyone in the world except hermits who live in caves in the Himalayas would already have it.

WHO HAS THE HIGHEST RISK FOR HIV?

- IV drug users (but all people who use illegal drugs are at risk)
- Anybody having unprotected sex with anyone (but people with many sex partners are especially at risk)
- People with a history of other sexually transmitted diseases
- Those who received blood transfusions, blood products, or organ transplants between 1977 and early 1985 *
- Children of HIV-infected mothers

* Since 1985, all donated blood used for transfusions and blood-clotting factor is tested for traces of the virus. That doesn't mean the blood supply is 100 percent HIV-free, but the risk is small. One way to make sure you don't get a contaminated transfusion is to donate your own blood in advance of any scheduled surgery.

SEX

HIV is commonly transmitted through unprotected sex—anal, vaginal, or oral. The virus is present in semen and vaginal fluids of infected men and women. During sex these fluids readily permeate the mucous membranes that line your vagina or rectum. The thin membranes and gums inside your mouth are also vulnerable. If semen or vaginal fluid from an infected person comes in contact with any openings in your skin, HIV can enter your bloodstream. It doesn't matter whether you're straight, gay, or bisexual.

Women are more likely to be infected by their male sexual partners than they are to infect men. If an infected woman is pregnant, she has a 25 to 40 percent chance of passing the virus to her fetus. Woman-to-woman sexual transmission is also possible but far less likely.

DRUG INJECTORS

All drug injectors are at high risk for HIV infection. During an injection, a small amount of blood is sucked up into the syringe. When needles are shared, HIV is pulled from one person's bloodstream, passes into the syringe, then enters into the next injector's bloodstream, with barely any exposure to air, making it a highly efficient method of transmission.

Many scientists and AIDS activists are convinced that all drugs, regardless of how they are used, suppress the immune system and leave the user especially vulnerable to HIV and AIDS if that person engages in unprotected sex.

PREVENTION

SAFER SEX

Abstinence—the "just say no" approach—has been recommended by a number of organizations, especially with regard to teenagers. By all means, preach abstinence to your kids. But be realistic: Make sure they know how to protect themselves, too.

The key to safer sex is that latex device, the condom. (Lamb-skin condoms can prevent pregnancy, but the HIV virus permeates them.) Using a latex condom coated with nonoxynol-9 *every time you have intercourse* is your best protection against HIV infection. Man or woman, carry latex condoms with you, especially if you're going out drinking or getting high. Alcohol and drugs can make you careless and put you in the position of having unsafe, unprotected sex.

What if you're certain that both you and your partner are HIV-negative? If you've been with the same uninfected person for years, and neither of you has had sex with anybody else, and you've both *tested negative a couple of times,* then you can feel pretty sure that you don't have to use a condom. (Since it can take several months for the antibodies that reflect HIV status to show up, you should get tested twice.) If either of you has used IV drugs in the past (or present), your risk of getting HIV soars. Your partner may never have sex with anyone else, but if he or she is having an affair with the needle, you're both in danger.

If it's so easy to stop HIV transmission, why isn't everyone using condoms? Some reasons men give: "they get in the way"; "they're uncomfortable"; "sex doesn't feel as good"; "they don't fit." Women say they're afraid to suggest condoms because the man may think they have a venereal disease or AIDS. Some women and men say condoms ruin spontaneity.

Using a condom doesn't have to interfere with foreplay if you make it a part of foreplay. There are condoms to fit every size. If it's tight or dry, you can lubricate it. Used routinely, condoms can be as natural and spontaneous as anything else that happens during sex. A few men are sensitive to latex. In that case, wear two condoms, a lambskin next to the skin and latex over it.

For oral sex: Yes, you need to use a condom, even for oral sex, because HIV can enter your bloodstream through invisible cuts in your gums or mouth.

PREVENTION FOR DRUG INJECTORS

If we hope to stop AIDS from killing every one of us, we have to come to terms with IV drug use. Today, a woman can get

AIDS just because her boyfriend stuck a needle in his arm when he was a teenager. Every man or woman with whom that person has sex is in danger, and so is every baby born to an infected mother. AIDS is more lethal than drug use.

Obviously, the best solution is for drug users to get themselves into a treatment program and stop using drugs. But if you or someone you know cannot or will not stop, there are steps that will at least reduce the risk of contracting HIV.

Don't share works if you can avoid it. If you do share, always flush the whole set (syringe and needle) with bleach and water—bleach first, then the water. Do it twice. If you got your set from a needle-exchange program or straight out of the box, you can be pretty sure it hasn't been used before. But if you just bought one from somebody on the street, chances are good that it's been used. As you probably know, people selling works are not above selling used for new. It only takes a couple of seconds to clean the set before use, and it can help save your life.

Needle-exchange programs are controversial in every community, but they are especially troublesome to blacks. The primary grievance of those against these programs is that city governments would use them as substitutes for treatment programs. If treatment was available, they say, we wouldn't need needle exchanges because drug use would automatically go down.

This is certainly true, but the clock is ticking fast on AIDS. By the time we are able to fund and implement these programs, which I agree should be a top priority, hundreds of thousands will be infected with HIV and dying in the streets. It's crucial that we air this issue now and experiment with some objectively monitored pilot programs. We need solid information on which to base the next step in the fight against AIDS—and fast.

At the turn of the century, new vaccines and other newly discovered medical therapies stemmed the awful tide of disease that threatened us. We hope the same thing will happen to contain and eradicate AIDS. Until then, I believe we have to use every weapon in our power to save ourselves and protect the future of our families.

Drug use and AIDS is an important issue for all of us. Plenty of people who never use drugs themselves have friends or relatives who do. Get involved; let your opinion be known. Action is imperative. If you think needle exchange is wrong for us, what other ideas do you have that might help? There is room for everybody in the fight against AIDS. By hearing different points of view, we may be able to come up with an effective, workable compromise. For example, I know that some black leaders would accept needle exchanges if clean needles were offered along with a full range of drug-treatment programs.

SHOULD YOU GET TESTED?

There are two important reasons to get tested:

1. People in the first stage of HIV infection may not be aware of their positive status and can infect others unknowingly.
2. The sooner you know what's happening, the quicker you can get treatment.

That said, not everyone agrees about testing. Since there is no cure, some think that there is no advantage to knowing. They would rather live without fear until symptoms of AIDS begin. Others worry about reactions of family, friends, employers, insurers, neighbors, and landlords. There have been too many instances of discrimination against HIV carriers and those with full-blown AIDS.

Still others believe that too little is known about AIDS to label someone as a carrier based on HIV status.

Despite these controversies, I still believe that if you're in a high-risk group, knowing your HIV status will help the fight against AIDS. If you test positive, you can keep the test results to yourself. You are under no obligation to share the information with anyone except those to whom you might transmit the infection. That means telling all of your sexual partners and all medical and dental personnel who treat you. If this is something you cannot face, a physician or public-health officer can do it for you.

What Does HIV-Positive Actually Mean?

The test does not detect the presence of the HIV virus, only antibodies in the blood. A positive test result means that you have been exposed to the HIV virus in the past and that your body has tried to fight it off by manufacturing antibodies against it.

Do HIV-Positive People Still Carry the Virus?

It is presumed that they do. An infection with the virus usually begins with a sudden flulike illness, but then the virus virtually disappears. Individuals may look and feel well for up to eight to ten years. It is now known that during this long latency period the virus is concealed in lymph nodes, quietly reproducing itself in nearby white blood cells. People who are HIV-positive are monitored to measure CD4 immune cells; the virus is active when the CD4 count begins to fall. As the immune system slowly collapses, the virus shows up in ever-increasing quantities in white blood cells and floating freely in the blood.

Do All HIV-Positive People Get AIDS?

The CDC predicts that 80 percent of HIV-positive people will develop AIDS within ten years.

With new drug therapies and new information on how to fight AIDS, people with HIV are living longer. Some people diagnosed HIV-positive twelve years ago are still living healthy lives.

Where Do You Get The Test?

To find a source, call any local AIDS information number. In most parts of the country, tests for the virus are free and anonymous. If anonymous testing is unavailable where you live, it's possible to get tested in another city.

If the first test is positive, it should be repeated. If the second is positive, still another test—called the Western blot or immunofluorescent assay—is done to confirm the results.

If the first test is negative but you think you've been exposed to the virus, get a repeat test in two to six months.

In the meantime, practice the precautions followed by people who know they are HIV-positive. (Follow these rules also if you fall into a high-risk category and have chosen not to get tested.)

- Refrain from donating blood, sperm, or body organs or tissues for transplant.

- Protect yourself and your sexual partners by practicing safer sex (important even if your partner is already HIV-positive, because you could be transmitting a different strain of the virus to your already-immune-weakened partner—to say nothing of what he or she could be transmitting to you).
- Do not breast-feed an infant.
- Do not share razors, toothbrushes, or other items that could be contaminated with blood and might come in contact with someone else's bloodstream.
- Follow a healthy, drug-free lifestyle.

How Else Might You Know If You Have HIV?

HIV-positive people may appear as healthy as anybody else. The virus often has a long latency period in which no signs of infection are evident. Unusual purplish-colored lesions on the skin might be a sign of Kaposi's sarcoma. Other early warning signs include:

- Diarrhea: several times a day for several weeks
- Unexplained weight loss: loss of ten pounds or more despite normal eating habits
- Chronic fatigue: being constantly tired despite plenty of sleep
- Night sweats: with or without fever, sweating so much that you soak the sheets
- Persistent fever: prolonged 99 to 100 degree fever without any obvious cause such as a cold or flu
- Cough: weeks of dry coughing not due to illness or smoking
- Skin rash: itchy, scaly bumps or ulcers appearing anywhere on the body, which often spread
- Mouth problems: slow-healing sores or persistent white patches (also known as thrush) on the gums, tongue, or palate
- Swollen glands: enlarged, sore, or tender lymph nodes in the neck, groin, or armpit
- Genital infections: recurrent yeast infections or warts or ulcers in and around the vagina, penis, or rectum
- Multiple allergic reactions: such reactions as fevers, rash, swelling, or itching to common medications or insect bites

GETTING MEDICAL HELP

Anyone who has been identified as HIV-positive should have their status periodically checked for two important reasons. First, he or she may choose to receive drug therapy against the virus. Second, such checks enable people to be alert for opportunistic infections in order to receive early treatment.

This is easy to say and not so easy to do, particularly for poor black and Hispanic IV drug users. These people are already out of the health-care loop and unlikely to get back in. Most must rely on public hospitals, which are already straining under the weight of other urgent health problems. Although there are clinics that specialize in treating HIV infection in many poor neighborhoods, these facilities have been quickly overwhelmed. Even those who can afford private medical care may have trouble finding doctors who will treat them.

These problems keep many people from getting the help they need until the disease has reached an advanced stage, one reason that on an average black people with AIDS live only one year beyond AIDS diagnosis (for whites, the average is eighteen months).

Until recently, there was a tendency to exclude women and people of color from clinical research trials, one of the few places where AIDS victims can get regular medical supervision and also be on the cutting edge of new developments. Researchers said that these patients often failed to keep appointments and were not reliable for follow-up. It's true that poor people have trouble keeping appointments—homelessness, hunger, lack of transportation to clinics, and lack of child-care facilities are all reasons for unreliability.

Why is it so important for blacks to participate in research trials? First, the drugs being tested may act differently in different people, so from a research point of view, it's important to test their effectiveness in various groups. Equally important, participation means that HIV-positive people have early, free access to new therapies that may prolong their lives or ease their pain. (To join a research trial, see Resources on page 290.)

THERAPY AGAINST HIV AND AIDS

DRUGS THAT SLOW THE PROGRESS OF HIV

AZT: Also known by its brand name of Retrovir, or zidovudine, AZT may help delay the progress of HIV and improve CD4 counts for some people, but it cannot be used indefinitely because of side effects and because it eventually stops working. Side effects include fatigue, nausea, insomnia, headache, or muscle pain. The manufacturers of AZT say its worst side effects were associated with the original higher doses, and that the new lower regimens cause fewer problems and can be used longer.

Some doctors have been prescribing AZT as soon as someone is diagnosed with HIV, before they have developed symptoms of full-fledged AIDS. However, one important new study from Europe, called the Concorde study, jointly sponsored by the Medical Research Council of Britain and the National AIDS Research Agency of France, showed that such early treatment does not improve life expectancy.

AZT does not work for everyone. Recent research reported in *The New England Journal of Medicine* in April of 1993 shows that some people are infected with strains of HIV that are already resistant to AZT.

Many AIDS activists agree that even when AZT initially improves CD4 counts, in the long run the drug doesn't prolong life. Some feel that drugs of any kind only make it that much harder to fight off infections. But those who believe in AZT's usefulness say that it may yet prove to be part of the answer to AIDS treatment when it is combined with other drugs.

ddC: Also called HIVID, ddC is approved for use only in combination with AZT. It is not very effective alone.

ddI: Short for dideoxyinosine and also known as Videx, ddI is used by people who can't take AZT any longer. Similar to AZT but with a different group of side effects, ddI has not shown a greater survival advantage in clinical trials.

A few unapproved drugs such as Kemron, which has been hailed as a wonder drug in Kenya (the country where it is made), may help, if you can get them; other unapproved drugs such as

Compound-Q from China have already been shown to cause more harm than good.

Combination therapy—the use of several drugs together—is the approach many AIDS specialists recommend. HIV is an extremely complicated virus, with many steps in its life cycle. As it reproduces, it sometimes makes copies with slight variations. These differences can make the virus resistant to certain drugs. Using several different drugs at one time means that even if the virus is resistant to one drug, it can be attacked with another.

DRUGS THAT FIGHT INFECTION

A huge variety of illnesses can attack when the immune system fails, including many cancers. Treatments are available for many of these diseases, particularly opportunistic infections. To take advantage of these drugs, it's important to obtain prompt medical help as soon as any sign of illness appears. Below are a few of the most common infections that strike people with HIV and full-blown AIDS.

PCP (Pneumocystis carinii *pneumonia)* is the most common HIV-related infection in the United States and one of the first signs of full-blown AIDS. PCP is a lung infection characterized by a dry cough, shortness of breath, fever, and fatigue.

Today, many doctors recommend that HIV-positive people whose CD4 cell count has fallen below the significant two hundred level begin inhaling small doses of antibiotics on a regular basis to prevent PCP from invading the respiratory system. There's a catch: Some scientists believe that with continued exposure to the antibiotic, people will become immune to its beneficial effects; thus, when they eventually fall sick with PCP, drug therapy won't help. It's very important for anyone who is HIV-positive to stay informed about new developments in preventive AIDS treatments.

Thrush is a fungus that grows in the mouth. It may spread to the throat or respiratory tract, making it difficult to swallow or breathe (also known as *Candida esophagitis*). It is treated with antifungal medications, often intravenously in a hospital setting, although a new antifungal agent can be given by mouth, which means fewer days in the hospital.

Toxoplasmosis: Toxoplasma is a parasite that invades the intestinal tract of many animals, particularly cats. When transmitted to humans with a weakened immune system, it can cause loss of coordination, blindness, or dementia.

Wasting syndrome is indicated by the unintentional loss of 10 percent or more of body weight due to loss of appetite, diarrhea, fever, and vomiting. The underlying cause of these symptoms includes infection of the gastrointestinal tract by viruses, bacteria, and parasites.

MAC (Mycobacterium avium *complex)* is an infection of the respiratory and gastrointestinal tract that produces fever, night sweats, severe weakness, and wasting.

HELPING YOURSELF
IF YOU'RE HIV-POSITIVE

Anger and depression are natural and common reactions to a diagnosis of HIV. Those who have had to face HIV say that sharing feelings with family, friends, or members of an AIDS support group can ease the anguish. If one is so overcome by depression that he or she is unable to take constructive health action, counseling by a mental-health professional may help. Counselors, like doctors, are required to protect their client's privacy.

Support groups and community organizations that specialize in HIV/AIDS issues for African Americans have sprung up around the country. These organizations help people find a doctor, provide information on drugs and treatments, can help with psychological counseling and information on insurance, or simply provide someone to talk to. Almost any organization that supplies HIV testing also can put you in touch with one that can help you. You're not alone and you don't have to fight HIV by yourself.

In the rare event that you reach out to an AIDS group for help and meet indifference or rudeness on the other end of the telephone, ask to speak to the person's supervisor or hang up and call the next name on your list (see Resources on page 290). You never have to accept a bad attitude.

Many people with HIV have said they began living their lives more fully, doing things they had only dreamed about before. The best thing you can do if you or someone you love is HIV-positive is to stay informed. New information is available all the time. The more you know, the better your chances of staying healthy.

STAYING HEALTHY WITH HIV

Treatments against HIV don't have to be limited to AZT and other drug therapies. You can help keep yourself healthy by improving your nutrition and paying attention to your overall health. Green vegetables, fresh fruits and juices, whole grains and quality protein, all recommended on the Sankofa Program in Chapter 17, provide a good basis for protecting the immune system. At the same time, do not smoke and stay away from those who do. Eliminate alcohol, caffeine, colas, and sugary products from your diet. Give up any drugs that you use. All chemicals weaken the immune system.

Some people swear by acupuncture, which has been shown to help relieve HIV-related stress. Some long-term survivors recommend herbal remedies and tonics that you can find at the health-food store. If you choose to try these herbal products, be sure to inform your doctor, since they may alter the effects of prescribed drugs. Should an allergic reaction or side effect occur, it will also be easier for your physician to pinpoint the cause if all your treatments are known.

Regular exercise is also important to maintain your health. Some AIDS experts believe that staying in good physical condition may help suppress the virus and delay the onset of AIDS symptoms. All agree that exercise fosters an overall sense of well-being and releases natural substances called endorphins that have immune-boosting and stress-reducing properties.

Other valuable self-help measures include practicing one or more stress-reduction techniques, including meditation, yoga, prayer, visualization, massage, and progressive muscle relaxation.

You can't go around in a plastic bubble, but you should take extra precautions to protect yourself from opportunistic infections. Wash all fruits and vegetables thoroughly and cook eggs, fish, meat, and poultry well.

Also take precautions around the house. Don't touch the cat's litter box; if you must clean up after your pet, use a mask and disposable gloves. In the bathroom and kitchen, wash your hands often and use disposable and separate cleaning materials to protect yourself.

LOOKING TOWARD THE FUTURE

We may not see an actual cure for or vaccine against HIV/AIDS for years. More than a dozen experimental vaccines are being tested in small trials around the world, but, according to June Osborn, the chairperson of the National Commission on AIDS, education must remain at the heart of any coordinated effort to prevent HIV from spreading further. Does education work? It's already working in the gay community. In this country, gay men have led the fight against AIDS and their willingness to speak out, uncover new information, and help others in their community has helped people everywhere. While they are still at great risk for AIDS, the number of new infections among gay men has slightly decreased.

But it's not enough. In November of 1992, the World Health Organization announced that twenty times more money must be spent on AIDS prevention and research around the world. Some believe that HIV eventually may be looked on like diabetes or hypertension—you might not be able to cure it, but with new therapies you will be able to keep it from killing you. Every day, new treatments are being explored and the length of time that HIV-positive people can stay healthy grows longer. There is an enormous amount of work that remains to be done on all fronts —education, prevention, treatment—all over the world.

Every culture, in every country, has to look for ways to reach its own members with information about AIDS. Black people know how to pull together to survive, and there's room for each of us to contribute in his or her own way.

Talking about living with HIV a year after he was diagnosed, Magic Johnson said, "You've got to keep going, keep on work-

ing, fighting, and living life with the same attitude as before."
When he played in the All-Star game in 1991 a few months after
his diagnosis, he said that he wanted to show the world that
people with HIV could still run, jump, and play basketball. And
that you couldn't get the virus from "playing against us, hugging
us, kissing us, or knocking us down." No one did, either in the
All-Star game or in the Olympics. Still, the fears remained. Magic
planned to return to the NBA for the 1992–1993 season, but he
retired again, this time for good, after several players said they
were afraid to play against him. He said that over the long season,
the controversy could hurt the game. Magic will continue to fight
HIV with education and by taking care of himself and his family.
Life is a long season.

RESOURCES

NATIONAL ORGANIZATIONS

Centers for Disease Control and Prevention
The CDC National AIDS Hotline
(800) 342-2437
(800) 344-7432 (Spanish-speaking)
   Free national hotline for anyone with questions about AIDS. Confi-
dential and anonymous referrals to local health organizations, counselors, and support groups. Open twenty-four hours a day.

The AIDS Clinical Trials Information Service
(800)-TRIALS-A (weekdays, 9:00 A.M. to 7:00 P.M. EST)
   Information on federally funded clinical trials for patients with AIDS
or HIV, including eligibility requirements and location of study centers.

The CDC National AIDS Clearinghouse
PO Box 6003
Rockville, MD 20849-6003
   Free educational materials on HIV and AIDS; names, addresses, and
phone numbers of regional and local black organizations specifically
working with AIDS.

National Association for People with AIDS
2025 I Street NW
Washington, D.C. 20006

AMFAR
American Foundation for AIDS Research
Box AIDS, Dept. P
New York, NY 10016
(800) 521-8110
   Its compendium "Learning AIDS" lists or reviews seventeen hundred books, pamphlets, videotapes, and other educational materials available to the public ($24.95 in softcover).

National Urban League
   Virtually every local chapter of the Urban League offers some kind of AIDS program. Call your local chapter.

National Coalition of Black Lesbians and Gays
PO Box 2490
Washington, D.C. 20013
(202) 429-2856
   There are many local organizations of black lesbians and gays. You can write or call the National Coalition or the CDC National Aids Clearinghouse (listed above) for the names of chapters in your area.

LOCAL ORGANIZATIONS

   Here are the names of some—but by no means all—AIDS groups around the country that offer special programs for African Americans.

California

Bay Area Black Consortium for Quality Health Care
AIDS Minority Health Initiative
Case Management Services
1440 Broadway, Suite 403
Oakland, CA 94612
(510) 763-1872

Black Community AIDS Research and Education Project
405 Hilgard Avenue
1283 Franz Hall
Los Angeles, CA 90024-1563
(310) 206-5160

San Francisco Black Coalition on AIDS
1042 Divisadero Street
San Francisco, CA 94115
415-346-AIDS

Colorado

Black AIDS Project-at-Large
1525 Josephine Street
Denver, CO 80206
(303) 388-5861

Georgia

Minority AIDS Information
Network
800 Peachtree Street, NE, Suite
505
Atlanta, GA 30365
(404) 894-5730

National Black Men's Health
Network
250 Georgia Avenue, Suite 321
Atlanta, GA 30312
(404) 524-7237

National Black Women's Health
Project
1237 Abernathy SW
Atlanta, GA 30310
(404) 758-9590

Illinois

African American AIDS
Network
3020 W. Lexington
Chicago, IL 60612
(312) 326-4344

Kupona Network
AIDS Program
4611 S. Ellis Avenue
Chicago, IL 60653
(312) 536-3000

Maryland

Black Educational AIDS Project
1054 W. Baltimore Street,
Suite A
Baltimore, MD 22522
(301) 685-1204

New Jersey

Blacks Against AIDS
PO Box 7732
Atlantic City, NJ 08404
(609) 347-1645

New York

Black Leadership Commission
on AIDS
105 East Twenty-second Street
New York, NY 10010
(212) 614-0023
(212) 674-3500
Helps local community
groups that wish to provide
AIDS services.

Gay Men's Health Crisis
(GMHC)
129 West Twentieth Street
New York, NY 10001
AIDS Hotline: (212) 807-6655
AIDS Hotline-TDD (hearing-
impaired): (212) 645-7470

Minority Task Force on AIDS
505 Eighth Avenue
New York, NY
(212) 563-8340

People with AIDS Coalition
31 West Twenty-sixth Street
New York, NY 10010
(212) 645-4538
(212) 647-1420 (HOTLINE)
(800) 828-3280

Pennsylvania

BEBASHI (Blacks Educating
Blacks About Sexual Health
Issues)
1233 Locust Street, Suite 401
Philadelphia, PA 91907
(215) 546-4140

Innerpride
PO Box 42426
Philadelphia, PA 19101
(215) 849-7597

Texas
Black Effort Against the Threat
  of AIDS
411 Spriggsdale Street
San Antonio, TX 78220
(512) 271-3997

Ebony Connection
227 Congress Avenue, Suite 125
Austin, TX 78767
(512) 459-4772

Inner City AIDS Network
912 3rd Street, NW
Washington, D.C. 20001-2511
(202) 789-4226
(202) 789-ICAN

Spectrum
401 New York Avenue, NE
Washington, D.C. 20002
(202) 675-2115
(202) 775-1770

Washington, D.C.
Best Friends of District of
  Columbia
3415 5th Street, SE
Washington, D.C. 20032
(202) 364-4074

RECOMMENDED READING

There are many good books being published about AIDS-related issues. Only a few are listed here. Visit your library or bookstore for
more.

Positively Aware, a monthly journal published by Test Positive Aware
Network, which provides programs and resources for people in the
Chicago area who have HIV or AIDS. You can subscribe to their journal
by writing or calling:

TPA Network
1340 W. Irving Pk., Box 259
Chicago, IL 60613
(312) 404-TPAN

Early Care for HIV Disease, 2nd ed. A paperback by Ronald A. Baker,
Ph.D., Jeffrey M. Moulton, Ph.D., and John Charles Tighe, published
by the San Francisco AIDS Foundation. It is $12.95 at bookstores and
can also be ordered by calling Impact AIDS at (415) 861-3397; add $4
for mailing.

The Guide to Living with HIV Infection is a paperback developed in 1991
at the Johns Hopkins AIDS Clinic by John G. Bartlett, M.D., and Ann
K. Finkbeiner. Available for $15.95 at bookstores or from the publisher,
Johns Hopkins University Press, 701 West 40th Street, Suite 275, Baltimore, MD. 21211; phone (800) 537-5487.

Positive Thinking is a twenty-seven-page booklet written especially for those newly identified as HIV-positive. Published by the American Social Health Association, it can be obtained without charge from the association by sending a self-addressed business-size envelope with 52 cents postage. The address is PO Box 13827-PL, Research Triangle Park, NC 27709; phone (919) 361-8400.

Surviving AIDS is by Michael Callen, a longtime survivor. It profiles the way he and other longtime survivors have stayed alive. Harper Perennial, a Division of HarperCollins Publishers, New York, 1990.

22

CANCER

A fter heart disease, cancer is the second-leading cause of death in the United States. According to the American Cancer Society, approximately 1 million Americans get cancer each year, and each year nearly 500,000 die. African Americans, especially men, are more likely to get cancer—and more likely to die from it—than members of any other group in the United States. (Other ethnic Americans have a *lower* than average total incidence of cancer than the general population. Native Americans have the lowest rate of all.)

The incidence of cancer is growing across the United States, particularly among blacks. Since 1950, the overall cancer incidence has increased by 12 percent among the general population and by 27 percent among blacks. Our death rates are even worse: In the last forty years, the number of cancer deaths in the total population has increased 10 percent, but the number of deaths among black cancer victims has jumped 50 percent—and the cancer death rate among black men has risen 88 percent.

Of all diseases, cancer is the most frightening. Many people believe that cancer is inherited—that there's nothing we can do to prevent it and, if we do get cancer, that it cannot be cured. Although it's true that some cancers, such as breast cancer and prostate cancer, seem to run in families, most cancers are not inherited. Cancer often can be prevented and, with early diagnosis and treatment, it often can be cured.

REDUCING YOUR RISK

If one of your parents or another close relative had cancer, you should be especially careful to follow cancer-prevention techniques. But family history is only one risk factor; it doesn't mean that you will get cancer. On the other hand, if no one in your family has ever had cancer, you don't necessarily have a free pass, either. *Everyone needs to pay attention to cancer prevention.*

WHAT IS CANCER?

Cancer is not one but, rather, many diseases characterized by the unrestrained growth of abnormal cells in the body. Normally, as old body cells are worn out, they are replaced by new cells. The renewal process then stops until the cells wear out again. In cancer, new cell growth continues unchecked, a process triggered by cancer-causing substances called carcinogens, which damage the reproductive machinery, or DNA, of the cells.

Carcinogens exist all around us—in tobacco smoke, pollution, food, sunlight, soil, chemicals, and even in our own bodies during digestion. Although everyone is exposed to carcinogens, not everyone gets cancer, because the body has natural defenses against it.

Researchers believe that when our innate ability to resist cancer is impaired, cancer begins. For example, we know that every cell in the body has checkpoints that watch over it. The most potent guardian is a gene called p53. If a cell is damaged by a carcinogen, such as cigarette smoke, p53 detects the damage and stops the cell from dividing until the body can repair it. In this way, the initial small error is fixed before the damaged cell can pass the mistake on to new cells. Once corrected, the orderly division of cells resumes. Apparently, some people either do not have a p53 gene or have somehow lost it. Without the p53 guardian, abnormal cells readily reproduce and one small error is magnified into mayhem.

If scientists can discover why the p53 gene becomes lost or deactivated, it may be possible to restore it. Genetics may be involved, which may also help explain why some cancers appear to run in families.

THE CAUSES OF CANCER

Specific causes of cancer have been clearly identified. They are:

- *High-fat, low-fiber diet—35 percent of all cancers*
- *Tobacco—30 percent*
- *Sexual and reproductive history*—7 percent*
- *Occupational hazards—4 percent*
- *Alcohol—3 percent*

Other recognized causes are:

- *Food additives*
- *Viruses*
- *Pollution*
- *Overexposure to sunlight (skin cancers)*
- *Excessive radiation*
- *Radon †*
- *Drugs*

The percentages given above are "best guesses" by reputable researchers. All researchers agree, however, that the two leading causes of cancer are tobacco and diet—which means that between 60 and 70 percent of all cancers could be prevented by quitting smoking and changing the way we eat.

* Women who have multiple sexual partners have a higher risk of cervical cancer; women who have children at a young age have a lower risk of breast cancer.
† Radon is an odorless, tasteless radioactive gas produced by the radioactive decay of radium. It occurs naturally in rocks and soil, enters buildings through cracks in foundations or basements, and, when inhaled, releases ionizing radiation that can cause damage to lung tissue and lead to lung cancer.

WHY ARE BLACKS SO VULNERABLE TO CANCER?

Why do we get cancer more often? And why are we more likely to die from it? Is it something about the disease itself or is it something in our environment or lifestyle that makes us especially vulnerable?

Recent surveys conducted by the National Medical Association, the premier medical society of black doctors, isolated two important cancer facts:

The majority of African Americans do not know the major warning signs of cancer. Only 13 percent can identify even one.

Blacks are less likely to participate in screening programs that might reveal early treatable cancers. For example, fewer black women have an annual Pap smear, which can diagnose early cervical cancer, and as a result twice as many black women die of this disease.

A third important factor contributes to our low survival rate from cancer: low income. Low income often goes hand in hand with a less nutritious diet and inadequate access to doctors. It also means we receive less information about cancer. For example, according to the survey, less than half of black adults are aware that eating a high-fat diet increases cancer risk.

While the way we live and the foods we eat may account for some of our greater cancer risk, they don't tell the whole story. For example, prostate cancer is two to three times more common in black men than white—regardless of lifestyle, diet, or income. It's possible that our high incidence of other diseases, such as high blood pressure and diabetes, may somehow interfere with the body's natural immunity to cancer.

There are more reasons. All the causes of cancer (see the box on page 297) affect everyone regardless of color. But black people are exposed to more carcinogens than others. More than half of American blacks now live within the limits of smog-choked cities, many near expressways and major thoroughfares, and in industrial areas.

Blacks also have always been accorded the dirtiest industrial jobs, exposing them to unusually high amounts of toxic chemicals. While only 4 percent of cancers are said to be caused by occupational hazards, this figure might be much higher among blacks. Attempts to clean up workplaces have reduced occupational hazards, but many potentially harmful chemicals and pollutants have yet to be tested. Therefore, when it comes to blacks and cancer, occupational hazards are an important area of research.

CANCER-CAUSING JOBS
Your cancer risk increases if your job exposes you to:

- *Chemicals, dusts, or harmful gases*
- *Sewage/chemical waste*
- *Sunlight (fair-skinned blacks are vulnerable)*
- *X rays*
- *Regular low-level radiation*
- *Asbestos*

Some jobs that may put you at risk:

- *Welding (exposure to lead, chromium)*
- *Construction work, shipbuilding (asbestos)*
- *Industrial workers (asbestos, silica, dust, tar derivatives, radioactive compounds, polyvinyl chloride PVC)*
- *Coal mining*
- *Radiology*
- *Furniture and cabinetmaking (dust)*
- *Quarry work*
- *Agricultural work*
- *Gas station work (benzene, liquid condensed by compressing oil gas)*

You can significantly reduce your risk of getting cancer by avoiding factors known to promote cancer—and emphasizing those known to inhibit cancer.

CANCER PROMOTERS

Cancer is promoted by smoking, fat in the diet, alcohol, nitrates, and charbroiling.

Smoking and Alcohol. Cigarette smoking is directly related to cancers of the throat, mouth, lung, and bladder. Black Americans smoke more than whites and are at greater risk of developing lung cancer. (Forty-one percent of blacks over the age of twenty smoke cigarettes, as compared to 32 percent of whites.) Twenty-seven percent more blacks than whites die of lung cancer.

If you smoke *and* drink, your risk of cancer is many times greater. Besides alcohol, smoking combined with other substances also puts people at risk. Industrial workers who smoke are more vulnerable to the toxic effects of radon, fumes from rubber and chlorine, and dust from cotton and coal. Smokers exposed to asbestos have a lung cancer risk nearly sixty times greater than nonsmokers.

Secondhand smoke has now joined the list of powerful human carcinogens. Secondhand smoke is thought to cause 53,000 deaths annually, 4,000 from lung cancer.

Smokeless tobacco—plug, leaf, and snuff—is also a big problem, especially among teenage boys and young adult males. "Dipping snuff" (tucking coarse, moist tobacco between the cheek and gum) is a highly addictive habit that exposes the body to the same levels of nicotine as cigarettes. The nicotine, along with other carcinogens in the snuff, is absorbed through the mouth tissues, which can lead to cancer of the mouth.

If you are a smoker and quit now, you immediately reduce your risk of contracting lung cancer. Although quitting is beneficial at any age, the younger you are when you quit, the more your risk profile will improve.

Fatty Foods. The higher your daily fat intake, the greater your risk of cancer. Colon cancer is most clearly associated with fat intake, but other cancers—cancers of the breast, pancreas, prostate, rectum, ovaries, and uterus—have also been linked to high-fat diets. Lung cancer is the latest disease to show an association with excess fat intake.

All types of fat, except fish oil, are involved. Too much animal protein has also been linked to some cancers, but it's difficult to know whether it's the protein or the fat in animal products that causes the problem.

How fat promotes cancer is unknown. However, a high-fat diet is usually low in fiber, which seems to establish a cancer-causing pattern. Adding vegetables, fruits, and grains to your diet, while limiting animal protein, automatically breaks this pattern.

Nitrates/Smoked Foods. Nitrates are food additives used to preserve bacon, sausage, luncheon meats, and other smoked, salted, or cured foods. When you digest these foods, nitrates spontaneously turn into nitrites, which then produce a compound called *nitrosamines.* Nitrosamines may induce cancer anywhere in the body, particularly in the stomach and esophagus, two cancers that are especially high among American blacks.

Vitamin C and vitamin E can help prevent the conversion of nitrates/nitrites into nitrosamines. But extra vitamins alone cannot do the whole job, so it's wise to limit these foods in your diet. *Charbroiled Proteins.* Charbroiling on gas or charcoal grills, or over an open fire, produces carcinogens in protein foods such as meat, fish and poultry.

One group of carcinogens, called PAHs (polycyclic aromatic hydrocarbons), is formed when dripping fat hits the heat and splatters back onto the food. Another type of carcinogen is formed when protein foods are cooked for long periods over high heat.

You can still enjoy outdoor cooking if you take some precautions:

- Remove the skin and fat from poultry and meat before cooking.
- Partially cook foods in the oven first to reduce grilling time.
- Cover the grill with foil to prevent splash-back of fat.
- Baste with nonfat liquid marinade.

WHERE DO MOST CANCERS OCCUR?

Cancer may develop in any organ of the body, but in the general population it occurs most frequently in the lungs, colon/rectum, breast, skin, prostate, and bladder.

For blacks, however, the major sites of cancer are somewhat different. In order of incidence, we are most likely to develop cancer in the prostate, lung, breast, colon/rectum, esophagus (throat) and mouth, and stomach.

WHERE THE BIGGEST GAPS ARE

When we look at where the biggest *differences* occur between blacks and other groups, the picture changes. For example, we have four times the rate of cancer of the esophagus, twice the rate

---

CANCER INHIBITORS
Specific compounds in plants are now known to act as potent anticancer agents. Scientists call these substances phytochemicals, derived from the Greek word phyton, *which means plant, or "that which grows." Several compounds are presently being studied by the National Cancer Institute.*

- *Carrots, celery, coriander, parsley, parsnips*
- *Cabbage family: broccoli, brussels sprouts, cabbage, cauliflower, collard greens, kale, mustard greens, rutabaga*
- *Garlic, onions*
- *Licorice-root extract**
- *Foods high in vitamin C (all citrus fruits, dark green leafy vegetables, peas, potatoes)*
- *Foods high in vitamin A and beta carotene (all dark green and bright orange vegetables)*
- *Vitamin E, vitamin B₆, selenium, folacin, calcium*
- *Fiber*

* Not recommended. May cause hypertension if ingested in large quantities.

---

of stomach cancer, and about one and a half times the rate of lung cancer and pancreatic cancer.

	Per 100,000 population*	
	Blacks	*Whites*
Esophagus	*9.1*	*2.6*
Cervix	*8.7*	*3.1*
Prostate	*43.9*	*21.1*
Stomach	*10.0*	*5.2*
Lung and bronchus	*51.3*	*41.6*
Pancreas	*11.2*	*8.4*

* Adapted from American Cancer Society, 1991.

WARNING SIGNS OF CANCER*

- *Lump or bump in the breast or elsewhere*
- *Unusual bleeding or discharge anywhere*
- *Change in bowel or bladder habits*
- *Change (color or size) in wart or mole*
- *A sore or scab that does not heal*
- *Persistent hoarseness or cough*
- *Difficulty in swallowing*
- *Rapid weight loss without apparent cause*
- *Severe recurrent headaches*
- *Change in shape or size of testicles*
- *Persistent abdominal pain*

* Adapted from the American Cancer Society. Specific cancers have specific warning signs. Read the rest of this chapter carefully to learn more about those cancers that affect blacks more often than others.

Let's take a brief look at the cancers that are most deadly to African Americans—and also the ones in which the gap between us and other Americans is the greatest: prostate, lung, esophagus, breast, cervical, colon-rectal, and stomach cancer. Even if you've never had cancer, even if no one in your family has ever had cancer, it's important that you read this information—because in the next few pages, we're going to talk about how you can prevent these potentially deadly diseases from knocking on your door.

PROSTATE CANCER

The incidence of this cancer is growing so rapidly that today prostate cancer is the most common—and the most ignored—cancer among American men. After lung cancer, it is the second-leading cause of cancer death among men. African-American men have the highest incidence of prostate cancer in the world (one in nine), two to three times higher than white males. And the survival rate for black men is 13 percent lower than for whites.

WHAT IS THE PROSTATE GLAND?

The prostate is a walnut-sized gland that grows out of and encircles the upper part of the urethra, the canal that carries both urine from the bladder and sperm from the testicles out through the tip of the penis. The prostate gland produces seminal fluid to transport sperm.

WHAT CAUSES PROSTATE CANCER?

The cause is unknown, although there are some intriguing ideas. For example, like breast cancer in women, prostate cancer can be stimulated by sex hormones. In women, these are estrogens; in men, they are androgens such as testosterone. This may account for the high incidence of prostate cancer among blacks who, on average, have higher testosterone levels than white men do. While the cause is unknown, there are some potential risk factors:

• Over age 40
• Family history of prostate cancer
• Having sex at an early age and multiple sex partners
• High-fat diet
• Toxic job hazards
• Vasectomy

SYMPTOMS

Prostate cancer may not produce any symptoms at all until it is too late. Men who have any of the warning signs below are urged to see a doctor without delay. None of these symptoms necessarily means prostate cancer is present. Several other harmless conditions, such as an enlarged prostate gland, may produce similar symptoms. The only way to know for sure is to have a proper checkup by a physician. Warning signs include:

• Inability to urinate
• Frequent urination, especially at night
• Pain or burning sensation when urinating or ejaculating
• Blood or pus in the urine or semen

• Persistent pain in the back, hips, and pelvis; fatigue; and anemia—all suggest prostate cancer even when other symptoms are absent.

EARLY DETECTION

The most effective way to stop this cancer is to catch it at an early stage when it is very responsive to treatment. Treated soon enough, prostate cancer can be cured in more than 90 percent of cases. Yet many men, particularly black men, fail to receive the simple examination that can detect prostate cancer early enough to save their lives.

The best prevention is to have a yearly rectal exam, including a digital exam, a blood test, and an ultrasound probe.

If you are over age forty, ask for a prostate exam every time you see a doctor. The doctor inserts a gloved hand into the rectum and feels the prostate gland; if it is hard and knobby, it may be diseased.

At that point, the doctor usually refers the individual to a urologist, who will probably order a biopsy. If the biopsy reveals cancer, further tests—chest X ray, bone scans, X rays of the urinary tract, blood tests—are performed to see how far the disease has spread. The treatment selected depends on the results of these tests.

EARLY TREATMENT

For small localized tumors, surgery to remove the tumor usually results in a cure. Afterward, men can resume their usual sexual activity; impotence seldom occurs. Urinary incontinence is usual right after surgery, but most men regain normal urine control within six months of surgery.

Radiation. Radiation therapy is often recommended as an alternative for older patients who wish to avoid surgery. Radiation may be either external or internal. Neither form causes urinary incontinence; however, external radiation may cause impotence.

The most important key to a successful outcome after treatment is to continue to have annual checkups even after all traces of cancer are gone.

LATE TREATMENT

If undetected and untreated, prostate cancer may spread to almost any organ of the body, most commonly to the bones and lymph nodes. But even in these advanced stages, progress has been made. Drug therapy, sometimes combined with surgery or radiation, can be used to slow the growth of the tumor and relieve symptoms. Drug therapy may be either chemotherapy or hormone therapy. Chemotherapy kills cancer cells throughout the body. Hormonal therapy blocks the production of male hormones that stimulate tumor cells. Drug treatment often results in diminished sex drive and impotence, but it can put some men in remission for a decade or longer.

TREATMENT CONTROVERSIES

Not every prostate cancer requires aggressive treatment. In some cases, especially in older men, the cancer grows so slowly that a man often dies of something else before the cancer becomes a problem. However, there's no way to know which tumors will spread rapidly and which will not. In men under sixty, the growth of a malignant prostate tumor can be fast and devastating.

In black men, the death rate from this cancer is so high that most experts agree that treatment is essential in all but the very elderly.

LOOKING TOWARD THE FUTURE

Most scientists believe the best hope for the future is earlier detection and more aggressive treatment. Two new diagnostic aids can be used to improve detection during a rectal exam: a simple blood test and a small ultrasound probe that scans the prostate for tumors.

New kinds of therapy may also lie just over the horizon as subtle differences between types of cancers are better understood. Until these procedures are perfected, however, all black men over forty are urged to have yearly rectal exams.

PROBLEMS YOU MAY FACE

Many men shun the digital rectal exam unless they're having a specific problem. The new blood test and the ultrasound probe have made screening more attractive, but most experts agree that all three exams should be done together.

It's important for black men to overcome their natural reluctance and begin to have rectal exams on a regular basis. The minor discomfort attached to such exams is surpassed by the potential benefits.

A reminder: Most men who have prostate surgery are able to resume a normal sex life. Only in advanced cases, where drug therapy must be used to shut down hormone production from the testicles, are sex drive and potency affected.

CANCER OF THE ESOPHAGUS

Black men and women are four times as likely to develop this type of cancer as whites are—and twice as likely to die from it. *This is one of our most dangerous cancers, and it is almost entirely preventable.*

The risk factors associated with this cancer are smoking and drinking. Difficulty in swallowing is a warning sign. The best means of preventing this disease are to give up cigarettes and alcohol. If you can't quit both, stop smoking and reduce alcohol consumption.

HOW ESOPHAGEAL CANCER IS DIAGNOSED

A barium drink is used to locate the site and often the type of obstruction. Then the physician inserts a tube (endoscope) into the esophagus to view the obstruction and collect a small tissue sample for biopsy. About 90 percent of tumors are malignant.

TREATMENTS

Removing the esophagus (an esophagectomy) usually gives the best result. This is major surgery, involving incisions in the abdomen, chest, and sometimes the neck. In older patients, radiation or chemotherapy is often recommended instead of surgery. In the meantime, intubation—inserting a tube through the tumor, which is blocking the passage of food down the esophagus—may allow the individual to swallow some liquid or semiliquid food.

The outlook is poor for this cancer. Only 5 percent of all patients survive for more than five years. Experts believe that the delayed detection probably accounts for the lower survival rate among black men and women. As with most cancers, your best chance lies in early diagnosis and treatment.

COLON CANCER

Colon cancer, also called colon-rectal or colorectal cancer, is responsible for about 20 percent of all cancer deaths in the United States each year, and the incidence is equally high for both blacks and whites. Risk factors include:

- Previous family history of colon cancer
- Family or personal history of polyps
- Inflammatory bowel disease
- Diet high in fats, low in fiber

SYMPTOMS

Colon cancer may not produce any symptoms until late in the disease. However, any change in your usual bowel movements may be a warning, especially if you are over age fifty. Warning signs include:

- • Constipation or diarrhea for more than ten days
- Blood in the feces
- Pain or tenderness in the lower abdomen

PREVENTION

Always tell your physician if someone in your family has had colon cancer so he or she can routinely check you for precancerous polyps. *Virtually all colon cancers start out in this benign form.* Many physicians believe that everyone over fifty should have a thorough examination of the colon every year. This includes a simple laboratory test to examine stool for hidden traces of blood, as well as the direct examination of the colon using a flexible sigmoidoscope, a narrow bendable tube with a viewing instrument on the end that allows the physician to look directly at the colon. Any polyps or growths often can be removed through the tube.

The best way to prevent this disease is by maintaining a high-fiber, low-fat diet.

How Colon Cancer Is Diagnosed

Tests used to diagnose colon cancer are the examination of feces, barium X rays, sigmoidoscopy, and colonoscopy.

Treatments

If the tumor is local, surgery to remove the cancer and a small amount of surrounding tissue—called a colectomy—is the most effective treatment. More than half of all patients are cured with this procedure.

When the cancer has spread, surgery may not be possible. However, other therapies can be used to slow or arrest its growth.

LUNG CANCER

Lung cancer is the leading cancer killer in the United States. Of all groups, blacks have the highest incidence and the highest death rates. While the lung cancer rate is dropping among white men, it is increasing among black men and women. In fact, women of every color are catching up in this deadly race: Their death rate from lung cancer has increased by more than 300 percent over the last thirty years.

Risk Factors
- Smoking
- Exposure to secondhand smoke
- Exposure to asbestos and natural radon gas
- High-fat diet

Early Warning Sign
- Persistent cough

Later Warning Signs
- Bloody sputum
- Shortness of breath
- Chest pain

Best Prevention
- Stop smoking.
- Avoid breathing secondhand smoke.
- Protect yourself from hazardous work sites.
- Eat less fat and more fiber.

HOW LUNG CANCER IS DIAGNOSED

Lung cancer is usually diagnosed by a chest X ray, in which a shadow appears on the lung. A CAT scan (computer axial tomography) or MRI (magnetic resonance imaging) may detect the tumor. Phlegm may be tested for cancer cells or tissue samples may be taken for biopsy.

TREATMENTS

When the tumor is still small and confined to one lung, surgery is the usual treatment. Drugs and radiation therapy may be used —alone or in addition to surgery—to destroy cancer cells.

Once the cancer has spread, there is little likelihood of a cure. Only about 13 percent of all those diagnosed with lung cancer survive five years. For blacks, the survival rate is only 11 percent.

BREAST CANCER

Breast cancer is the most common cancer killer in women. Approximately one of every ten women will develop breast cancer in her lifetime, and that number is going up. By the year 2000, it is estimated one out of every eight American women will develop breast cancer.

The incidence of breast cancer in black women is actually lower than in white women, but the mortality rates are the same. This is an important discrepancy. If our incidence is lower, then the death rate should also be lower. One obvious reason for the higher death rate is that breast cancer is discovered at a more advanced stage in black women.

No one knows exactly what causes breast cancer or how to avoid getting it. Women's groups are pressuring government medical institutions to make a consistent planned attack on this disease that is growing in incidence every year. Several studies have shown a link between high-fat diets and breast cancer, but one important new study failed to show a connection. There is also disagreement about whether fat alone or excess weight is the critical factor.

It's also known that breast cancer rates are higher in certain communities, which suggests an environmental cause, but no one knows exactly what that cause might be. A new study published in *The Journal of the National Cancer Institute* in April of 1993 showed that women who had the highest exposure to the pesticide DDT had four times the breast cancer risk of women with the least exposure. Even though the use of DDT was banned in 1972, residues of the pesticide are stored in the body—*in fatty tissue* —for decades. Most Americans still carry DDT residues and DDT also remains in the food chain, in the earth, and in animals. If confirmed, the findings could provide a possible explanation for the puzzling rise in the incidence of breast cancer in recent decades.

RISK FACTORS

While the exact cause of breast cancer remains a mystery, a number of studies explored breast cancer in different countries and identified three common risk factors: age, family history, and previous breast cancer.

- Over age fifty: Two-thirds of all breast cancers occur among older women. However, *youth does not protect you against this cancer; it merely reduces your risk.*

- Family history: Women whose mothers or sisters have had breast cancer develop the disease at about twice the average rate. If a mother's cancer occurred before menopause, her daughters have a somewhat higher risk.
- Previous breast cancer: Women who have had cancer in one breast are three times more likely to develop cancer in the other breast.

Other possible risk factors include:

- Previous breast biopsies showing unusual cell growth
- Never having given birth to a child, or bearing the first child after age thirty-five
- Having a distant relative—maternal aunt or grandmother— with breast cancer
- Onset of menstruation before age twelve
- History of fibrocystic breast disease (a nonmalignant growth in the breast)
- Obesity or a high-fat diet, possibly because these lead to additional production of hormones that are linked to some breast cancers
- Previous endometrial cancer
- Menopause after age fifty-five
- Previous mammograms that looked suspicious to the radiologist

The best way to prevent this disease is to maintain a low-fat diet and a desirable weight.

EARLY DETECTION

Because breast cancer is so deadly, it's important that every woman—even if she has no risk factors—pay special attention to detecting the disease. The earlier breast cancer is discovered and the smaller it is at the time of discovery, the better the chance for a cure.

Various medical organizations have different guidelines concerning breast exams and mammograms. Here are the recommendations from the American Cancer Society:

Starting in her teens, or as soon as her breasts start to develop, every woman should begin to examine her own breasts for lumps each month (see page 314).

After age eighteen, all women should continue monthly self-exams and also have their breasts examined by a physician every year. A breast exam is a routine part of every gynecological checkup.

At age thirty-five, mammography is recommended to provide a baseline for future comparison (every year thereafter for women who have had previous breast cancer).

Between the ages of forty and forty-nine, women should have a mammogram every one to two years (every year for women with a family history of breast cancer).

Age fifty and over, women should have a mammogram every year.

MONTHLY BREAST SELF-EXAMINATION

Monthly self-examination is key to diagnosing cancer at an early stage. Black women especially need to tune in to monthly self-exams, since late discovery is the major factor in our high death rates from this disease. With monthly examination, you will get to know the normal appearance, shape, and feel of your breasts so you will be able to notice changes if they occur.

Each month, one week after your period ends, examine your breasts. (If you are past menopause and no longer have periods, set any day, such as the first of the month.) If you have had one breast treated for cancer, you should examine the opposite breast regularly, as well as the treated breast.

A self-exam is divided into two parts—first, looking at your breasts; second, feeling each breast for lumps. Look for:

- Swellings or depressions
- Moles or dark or reddened areas
- Puckering or dimpling
- Any skin irritation that persists
- Any change in the nipple—whitish scale, distorted shape, inverted nipple, or dark discharge.

Next, you want to feel your breasts for any lump or thickening. It's best to do this while lying down on your back. Put your left hand under your head; examine your left breast with your right hand, using the flats of your fingers.

1. Start with the upper part of your breast and stroke your fingers down toward the nipple. Feel all around the nipple and gently squeeze it to detect any discharge.
2. Feel the lower breast the same way, working from underneath up toward the nipple.
3. Examine both sides of the breast, working from the outside toward the nipple.
4. Feel carefully around the upper portion of the breast near your armpit.
5. Finally, feel inside the armpit for any unusual lumps. Some women normally have lumps there in the lymph nodes: *What you're looking for is any change from your normal condition.*

Switch sides and repeat the exam for the right breast.

If you feel a new lump in either breast or if there is a discharge from either nipple, immediately report it to your physician.

SYMPTOMS

A lump in the breast or a dark discharge from the nipple are the most common symptoms of breast cancer. Most lumps, bumps, and alterations are not malignant, but the only way to know for sure is to have them checked out by your doctor. Never assume that a lump will just disappear.

If you or your physician discovers a lump in your breast, a mammogram or breast X ray is often the next step. A biopsy will determine whether the lump is malignant. The doctor may insert a needle into the breast to remove a bit of tissue for examination, or you may decide to have the whole lump surgically removed. About 80 percent of breast lumps are benign. However, if the tumor is malignant, further tests will be conducted to see whether the cancer has spread and, if so, how far.

TREATMENTS

The medical community is at odds with itself over the proper treatment for breast cancer. Right now, the treatment suggested may depend more on which doctor you see than on your particular condition.

Surgery is still the most common treatment of breast cancer. There are two types of operations: a mastectomy, in which the entire breast is removed, and a lumpectomy, in which the tumor alone is removed.

Many surgeons now believe that lumpectomy, in combination with radiation or anticancer drug therapy, is as effective as mastectomy, and much less disfiguring. (If the cancer has spread, having a radical mastectomy won't stop it.) Your age, the size of the tumor, and whether the cancer has spread are all part of the treatment decision. Early-stage breast cancer is curable in about one in three women. After surgery, monthly breast self-examination, regular doctor visits, and periodic mammograms are critical follow-up procedures.

CERVICAL CANCER AND OTHER GYNECOLOGICAL CANCERS

While most women are generally aware of breast cancer, many of us are less knowledgeable about cancers of the cervix, the ovaries, and the uterus. Gynecologic cancers produce few symptoms until the disease is advanced. Regular gynecological checkups are the only prevention strategy, and they are designed to pick up specific cancers: A pap smear identifies cancer of the cervix; a pelvic exam detects ovarian cancer; a rectal exam detects cancer of the rectum.

If the gynecologist suspects a problem, other tests may include a biopsy of tissue samples, blood tests, or imaging studies. All gynecological cancers are important, but cervical cancer is the most dangerous for black women.

CERVICAL CANCER

The cervix is a hard, movable valve between the vagina and the uterus. It measures about one and one -half inches across, with a small depression in the middle. The depression is actually a small hole through which sperm enter the uterus during intercourse. Blood flows out through the hole during menstruation, and babies push through it during childbirth.

Cervical cancer is one of the most common—and most treatable—of all cancers. Yet black women, who have twice the incidence, are also twice as likely to die from cervical cancer.

The cause of cervical cancer is unknown, but several risk factors may set up an environment in which it is easier for this cancer to take hold. Risk factors include:

- Early age at first sexual intercourse
- Multiple sexual partners
- Contact with herpes and papilloma viruses, passed on from sexual partners
- A history of venereal diseases
- Smoking, which may also play a role in this type of cancer, possibly because it weakens the immune system and leaves the cervix vulnerable to viral infections

PREVENTION AND DIAGNOSIS

Every women who is sexually active should have a simple Pap (Papanicolaou) test every year. The test takes only a few seconds: a nurse or doctor wipes a swab like a Q-Tip across the surface of the cervix, inside your vagina. Cells caught on the swab are examined at a laboratory. This test can detect abnormal precancerous cells; if present, they can be treated and cured completely *before* any cancer appears.

All women should have full access to a yearly Pap test, and yet we know that all women do not. A recent study by the American Cancer Society revealed that only 76 percent of black women were even aware of the Pap test, and only 70 percent had ever had one, compared to 92 percent of white women who knew about the test and 85 percent who had had it at some time.

There are no early warning signs for cervical cancer, but symptoms occurring later are vaginal bleeding and pain in the pelvic region.

TREATMENTS

Cervical cancer also can be detected by a biopsy or by colposcopy, in which the cervix is examined with magnified light. When caught early enough, the cancer can be destroyed with either heat or cold techniques: electrocoagulation, diathermy, laser treatment, or cryosurgery. Fifty to 80 percent of all patients with early-stage cervical cancer can expect a full recovery.

In later stages, radiation therapy or surgery may be recommended, depending on your age and the extent of the cancer. In these cases, the survival rate drops dramatically—to 10 to 30 percent. Radical surgery—in which the cervix, vagina, uterus, bladder, and rectum may all be removed—improves the survival rate to between 30 and 50 percent.

STOMACH CANCER

While other cancers have increased in incidence or remained the same, the number of new stomach cancer cases in the United States has actually declined over the last sixty years. No one knows exactly what causes stomach cancer, but it has been linked to the way food is preserved. For example, before home refrigeration, many foods were preserved through salting, pickling, and smoking; fresh fruits and vegetables were often unavailable much of the year. In 1930, stomach cancer was the leading cause of cancer death among men, and the third-leading cause among women. Refrigeration has changed the way foods are preserved and better transportation has made fresh foods available year-round. This type of cancer is disappearing in the United States. Yet 24,000 new cases of stomach cancer are still diagnosed each year, claiming about 14,000 lives yearly. This is an important cancer for us to talk about because twice as many blacks as whites develop the disease.

Family history may play a part in this disease. The risk appears to be highest for people whose mother or father developed stomach cancer at an early age. But it's difficult to distinguish between environmental factors and genetic influences when families live together.

Exposure to certain dietary factors *early in life* may be partly responsible. For example, adults immigrating to the United States have stomach cancer rates similar to the rate in their home country. But their children, born in the United States, have stomach cancer rates similar to other Americans. Risk factors include:

- Over age fifty
- Diet high in smoked or cured foods
- Diet low in fruits and vegetables
- Family history
- Pernicious anemia, a form of anemia in which the body cannot absorb vitamin B_{12}
- Chronic gastritis

SYMPTOMS

Stomach cancers cause few symptoms in their early stage, and when symptoms do occur, they are easy to ignore—vague indigestion, a feeling of fullness, and loss of appetite. Only later in the disease, when the cancer has spread widely, do symptoms such as severe pain in the upper abdomen, weight loss, and frequent vomiting develop. Anemia (resulting from prolonged bleeding from the cancer) and bloody vomit and feces also appear in the later stages.

Consult your doctor without delay if symptoms of indigestion occur for the first time in your life or if your usual indigestion changes in character.

HOW STOMACH CANCER IS DIAGNOSED

The diagnosis is made by inserting a gastroscope down the throat to give a direct view of the inside of the stomach and also to remove tissue samples for biopsy.

Most stomach cancers develop in the lower portion of the stomach. If all of the affected area can be removed, a cure is possible. Very often, however, the cancer has spread to other organs such as the lungs, bones, or liver before the diagnosis is made. In the late stages of this disease, cancer cells may spread to any organ in the body. Surgery may still be recommended to relieve the symptoms; chemotherapy and/or radiation therapy will also be used to reduce the tumor size and extend survival.

While you cannot fully protect yourself against cancer, you can reduce your risk by improving lifestyle practices and getting an early examination should warning signs appear. And if you do get cancer, you have a better chance of a full recovery if you seek treatment early.

RESOURCES

Cancer Information Service
1-800-422-6237 (1-800-4-CANCER)
Alaska: 1-800-638-6070
Hawaii (Oahu): 524-1234 (on neighboring islands, call collect)

This cancer hotline answers questions about cancer seven days a week. There is a Spanish-speaking staff member available during the day.

23

CHRONIC LIVER DISEASE

Of all the leading causes of death among African Americans, chronic liver disease, or cirrhosis, gets the least attention. And yet cirrhosis of the liver is the number-seven killer among blacks and it is almost entirely preventable. Chronic liver disease can be caused by hepatitis, parasites, toxic chemicals, and congestive heart failure, but its most common cause is alcoholism. Cirrhosis of the liver caused by alcoholism accounts for about thirty thousand deaths each year; black men and women have twice the rate of other groups.

Cirrhosis is the final stage of the long, slow deterioration that occurs with liver disease. The liver, located in the upper-right portion of the abdomen, is the biggest gland in the body, weighing nearly four pounds in an adult. It is the key organ of human metabolism. Like a giant chemical plant, the liver carries out about five hundred tasks to detoxify ingested food. Once blood has circulated through the liver, it is safe and ready to nourish all the millions of cells in the body.

About a quarter of our total blood volume is in the liver at all times. To a certain extent, the liver can repair itself if it is damaged, but when the liver dies, the body dies.

The death rate associated with liver disease directly corresponds to alcohol consumption. For example, during Prohibition in the United States, and when wine was rationed in France during World War II, the incidence of death from liver disease fell dramatically. Modern data show that countries that have the highest per capita alcohol consumption also have the highest rates of death from cirrhosis. In the United States, the incidence rate of cirrhosis has risen steadily since 1950, particularly among black men.

A person who drinks seven ounces of alcohol every day (the amount contained in about three-quarters of a bottle of wine) has a 50 percent chance of developing cirrhosis within twenty years. The risk goes down as the amount is reduced, and goes up as the amount is increased. Prolonged, heavy intake of alcohol almost inevitably leads to cirrhosis.

As liver cells die, scar tissue erodes the liver and it loses its ability to function. As long as the individual continues to drink, the disease progresses, eventually leading to liver failure. But if the person stops drinking before the liver is destroyed, in time liver function improves.

SYMPTOMS

In the early stages, when there are still plenty of healthy liver cells, cirrhosis may produce no symptoms. As the disease progresses, mild symptoms begin to appear:

- Appetite loss and weight loss
- General weakness, nausea, indigestion, and stomach bloating. Vomiting may occur.
- Easy bruising and nosebleeds
- Small red spidery veins, called spider nevi, on the face, arms, and upper body

In later stages:
- Jaundice
- Decreased sex drive
- Cessation of menstruation
- Fluid buildup throughout body, particularly in the abdomen and ankles
- Impaired memory, poor concentration, confusion
- Trembling in the hands
- Spitting up blood

Cirrhosis cannot be cured, but symptoms improve as soon as treatment begins. The best hope is to arrest the progress of the disease before it reaches its final stage.

HOW LIVER DISEASE IS DIAGNOSED

Liver disease is easily diagnosed by a physical examination, blood test, and a liver biopsy to confirm the diagnosis. X rays, CAT scans, and MRIs can also be used to aid the diagnosis.

COMMON TREATMENTS

How cirrhosis is treated depends on how far it has progressed. The most important first step is to stop drinking, which immediately slows down the progression of the disease. (See Chapter 5.)

The second step is to improve nutritional status. It's common for people suffering with liver disease to be poorly nourished because they drink instead of eat. Although the number of total calories in alcohol may be high, the nutritional value is almost zero. Those who drink to excess are facing a nutritional wasteland: They consume fewer nutrients, and the ones they do consume cannot be absorbed.

Nutritional recommendations depend on how much liver function has been lost. Modifying the diet cannot cure the disease, but it can relieve some of the worst symptoms and slow down the progress of the disease.

Overall, calories need to be increased to two to three thousand, with lots of complex carbohydrates, moderate protein, mostly from vegetable sources, and a total fat intake of no more than 30 percent of calories. Vitamin and mineral supplements are often recommended, especially vitamin B complex, vitamins C and K, and magnesium. Mild to moderate salt restriction is usually recommended if fluid retention is a problem.

These dietary modifications may seem like a lot of effort to those who are used to drinking their meals, but in fact they constitute a well-balanced, nutritionally sound diet that everyone should follow. The Sankofa Program described in Chapter 17 can be followed safely by most people suffering from liver disease.

Medication also may be used to relieve some symptoms. Diuretics can reduce fluid retention, and antibiotics can reduce the number of bacteria in the intestines. Bleeding veins in the esophagus can be stopped by injecting them with medication; surgery can also be carried out to relieve pressure on the veins. In some cases, steroids or other immunosuppressive drugs may be prescribed.

The individual who stops drinking and eats a nutritious diet should be able to lead a fairly normal life. But the alcoholic who will not, or cannot, abstain will eventually develop liver failure.

Hospital treatment with an intravenous drip that contains drugs and nutrients can usually bring about some improvement, but repeated episodes of liver failure eventually make this treatment progressively less effective.

Liver transplants. The prospects for a person with cirrhosis have improved dramatically with advances in liver transplants. A person who has developed cirrhosis as a complication of hepatitis may be restored to normal health by a successful transplant. However, transplants are not always recommended for a person who has advanced cirrhosis caused by alcohol, since the alcohol may also have damaged the heart, brain, and other organs. Because donor organs are so scarce, most medical professionals will not recommend a liver transplant for an alcoholic who has not stopped drinking.

HIGH-PROTEIN, AMMONIA-PRODUCING FOODS TO AVOID

One of the substances an ailing liver is unable to process is ammonia, a by-product of a high-protein diet, which normally it handles very well. Therefore, people suffering chronic liver disease are usually advised to reduce their consumption of foods that typically produce ammonia in the bloodstream. These include:

Cheese	*Chicken*
Buttermilk	*Gelatin*
Hamburger	*Ham*
Potatoes	*Onions*
Peanut butter	*Salami*

STAYING SOBER

Dietary changes can do more than arrest the progress of liver disease and relieve symptoms. There's ample evidence that making dietary changes can also reduce the craving for alcohol and make it easier for alcoholics to stay sober.

In one study, thirty-two patients with high blood pressure followed a diet averaging 62 percent raw vegetables and fruits for six months. Four out of five of those who usually smoked and drank naturally stopped doing both. Chronic alcoholics who followed a nutritious diet and took a multivitamin supplement found it much easier to stay away from alcohol than those who continued their regular pattern of eating.

24

DIABETES

Diabetes is the third-leading cause of death among black Americans, which makes it one of our most pressing health problems. Before 1940, diabetes mellitus (commonly called diabetes) was thought to be relatively rare among African Americans. But today, we have higher rates of diabetes than white Americans at all adult age levels.

Our vulnerability to this disease begins early and increases as we grow older. Between the ages of forty-five and sixty-five, one in ten black Americans suffers from diabetes, twice the rate of whites of the same age. Over the age of sixty-five, we have almost three times the incidence. The disease is especially common among older black women: Over the age of fifty-five, one out of four has diabetes.

We also experience higher rates of three of the most serious complications of diabetes: blindness, amputation, and kidney failure. And our death rate is 132 percent higher than whites'; it may be even higher, because diabetes is not always recorded as the cause of death, especially among older people who have other chronic ailments.

(We are not alone in our struggle with this disease. The National Center for Health Statistics reports that other minorities in the United States have even higher rates of diabetes than we do.)

As overwhelming as this disease is in our community, it often can be prevented. And even if you do develop diabetes, it is still possible to live a long and healthy life. The aim throughout this book is not just to bemoan our health status but actively to find ways to promote our good health.

WHAT IS DIABETES?

To have this condition means that your body doesn't properly make or use insulin. Insulin is a hormone that lets cells absorb glucose from the food you eat; without it, cells starve. Here's how it normally works: most of the food you eat and digest is turned into glucose; glucose then travels through the bloodstream to cells throughout the body. Even as you're eating, the pancreas, a gland that sits behind the stomach, begins to produce insulin. As the glucose from food builds up in the blood, the pancreas releases the insulin; in turn, the insulin helps the glucose enter the cells, and the glucose level in the blood goes back down. Throughout the day, glucose levels rise and fall within a fairly steady range.

If this system goes wrong—if the pancreas doesn't produce enough insulin, or if the insulin it does make doesn't work properly—cells are deprived of nourishment and glucose builds up in the bloodstream.

Initially, a glucose overload in the blood may make a person feel only mildly ill. But over time, diabetes can seriously damage many body organs and functions. Almost half of all diabetics eventually develop hardening of the arteries and veins in the legs, which can cause ulcers on the feet or ankles. This condition may become so bad that amputation is necessary.

Fortunately, with modern medical management, much of this wholesale damage can be avoided or at least reduced. If you do not have diabetes but your family history puts you at risk for the disease, it may be possible to prevent its onset.

Although researchers don't yet know exactly what triggers diabetes, they suspect a genetic flaw may carry it from generation to generation. And some researchers theorize that shifts in the body's metabolism, or even a virus, may trigger diabetes in susceptible people.

THE TWO TYPES OF DIABETES

There are two main types of diabetes:

Type I, also known as juvenile-onset or insulin-dependent diabetes (IDDM), usually begins abruptly in childhood or adolescence, and sometimes in adults under the age of forty. When Type I diabetes strikes, the body abruptly halts insulin production completely. The body, seeking other fuel sources, starts to convert fat and protein into energy. This drain of nutrients can cause the individual to lose weight rapidly. The heart, nerves, eyes, blood vessels, and virtually every other part of the body can be damaged. Without prompt treatment, coma and even death can result.

To survive, these patients must inject themselves daily with insulin all their lives. About 10 percent of the 11 million diabetics in the United States have this type of diabetes, although the incidence is slightly lower among blacks. At present, there is no way to prevent Type I diabetes, but there are ways to control the condition. Daily insulin treatment, a special diet, and exercise help keep blood-glucose levels balanced.

It is the second type of diabetes that we are most concerned with. *Type II diabetes,* also called adult-onset or non-insulin-dependent (NIDDM), accounts for more than 90 percent of all cases of diabetes among blacks. In this type of diabetes, whose overwhelming occurrence is in people who are overweight, the pancreas may actually produce normal levels of insulin, but for some reason the body is unable to use it. Sometimes insulin levels are insufficient and the pancreas gradually loses more and more of its capacity to produce the hormone. The devastating results are similar to those that can occur in Type I, but development of this disease is slower. Sometimes Type II diabetes is diagnosed only after complications such as heart, eye, kidney, or nerve damage are discovered. For this reason, it may actually be more dangerous.

On the bright side, people with Type II diabetes often can control the disease through diet for weight control, exercise, and possibly oral medication. To manage diabetes in this way, often without insulin injections, requires careful attention and medical supervision, but it is worth it.

Gestational diabetes is a form of Type II diabetes that sometimes occurs in pregnant women. These women are on average twenty pounds heavier before pregnancy than women who don't develop it. Since black women already have especially high rates of obesity and diabetes, as well as a high rate of infant mortality, screening for this type of diabetes during pregnancy is especially important for them.

Black diabetic women are three times more likely to lose their babies during or immediately after childbirth than white diabetic mothers, and 8.5 times more likely to lose their babies than non-diabetic white mothers.

Babies who survive may be excessively large at birth and are at risk for a host of medical problems, including congenital malformations, low blood sugar, and respiratory distress syndrome. If you are an overweight woman of childbearing age, it's important that you take special care of yourself throughout the course of your pregnancy. (See Chapter 29.)

WHY IS DIABETES INCREASING AMONG BLACKS?

The rise in the incidence of diabetes among blacks is partly due to better screening and reporting methods, but other factors may also be involved, according to a government-sponsored diabetes conference chaired by Dr. Louis W. Sullivan in 1988.

Obesity—the most common risk factor for diabetes—is significantly higher among blacks. Obesity reduces the sensitivity of cells to insulin and makes it harder for glucose to enter them. *But, for unknown reasons, we have higher rates of diabetes at all weight levels.*

The types of foods we eat contributes to the problem. Although our total intake of calories and fat are lower than whites', we consume more cholesterol and *less fiber.* Fiber is thought to help control levels of glucose in the blood.

We have an exceptionally high rate of hypertension. Hypertension often appears with diabetes, either independently or as a result of the diabetes, and affects the same target organs. When both diseases are present, the impact may be more than double.

Lack of consistent treatment worsens the outcome of the disease. Black people have less access to consistent health care and self-help education, which are the hallmarks of diabetes management.

On the whole, we average fewer visits to doctors each year. When we do go to doctors, studies have shown that we often don't get the simple, routine blood-glucose tests that could detect diabetes in its early stages.

Finally, diabetes is one disease whose management is day by day, hour by hour, which means that proper self-care is absolutely essential to success. Yet few self-help educational materials about food, cooking methods, taking medication, and doctor visits reflect black lifestyles and culture.

ARE YOU AT RISK?

Type II diabetes often runs in families, so if your parents or brothers or sisters have diabetes, your risk is immediately greater. However, there are other risk factors, particularly if you have a family history of diabetes, too.

• Over age forty
• 20 percent or more over ideal weight
• Little exercise
• Stress
• Being female
• Being pregnant

Risk factors are important, but they may not tell the whole story. Dr. Loren G. Lipson and his colleagues at the Division of Geriatric Medicine at the University of Southern California School of Medicine in Los Angeles point out that black Africans have a much lower rate of diabetes than black Americans. That means that some aspect of the environment must be at play. It's possible that there are differences in the environment that are difficult to demonstrate. Or, as Lipson suggests, black Americans may have a genetic predisposition to diabetes that is expressed only when they are exposed to certain aspects of American life.

YOU CAN REDUCE YOUR RISK

Lose weight. Controlling your weight is the single most important action you can take to prevent the onset of diabetes. (Diabetes experts estimate that by preventing obesity, the incidence of diabetes would be cut in half.) Read Chapter 6 carefully and get started on the Sankofa Program, which is the centerpiece of this book.

Take time out for daily exercise. Exercise helps burn calories and also helps your body use insulin more efficiently. (See Chapter 7.)

Don't wait for symptoms to develop. If you have a family history of diabetes, inform your doctor *now* so you can receive routine blood-glucose tests. (The test is easy and inexpensive.)

The more recent the onset of diabetes, the more responsive a person is to treatment. Weight loss, for example, is more effective in people who have recently developed diabetes than in individuals where the disease is established.

SYMPTOMS OF DIABETES

What should you be on the lookout for? When glucose cannot be absorbed by the cells in your body, you will begin to feel weak and tired. As the glucose builds up in the bloodstream, you will urinate more frequently as your body tries to eliminate the excess sugar, which will make you feel constantly thirsty. (There are many other causes of frequent urination, however, so if you experience this symptom, it does not necessarily mean you have diabetes. See your doctor.)

High levels of glucose in your blood may also interfere with your ability to fight off infection, making you vulnerable to various ailments. Simple sores and cuts take longer to heal. Diabetes also has an adverse effect on your retina and other eye structures, so you might notice a change in your vision.

COMMON TREATMENTS

Treatment is most effective when it is tailored to your unique personal needs and cultural beliefs, since what works for somebody else may not fit your lifestyle.

Many Type II diabetics, especially if the diagnosis is made early, can control their disease simply by losing weight and following a dietary and exercise regimen designed to stabilize blood glucose. Others may also require oral medication that improves the body's use of insulin.

WARNING SIGNS OF DIABETES
Type I *(these symptoms will occur suddenly)*

• *Excessive thirst*
• *Extreme hunger*
• *Severe weight loss*
• *Muscle weakness*
• *Irritability*
• *Frequent urination*
• *Nausea and vomiting*

Type II *(these symptoms may occur gradually)*
• *Any of the Type I symptoms*
• *Blurred vision*
• *Drowsiness*
• *Urinary-tract infections*
• *Vaginal yeast infections*
• *Skin infections*
• *Boils*
• *Tingling or numbness in the hands and feet*
• *Slow healing of cuts*

Pills for diabetes (oral hypoglycemia agents), sometimes called oral insulin, do not actually contain insulin, nor are they a substitute for good nutrition and exercise. Instead, oral diabetes drugs help lower blood sugar by stimulating insulin secretion and by making the body's cells more sensitive to the hormone.

Some Type II diabetics need daily insulin shots to improve the body's uptake of glucose. Your requirements for medication are likely to change as you grow older, which is one reason that continued medical supervision is so important. The goals of treatment are to relieve symptoms, prevent complications, and extend life. Success depends on keeping the level of glucose in the blood normal at all times.

SELF-HELP TO MANAGE DIABETES

Diabetics who fare best are those who participate fully in their own treatment. Your dietitian or physician can help you make a dietary plan that will help maintain your health and fit your life, but you're in the driver's seat.

For example, you can monitor your own blood glucose several times a day with do-it-yourself testing kits. Using these kits lets you quickly detect the effect of food, exercise, and stress on your condition and gives you a chance to make early adjustments in meals and medication that day.

Every diabetic requires an individualized eating and exercise program. In the beginning, you will work with a doctor and dietitian to set your ideal weight and devise a diabetes-conscious plan on how to get there. Even moderate weight loss begins to reduce blood glucose toward normal levels.

An important part of your eating plan is to get used to eating on a schedule that keeps levels of glucose in the blood fairly constant. For juvenile or Type I diabetics, this means eating several smaller meals a day. For most people with Type II diabetes, it means eating three main meals with additional snacks between meals and at bedtime.

DIABETES AND FOOD

The focus of any diabetic diet is to maintain a healthy weight and eat foods that make it easier for insulin to do its job. That means stabilizing the amount of sugar in your blood so that it is never too high or too low.

Over the decades, various formulas to control blood sugar have been tried, but none has proved ideal. Some doctors believed high-protein diets were best, with no sugar and few complex carbohydrates such as bread, cereal, rice, or other grains. Theoretically, this diet would force down glucose in the blood. More recently, high-carbohydrate diets have been recommended. The idea here is that because extra carbohydrates raise blood sugar, the pancreas is forced to work harder to produce insulin. Scientists now believe that complex carbohydrates may have other important effects on blood sugar, as well.

Complex carbohydrates are high in fiber, which slows down the absorption of food. Because food is then absorbed more slowly, blood sugar remains fairly level, without any big dips.

An added benefit of complex carbohydrates is that fiber, again particularly soluble fiber, also has a beneficial effect on cholesterol levels, which are important to everyone, especially diabetics, who have a greater risk for coronary heart disease. (See Chapter 14.)

Here are the newest dietary recommendations from the American Diabetes Association, which I follow with my patients. They are in line with the Sankofa Program described in Chapter 17.

Carbohydrates: 55 to 60 percent of daily calories

Protein: 10 to 15 percent of total calories per day

Fats: 20 to 30 percent of calories

Cholesterol: three hundred milligrams per day

Fiber: forty grams per day

Sodium: no more than three thousand milligrams per day. (This is mild salt restriction recommended for diabetics. Diabetic patients with high blood pressure may have their salt limited to two thousand milligrams or less.)

ABOUT SUGAR AND DIABETES

Do you have to eliminate all sugar? It depends. It's a good idea to omit ordinary sugar from your diet, both to help control weight and to balance blood glucose.

In general, you want to avoid all products that contain glucose, dextrose, corn syrup, or glucose syrup. All cause a rapid and high rise in blood sugar. Honey is not appropriate because of its high glucose content.

So what kinds of sweeteners might you be able to use? As a general rule of thumb, most diabetics can use noncaloric sugar substitutes, such as Aspartame (Equal) and saccharin (Sweet'n Low).

Foods labeled "sugarless" may contain fructose or sorbitol. If your diabetes is well controlled, these caloric sweeteners may be acceptable.

Fructose, which occurs naturally in fruit, doesn't require insulin to enter cells. Words ending in *tol*—sorbitol, mannitol, and xylitol —are sugar alcohols that contain the same number of calories as table sugar. However, because they are absorbed into the blood more slowly than regular sugar, they often can be used in well-controlled diabetes.

Always check with your doctor or dietitian to see which sweeteners you can safely use.

ALCOHOL

What about alcohol? Some diabetics cannot use any alcohol at all because it may interfere with medications and worsen blood-glucose levels. Talk to your dietitian or physician honestly about how much alcohol you usually drink and what kind. Alcohol is generally not recommended for diabetics, but the doctor may allow some people two or three drinks a week. Food intake has to be adjusted, however.

VITAMIN SUPPLEMENTS

Unusual vitamin supplements, other than those recommended for everyone in Chapter 16, are unnecessary unless for some reason the variety of foods you eat is limited.

EXCHANGE LISTS

To help make meal planning easier and more flexible for diabetics, the ADA has devised a system called exchange lists. Food exchange lists were developed to provide optimum nutrition and to allow you to monitor your carbohydrate intake. This simple method divides foods into six groups:

- Starch/Bread
- Vegetable
- Fruit
- Meat and meat substitutes
- Milk (skim, low-fat, whole)
- Fat

Within each group, each serving listed contains similar amounts of calories, carbohydrates, protein, and fat, even though the serving sizes may vary. In addition, there is a "free foods" list, which includes foods and beverages that contain less than twenty calories per serving.

Learning how to use exchange lists requires help from a trained nutritionist, but once you get the hang of it, this system helps you manage your diabetes in your own way. Exchanges for processed foods or combination foods have been developed over the years in order to include foods that are commonly eaten or those that are culture-oriented.

Exchange lists are the most common method employed by nutritionists to help diabetics plan menus, although other counting systems and sample menus are sometimes used. Your dietitian will try to find the method that works best for you.

MEDICAL SUPERVISION

Self-management is important, but it is equally important that you visit your doctor regularly so that he or she can adjust your medical regimen. Diabetics should also carry medical ID tags with them at all times. If you should ever need emergency medical help for any reason, the medical personnel who treat you will know that you may require care for your diabetes.

PROBLEMS YOU MAY HAVE

It isn't always easy to change eating habits. Often, the foods that many of my patients enjoy most are exactly the ones they need to give up. Diabetics often say they enjoy sugary foods, just as those allergic to certain foods seem to crave the foods that cause the reaction.

Reducing stress may also be hard to do. And exercise can be a problem, too, particularly for people living in urban areas where outdoor exercise feels dangerous as well as difficult.

When I sit down with my diabetic patients, the first thing we do is consider their whole life picture—their stress load, lifestyle, cultural concerns, and food preferences. I always invite family members or others who will support the patient in choosing foods to sit in. When diabetics feel they're still part of the family and can enjoy most of the same foods, they have a much better chance of making a smooth transition. To make it a reality means talking about it and thinking about it, literally saturating yourself with this new knowledge and letting it get under your skin.

I always ask patients about stress, which can be crucial when it comes to controlling diabetes. Stress not only makes it difficult for diabetics to concentrate on nutrition; it also interferes with blood-sugar control. In some situations where stress is making the diabetes spin wildly out of control, the physician may want to add a social worker or psychologist to the team.

The physician also will recommend a certain level of exercise based on the individual's age, overall medical condition, and life-style factors. Diabetics who also suffer from hypertension will have to work closely with their doctors to ensure that they are able to exercise safely.

INACCURATE INFORMATION

Not everyone is lucky enough to have an experienced diabetic management team. Self-help information about medications and diet is sorely lacking in the black community. Therefore, to cure their "sugar diabetes," many people try remedies that they pick up from around the neighborhood. Or they purchase quantities of vitamins.

One misconception is that medication can be stopped when symptoms disappear. It can't. Diabetes cannot be cured, although it can be controlled by proper medical and nutritional management. Too many diabetics accept that they are ill only when serious complications develop.

It's easy to say that the key to managing diabetes is consistent medical supervision. What are you supposed to do if you cannot afford health care? Or what if your only source of care is a crowded clinic where you may have to wait several hours each time you go, and when the doctor you see may not be the same person who treated you before? The truth is, it may be hard for you to get the kind of quality care a diabetic needs to stay healthy.

You can go a long way toward taking care of yourself, but you can't do it entirely alone. Your best help is to educate yourself about diabetes, stay informed, and make the effort to search out help in your community. Even if you go to a clinic, your records are on file and every doctor who treats you can and should refer to them.

If you can get off on the right foot once you've been diagnosed with diabetes—if you have a proper medical evaluation, get started on a management program and continue to follow it—it will be easier. A warning: Even if your diabetes comes under control and even if you continue to follow your diet and exercise regimen carefully, your condition may change as you grow older. Therefore, it is essential that you continue to get medical supervision for the rest of your life.

RESOURCES

American Diabetes Association
Diabetes Information Service
  Center
1660 Duke Street
Alexandria, VA 22314
1-800-ADA-DISC

National Diabetes Information
  Clearinghouse
Box NDIC, 9000 Rockville Pike
Bethesda, MD 20892
301-468-2162

American Dietetic Association
216 West Jackson Boulevard,
  Suite 700
Chicago, IL 60606
312-899-0040

Many books, cookbooks, and other publications to help you learn how to control diabetes with diet are available at your local bookstore. Others are available by mail.

Understanding Your Diabetic Diet, vol. 1 (video). $19.95 by mail from Nutrition World Enterprises, 2303 Government Street, Baton Rouge, LA 70806 1-800-223-3109

Also by mail:

Exchange Lists for Meal Planning, 1989. Order from American Diabetes Association (above).

Diabetes and Food: A Guide for People with Non-Insulin-Dependent Diabetes Mellitus, 1990. Order from the American Dietetic Association (above).

25

HEART DISEASE

Deaths from heart attacks declined 24 percent in the United States in the 1980s, according to the federal Centers for Disease Control and Prevention. A decline in risk factors such as smoking and high cholesterol might account for much of the improvement, but doctors have also improved their ability to treat heart attacks in the first few minutes after an attack and to provide long-term care.

Despite its decline, coronary heart disease, or CHD, is the number-one cause of death among all Americans today, regardless of race or ethnic background. Every year, according to the Center for Health Statistics, more than 6 million Americans experience the symptoms of CHD, and nearly 600,000 die from the disease. While Africans Americans have about the same incidence, we have not shared in the progress medical science has made. Although death rates from heart attack and stroke have declined among both blacks and whites, the drop among black Americans has been smaller: *In fact, our death rate from heart attack and stroke is one of the highest in the world.*

While we know a great deal about coronary heart disease and other cardiovascular diseases among white males, comparatively little research has been done among other groups.

1. Black men may, in fact, have lower heart disease rates than white men, and it's been suggested this is because their levels of beneficial HDL cholesterol are higher. (See Chapter 11.)

2. On the other hand, black women appear to have significantly higher rates of heart disease than white women. Is greater obesity among black women the cause?

3. Is socioeconomic status—a catchall word for less access to medical care, less education, less money, poor housing, inadequate diet, and more stress—a risk factor for heart disease in blacks? Can it be separated from other risk factors?

4. Is the high incidence of hypertension the most important factor in the development of coronary heart disease among blacks?

5. Is heart disease different in blacks than in whites? For example, African Americans have a higher rate of "silent" (undetected) heart attacks, in which no obvious symptoms are reported. The ECGs of all blacks seem to show certain types of abnormalities more often than whites'.

6. We are also more likely to die from a heart attack than whites. Is that because the heart attack is different in some way? Or is it because we are less likely to receive immediate medical treatment that could save our lives?

HOW RISK FACTORS WERE DISCOVERED

In 1948, the National Heart Institute selected the citizens of Framingham, Massachusetts, for a long-term study to determine who was at risk for heart disease and how they would respond to various treatment approaches. When the study began, the five thousand volunteers had no sign of heart disease. The investigators scrutinized every aspect of their lives—and each volunteer received a thorough physical exam every other year. After fourteen years, the original data were analyzed in terms of who developed heart disease and who did not. From this initial study, the risk factors for heart disease were first documented: Smoking, obesity, high levels of cholesterol and other fats in the blood, and lack of physical exercise were all strongly implicated. *The major risk factor was hypertension.* Those Framingham subjects who developed hypertension had between three and five times the number of heart attacks as the volunteers with normal blood pressure.

This critical finding about the effect of hypertension on the heart is thought to be one important reason why blacks have such a high incidence of heart disease.

The Framingham Heart Study, however, involved mostly white volunteers. Our high death rate from heart disease would seem to be due to an extraordinary accumulation of risk factors. Hypertension, diabetes, high cholesterol levels, smoking, obesity, and stress are *all* higher in the black community. However, according to Dr. Michael H. Alderman, professor and chairman of the Department of Epidemiology and Social Medicine at Albert Einstein College of Medicine in New York, American blacks are at no greater risk for heart disease associated with hypertension— and at no greater risk for premature death—when they have *equal access to treatment. Treatment is a key factor in preventing heart disease and premature death for everyone.*

WHAT IS CORONARY HEART DISEASE?

Coronary heart disease, the most common form of heart disease, is caused by a narrowing and hardening of the arteries (atherosclerosis) that feed the heart muscle. It is unrelated to congenital types of heart disease, which are caused by abnormalities in the heart muscle itself, present from birth.

Atherosclerosis is a slow process, probably beginning early in life and worsening until it begins to cause symptoms of pain (angina) or heart attack in middle age. Cholesterol and fatty plaque build up along the interior walls of the arteries that supply blood to the heart; as these sludgy deposits harden, the increasingly narrow arteries become rigid, losing their ability to expand and contract.

When the heart is deprived of oxygen, a condition called myocardial ischemia (literally, lack of oxygen to the heart muscle) can cause chest pain (angina pectoris).

Often, however, there are no symptoms until an artery becomes completely blocked, which often happens if even a small clot forms. At this point, oxygen to the heart muscle is cut off and acute myocardial infarction—heart attack—occurs.

NO HEART DISEASE IN
NOMADIC AFRICANS

In a fifteen-year study of 23,000 nomadic Africans, researchers found no evidence of heart disease. According to chief investigator Dr. M. John Murray of the University of Minnesota, participants included tribal societies in Ethiopia, Nigeria, and Kenya. Dr. Murray found that the tribal diet of grains and vegetables led to a diet low in overall calories; only about 10 percent of the calories were derived from fat. The Africans all had a low cholesterol level—an average of 131, compared with the average American's level of 210 to 220.

RISK FACTORS AND
BLACK AMERICANS

There are two sets of risk factors for heart disease. The first—*male sex, advancing age, and family history*—is beyond our control. However, it's extremely important to be aware of these risks so that you can take extra precautions to maintain your health.

GENDER AND AGE

Although heart disease is the number-one cause of death among women, men have a higher incidence. The heart disease gap between men and women narrows when a woman reaches menopause. Her body produces less estrogen then, and estrogen has been thought to protect women's hearts by helping to lower cholesterol, which in turn helps prevent atherosclerosis. (That assumption, too, is now being challenged.)

Although coronary heart disease primarily affects middle-aged and older adults, its foundations are laid early in life. Maintaining a healthy lifestyle from youth can reduce your risk of developing heart disease later in life.

FAMILY HISTORY

Heart disease appears to run in families. If one of your parents or siblings has suffered a fatal heart attack before age fifty, your own risk of heart disease is higher. My father died of a heart attack in his forties, which makes family history an important risk factor for me. But while it's been observed that family history plays a role in heart disease, the mechanism is not at all certain. We know that blacks have higher rates of diabetes and hypertension, which may be inherited and can lead to heart disease. Some people appear to inherit high cholesterol levels. It's always difficult to separate heredity from environmental factors. In practical terms, however, anyone who has a family history of heart disease that occurred early, before age fifty-five, should be especially careful to reduce all of their other risk factors.

The second set of risk factors are the ones you can control.

SMOKING

Smoking has the same devastating effect on the heart regardless of what color a person is. But black Americans continue to smoke more than whites. Smoking more than doubles your chances of developing heart disease, and it is responsible for 30 to 40 percent of all deaths from heart disease in this country each year.

A combination of smoking and stress pushes the already-elevated heart attack risk of smokers even higher. Smokers' hearts are starved for blood during times of physical and emotional stress because of the damage that smoking does to tiny blood vessels.

Cigarette smoke also appears to encourage fatty deposits around the arteries. In animal studies conducted at the University of California at San Francisco, researchers found that fat deposits covered more than half the surface of the aortas of rabbits exposed to a heavy dose of *secondhand smoke,* which is about two to ten times the level of smoke typically found in social situations.

Many people believe that if they smoke cigarettes lower in tar and nicotine, they are playing it safe. According to the latest studies, which show a comparable risk among all smokers, this is not so.

If you quit smoking, you immediately lower your risk. The longer you are smoke-free, the better your risk profile becomes. (See Chapter 5 for help in quitting.)

Fibrinogen. This is a component of blood that helps clotting. People with high levels of fibrinogen may be more prone to clots in their arteries, thus having an increased risk of heart attack or stroke. Recently, the Framingham Heart Study has named fibrinogen an independent risk factor for heart disease. Fibrinogen levels are affected by two factors—age and smoking. Obviously, you cannot change your birth date, but stopping smoking will help lower fibrinogen levels in your blood.

OBESITY

Being 20 percent or more above your desirable weight doubles your risk of developing heart disease. Obesity is a special problem for black women, though there is no clear reason why we gain more weight than white women in the same age group. Part of the risk appears to be indirect—due to hypertension, diabetes, and other problems associated with obesity. However, the link may be more subtle: A woman who gains weight in the typical male weight-gain pattern—around the upper middle—has a higher risk of heart disease than a woman who gains weight in her bottom and thighs. (See Chapter 6.)

SEDENTARY LIFESTYLE

Regular exercise reduces the risk of a heart attack and improves the chances of survival if one does occur. Regular exercise, such as brisk walking, aerobics, and jogging, helps your heart in a variety of ways. Exercise helps increase the amount of good HDL cholesterol, which in turn helps keep your arteries free of fatty deposits. Exercise can also help you lose excess weight, relieve stress, and enable your heart to work harder while using less energy.

Traditionally, African Americans were thought to be more active physically than whites because we were more likely to work at jobs that required hard physical labor. This is an outdated per-

ception. In fact, we may be getting less exercise than other
groups, since we don't seem to have joined in the fitness phenomenon that has captured the attention of much of the white community. (See Chapter 7.)

HIGH CHOLESTEROL AND OTHER BLOOD FATS

Large epidemiological studies have shown that the higher the
cholesterol, the more likely one is to suffer a heart attack. A total
blood-cholesterol level of 240 or greater doubles your risk of heart
disease. Conversely, lowering cholesterol lowers your risk.

We don't know yet all we need to know about cholesterol. But
since heart disease is the number-one killer and cholesterol is a
major risk factor for heart disease, it seems beneficial to lower
high levels of cholesterol. Even if you have no other risk factors,
you will want to start a cholesterol-lowering program.

Here is one point where we may get a break. While elevated
total cholesterol is roughly the same among blacks and whites,
some studies have shown that blacks have higher levels of HDL,
the beneficial cholesterol. Whether this actually helps us is not yet
clear.

Most people can improve their cholesterol profile by changing
their lifestyle habits: Reduce fats in your diet; reduce alcohol if
you are a heavy drinker; exercise regularly; and stop smoking. If
these measures alone cannot do the job—and in some people who
have the inherited form of elevated cholesterol and triglycerides,
they don't—cholesterol-lowering drugs may be recommended.
(See Chapter 11 for special guidelines for African Americans.)

Triglycerides. Usually when a person has a poor cholesterol profile
—low HDL and high LDL—triglycerides, another blood fat, are
also high. It is possible that triglycerides may destroy the beneficial HDL. The Framingham Heart Study found that high tri-
glyceride levels were a risk factor for women but not men. The
reason is uncertain, but high triglycerides levels are also common in obese people and in persons with diabetes—two conditions more common in women, particularly black women, than
in men.

HYPERTENSION

Controlling high blood pressure dramatically reduces your coronary risk. *This is the number-one risk factor for black people.* Not only is our incidence of hypertension higher than that of other groups but we suffer more from the consequences of the disease. We are also more likely than whites to have heart enlargement (see below) as a result of hypertension and ultimately to have congestive heart failure. (For an in-depth discussion of hypertension, see Chapter 21.)

Left Ventricular Hypertrophy (LVH). An enlarged left ventricle— the chamber of the heart that pumps blood to all parts of the body except the lungs—is prone to develop heart failure, erratic heartbeat (arrhythmias), and to cause sudden death. Since an enlarged heart is a common result of hypertension, it is *a particular problem for African Americans.* Successful treatment of hypertension helps to reduce the size of the left ventricle and thus to reduce the risk of heart failure.

DIABETES

People who develop diabetes have a highly increased risk of heart disease. Diabetics are often overweight and also have a higher incidence of hypertension and higher total cholesterol levels. All of this makes diabetes a particular problem for African Americans, since we have high rate of this disease. (For more information about diabetes, see Chapter 24.)

ANGER

Researchers have also been looking at the effects of explosive anger, hostility, and other stress on the heart—with mixed results. Not every study links these to a heightened risk of early death from heart disease. The problem is that there is no blood test that can measure hostility, and researchers still have a long way to go in their understanding of how emotions affect heart health.

But all of this newer research is of particular importance to black Americans. We are just beginning to learn about the destructive effects of stress—and subsequent rage and anger—on our bodies. It's logical that racial prejudice, along with the devastating effects of poverty that many of us live with, could lead to a hostile attitude and behavior in some people.

Those researchers who do suspect that relentless anger and mistrust harm health have turned their attention to stress-reduction techniques. Dr. Dean Ornish of the Preventive Medicine Research Institute in Sausalito, California, has concluded that diet and exercise alone cannot reverse coronary heart disease, but when combined with stress-reduction techniques, lifestyle changes can begin to reverse clogged arteries—without the use of cholesterol-lowering drugs.

As a result of this and other studies relating hostility and anger to heart disease, stress reduction is becoming a recommended part of prevention and therapy. It is especially important for black patients, who have many hidden sources of stress in their lives and less opportunity to relieve it. (See Chapter 4.)

COCAINE

Cocaine use is a major risk factor for everyone, regardless of age or race. Cocaine has a direct effect on the heart. It can cause angina, abnormal heart rhythms, high blood pressure, heart attacks, and death—even in healthy young adults (see Chapter 5).

FACTORS THAT MAY BE GOOD FOR YOUR HEART

ALCOHOL

Alcohol in small amounts is thought to protect the heart by raising HDL cholesterol. One or two drinks a day appears to lower the risk of heart attack by 25 to 45 percent. This is good news for people who drink alcohol, but if you don't drink at all, there's no evidence to suggest that you should take it up. Moderate and heavy drinking have a negative effect on the heart, raising blood pressure and increasing your risk of liver damage and other serious complications. This warning about moderate amounts is particularly important for African Americans because studies indicate that we are more likely than whites to be heavy drinkers— or total abstainers.

ASPIRIN

A half tablet of regular aspirin or one baby aspirin has been shown to lower men's risk of heart attacks or to prevent a second heart attack because it makes a blood clot less likely. More recent studies have confirmed the heart benefits of aspirin in women over age fifty. Aspirin alone is not the answer to preventing heart attacks, but apparently it can be a useful adjunct. However, people who have a history of stomach problems such as ulcers should not take daily aspirin. For most people, aspirin usually does no harm and may help prevent a heart attack, but always ask your doctor first.

PREVENTION TIP: ECGs

The American Heart Association suggests that even men and women with no symptoms of heart disease should have a resting ECG done at ages twenty, forty, and sixty.

An electrocardiogram (ECG) is a painless, nonintrusive way to measure the electrical activity of your heart. Electrodes are applied to the chest, wrists, and ankles by using conducting jelly as a sort of glue. The other end of the electrodes are attached to a recording machine that displays the normal or abnormal activity of the heart.

Some cardiologists suggest that people who have two or more major risk factors for heart disease also have a stress test—an ECG given during controlled exercise such as running on a treadmill or exercising on a stationary bicycle. Others believe a stress test isn't necessary unless the individual has specific symptoms of heart disease, such as pain.

WOMEN AND HEART DISEASE

According to the American Heart Association, of the 600,000 heart attack deaths each year, almost half occur in women. While heart disease in women is similar in many ways to heart disease in men, differences do exist. Because there has been little research done in women, it's anybody's guess how important these differences might be. (The National Institutes of Health recently mandated that all researchers receiving NIH grants must also include women in their studies; the NIH has also created an office of Research on Women's Health.)

- Between the ages of forty-five and sixty-four, one in nine women has some form of cardiovascular disease—hypertension or atherosclerosis.

- Above the age of sixty-five, that figure goes up to one in three women.

- Women who have a heart attack are twice as likely to die within the first two weeks as men are.

- Within the first year of a heart attack, 39 percent of women die, compared with 31 percent of men.

- Black women have even less chance of survival.

Lately, researchers have been wondering about the disparity in survival between men and women. It's possible that therapies that work well in men may be less successful in women. Or it may simply be because women are typically older than men when they have heart attacks; heart attacks are always more dangerous for older people. Their age may also explain why doctors are more reluctant to give them risky treatment, such as bypass surgery. Some researchers believe that women may receive less aggressive treatment because doctors fail to realize soon enough that they are having heart attacks. That's because women seem to experience heart attacks differently: While men typically have crushing pain in the middle of the chest that radiates to the left arm, women may have nausea and vague chest discomfort. These unclear signs can delay treatment.

WHAT ROLE DOES IRON PLAY?

A 1992 study conducted by Dr. Jukka T. Salonen of the University of Kuopio in Finland suggests that high levels of iron may double the risk for heart attacks in men. This report offered an intriguing potential explanation for why heart attacks are rare among women before menopause. Iron may help form the plaque that hardens artery walls, blocking blood flow to the heart. Before menopause, women lose iron when they menstruate each month, which might explain why young women suffer fewer heart attacks than men of the same age. A woman's iron levels—and correspondingly her risk of heart attack—rise after menopause.

However, the role of iron in heart disease remains unclear; the issue engenders lively debate and the jury's still out. Several researchers agree at least that men and postmenopausal women might be able to protect themselves against heart attacks by keeping their stored iron levels low. Do not take vitamins with iron unless these are specifically prescribed by your doctor.

THE SYMPTOMS OF HEART DISEASE

The first symptoms of heart disease are either pain in the chest (angina pectoris) or a heart attack (also known as acute myocardial infarction, AMI, or coronary thrombosis).

Angina occurs when your heart is working hard but isn't getting enough blood to sustain the effort, so it is most often brought on by physical effort or strain. The pain is usually felt as a dull ache or pressure in the middle of the chest; it may extend to the neck and down the arms, especially on the left side. Sometimes it is felt only in the neck or arms. Angina usually subsides when you stop the effort that induced it.

By contrast, a heart attack—which occurs when the blood supply to the heart muscle is completely blocked—may occur suddenly and without warning. The intense chest pain of a heart attack may be unrelated to physical effort, and it doesn't stop when you rest. The victim may experience nausea, weakness, extreme cold or sweating, eventually losing consciousness. Often, quick treatment can make the difference between life and death.

At the other extreme are heart attacks that are so mild that the individual doesn't even know a heart attack has occurred. Usually, however, the pain and consequences of a heart attack are self-evident. Various methods are used to diagnose and confirm heart disease, including ECGs and heart-imaging techniques.

An angiogram may be used to assess the arteries and blockages. In this technique, dye is injected into the arteries, and then an X ray is taken to determine the nature and extent of the blockage. Data gathered from these techniques help determine the best course of treatment.

COMMON TREATMENTS

How coronary heart disease is treated depends wholly upon the nature and severity of each case. One or more of three treatments is usually chosen: lifestyle changes, drug therapy, and surgery.

Lifestyle changes not only can prevent heart disease; they can also improve the condition of clogged arteries. Such changes should include a low-fat diet and regular exercise, no smoking, alcohol in moderation, and stress-reduction techniques.

Drugs, particularly drugs that lower blood pressure, are often used in conjunction with lifestyle changes. If lifestyle changes and drug therapy are not sufficient to relieve the symptoms of heart disease, *surgery* may be recommended. In emergencies, when a heart attack is actually in progress, immediate surgery to open the blocked artery may be undertaken if the patient is in the hospital. In most cases, however, surgery is planned well in advance. There are two major types of surgery for coronary heart disease:

Balloon angioplasty—transluminal angioplasty—involves locating the narrowest part of the artery, sending a balloon to the site, and inflating it. The pressure of the inflated balloon forces the artery to widen.

Bypass surgery is complicated and often lasts several hours. During it, the surgeon removes a vein from the patient's leg and attaches it to the coronary artery at a point above and below the blockage, so blood can flow around it.

HEART-HEALTHY VITAMINS

The newest weapons against heart disease may be ordinary vitamins. The idea is based on the fact that LDL cholesterol must be oxidized before it can begin to build up artery-clogging plaque. Antioxidant vitamins such as E, C, and beta carotene have been shown to block the oxidation process. Two major studies over the last ten years—one involving women and one involving men—have shown that taking daily doses of vitamin E appears to cut the risk of heart disease by one-third to one-half. The studies were conducted at the Harvard School of Public Health in Boston. In both, the men and women took at least one hundred international units of vitamin E per day, the amount in a single vitamin supplement. (For information about vitamins and heart disease, see Chapters 14, 16.)

PROBLEMS YOU MAY HAVE

Newer studies have confirmed that blacks are less likely to have angiography, bypass operations, and angioplasty, even though their heart disease is just as severe as that of whites. Maybe we sometimes refuse to accept these procedures, reflecting our continuing distrust of the medical establishment. If this is the case—that we resist treatment—the problem might be solved with better communication and better information between doctors and patients. Heart surgery is a frightening prospect for everyone. When doctors talk about opening the chest to perform a bypass or threading wires through arteries reaching into the heart, it's scary stuff. If the benefits of these techniques were thoroughly and patiently explained, acceptance would probably improve.

RESOURCES

The American Heart Association, which provides extensive information and literature to the public, has offices in every state. Check your local telephone directory or contact:

The American Heart Association
7272 Greenville Avenue
Dallas, TX 75231-4596
(214) 373-6300

26

HYPERTENSION

Hypertension, also known as high blood pressure, is one of the most common—and most serious—chronic adult illnesses. Untreated, hypertension can increase your risk of stroke, heart attack, and kidney failure.

Approximately 50 million Americans have hypertension, but the disease has its harshest effect on blacks: one out of three black Americans, and 71 percent over the age of sixty, have it. Not only do we develop hypertension more often than whites; we tend to get the disease at a younger age and suffer its severest consequences. And for reasons that are not well understood, we don't seem to respond as well to standard treatment.

The strangest part about this life-threatening disease is that you almost never know you have it until years after it has done its worst damage. Fortunately, it's easy to diagnose and treatment in the form of lifestyle changes and oral medications is very effective. Hypertension cannot be cured, but it can be controlled, *and treatment must be every day for the rest of your life.*

If you are black, its a good idea to have your blood pressure checked every six to twelve months, especially as you grow older.

HYPERTENSION BASICS

Blood pressure is the force exerted by the blood on the walls of the arteries. Systolic pressure, the higher number of your blood pressure reading, is the amount of pressure present as your heart pumps; diastolic pressure, the lower number, is the amount of pressure present as your heart relaxes between beats. It's normal for blood pressure to go up and down throughout the day in response to various activities, but generally it stays pretty much within an average range. The classic good blood pressure profile has always been 120 systolic over 80 diastolic, or less. But anything below 140/90 is considered within normal range.

When blood cannot flow easily through vessels, pressure increases. In general, systolic and diastolic pressures tend to rise together; when one is high, the other is likely to elevate, as well. But if one should rise while the other remains normal, this is still considered high blood pressure and should be treated.

STAGES OF HYPERTENSION
Stage 1 hypertension (formerly called mild) is a systolic pressure of 140 to 159 and a diastolic of 90 to 99.
Stage 2 (formerly moderate) is a systolic of 160 to 179 and a diastolic of 100 to 109.
Stage 3 (formerly severe) is a systolic pressure of 180 to 209 and a diastolic of 110 to 199.
Stage 4 hypertension is a systolic of more than 210 and a diastolic pressure higher than 120.

TARGET ZONES

High blood pressure does its damage silently and methodically over a period of years. Untreated, it almost always results in permanent damage to the major target organs of the body.

THE BRAIN

High blood pressure is particularly hazardous to the delicate arteries of the brain. Like the kidneys, the brain takes a lion's share of cardiac output—one fourth of the blood of each heartbeat goes to the brain. High blood pressure affects the brain either directly —by rupturing blood vessels—or indirectly—when atherosclerosis clogs brain arteries.

A direct effect can cause a blowout. Often when high blood pressure has been pounding through arteries, the walls begin to weaken; eventually, they may give way and finally blow out. A blowout can happen in any artery, but it occurs most frequently in the brain, where arteries are more fragile.

An indirect effect is stroke, which is more likely to occur. A stroke occurs when blood flow to the brain is interrupted, often caused by a blood clot or a buildup of plaque in the arteries. Sometimes the onset of stroke occurs over a matter of hours; other times, it seems to cut a person down in midsentence. Stroke victims may be unable to walk or speak. They may lose their memories. And they may die.

My mother was only in her early forties when she had a stroke. I remember her speech became slurred and she had trouble walking. None of us understood what was happening. We didn't know she had high blood pressure, because she never mentioned it to us. I don't remember that she took any medications for hypertension or followed any special diet. She had a second stroke soon afterward, and this one forever changed the quality of her life. She walked with a cane or a walker for the rest of her life. Her own mother had suffered a stroke at the age of thirty-nine.

There are many causes of stroke, but hypertension and smoking are the clearest risk factors. Although death rates have fallen for everyone, African Americans still die nearly twice as often from stroke. Black women have a 43 percent higher death rate from stroke than white women. Black men have the highest incidence —47 percent higher than among white men, probably because they have a higher rate of hypertension and cigarette smoking.

If you have high blood pressure that is well controlled, chances are excellent that you will never have a stroke. If you do have a stroke, the fact that your blood pressure is controlled will help you recover and help ensure against your having a second, fatal event.

If hypertension is undetected or uncontrolled and you suffer a nonfatal stroke, lowering the blood pressure can keep you from ever having another one. Many stroke victims also have been able to achieve partial and sometimes full recovery with new methods of stroke rehabilitation. Coupled with adequate control of blood pressure, the outlook for stroke patients is optimistic.

STROKE: WARNING SIGNS

The symptoms of minor strokes are slight and often disappear before you even know that stroke has occurred. Major stroke, however, makes itself known in a drastic manner: dizziness, sudden weakness or paralysis in the limbs or face, speech loss, loss of vision. Symptoms may occur all at once or over a period of several hours. Emergency treatment is most effective if it begins within the first six hours after symptoms begin.

If you have any of these symptoms or warning signs, call 911 immediately:

- *Numbness, weakness, or paralysis of face, arms, or legs, especially on one side of the body*
- *Suddenly blurred vision in one or both eyes*
- *Difficulty speaking or understanding simple statements*
- *Loss of balance or coordination, when combined with another warning sign*

THE HEART

When blood pressure rises, the heart pumps harder. This extra work load causes the heart muscle to grow. As the heart enlarges, it demands more blood from its own coronary arteries to nourish itself. If it doesn't receive this extra nourishment—and narrow or clogged arteries may prevent it—the cells of the heart muscle begin to die and the oversized heart is susceptible to angina and heart attacks.

HEART ATTACK: WARNING SIGNS

Victims of heart attacks have described the feeling as a severe gripping pain in the center of the chest that doesn't subside. If you move or take a deep breath, the pain doesn't get worse. It just stays the same. The pain often travels up from the chest to the neck or jaw or radiates through the shoulders and arms. Sweating, dizziness, shortness of breath, and nausea and vomiting frequently occur. Immediate medical treatment is often the difference between life and death. (See Chapter 25.)

Congestive Heart Failure. Eventually, the heart becomes exhausted. It continues to beat, but its action is weak and less blood is pumped out. The result is congestive heart failure, a condition where the heart muscle cannot pump enough blood to circulate to all the body's tissue.

Congestive heart failure can be deadly. Deprived of an adequate blood supply, the kidneys cannot function properly. Excess water accumulates in body tissues and backs up into the lungs; the body begins to swell.

THE KIDNEYS

The normal kidney helps maintain adequate blood pressure levels in the body. As blood vessels become narrow after years of high blood pressure, the blood supply to the kidneys is reduced. To increase its blood supply, the kidneys begin to secrete hormones that raise blood pressure. This makes the hypertension even worse. The kidneys become so damaged that they are unable to filter waste products from the blood. Fluid accumulates in the body and overburdens the heart, leading to congestive heart failure.

THE FOURTH TARGET ZONE

The brain, heart, and kidneys are the best-known target zones affected by high blood pressure. But there is a fourth—the eyes. With elevations of blood pressure, for example, the arteries in the eye show a slight narrowing. As the blood pressure continues to rise, these arteries become so narrow that they are barely visible. Eventually, the capillaries in the eye begin to deteriorate and hemorrhage, and blindness may occur.

DIFFERENT KINDS OF HYPERTENSION

Ninety-five percent of all hypertension is *essential* or *primary,* meaning that it does not stem from any known cause. But there is a small segment of the hypertensive population, the other 5 percent, in whom we can identify the cause of the elevation and, in most cases, cure it. This is called *secondary* hypertension, meaning that it is a side reaction to a known abnormality—such as an obstruction in the arteries of the kidney, or a tumor in the adrenal gland that produces hormones that make blood pressure rise. When the abnormality is cured, the high blood pressure automatically returns to normal.

Essential hypertension is the one we will be talking about in this chapter. Clues surrounding this mysterious disease have tantalized investigators for decades. But each answer provides only more questions. Who gets it? Anyone and everyone. When? Anytime, although most people who have hypertension first show high pressures in their thirties. If a person past fifty suddenly shows elevated blood pressure, it is assumed that he or she had some rise before and didn't know it. However, there are always exceptions. High blood pressure has been known to develop at any age, sometimes beginning in infancy, and sometimes developing in old age.

Because the cause is unknown, it's impossible to know why blacks are more likely to develop it than other groups, although there is no shortage of theories.

We know that hypertension runs in families. Regardless of your skin color, income, or education, if your parents or grandparents had it, you are likely to have it, too. We also know from studies carried out in various neighborhoods in Detroit that the higher the stress level in the environment—characterized by overcrowding, high crime rates, and broken families—the greater the risk of developing hypertension. Therefore, it may be that both heredity and environment are involved.

THE BLACK EXPERIENCE

There are many theories about why we have more hypertension than other groups. Dr. Elijah Saunders of the Division of Hypertension at the University of Maryland School of Medicine in Baltimore believes we develop hypertension for the same reasons that other people do—it's just that those reasons occur more often in our lives.

The genetic theory comes primarily from evidence that some people, black and white, tend to retain salt under stress. The tendency appears to be more common among blacks. Dr. Clarence E. Grim, professor of medicine and director of the Charles R. Drew UCLA Hypertension Renal Clinic in Los Angeles, believes that salt sensitivity in blacks is one more terrible legacy of slavery.

Studying ships' logs and other documents, Dr. Grim and his colleague Dr. Thomas Wilson estimate that approximately 25 percent of Africans sweated to death on forced marches from the African interior to the coast. Another 10 percent died while being held in crowded pens and dungeons waiting to go to America; and 10 percent died of diarrhea and massive fluid loss during ocean crossings as they were chained in airless holds. More died working on American plantations, where diarrhea was epidemic.

Who survived death from sweat loss and diarrhea? According to Grim and Wilson, those whose kidneys naturally retained substantial stores of salt. Dr. Grim calls this theory "rapid natural selection."

What helped slaves survive a harsh environment has become a health risk for us, their descendants, who inherited this tendency.

It is estimated that 75 percent of blacks with hypertension are salt-sensitive and can be treated with diuretics, drugs that help excrete water—about twice the rate of whites.

The salt theory doesn't account for all of the genetic possibilities. High blood pressure is known to have a strong family relationship, even when family members are not salt-sensitive. This suggests that other, unknown hypertension-causing mechanisms may be inherited.

Not every researcher buys this theory of inherited hypertension, mostly because they fear it ignores the many other factors present in the lives of black Americans that may contribute to hypertension. Spearheading the other side of the debate is Dr. James Lynch, a psychiatrist and professor at the Johns Hopkins University Medical School who also operates the Life Care Health Foundation in Baltimore. Dr. Lynch believes that black hypertension is the result of the emotional toll of racism, poor socioeconomic conditions, and stress. The problem, he believes, can be reduced to self-esteem. Dr. Lynch and several other researchers believe that focusing on a genetic cause simply promotes further racism.

Dr. Lynch is well known for a unique study: He found that blood pressure naturally goes up, about 10 to 15 percent, when you speak—how high depends on whom you're talking to. When college students talked to people they thought were physicians, their blood pressures rose more than when they talked to people they believed to be other students.

Dr. Lynch connects this finding to the lives of many blacks in American society, a society that constantly tries to make them feel inferior. The lower the self-esteem, the greater the stress. It's normal for blood pressure to go up and down in response to stress, but in blacks, whose stress load is more or less permanent, blood pressure finally loses its ability to adjust and simply stays high all the time.

The self-esteem theory is closely linked to anger, which is heightened by racism, or even perceived racism. Dr. Earnest H. Johnson, associate professor of psychology at the Behavioral Medicine program, University of Miami, has conducted several studies on the relationship of anger to high blood pressure. He found that the emotional factors—in particular suppressed anger—are significantly related to elevated blood pressure in adolescents.

Simply living in an urban environment may contribute to high blood pressure. Studies of Kenyans found that they had no hypertension until they moved to urban areas. Dr. Johnson's observations are supported by the Detroit neighborhood studies carried out in 1973 by Dr. Ernest Harburg, who measured blood pressure among people living in high-stress neighborhoods, where poverty, crime, and overcrowding were the norm. He compared the results with blood pressure measurements of people living in neighborhoods classified as low-stress. Across the board, people from the high-stress neighborhood had higher blood pressure than others, and the association was stronger among African Americans than whites.

Apart from this sharp division of opinion—racism, self-esteem, rage versus such genetic factors as salt retention—other researchers believe that *both* heredity and environment are necessary to produce high blood pressure. We inherit a predisposition to high blood pressure but, depending on our environment, may or may not develop it. Environment and genetics may be so closely linked as to be inseparable, and there's every reason to believe that both elements may be involved.

HOW RISK FACTORS AFFECT HYPERTENSION

If you don't have high blood pressure, controlling risk factors may help prevent you from ever getting it.

If you do have high blood pressure, controlling risk factors will often reduce your need for drug therapy, and in some instances it may eliminate medication altogether. Controlling risk factors will also reduce your risk of complications. Should you have a heart attack or stroke, your chances for recovery are much better if your risk factors are low.

SMOKING

For the person with high blood pressure, cigarette smoking is the most dangerous single risk factor for increasing disease and early death. A person with untreated hypertension who also smokes cigarettes is five times more likely to have a heart attack than a nonsmoker whose blood pressure is normal. And that person is sixteen times more likely to have a stroke. (See Chapter 5.)

OBESITY

Since we don't know the cause of high blood pressure, we cannot lay its origin at the doorstep of obesity. But people who are overweight are more likely to have hypertension than those who are of normal weight.

The same is true for children. A child who is overweight is much more likely to have high blood pressure than a child of normal weight and is more likely to suffer from complications from the disease.

If you have high blood pressure and are overweight, there is a strong possibility that when you lose weight your blood pressure will go down. In the Framingham Heart Study, elevations in blood pressure seemed to parallel the degree of obesity; when obese hypertensive people lost weight, there was a corresponding reduction in blood pressure. The decreased pressure may be due to the weight loss itself or to a loss of excess salt.

The important part is to keep weight steady at a normal level. Losing and then gaining weight back is ineffective for hypertensives because it doesn't allow enough time to let the layers of cholesterol work themselves out of the arteries. Each time you gain, new layers of cholesterol are added.

CHOLESTEROL

A high level of cholesterol in the blood can be destructive to the body because it contributes to atherosclerosis. When you have high cholesterol *and* high blood pressure, you are particularly susceptible to heart attack and stroke. As excess cholesterol builds up in the blood, a hard pastelike substance forms inside artery walls. High blood pressure pounds this plaque into the walls of the arteries. For this reason, it's important for people with high blood pressure to be aware of their cholesterol level and to work toward keeping it within normal range. (See Chapter 11.)

LACK OF EXERCISE

Obesity is invariably associated with inadequate exercise and a poor fitness profile. By contrast, we know that physically active people are less likely to develop heart disease. And if they do have a heart attack, they are much more likely to recover. There's also some evidence that exercise may help lower high blood pressure.

SALT

Research done in the 1960s concentrated on examining high blood pressure among populations in which the lifestyle was simpler, free from stressful technology. Native communities throughout the world—in Africa, New Guinea, the Solomon Islands, and Central and South America—where salt is almost never used have almost no incidence of high blood pressure. The Kang bushmen, a primitive tribe of Africa, have normal blood pressure even in old age. These people use almost no salt in their diet. But researchers could not tell whether the beneficial factor was lack of stress or lack of salt.

STRESS

Tension or stress does not cause hypertension—at least not directly. Stress causes temporary rises in blood pressure. However, constant exposure to stress—particularly the hidden stress that many black people live with—may contribute to eventual sustained elevation of blood pressure.

ALCOHOL

Too much alcohol also contributes to hypertension. The question is, How much is too much? Studies have shown that on a daily basis, more than one glass of wine, one ounce of hard liquor, or two twelve-ounce cans of beer raise both systolic and diastolic blood pressure.

YOU CAN REDUCE YOUR RISK

Many people ask whether hypertension can be prevented. Unfortunately, the answer is no. It is possible to have none of these risk factors and still develop hypertension. This most often happens when you have a history of hypertension in your family. But it is possible to reduce your *risk* of ever developing hypertension and its complications. For the person with a family history of hypertension, reducing risk factors—obesity, smoking, stress, and salt—is like taking out insurance: You may still get hypertension, but you will have easier control and less danger of complications.

Exercise can also help you control your weight and reduce stress. Aerobics are the best exercises for helping circulation to the lungs and heart. Walking, running, bicycling, swimming, dancing, and tennis are all good choices. Light weights are probably okay to lift for most people—but in general, hypertensives are advised to steer clear of weight lifting and other isometric-type exercises, which tend to increase blood pressure. More important than the type of physical exercise you choose is the regularity with which you do it. A brisk walk every day is much better than a game of tennis once a week.

The most important thing is to begin an exercise program that does not overtax your physical ability. The hypertensive person is not an invalid, but he or she should always discuss the appropriate exercise with a physician. (See Chapter 7.)

Reducing stress is especially important when it comes to controlling high blood pressure. Many studies have shown that relaxation techniques such as meditation can lower blood pressure. The benefit extends far beyond the period of relaxation. Try to enlist the support of your family to reduce stress, and tap into the resources of local community organizations. (See Chapters 4 and 5.)

SYMPTOMS

You can have hypertension for many years without ever experiencing any symptoms. However, symptoms may develop as the disease advances. The most common symptom is a headache, which typically occurs in the morning and fades as the day goes by.

The second most common symptom is fatigue. You may feel irritable or nervous. Dizziness and vertigo can be clues that you are suffering from high blood pressure. Frequent nosebleeds, chest heaviness, shortness of breath when walking up stairs, and pains in various parts of your body are all warning signs.

WARNING SIGNS

If you are being treated for high blood pressure, you needn't constantly be looking for symptoms. Chances are good that you will never have a complication from your disease. Any symptoms that you do experience most likely will be in response to medication and usually can be adjusted to relieve discomfort.

However, should you notice any new symptoms or a replay of old ones, you should advise your doctor. There are three warnings signs that are important if you have hypertension. Call your doctor if you experience:

• Noticeable fluid retention: Swollen hands and feet, sudden weight gain, and feeling bloated are signs of water buildup in your tissues.
• Shortness of breath or wheezing, especially in the middle of the night, is another warning sign.
• Muscle cramps or weakness in your legs: This is usually caused by drug side effects and is reversible with an adjustment in the dosage of your medication.

DIAGNOSIS AND TREATMENT

Early diagnosis is our top priority. When hypertension is left untreated for several years, its deadly complications cannot be avoided or reversed. High blood pressure can be successfully treated by a combination of lifestyle changes and drugs.

If your pressure is only slightly elevated, you should use self-help methods to cut risk factors. These almost always help bring the pressure into normal range: Get your weight down; reduce salt intake; engage in regular aerobic exercise; stop smoking; and drink only in moderation. It's important to bring even slight elevations down to within normal range. With hypertension, a little can be as bad as a lot. This requires lifelong attention.

If changes in lifestyle are not enough to lower blood pressure, your doctor will prescribe medication. Several researchers have observed that the drug regimens effective for whites may not work as well for black patients. For example, many blacks do not respond well to *beta blockers* and *ACE inhibitors*. In contrast, many African Americans respond well to treatment with *diuretics* and *calcium-channel blockers*. Diuretics lower blood pressure by lowering fluid in your body. Calcium-channel blockers seem to be especially effective in people who have the low-renin, salt-sensitive type of high blood pressure, which is most common in the black population.

Finally, getting your family involved in helping you to control high blood pressure can be a very positive act. As a family, you can switch to a healthier low-salt, high-calcium diet. Family members will also become more aware of their own blood pressures.

OTHER FACTORS THAT MAY AFFECT HYPERTENSION

- Low intake of calcium
- Low intake of potassium
- Diabetes: New studies suggest that the body's inability to use insulin may increase blood pressure. If this proves true, it has special significance for blacks, who have high rates of diabetes and in whom hypertension and diabetes often go hand in hand.

PROBLEMS YOU MAY HAVE

African Americans may have special problems in preventing and treating high blood pressure because they tend to lack health-care information and don't have access to *regular* medical care. Cost can be a problem; the newer antihypertensive drugs tend to be very expensive. Fortunately, diuretics, which are effective in many blacks, are less expensive because they have been on the market long enough to be available in generic form.

If you're in a clinic situation and see a different doctor on each visit, you can help the doctor by keeping track of your visits. Write down the dates of each visit, the drugs prescribed, and any side effects or other symptoms experienced. Tell your doctor if you have any trouble adhering to the drug schedule, if you can't remember to take the drug, can't afford it, or miss a dose for any other reason. Before your next appointment, write down any questions you have.

DRUG SIDE EFFECTS

When you start medication, you may not notice any reactions at all. On the other hand, some people experience a variety of side effects. Antihypertensive drugs may produce different side effects in different people. *You do not have to live with the side effects.* If you experience side effects from medications, tell your doctor immediately. Sometimes your dosage can be adjusted; sometimes the medication can be changed. There is a wide choice of drugs available to treat hypertension today.

LOOKING TOWARD THE FUTURE

CHECK YOUR FOOD LABELS

In October of 1992, federal health officials launched a major drive against high blood pressure. Among other things, the program challenges the food industry to lower the amount of salt and calories in processed foods, to increase public education programs, and to label salt and calorie contents of foods.

GO FOR SCREENINGS

An important advance in the treatment of hypertension is community-based blood pressure screening. Dr. Elijah Saunders was instrumental in piloting the concept of church-based blood pressure control centers in Baltimore, and the idea has taken off around the country. Other community groups have organized blood pressure screening in barbershops, gyms, mobile vans, malls, and on street corners. Members of the community take your blood pressure and provide information on getting follow-up treatment.

If you have high blood pressure, regular checkups are going to be a part of your life—*even after your pressure is controlled*. Blood pressure may go down too far or it may start to go up again. The objective is to keep your medication adjusted properly so that the pressure continues to be stable.

27

SICKLE-CELL DISEASE

Frequent pain and hospitalizations have been longtime common associations with sickle-cell anemia (SCA). The future of those afflicted with the disease has always been considered bleak and no known cure is yet available. Not long ago, it was hard to find anyone with sickle-cell disease (SCD) who lived past age forty. But today, thanks to new knowledge about managing the disease, SCA patients are living a full life for a much longer time. People who suffer with this disease will tell you how much they now enjoy the many good days between crises. The many children with sickle-cell disease can look forward to a longer, more normal life, *provided they receive appropriate medical management.*

Sickle-cell disease has always been neglected, primarily because it affects mostly African Americans. About fifty thousand black Americans have SCA, and each year about one out of every four hundred black infants is born with it. *But it is not solely a "black disease."* It can be found, although to a lesser degree, among southern Italians, Greeks, East Indians, and many Hispanic people around the world, particularly in South America, Cuba, and Central America. According to the March of Dimes, one in every one thousand to fifteen hundred Latinos living in the United States has sickle-cell disease.

Many more people, including one in twelve black Americans, carry the sickle-cell trait (SCT)—meaning they can pass the defect on to their children, although they remain healthy. (You cannot catch sickle-cell disease. It is transmitted genetically by two parents, each of them a carrier of the sickle-cell trait.)

It's almost certain that sickle-cell disease arose as an evolutionary mutation in places that had a problem with malaria. Children born with the trait for sickle-cell disease are protected against the severe form of malaria. As populations migrated, sickle-cell disease moved throughout the world. Although no one knows for certain where sickle-cell disease originated, scientists have identified four separate types, each associated with a different geographic area. This suggests that the sickle-cell gene mutation occurred at different times and at different sites, perhaps accounting for the wide variation in manifestations of the disease. Some people with sickle-cell disease rarely have crises. Others have frequent, very prolonged, severe crises.

Sickle-cell disease was first described in 1910 by Chicago physician Dr. J. B. Herrick, who observed unusual crescent-shaped, or sickled, blood cells in a blood sample of a twenty-year-old black man from the West Indies. In 1922, sickle-cell disease was recognized as a disease and given a name in an article by Dr. Verne Mason in *The Journal of the American Medical Association*. Four years later, sickle-cell anemia was distinguished from sickle-cell trait: those with sickle-cell anemia show painful symptoms of the disease, while those who have the trait are perfectly healthy.

Dr. Mason made it clear that the disease was much more common than previously thought. But scant attention was paid the disease until the 1970s. I personally remember Dr. Roland Scott, one of the leading researchers in sickle-cell disease from this period, from Freedmen's Hospital in Washington, D.C. Dr. Scott's research was instrumental in the formation of the Sickle Cell Anemia Foundation. During my dietetic internship at Freedmen's, I was assigned to the pediatric ward, where we saw many young patients admitted with sickle-cell disease. I remember how helpless we all felt. Unfortunately, there wasn't much we could do to help in those days, but I remember trying to make up for it by providing the children with their favorite foods to encourage them to eat.

The National Sickle Cell Disease Program has inaugurated sickle-cell centers at medical schools around the country in order to develop programs for research, public education, and screening, but this disease remains a serious problem for the black community. I want to talk about sickle-cell disease from our personal perspective—what do we need to know to protect our children from being born with this disease, and if they are born with it, what can we do to help them live healthy, pain-free lives?

WHAT IS SICKLE-CELL DISEASE?

Scientists eventually discovered that the peculiar sickling observed by Dr. Herrick and Dr. Mason in the early years of this century was caused by a defect in hemoglobin, a special molecule found in red blood cells. Hemoglobin takes oxygen from the lungs and transports it to other parts of the body. Any defect in the hemoglobin molecule can ruin the blood cell.

Normally, red blood cells are soft, round, doughnut-shaped cells that can squeeze through the tiniest blood vessels in single file, reaching every single part of the body. But defective hemoglobin molecules are long and rigid, causing cells to take on the characteristic sickle shape. Instead of squeezing softly through the blood vessels, the stiff cells get caught together, clogging tiny vessels and blocking the flow of blood.

"Sickling" leads to anemia: Red blood cells normally live 120 days; sickled red blood cells survive only 10 to 20 days in the bloodstream. The sickled cells are removed faster than the bone marrow can produce new ones. Sometimes the anemia is mild and can be corrected with diet and supplements; in other cases, it can be devastating, requiring many blood transfusions.

When blood-oxygen levels get critically low, a crisis occurs, most often caused by the plugging of the vessels as a result of the sickling phenomenon, but sometimes it is caused by the anemia itself. Sickle-cell clots can be life-threatening, depending on where they occur. For example, blockage of blood vessels in the brain can cause seizures or stroke. Blockage in the lungs causes respiratory complications. Other clots may damage such vital organs as the heart, kidney, liver, or eyes.

Crisis attacks are unpredictable; they often occur abruptly and can last anywhere from a few hours to several days. Pain in the abdomen and chest is the most common symptom, but the whole body may be affected, particularly the joints and spine.

If the crisis is caused by severe anemia, which is most common in infants, the baby can go into shock and die.

A third type of crisis situation is infection. Infections in babies with sickle-cell anemia are the number-one killer in this disease. In infants, infections can go from the onset of fever to death in as little as nine hours. A study in Los Angeles found that some babies thought to have died from sudden infant death syndrome (SIDS), a condition uncommonly high among black infants, actually had undiagnosed sickle-cell anemia and a related infection.

Symptoms vary widely in severity. Not all patients have every complication, and even two children in the same family can be affected in dramatically different ways.

One common type of complication in children is a clot forming in the hands or feet, known as hand-and-foot syndrome. Pain, swollen fingers or swollen feet, and fever are typical symptoms. As children mature, the blood supply to the long bones such as the spinal column or hip is usually inadequate. Pain can be severe in these joints. Retarded growth is common and sexual maturity is usually late.

As patients grow older, some experience painful episodes only once a year; others may have as many as fifteen to twenty episodes a year. These painful events can be so severe that hospitalization is required for several days to give intravenous fluids and pain-killers.

As the disease progresses, crises occur more often and major organs sustain damage, particularly the heart, liver, and spleen. Older patients continue to be vulnerable to infection. Lung clots also make them more susceptible to pneumonia or chronic lung disease. Gallstones are common and may require surgical removal. The eyes often look yellow due to jaundice caused by the rapid breakdown of red blood cells. Blindness may result from sickle-cell blockage of the retina.

TRAIT OR DISEASE?

There is a big distinction, as I've said, between someone with the sickle-cell trait and someone who has the disease. Because the gene for sickling disease is recessive, a child must inherit it from both parents in order to develop the full-blown illness.

Even when both parents are carriers, however, it doesn't mean that their child will necessarily have sickle-cell disease.

Here are the odds if both partners are carriers:

- A 25 percent chance that your child will have sickle-cell disease.
- A 25 percent chance that your child will have neither the trait nor the disease.
- A 50 percent chance that the child will have the sickle-cell trait. The child will not develop sickled cells (unless subjected to extreme stress) and will live a normal life. However, he or she can pass the sickle gene on to offspring.

If only one parent has the trait, each child has a fifty-fifty chance of having the trait but cannot have the disease itself.

Other Types of Sickle-Cell Disease. There are several variations of sickle-cell disease, principally sickle-cell hemoglobin C and sickle-cell thalassemia. They are generally less severe.

MANAGING SICKLE-CELL DISEASE

The choice of therapy depends on the situation and the individual's overall medical status.

HOSPITALIZATION

The usual treatments in the hospital include oxygen, IV fluids to prevent dehydration, antibiotics to control infection, medication to relieve pain, and blood transfusions to replace hemoglobin and prevent recurrent strokes. Anticoagulant drugs can help prevent blood from becoming too thick and other drugs can be given to dilate the blood vessels.

CHILDREN

Infants are at great risk of being overwhelmed by infection from the age of three months to five years. Two approaches are used to prevent this. First, babies can be screened at birth to find out whether they have sickle-cell disease. This is a simple, inexpensive test that should be performed before the baby leaves the hospital and repeated in about a month to be certain of the diagnosis. If the baby has sickle-cell anemia, he or she should be entered into a pediatric program, seen frequently, and, most important, be given penicillin every day. Studies have shown that babies given this kind of care had their risk of infection reduced by 84 percent and none died.

A whole medical team—including physician, nurses, and social workers—works with the family to keep the baby well. Immunizations are especially important. Pneumovax prevents a large number of the pneumococcal infections that sickle-cell children often develop. Beginning at two months of age, another vaccine, called anti-Hemophilus influenza-B, can be given; it prevents another type of serious infection in these children.

Parents learn to feel for spleen enlargement, common in children with sickle-cell anemia, which can lead to severe anemia if the spleen becomes so enlarged that it traps a huge amount of the circulating red blood cells.

NUTRITION

Nutrition plays an important part in managing sickle-cell disease. The nutritional keys are folic acid, zinc, vitamin E, and cyanate.

Folic acid. It helps support the immune system, typically weakened by sickle-cell disease. The dietary goal is to derive four to six hundred milligrams of folic acid each day from food. In addition, supplements at a dosage of 250 milligrams a day are recommended.

Zinc. Researchers have also observed symptoms of zinc deficiency among patients with sickle-cell disease: delayed puberty, short stature, low body weight, rough skin, and poor appetite. Dr. Ananda Prasad and his colleagues from the Department of Medicine at Wayne State University in Detroit found that giving zinc supplements to sickle-cell patients helps them resume normal growth, gain weight, and improve testosterone levels and night vision. Zinc acetate is less irritating to the stomach than zinc sulfate. But these studies also indicate that zinc supplementation must be carefully monitored to prevent copper deficiency; although an important nutrient, copper is needed only in small amounts. Adding copper supplements (0.5–1.0) to zinc therapy can correct the imbalance.

Vitamin E. New research has shown that vitamin E is a powerful antioxidant that helps the body use oxygen more efficiently. Since sickled cells interfere with the body's getting enough oxygen from blood, vitamin E is an obvious choice to help.

Cyanate. There is one more promising dietary phenomenon to help treat sickle-cell disease, although it has received scant attention. We have to go back to the origins of the disease to appreciate the significance of cyanate. In Africa, an estimated 25 percent of the population carry the sickle-cell trait, yet the incidence of sickle-cell disease itself is rare. In fact, from 1925 to 1950, it was estimated that fewer than one hundred cases of sickle-cell anemia were reported throughout the continent. In an article that appeared in *The American Journal of Clinical Nutrition* in 1974, scientist Robert Huston theorized that diet might be the reason. Several foods commonly eaten by Africans contain rich sources of cyanate, a substance known to inhibit cell sickling. Cyanate is a nontoxic relative to the poisonous chemical cyanide. African Americans typically consume only about twenty-five milligrams of cyanate each day, but the average African gets about one thousand milligrams of cyanate in the diet each day—derived largely from yams and cassavas, staples of the African diet. In Central America and the Caribbean, just about every part of the cassava is eaten, from the dark green leaves to the roots. Cassava can be boiled, fried, roasted, ground into a powdery white flour, or mashed like potatoes. African yams are quite different from the sweet potatoes we call yams here. In fact, the true yam and the sweet potato don't even belong to the same plant family. The true yam is seldom grown in the United States because it is not hardy north of North Carolina, but it is sometimes imported. These foods can be found in specialty stores in major cities, especially cities with large populations of West Indians and Africans. In the United States, other foods that contain cyanate are radishes, carrots, millet, sorghum, cabbage, kidney beans, lentils, and legumes. I feel there are enough demonstrated benefits of cyanate to indicate that sickle-cell patients can easily and safely include cyanate-rich foods in their diet.

In addition to these supplements, of course, your diet should be well balanced and varied. If you don't have much of an appetite, common during crises, you still want to try to eat a variety of foods. During these periods, eat smaller portions in several meals throughout the day. If you find you're losing weight since you're eating less, ask your doctor or nutrition counselor for suggestions on ways to keep your weight up.

PRECAUTIONS

- *Avoid situations where oxygen may be in short supply—flying in unpressurized airplanes, deep-sea diving, mountain climbing.*
- *Avoid becoming pregnant without the support and counsel of your physician before trying to conceive.*
- *Take care to avoid cuts or injuries, especially to the arms, legs, toes, and fingers. If you do sustain a cut or abrasion, get treatment immediately to avoid infection.*
- *Get the approval of your doctor before participating in physical exercise or other activities.*

TESTING AND GENETIC COUNSELING

In the past, many people with the sickle-cell trait felt they should not marry or have children, for fear the children might develop the disease. This is not what genetic counseling is all about. People who think they may carry the sickle-cell trait may be tested for it and counselors may give advice if they are asked, but the ultimate decision to have children is up to the parents—as is true with regard to any genetic disease. Testing and counseling can take place at several points along the arc of SCD: before pregnancy, during pregnancy, and immediately after a child is born.

Before pregnancy: Both partners can be tested to discover whether they carry the sickle-cell trait. It's important to know what your odds are so you can make your own decision about pregnancy.

During pregnancy: If both partners are known to carry SCT, fetal testing is recommended.

A woman can receive an early diagnosis at about nine weeks through a procedure called chorionic villus sampling. Unlike amniocentesis, in which only a bit of fluid surrounding the fetus is withdrawn, this procedure captures a bit of tissue from the membrane surrounding the fetus. This is the only procedure available that offers very early diagnosis and gives a woman a safe option for abortion if she chooses. There is some concern that in rare instances chorionic villus sampling might cause a miscarriage. So far, the test has not been widely used; it is usually recommended only to test for sickle-cell disease or thalassemia.

Amniocentesis, which can be carried out at about fifteen weeks after conception, gives a pregnant woman a second, albeit much later, opportunity to determine whether to continue the pregnancy. If she chooses to continue the pregnancy, she can take all the precautions to protect her baby from birth and can also begin to learn how she will manage medical care throughout her child's life.

At birth: If you and your partner carry the sickle-cell trait and have not had the fetus tested before birth, it's *crucial* to have the baby screened immediately following birth. The infant can receive antibiotics to protect it against life-threatening infection; and you and your partner can receive counseling that will help prepare you to manage your baby's health in the future.

In childhood: At the time initial symptoms of the disease occur, usually around age six to twelve months.

ABOUT GENETIC COUNSELING

Genetic counseling never involves telling anybody what to do; it simply provides information. The goal of counseling, says Dr. Charles F. Whitten, director of the Comprehensive Sickle Cell Center and founder of the National Association for Sickle Cell Disease, Inc., is to provide information so a woman can make a decision that is right for her—and to do so in an environment free of criticism. Women who decide to have an abortion should be able to do so without being exposed to disapproval from health-care professionals. "Similarly," says Dr. Whitten, writing in *Health Issues in the Black Community,* "women who decide to continue their pregnancies and later have a child who experiences a great deal of difficulty with the disease should not be humiliated by insensitive health care providers who believe that a chance was missed by not aborting." *In other words, the decision is up to the parents.*

PROBLEMS YOU MAY HAVE

Unfortunately there is no national program to make sure that screening at birth is offered. Forty states have passed laws that require sickle-cell testing in newborns, but they don't all provide the money to implement the testing programs effectively. Family physicians are the ones who usually recommend screening for babies they consider at risk for the disease—that is, babies born to parents of African, Caribbean, and Mediterranean descent.

Sickle-cell anemia, like other chronic illnesses, creates a host of problems that affect the entire family. Frequent hospitalizations and special health-care requirements in between visits can cause a good deal of stress. Very little research has been done about the impact on families of coping with this particular disease, but I can tell you from my experience with families in my private practice that the stress load can be enormous.

Children with SCA tend to be overprotected and think of themselves as always ill. Says Dr. Whitten, "They become 'programmed' to live a life of dependency rather than one of self-sufficiency. This results in many having neither the education nor the vocational skills that would render them employable."

Some parents do very well raising their SCA children on their own, but it would be a huge help if in addition they had some standard guidance and counseling on coping with the disease— Helpful programs might include advice on how to get tutoring if the frequency and duration of pain attacks make it hard for their child to keep up in school; career guidance; scholarships or vocational training grants their child may be eligible for; and vocational rehabilitation. In some cities, these programs are available, but often they are not.

Another problem is the biases of employers who are reluctant to hire people who may have a high rate of absenteeism. Although it's true that people with SCA are at risk for unpredictable pain attacks, most do not have crises frequently enough to disqualify them for employment. Dr. Whitten's organization would like to educate employers to evaluate each case individually, not to judge people with SCA universally. Many times, says Dr. Whitten, the pattern of an individual's disease is compatible with employment.

Other kinds of stress can come from unexpected sources. For example, when adults with SCA seek relief of pain in hospital emergency rooms, they are often suspected of being drug abusers; this means that health-care providers may treat these very sick individuals with callous disregard.

I remember asking one of our sickle-cell patients how she coped with the disease. She told me that despite the many medical complications and hospitalizations, she felt she had control over it. "I can handle it," said the twenty-nine-year-old. "I don't feel as helpless as I did when I was young. I can generally tell when a crisis is going to come on." She said crises usually occur when she has neglected her body—when she has worked herself too hard or let a cold linger untreated. She also wishes people wouldn't feel sorry for her. "I wish more people understood the disease and why I visit the doctor so often, so I wouldn't have to keep explaining all the time. Sometimes I feel sickle cell is all I talk about."

Over the years, her chief concern was not to become addicted to pain medication as some others she knows with the disease have. She makes an effort not to take a pain pill unless she really needs it. She says that during a crisis the pain is very bad, at times almost unbearable, but she has learned to tolerate it better. "Your mind can ease the pain and faith can keep you going."

We have another patient in our clinic who is the oldest living sickle-cell patient in the state of Louisiana. Burgess White is past fifty. He worked for many years and always has a pleasant smile and greeting for everyone. Except for his short stature and the stiffness in his joints that impairs his gait, you would never know he has sickle-cell disease. Mr. White is an inspiration for everyone who lives with sickle-cell disease.

LOOKING TOWARD THE FUTURE

Since red blood cells are manufactured in the bone marrow, modern research has focused on bone-marrow transplantation. This process is still in the experimental stage and has been tried only in a limited number of people. It's a difficult procedure at best because the donor must be a perfect match.

In gene therapy, another target for new research, the gene for sickle hemoglobin is replaced with a gene for normal hemoglobin. This technique is still highly experimental and has not yet been successfully achieved. In the long run, the prospects for a cure using bone-marrow transplantation or gene therapy are excellent because the same research can be applied to many other diseases besides SCA, which means that funding is more generally available.

A few new drugs are also being tried. Chemotherapy agents such as azacitidine, cytarabine, and hydroxyurea have been shown to stimulate the production of new and healthy red blood cells, but they have toxic side effects. Researchers continue to look for therapy that is less harmful.

In January of 1993, a group of physicians reported in *The New England Journal of Medicine* a promising treatment using a natural fatty acid called butyrate, which can be used as a stimulant to produce new red blood cells. Butyrate, a widely used flavor enhancer, was shown to overcome the basic cause of the disease. Apparently, the chemical reactivates the gene that produces a form of hemoglobin that is used by the baby in the womb (called fetal hemoglobin, or hemoglobin F) but shuts down soon after birth. Turned on again, the gene directs the manufacture of enough fetal hemoglobin to compensate for the defective adult variety. Since butyrate is a natural substance, it has a low level of toxicity. This initial study included only six patients, so obviously more work is needed, but this is a very promising new treatment.

At present, community organizations—including the seventy-five chapters of the National Association for Sickle Cell Disease, the only national black health organization devoted to sickle-cell issues—must carry out their work supported almost entirely by private funding. The NIH does support ten Comprehensive Sickle Cell Centers, which provide public education, testing, and counseling. Some testing is done, too, by private physicians and those working in HMOs, but typically such testing is not accompanied by counseling. Dr. Whitten, founder and past president of the NASCD, says that overall, available services are grossly inadequate to meet the need. The know-how is there, but the money isn't. Whether the quality of life for those families struggling with sickle-cell disease is enhanced seems to depend largely on fresh funding from government sources.

On April 27, 1993, a federal panel recommended that all newborns, regardless of race, be screened for sickle-cell disease and that those in whom the disease is diagnosed receive daily treatment with penicillin to prevent infections. The new guidelines have been endorsed by several medical groups; hopefully, they will soon become mandatory in every state.

RESOURCES

Copies of the sickle-cell treatment guidelines for newborns and infants are available in versions for parents, doctors, and health-care professionals. Write to:

Sickle Cell Disease
AHCPR Publications Clearinghouse
PO Box 8547
Silver Spring, MD 20907
1-800-358-9295

Research in SCD is conducted by two groups—scientists working through the National Heart, Lung and Blood Institute and those working in one of the ten regional sickle-cell centers. For information, contact:

Sickle Cell Disease Branch
National Heart, Lung and Blood Institute
Federal Building
7550 Wisconsin Avenue
Bethesda, MD 20205

SICKLE-CELL TREATMENT CENTERS

Since 1972, ten regional Comprehensive Sickle Cell Centers have been established to conduct basic and clinical research and also to provide educational information and testing.

Boston City Hospital
818 Harrison Avenue
Boston, MA 02118
(617) 424-5727

Medical College of Georgia
1435 Lancy Walker Blvd.
Augusta, GA 30912
(404) 828-3091

Howard University
2121 Georgia Avenue NW
Washington, D.C. 20059
(202) 636-7930

University of Illinois
1959 West Taylor Street
Chicago, IL 60612
(312) 996-7013

Children's Hospital of Michigan
3901 Beaubien Boulevard
Detroit, MI 48201
(313) 494-5611

San Francisco General Hospital
1001 Potrero Avenue
San Francisco, CA 94110
(415) 821-5169

St. Luke's Hospital Center
419 West 114th Street,
   Room 403
New York, NY 10025
(212) 870-1756

University of Chicago
950 East 59th Street
Chicago, IL 60637
(312) 947-5501

Children's Hospital
   Medical Center
Elland and Bethesda Avenue
Cincinnati, OH 45229
(513) 559-4534

University of Southern
   California
1129 North State Street,
   Trailer 12
Los Angeles, CA 90033
(213) 226-3853

Part Six

BUILDING
OUR FAMILIES

28

GETTING READY FOR PREGNANCY

Pregnancy and birth is the everyday miracle, a few short months in which a new human being develops from a cell no bigger than a grain of sand. Couples come face-to-face with all the issues of life and death, joy and pain. Maternity care today is complemented by technological advances that make childbirth safer than ever before.

Despite these new advances, and despite the eagerness with which we look forward to a new life, childbirth and early infancy pose some of the most dangerous health hazards black Americans must face. In the United States today, black infants are twice as likely as white babies to die before their first birthday. The statistics reflect a tragic reality. A black child born in certain areas of Boston has less of a chance to live than an infant born in Panama or Korea.

Infant mortality is defined as the number of babies out of every one thousand born who die before they reach the age of one. If we examine the nationwide statistics, in 1981 the United States, which spends a higher percentage of its gross national product on health care than any other nation, ranked sixth in preventing infant mortality among developed countries; today, we have fallen to an abysmal twenty-second.

The direct medical causes for most cases of infant mortality are clearly recognized. The most important factor is low birth weight. A low-birth-weight baby is defined as one weighing less than five and a half pounds at birth.

BABIES WHO ARE BORN TOO SMALL

Low birth weight may be due to premature birth—the mother has carried the fetus for only about six months or less. However, many low-birth-weight babies spend a full nine months in the womb, yet for some reason they fail to grow at a normal rate and are born too small.

Babies born too small are more likely to have birth defects, physical and mental handicaps, and respiratory and other infectious diseases; if they survive, they may also suffer from behavioral problems. The lower the birth weight, the higher the risk—infants weighing three pounds or less at birth (referred to as very-low-birth-weight babies) have the poorest chance of survival and account for half of all deaths among newborns. Why do so many black infants weigh so little? In October of 1992, Dr. Allison Kempe and her colleagues from Harvard Medical School published a study that reviewed 1,299 infants born over a six-year period in Boston, St. Louis, and rural east-central Mississippi. Black infants in these areas were two to three times more likely than whites to weigh less than three pounds at birth. Four common pregnancy problems accounted for 90 percent of the extra risk among black mothers: infection or rupture of the amniotic membranes, 38 percent; premature labor for no apparent reason, 21 percent; high blood pressure, 12 percent; hemorrhaging, 10 percent.

Black women were *three times* as likely as whites to experience these difficulties during pregnancy.

We can learn two important facts from this study. First, these are the same conditions that cause dangerously undersized babies among all women, regardless of race or ethnicity. Second, a wide array of risk factors are involved, not just one health factor.

RISK FACTORS

The major risk factors for having a low-birth-weight baby include smoking or drinking during pregnancy, little or no prenatal care, and being too young when you become pregnant. Poverty and all of its ramifications make up a big part of the story, because risk factors such as poor nutrition and anemia occur more often among poor women. Health problems suffered by the mother can also contribute to a baby's birth weight: diabetes and hypertension, too low or too high prepregnancy weight, and a history of multiple pregnancies or previous low-birth-weight births.

Preventing or treating these risk factors could make a huge difference in our rate of infant mortality. However, not every low-birth-weight infant is the product of a high-risk pregnancy. A healthy woman with good nutrition, good prenatal care, and no harmful social habits may also deliver a low-birth-weight baby, and nobody really knows why. And twice as many black women and their babies fall into this category. Researchers speculate that low birth weight in these cases may stem from the cumulative effect of generations of poverty, or it may reflect a mother's poor nutrition during adolescence. Or perhaps these women have smaller babies because they suffer from chronic stress.

Although these issues are complicated, we don't have to wait for all the answers before we take steps to improve our babies' chances. All studies clearly show the need for three vital pregnancy goals: good maternal nutrition *before* and during pregnancy, early and consistent prenatal care, and quality care during delivery.

Black mothers, particularly teenagers, are much less likely to receive early prenatal care. According to some estimates, the health-care system could prevent one-quarter of all infant deaths simply by increasing prenatal care programs and continuing campaigns to curb smoking and alcohol abuse. Aside from the tragic loss to our families and to society at large that infant mortality causes, improving the health of newborns is more practical than paying the huge price tag for the medical care of sick babies. The Academy of Pediatrics estimates that every dollar spent on prenatal care could save ten dollars on hospital intensive care. Medical costs increase as birth weight falls: The medical bills for a baby who weighs less than a pound and a half can be as much as $150,000.

The first step you can take to reduce your chances of having a low-birth-weight baby is to plan your pregnancy. Every baby deserves to be wanted and nurtured from its earliest days in the womb. It's the unplanned and unwanted pregnancy that is most likely to go uncared for, and consequently the one much more likely to produce a small baby.

Everyone knows that teenage pregnancy is a common phenomenon in our community. Black teenagers are having babies as soon as they start menstruating. Not only is this far too early to conceive safely—teenagers often give birth to premature and very low-birth-weight infants—but having a baby constitutes a financial and psychological responsibility that all too few teenagers are ready to shoulder. Teen mothers are likely to be poorly educated, to receive inadequate prenatal care, and to space children too closely.

When I counseled teenagers in a pregnancy clinic, I was shocked at how little they knew about their own bodies, not to mention the new lives growing inside. Misconceptions about sex and pregnancy abounded. Few used contraceptives, and if they did, they didn't use them properly. No one had discussed nutrition with them; their diets were poorly balanced; any prenatal vitamin supplements were taken irregularly, if at all. Most were frightened, abandoned by the fathers of their babies, and without a clue to future plans. And most did not come to the pregnancy clinic until late in their pregnancies. The saddest part about their predicament is that the girls I met got pregnant not only because they don't know how to protect themselves but because of a deeply felt need to have someone to love.

I know that some of our spokespeople have been reluctant to accept the predominant American view of black teenage pregnancy—that it is inevitably a negative phenomenon and that it should be countered with abortions and contraceptive education. Historically, racism has permeated this issue: In the past, birth-control advocates often were not as worried about the welfare of black mothers and babies as they were concerned with limiting the growth of our population.

Certainly, it is a fact that many black teenagers have done a great job of mothering under often extremely difficult circumstances. And I know how often pregnant teenage girls have felt themselves not the victims of an "accident" but the happy possessors of what they describe as "something for myself." And maybe it's true that the dominant white population has wanted to use the contraceptive discoveries of medicine in our time to reduce minority populations. This is something for us all to think about in terms of social policy.

But as a nutritionist, not a historian, my concern is to help black women to conceive and bear healthy babies. If we can take care of our pregnant sisters and our newborn babies, our families will increase and our children will grow into healthy adults. If we do not take care of them, their death statistics will continue to haunt us.

I advise young women to think carefully before engaging in sex. If a young woman chooses to become sexually active, she needs to start thinking about contraception and the possibility of pregnancy first. This chapter provides information about preventing pregnancy when the partners are not ready for parenthood, as well as getting physically prepared ahead of time when they are ready. This is the best way we know now to prevent low-birth-weight babies and infant mortality in our community.

CONTRACEPTION

A contraceptive said to be 90 percent effective means that ten women out of every one hundred using it will become pregnant within one year. The other important consideration is whether the contraceptive protects against sexually transmitted diseases (STDs) such as gonorrhea, syphilis, chlamydia, herpes, and HIV. You want to choose the one that suits your age and your life circumstances—and one that protects against STDs.

Condom.
A condom is a fine latex rubber sheath that covers a man's erect penis during intercourse. (There is a new female condom that women can use; it is bigger and more awkward, but it does offer similar effectiveness and protection, and it gives women an element of control.) Condoms are 90 percent effective if used properly—slightly more effective if used with a vaginal spermicide. They also offer protection against STDs. You will find condoms at drugstores.

Spermicidal Foams, Gels, Creams.
Put into the vagina, spermicides make a thick chemical barrier sperm cannot cross. Used alone, spermicides are only about 82%

effective; they are more effective when used with a diaphragm or condom. They offer some protection against STDs. You will find spermicides at drugstores.

Sponge.

This is a soft, disposable, synthetic vaginal sponge containing spermicide. It is inserted into the vagina before sex and left in for several hours. Repeated intercourse can take place as long as the sponge is removed within twenty-four hours. The effectiveness rate is less than 90 percent. Protection increases if used with a condom. The sponge provides some protection against STDs. It is available at drugstores.

The Pill.

The pill contains hormones that jam the hormonal axis that controls the release of eggs from a woman's ovaries. There are various combinations. If used according to instructions, the pill is 99 percent effective against pregnancy. It cannot be used by women over thirty-five, smokers, obese women, or those with a preexisting disease. *The pill offers no protection against STDs.*

Diaphragm.

This is a latex cup with a springy rim that fits securely in the vagina and covers the cervix. Another version is a solid rubber cervical cap. A diaphragm requires fitting by a health-care professional (family-planning clinic) and must be prescribed by a physician. The size of the diaphragm needs to be checked every couple of years, and care is required in handling in order to prevent tears. If properly fitted and used with spermicidal foam, gel, or cream, it is 92.8 percent effective. The diaphragm does not protect against STDs.

IUDs (Intrauterine Device, Coil, Loop).

A small piece of shaped plastic is placed inside the uterus, and it prevents a fertilized egg from implanting inside the uterus. However, in the past IUDs led to infections of the uterus and subsequent infertility. They are not manufactured by any American company, although their sale is legal. However, some women still have the devices in place, and they can be purchased in other countries. They are very effective—95 percent and higher. *They offer no protection against STDs, however.*

PREPARING FOR PREGNANCY

Whether you are in your teens or adulthood, pregnancy is a gift and a responsibility that requires good planning. Here is some information that can help *every woman* prepare herself for a healthy pregnancy.

If you are ready to have a baby, you can have a medical checkup before you conceive. A prepregnancy checkup is just like a first prenatal exam (see page 398). Simply tell the doctor you want to make sure that you're in good health because you're planning to become pregnant. This gives you an opportunity to discover whether you have diabetes or hypertension, to treat any infections you may have, to make sure your nutritional status, particularly your iron levels, are adequate, and to get your doctor's recommendations for extra vitamins and minerals.

Before pregnancy, you and your partner can reduce all of your primary risk factors, particularly smoking, drinking, and drug use. This is extremely important for two reasons: First, it takes time to give up these habits, so you don't want to wait until you're already pregnant to get started. Second, your baby is at its most vulnerable during the first eight to twelve weeks following conception—a time when you may be unaware that you're pregnant. Environmental hazards such as smoking may come from either the mother or the father. A man's heavy smoking and drinking, as well as certain diseases and drugs, may harm his sperm. You want to make sure that you are both clean machines at the moment of conception.

Let's take a look at those huge risk factors that interfere with the baby's life in the womb: smoking, alcohol, drugs.

SMOKING

Cigarette smoking is a major cause of infant mortality and low-birth-weight babies. There is no time that a baby is safe from smoking: From the moment of conception to the moment of birth and afterward, the baby is threatened by repeated assaults of cigarette smoke. Maternal smoking is linked to an increased risk of spontaneous abortion, separation of the placenta from the uterus (*placenta abruptio*), misplaced placenta (*placenta previa*), bleeding during pregnancy, and sudden infant death syndrome. Maternal smoking is believed to cause many fetal abnormalities, including brain damage.

When a pregnant woman smokes, chemicals in smoke reduce the amount of oxygen available to the baby, constrict the blood vessels feeding the placenta, and strip nutrients from the fetus; the baby's heart beats faster and breathing is abnormal. Even smoke she breathes in from other smokers can reach the fetus.

After birth, the baby can continue to suffer by receiving nicotine in breast milk or by inhaling secondhand smoke. The child is vulnerable to a host of ailments, including ear, nose, and throat infections, bronchitis, pneumonia, asthmatic attacks, and decreased lung efficiency.

To protect their baby, both parents should try to stop smoking several months before pregnancy and permanently stay off cigarettes once pregnancy is achieved. (See Chapter 7.)

ALCOHOL

A woman who drinks heavily during pregnancy (five to six drinks a day) runs the risk of giving birth to a baby with fetal alcohol syndrome, a cluster of severe physical and mental defects, including growth retardation, facial abnormalities, brain damage, abnormal development of various organs, including heart defects, and poor muscle coordination. Mild mental retardation, hyperactivity, and learning disabilities are also common. From 40 to 50 percent of babies born to heavy drinkers have fetal alcohol syndrome. Babies of mothers who drink heavily, especially early in pregnancy, are likely to suffer the most severe abnormalities; infants born to moderate drinkers may suffer more subtle fetal alcohol effects.

Low birth weight and miscarriage are also common among mothers who drink. Studies have shown that a woman who drinks as little as two drinks a week has a higher rate of miscarriage than a woman who doesn't drink. And a pregnant woman who consumes about ten drinks a week, classified as moderate drinking, doubles her risk of having a low-birth-weight baby.

Can you drink at all when you're pregnant? You probably should not. The FDA has handed down these guidelines: More than six hard drinks each day presents a major risk of serious problems to the fetus; two to six drinks per day carries a substantial risk of lesser abnormalities. *There is no known safe level of alcohol consumption below which no risk is present.*

Most doctors say give up drinking altogether—*before becoming pregnant.* If you drink and are unable to stop, reduce your intake to the lowest amount possible. Binges or sporadic drinking are particularly dangerous, since at these times a woman may consume especially large amounts of alcohol, which her body is unable to detoxify.

OTHER DRUGS

Babies born to drug-addicted mothers are also addicted, suffering withdrawal symptoms that may cause death. Those who survive may have developmental problems and long-lasting brain damage.

Based on estimates from the National Association for Perinatal Addiction Research and Education, one out of every eleven infants—approximately 375,000 babies a year—is born to a woman who abused drugs (cocaine, heroin, methadone, amphetamines, PCP, and/or marijuana) during pregnancy. Drug use during pregnancy is associated with spontaneous abortion, *placenta abruptio,* low birth weight, SIDS, and other problems. Experts say we are just now beginning to see the effects of drug-exposed babies as those who survive grow up and begin school. All too often, they are unable to learn, cannot pay attention for long, and often exhibit severe behavioral problems.

I know that a lot of pregnant women who drink or use drugs stay away from prenatal clinics because they don't want to tell the doctors and nurses about their substance abuse. They feel ashamed and also fear their babies may be taken away from them. But these are the women who need the most care. If you are hooked on drugs or alcohol, you've got a problem that requires help. You don't have to waste time blaming yourself, but do get help. Talk to someone you feel you can trust—your mom, your sister, your minister, or a friend. Better yet, take yourself to a treatment center. Tell them you're pregnant. People there can help you and work with your doctor. The idea is to get yourself alcohol- and drug-free—and to help your baby be born healthy. If you find yourself in this predicament, read Chapter 7 carefully. Don't be afraid to ask for help.

Smoking, alcohol, and drug use are three major factors that affect our babies. Nutrition is the fourth factor that can make an enormous difference in the outcome of a pregnancy.

NUTRITION

It's clear that poor nutrition increases the risk of producing an abnormal baby, and the risk is greatest for women who are already poorly nourished when they conceive.

YOUR WEIGHT BEFORE PREGNANCY

Your weight *before* you conceive is as important as your weight gain during pregnancy. Once you become pregnant, it's too late to start changing your basic body weight. If you are very thin or extremely overweight, it's not enough to adjust your weight; you also want to enhance your nutrition.

If You Are Overweight. A woman who is very overweight before pregnancy is more likely to develop serious complications during pregnancy and delivery that could jeopardize both mother and baby. If you're thirty or more pounds overweight, you need to try to lose weight—gradually—before becoming pregnant. *Do not go on a crash diet.* Any extreme dieting risks depleting essential nutrients that you need for a healthy pregnancy.

Read Chapter 6 carefully and follow the guidelines laid out in Part Three and you will be well on your way to achieving an ideal pregnancy weight.

If You're Underweight. If you are underweight before pregnancy, your baby is more likely to be born prematurely or dangerously small. Try to get your weight up before you conceive. The best way is simply to increase your daily intake of calories. Don't just go for empty calories; choose high-calorie *nutritious* foods: Whole nuts and seeds, dried fruits, sweet potatoes, and avocados are examples. You can add a daily drink of well-balanced high-protein powder.

If you are still underweight when you conceive, it may help to gain a little more weight than usual during pregnancy, but don't go overboard. Unless you're very underweight or are carrying twins or triplets, gaining more than forty pounds will not help you or your baby.

YOUR DIET BEFORE AND DURING PREGNANCY

Nutritional status is as important as weight. Optimize your nutrition before pregnancy so that in the first weeks following conception—when most women can't stand food—your nutritional stores will carry the baby through.

The most important nutrients for pregnancy are protein, calcium, folic acid and vitamin B complex vitamins, iron, vitamins C and E, and zinc. These are also the same nutrients most women lack.

Protein
High-quality protein is crucial to form healthy new tissue for you and the baby. *High quality* means a complete protein that contains all eight essential amino acids (found in eggs, meat, chicken, and fish). Body tissue cannot be built from incomplete vegetable proteins—unless they are properly combined. For instance, rice and beans combine to form a complete protein.

Calcium
You need extra stores of calcium during pregnancy for the baby's bones and tooth buds to develop. If you don't consume extra calcium, the developing fetus will drain it from your bones and teeth. Increasing your calcium intake before and during pregnancy may also help prevent certain complications, particularly a serious condition called toxemia, which causes blood pressure to rise.
Food sources. You're looking for at least twelve hundred to two thousand milligrams of calcium each day during pregnancy. A

quart of milk supplies twelve hundred milligrams, so you can see how much food you would have to consume just to get the minimum amount. Other good sources of calcium are dark green vegetables, tofu, canned sardines and salmon, and dried beans and peas.

Supplements. Calcium is one of the five important pregnancy vitamins/minerals that usually need supplementation; it's almost impossible to get adequate amounts from food without going overboard on dairy products.

Folic Acid and Vitamin B Complex

Too little folic acid is one of the most common and most serious deficiencies in pregnant women. When you are pregnant, you need twice as much vitamin B complex and folic acid as usual. These two vitamins work together to promote healthy red blood cells in the mother and the fetus. You can increase your vitamin B complex and folic acid intake before pregnancy and maintain it all the way through.

Food sources. Dark green vegetables, asparagus, legumes (especially lima beans), whole grains, nuts, salmon, and lean meats are all good sources. Vitamin B_{12} is found in fish, organ meats, egg yolks, and cheese.

Supplements. These vitamins are often supplemented during pregnancy. Four hundred milligrams of folic acid a day is usually recommended, even before conception. (Folic acid helps prevent neural-tube disorders, such as spina bifida, which develop in the early weeks of pregnancy.)

Iron

Your blood volume will double during pregnancy, and few women have enough iron stored in their bodies to meet this increased need. It's difficult to get enough iron from any source— only 10 percent taken in supplements or in food is actually absorbed by the body. Iron from red meat is absorbed better than iron from vegetables, enriched breads, or fortified cereals. Adding foods that contain a lot of vitamin C will also help your body absorb iron.

Food sources. Lean meats, dark green vegetables (especially parsley and kale), beets and beet greens, dried fruits, egg yolks, shellfish, molasses, and whole grains are good sources. Organ meats, such as liver, heart, and kidney, are also iron-rich, but make sure these come from organic sources free from chemicals. Dried beans and peas also provide some iron.

Supplements. Your doctor may recommend iron supplements during pregnancy.

Vitamin E

Vitamin E is the only fat-soluble vitamin needed in increased amounts during pregnancy. Years ago, vitamin E was known as the "antisterility factor" because it is associated with successful ovulation and fertilization. A pregnant woman needs twice as much vitamin E as usual, particularly during the second trimester.

Food sources. Meat, fish, grains, liver, yeast, nuts, and oils of wheat germ, soybeans, cottonseed, and corn are all good sources.

Supplements. The usual RDA for vitamin E is eight milligrams for women; it increases to sixteen milligrams during pregnancy. Your doctor may recommend more in the form of supplements.

Vitamin C

Proper amounts of vitamin C are needed both before and during pregnancy. It's important for the developing baby and for the mother's immune system.

Food sources. Vitamin C is found naturally in a wide variety of fruits and vegetables. Citrus fruits, papaya, mango, guava, cantaloupe, broccoli, brussels sprouts, green and red peppers, parsley, and strawberries are all good sources of vitamin C.

Supplements. Vitamin C supplements in low to moderate levels —up to one thousand milligrams daily—appear safe before and during pregnancy. Very high levels, in the thousands of milligrams a day, are not recommended because they are thought to create a transient vitamin dependency in the fetus. If you are used to taking greater quantities of vitamin C supplements and would like to continue through your pregnancy, discuss the amounts with your doctor.

Zinc

Zinc is crucial to the growth of the fetus. Too little zinc in the mother's diet is associated with retarded fetal growth, abnormal fetal development, and prolonged labor. Adequate amounts of iron, vitamin B$_6$, and tryptophan (an amino acid found in lean meats, fish, eggs, and dairy products) help the body absorb zinc. The amount of zinc recommended for nonpregnant women is fifteen milligrams a day; during pregnancy, this amount increases to twenty milligrams.

Food sources. Oysters, herring, whole grains, liver, lamb, beef, poultry, nuts, brown rice, peas, peanuts, milk, and eggs are all good sources of zinc. In most parts of the country where oysters are available, eating raw oysters every day is not a good idea because of the possibility of contamination. Try to get zinc from a variety of foods.

Supplements. Your doctor may recommend that your vitamin/ mineral supplements contain zinc.

Supplements

During pregnancy—when you need an even greater supply of nutrients than usual—supplements of key vitamins and minerals (calcium, folic acid, and other B vitamins) are recommended by most doctors.

If your diet has been deficient in the past, you can start supplements even before pregnancy; the same supplements can be continued throughout pregnancy. *But because each woman's needs are different, always consult your doctor before taking supplements during pregnancy.* (See Chapter 17.) Megadoses are out. Your doctor will recommend a combination of vitamins and minerals that's right for you.

How Many Calories

During pregnancy, you should plan to consume about 300 extra calories a day, for a total intake of at least 1,500 to 2,500 calories per day. The idea is to eat a variety of foods you like and increase the caloric content to fit your needs.

Using the guidelines in the Sankofa Program, *the best place to increase calories is in the protein category*—adding three hundred extra calories' worth of fish, skinless chicken, lean meat, skimmed dairy products or cheese, or a combination of legumes and grains that add up to quality protein.

Caffeine

No one knows for certain whether the caffeine in tea, coffee, chocolate, and some soft drinks is harmful during pregnancy. Scientists know that caffeine interferes with the body's ability to absorb and use certain nutrients, specifically iron and some forms of protein. Caffeine also crosses the placenta and is distributed to all fetal tissues.

The FDA has issued a warning to pregnant women to modify or stop their consumption of caffeine-containing foods and beverages, but it also states that evidence of harmful effects is inconclusive. Although harmful effects have not been proved, I recommend that a pregnant woman stop consuming caffeine or limit herself to one or two cups of coffee or other caffeine-containing drinks a day. Unfortunately, those who are hooked on caffeine usually consume much greater quantities. It's estimated that 13 percent of pregnant women drink five or more cups of coffee each day. Caffeine is a real addiction, and it takes time to break the habit. However, after going through a few days of feeling a little groggy and headachy, you'll quickly get back to normal. (For more about caffeine, see Chapter 15.)

How Much Weight Should You Gain?

No one weight-gain figure is right for every woman. Babies have a better chance of surviving if their mothers gain at least twenty pounds during pregnancy. The American College of Obstetricians and Gynecologists recommends that women entering pregnancy near their ideal weight should gain twenty-five to thirty pounds during pregnancy. If you are underweight when you conceive, you may need to gain as much as thirty-five pounds to ensure the health of the baby. If you are overweight, your obstetrician may advise you to gain *slightly* less than the recommended amount, as long as you eat nutritiously.

Ideally, you should gain weight gradually and steadily throughout pregnancy rather than in spurts. During the first three months, you should gain a total of two to five pounds, then three to four pounds a month thereafter. The weight you gain during the first half of your pregnancy goes into building up stores of fat and protein that can be used by your baby later in the pregnancy.

Some will be held over to sustain you after pregnancy and to help produce breast milk.

If you gain too much weight over the course of the pregnancy, *do not cut back toward the end.* The weight increase during the last three months represents mostly growth of the baby, so reducing calories at the end can compromise the baby's development.

Your Baby's Weight

Your diet during pregnancy sets up a chain reaction: What you eat directly affects the baby's weight. Your goal is to give birth to a healthy child who weighs more than seven pounds. A large study funded by the NIH found that babies weighing seven pounds six ounces or more had fewer diseases and were generally healthier than babies who weighed less.

Although bigger babies tend to do better, extremely large babies do not. Babies weighing more than ten pounds at birth have a somewhat higher than average number of problems during labor and delivery. Excessive size is usually caused by a mother's obesity before pregnancy, poorly controlled diabetes during pregnancy, family history of large newborns, or a pregnancy that lasts longer than forty-two weeks.

A baby's birth weight in relationship to its gestational age (how long it has been developing in the womb) is the best indicator of health. For example, a baby who is small because it has been born early will have less trouble than a baby who is born small after a full nine months. In other words, a six-pound baby born after eight months will have fewer health problems than if it weighed the same after nine months.

Returning to Your Normal Weight

After childbirth, you will not immediately lose all the weight you gained, because your body needs it to help you breast-feed. No matter how little weight you gain during pregnancy, your body will *still* store fat for milk production. If you don't consume enough calories during pregnancy for storage, your body will take away nutrients from the baby. So don't try to keep your weight down during pregnancy in the hope that you will be thin afterward.

During the first week after delivery, you can expect to lose about fifteen pounds. From then on, if you're nursing the baby, you can expect to lose about one-half pound a week. On average, breast-feeding mothers are back to their normal weight six weeks after delivery.

Bottle-feeding mothers tend to lose weight more slowly. If you're following the guidelines recommended in the Sankofa Program, weight loss will be automatic and stress-free. You may want to exercise more and eat a little less, but don't try to lose more than about half a pound to one pound a week. All new mothers, whether they breast-feed or bottle-feed, need to conserve energy. Avoid crash weight-loss programs.

NOW YOU'RE PREGNANT

PREGNANCY TESTING

A missed period is usually the first sign of pregnancy, although missing a period may be caused by other reasons. The only way to be certain is to have a pregnancy test. A doctor or clinic can perform the test, or you can do it yourself using a home kit. As soon as you suspect—or know for sure—that you are pregnant, see a doctor.

YOUR FIRST PRENATAL VISIT

You should have your first prenatal visit as soon as you suspect or know you are pregnant. (You can also have one before you conceive.) A prenatal examination includes a blood-pressure check, an internal vaginal examination, a breast exam, blood tests, and a urinalysis. The visit begins with your family medical history.

Medical History. You will be asked whether you've ever had a serious illness, including kidney disease, diabetes, German measles, high blood pressure, or pelvic inflammatory disease. Your doctor will want to know whether you have had any recent inoculations or if you take any medications.

A note will be made if there are any twins in your family. Twins are more common among black women than white. (If it turns out you are pregnant with twins, you will be a high-risk mother, meaning that you will need special prenatal care. The outlook for babies and mother is good, particularly if you have good nutrition, rest, and prenatal care.)

You will also be asked whether you have any history of birth defects or other serious illnesses in your family. If so, you may want to consult a genetic counselor to assess the chances of passing along the disorder.

If you have encountered any complications in a previous pregnancy, your physician will want to know about them. Miscarriage, premature birth, and toxemia are just a few of the conditions that may have a bearing on the outcome of your next pregnancy.

Your physician will also ask you to describe your menstrual pattern. Menstrual problems may be caused by endometriosis, erratic ovulation, unbalanced hormonal cycles, or premature menopause, conditions that may interfere with conception and pregnancy.

Height and Weight. Your weight gives the doctor a baseline to track your weight gain through pregnancy; measuring your height will reveal any postural problems that might affect your ability to carry the baby.

Pelvic Exam. The internal pelvic exam will detect any structural abnormalities of the pelvis, vagina, and cervix. During the exam, the physician can take cervical swabs for a Pap smear and test for sexually transmitted diseases.

Sexually transmitted diseases such as syphilis, gonorrhea, chlamydia, and herpes must be treated promptly for the health of both mother and fetus. If the mother has syphilis, she has an increased risk of miscarriage. Infants born infected with syphilis are at increased risk of premature death, low birth weight, mental retardation, and chronic health problems. Congenital syphilis is completely preventable when detected and treated in the mother.

Untreated gonorrhea can cause a buildup of scar tissue in and around a woman's reproductive organs. This means her chances of becoming pregnant are reduced, and if she does become pregnant, she may have a higher risk of miscarriage. Gonorrhea is easily identified, usually by a slide test in the physician's office.

New tests are now available that can uncover another common STD, chlamydia.

If a woman has active herpes at the time of delivery, her baby is usually delivered by cesarean section. A past history of herpes does not ordinarily threaten the developing fetus, but a flare-up at the time of delivery can expose the baby to the virus as it passes through the birth canal. Herpes infection in a newborn can cause mental retardation, blindness, neurological problems, and even death.

The doctor may ask whether you want to be tested for HIV, the virus believed to cause AIDS. The AIDS epidemic is having a devastating impact on African-American women and children. A woman with HIV has a significant risk of passing it on to her baby. (See Chapter 21 for full information on AIDS.) Even if you are certain you don't have HIV, it's still worth it to have the test. You or your partner may have been exposed years before and unknowingly carry the virus.

Urine Tests. Your urine specimen will be analyzed for the presence of protein, which may indicate kidney disease; glucose, which would indicate diabetes; ketones, which may indicate that you're not eating enough; pus or blood, which could mean kidney infection.

Blood Tests. A blood sample is analyzed to identify your blood group, in case you need an emergency transfusion, and to test for venereal diseases, anemia, and the rhesus (Rh) factor. (If you are Rh-negative and your partner is Rh-positive, you may potentially have a high-risk pregnancy. About 15 percent of the white population has Rh-negative blood, but the trait is less common among other groups.)

Your blood can be tested for sickle-cell disease and sickle-cell trait. (If you and your partner both carry the sickle-cell trait, you have a one-in-four chance of having a baby with sickle-cell disease, a severe form of anemia. For more information, see Chapter 27.)

Your blood may also be tested for toxoplasmosis—an infection that can severely affect fetal development—and rubella antibodies.

Rubella Vaccinations. Rubella, or German measles, is a relatively trivial illness in adults, but it can have serious consequences for an unborn baby. If a woman catches it during the first three months of pregnancy, there is a 20 to 30 percent risk that the baby's eyes, ears, brain, or heart will be damaged. Later in pregnancy, the risk to the baby is less, with damage usually restricted to hearing difficulties. The virus may also cause miscarriage, a low-birth-weight baby, or even a stillbirth.

Even if you think you have had measles or know you were vaccinated against it, ask your doctor to check that you are still immune. If you are not immune, you can be vaccinated *before* you become pregnant (it's important that you do not become pregnant for at least three months following the new vaccination).

After you conceive, you cannot be vaccinated, because the live vaccine might harm the unborn child. However, as long as you do not contract German measles during pregnancy, the baby will be all right.

At the end of your prenatal exam, you will have a chance to talk over anything that worries you. If you tend to forget your questions the minute you walk into a doctor's office, write them down beforehand and take them along.

Your doctor will work out the date the baby is due to arrive. The average pregnancy lasts thirty-eight weeks from the date of conception. Since it's impossible to know the exact time of conception, the doctor counts forty weeks, from the first day of your last period.

Your due date is only a best guess. Every woman doesn't menstruate on a strict twenty-eight-day cycle. Nor does every normal pregnancy last exactly the same number of days. Your labor may start a week before or a week after the estimated date and still be perfectly normal.

Doctor Visits During Pregnancy

After your first prenatal visit, you'll be seeing your doctor once a month for the first six months of pregnancy. The heartbeat and position of the baby will be checked on each visit; you will have a urinalysis and your blood pressure and weight will be recorded.

In the seventh and eighth months, you'll probably see your doctor every two weeks. And during the ninth month, you'll see the doctor every week until labor begins.

If you have any health problems that put your pregnancy in a high-risk category, you will probably see the doctor more often. These prenatal visits are crucial to your well-being and the health of your baby, so it's important to keep your regular appointments. If you experience any problems in between visits, don't hesitate to call your doctor.

It's important to be assertive about your prenatal care. I always ask my pregnant clients to keep a diary to record how they feel and how the baby feels inside. They can also jot down any questions. Journal keeping helps them and their doctor know how things are going.

SPECIAL HEALTH PROBLEMS

DIABETES AND PREGNANCY

Diabetes can be a dangerous condition in a pregnant woman. If the diabetes is not carefully controlled, the risks of stillbirth or congenital defects increase. The baby may grow larger than normal, contributing to difficulties at birth. This is a particular problem for us because black women have very high rates of diabetes, and for reasons that are unknown they also suffer more serious consequences from their disease. For example, black diabetic women are more likely to lose their babies during or immediately after childbirth than white diabetic mothers. If you have diabetes, your pregnancy is automatically identified as high-risk. You will need closer observation than the average expectant mother and blood-glucose tests will need to be carried out regularly. You will probably need a strict diet and insulin injections. As long as the diabetes is carefully controlled, the risks are greatly reduced.

Many women don't know they have diabetes until after they become pregnant, another important reason for black women to receive early prenatal care. *If you know you have diabetes, consult your physician before you become pregnant.*

One kind of diabetes, called gestational diabetes, develops only during pregnancy. It carries the same risks to the pregnancy as regular diabetes. Gestational diabetes can often be taken care of by a special diet, though in some cases insulin injections are necessary. (See Chapter 24.)

If your diabetes is very severe, you may be admitted to the hospital for the last days, or weeks, of the pregnancy, so that the diabetes can be precisely controlled and the baby's condition can be monitored.

HIGH BLOOD PRESSURE AND PREGNANCY

Extremely high blood pressure is associated with difficult childbirth and can harm the baby. High blood pressure may be discovered for the first time during routine prenatal visits. An expectant mother may have had high blood pressure for some time, or it may be caused by the pregnancy itself. It's normal for blood pressure to fall slightly during the middle weeks of pregnancy and to rise slightly at the end. Sudden elevations can be dangerous and may lead to a condition known as toxemia. Your blood pressure will be checked on each prenatal visit.

HIGH-RISK PREGNANCIES

Certain medical conditions automatically place a pregnant woman in a high-risk category, which means she will require close observation and monitoring throughout the pregnancy to ensure her own health and the health of the baby. Pregnancy may have an adverse effect on the disease; by the same token, the disease may affect the pregnancy and its outcome. Your age can also place you in the high-risk category. Your pregnancy is high-risk if you have any of these risk factors:

- Older than age thirty-five
- Diabetes
- High blood pressure
- Thyroid or neurological problems

Before becoming pregnant, high-risk women should consult with their doctors to make sure they get off to a good start. In some cases, the doctor may advise against pregnancy, but most of the time high-risk pregnancies can be successfully handled with proper care.

FINDING MATERNITY CARE

As soon as you know you're pregnant—or even before—you need to find maternity care. You are looking for two things: a doctor to care for you while you are pregnant and a place in which to deliver your baby. Read this section carefully; think about your own preferences and also ask yourself whether you know what's available in your community.

Most American women give birth to their babies in a hospital. Having medical technology instantly available ensures the safety of mother and child, because when things go wrong during delivery, they often go wrong suddenly and without warning. This is particularly true for high-risk pregnancies. But hospitals vary considerably in their approach to childbirth.

Many hospitals try to offer a personalized and caring approach toward pregnant women and their babies. If you know in advance that yours is a high-risk pregnancy, you will want to choose a hospital known for its superior technology and neonatal unit. You can call hospitals in your area and ask to visit their maternity floors. People who work in high-quality maternity units are usually very proud of their services and will welcome a visit. The hospital you choose can provide you with a list of affiliated obstetricians, from which you can choose a doctor for your prenatal care. The hospital itself may offer prenatal care in a special pregnancy clinic (see page 405).

The other way to go is to choose a doctor first and then plan to deliver your baby at the hospital where he or she is affiliated.

CHOOSING AN OBSTETRICIAN

You may choose a general practitioner, a family doctor, or an obstetrician. Many obstetricians are board-certified by the American Board of Obstetrics and Gynecology meaning that they have spent four to five years in resident's training after they have received their initial medical degrees and that they have passed several examinations.

The most important thing is to find a physician who is competent and caring, someone you can trust. It's also important to choose a doctor whom you can get to easily, because you don't want to miss any prenatal appointments, and if you develop any complication during pregnancy, you may need to have more frequent visits. (For more information about how to choose a good doctor, read Chapter 20 carefully.)

HOSPITAL PRENATAL CLINICS

Many hospitals have prenatal clinics, staffed by resident obstetricians, obstetrical nurses, and often nurse midwives. You visit the clinic just as you would a private obstetrician, beginning with prenatal checkups and going straight through delivery. Clinics also offer childbirth-preparation classes

Hospital maternity clinics have many different kinds of specialists available, which makes it an ideal setting for high-risk pregnancies. Another advantage is that clinic costs are generally lower than private care, although costs vary considerably.

BIRTHING CENTERS

A birthing center is a small childbirth facility, often located near a hospital. Most centers offer full maternity care, including childbirth classes and delivery, in a friendly, personal atmosphere. Only young, low-risk mothers are accepted for care at a birthing center, which is often staffed by midwives, with obstetricians on call for backup. However, there are only 125 such facilities nationwide, so you may be unable to find one near you. Look in the Yellow Pages of your telephone book under "Birthing Centers" or write to the American College of Nurse-Midwives (1522 K Street NW, Washington, D.C. 20005).

NURSE MIDWIVES

In the last two decades, midwifery has undergone a revolution that is bringing high quality and highly personalized maternity care to a growing number of women. Nurse midwives are registered nurses who have completed advanced training in gynecology and obstetrics. Those who are certified, known as C.N.M.s, and licensed can practice midwifery in all fifty states. They must first pass a national examination and then attend continuing-education programs.

About 87 percent of births attended by nurse midwives take place in hospitals. But nurse midwives also may deliver babies at birthing centers and attend home births. In some hospitals and birthing centers, the nurse midwife sees the mother through labor and an obstetrician comes in to deliver the baby; in others, the nurse midwife actually delivers the baby, but an obstetrician is available as backup in case of complications.

A growing number of obstetricians in private practice also have nurse midwives on staff. Today's midwives may perform a broad range of gynecological services, including Pap smears, breast and pelvic examinations, contraceptive and menopausal counseling, teenage pregnancy counseling, and assistance for new mothers.

Are nurse midwives a good choice for you and your baby? They certainly seem to be. A recent analysis of fifteen studies of low-risk births showed that babies delivered by the midwives fared as well as or better than those delivered by doctors.

In fact, the only problem with nurse midwives is that there aren't enough of them to go around. The American College of Nurse-Midwives has called for the training and certification of ten thousand nurse midwives by the year 2001, which would more than double the number now in practice.

Lay Midwives

Lay midwives mostly acquire their skills from direct experience rather than academic training. Black women have a long and rich history as lay midwives in this country. For hundreds of years, "grannies" have provided care to pregnant women, learning their skills from their grandmothers and mothers or from other older midwives in the community. Many other immigrant ethnic groups also had lay midwives. In the old days, lay midwives were often called in a spiritual sense and were usually very sensitive to cultural rituals surrounding pregnancy and birth in their communities.

Black grannies practiced everywhere; long after other ethnic midwives had disappeared, hundreds of black midwives continued to practice in the Deep South, their midwifery lineages extending as far back as slavery.

Obstetricians used to regard midwives as competition and backed state laws to forbid them to practice in or out of hospitals. It was fairly easy to get rid of the midwives, because they had no formal support. In the 1960s many black families were able to deliver their babies in hospitals for the first time. The grannies were getting old, and young black women no longer had reason to learn from them. As the older women retired, lay practices simply faded into history.

When the women's movement gained strength in the 1970s, the idea of midwifery was reborn in new generations, albeit in a somewhat different style. Today, some women's organizations and midwife groups believe that women should have the opportunity to become midwives without having to be registered nurses first. The modern lay midwife tends to be younger and politically active in the birth-alternatives movement. Lay midwives may practice legally in several states, but requirements for licensure vary from state to state. Lay midwives are often dedicated, experienced, and have superior skills. However, if you choose a lay midwife for your maternity care, check her qualifications just as you would those of any other health-care professional—and also check the qualifications of her physician backup. If she doesn't have medical support, no matter how good she herself is, it would be unwise to choose a lay midwife for maternity care. Too many things can go wrong during pregnancy and delivery to make this a safe option.

HOME BIRTHS

Home delivery is safe for normal births; the problem is that you can't really know ahead of time whether a birth will be normal. A close friend of mine who was thirty-five years old when she became pregnant planned a home birth with an obstetrician and nurse midwife in attendance. For eight months, everything about the pregnancy was normal. Suddenly, her labor began. Her husband rushed her to the hospital, where their baby was delivered by cesarean section. Everything turned out fine; the hospital took very good care of them all, and the father was present in the operating room to receive the baby girl into his arms when she was delivered. Both parents felt good about their unexpected hospital experience. Three years later, my friend became pregnant again and the second baby was born safely by vaginal delivery—at home.

YOUR BABY'S FIRST YEAR

If all goes well, the baby will weigh more than six and a half pounds and less than ten pounds. This healthy weight means that your baby is getting off to a vibrant start in life. I wish this wonderful outcome for every woman.

We've said that our biggest problem with infant mortality is low birth weight. Even if your baby is born at a healthy weight, or survives some initial health problems in the first month following birth, it is still very vulnerable.

Infant mortality is divided into two main components: death that occurs in the first twenty-eight days of life and death that occurs between twenty-eight days and one year, called postneonatal death. Black babies have an increased risk of dying in their first year, regardless of their birth weight. Accidents are one cause of postneonatal death, often related to poor living conditions and lack of quality care. Other risks may involve stress or infections, which are more common among poor mothers and babies who often do not have adequate medical care. However, the leading cause of postneonatal death is sudden infant death syndrome, which is significantly higher among black infants. Let me say first that no one knows why some babies die in their sleep; it is no one's fault. Even if you take every possible precaution, it can still happen. However, it's important that we take a look at this cause of black infant death. Here's what we know about SIDS.

SUDDEN INFANT DEATH SYNDROME

About ten thousand infants each year—about three out of every one thousand—die quietly in their sleep after being put to bed at night. Most deaths occur between the hours of midnight and 8:00

A.M. during the winter rather than the summer months. The baby is usually between two and four months old, rarely older than six months.

SIDS can happen to any baby. Asian babies appear to have the lowest risk, and black and native American babies have a particularly high risk. Boys die more often than girls. SIDS tends to occur more than once in families.

No one knows why these deaths occur or if SIDS is one disease or many. There's some evidence that such babies were not as healthy as they appeared.

It's normal for babies to have brief pauses in breathing as they sleep, but most do not die of SIDS. In fact, SIDS may not be related to such normal interruptions in breathing. Some victims of SIDS have been slow to grow after birth, but again, no one knows whether this is a contributing factor.

Studies of infants who died of SIDS show some slight abnormalities in the arteries leading to their lungs; their breathing and heart rate appeared to have been poorly coordinated, suggesting that heart and lung function was immature. But there is no clear picture of why these things occur. Factors that *seem* to increase risk are these:

• Maternal smoking
• Low birth weight or premature birth
• Maternal drug use
• A family history of SIDS or a near miss, when an infant was rescued after breathing stopped

Can you prevent SIDS from happening? If your doctor thinks your infant is at risk, your baby's breathing during the night can be tracked on a home monitor. The value of these monitors is still uncertain, and the fact is that it's just about impossible to predict which infants are vulnerable.

Right now, the most important aspect of dealing with SIDS comes after the tragedy has happened. Fortunately, doctors, police, and the public have become sensitive to the fact that SIDS is indeed an unexplained cause of death and no one is to blame, least of all the baby's parents.

We have discussed many issues that affect infant mortality in the black community. They all need attention, beginning with nutrition, early prenatal care, and elimination of risk factors that can damage the baby. We need to work on these problems as a community. As Virginia Davis Floyd, M.D., director of the Family Health Services Section, Georgia Division of Public Health, writes in *Health Issues in the Black Community,* "Children are the most precious resource of the African-American community. All children, born and yet to be born, deserve nothing less than a full promise of tomorrow."

RESOURCES

Planned Parenthood
810 Seventh Avenue
New York, NY 10019
(212) 603-4600

American College of Nurse
  Midwives
1522 K Street NW, Suite 1000
Washington, D.C. 20005
(202) 289-0171

National Black Women's Health
  Project
1237 Abernathy SW
Atlanta, GA 30310
(404) 758-9590

Women's Health Network
1325 G Street NW
Washington, D.C. 20005
(202) 347-1140

The information offered in this book is only the beginning. Our goal was to talk about the most urgent problems that are causing our people to die too soon. I wish my parents could have had the same kind of information; I believe that if they had they would be alive today. It's too late for them. But there's still time for us and for our children. The investment you make in learning and adapting your life to a good health program will pay off—and pay off repeatedly—for the generations who follow. As we ourselves are products of our African ancestors, so our children and their children will be products of the healthy changes we make now.

INDEX